*Wilber "Bullet" Rogan
and the Kansas City
Monarchs*

Wilber "Bullet" Rogan and the Kansas City Monarchs

Phil S. Dixon

McFarland & Company, Inc., Publishers
Jefferson, North Carolina, and London

LIBRARY OF CONGRESS CATALOGUING-IN-PUBLICATION DATA

Dixon, Phil.
Wilber "Bullet" Rogan and the
Kansas City Monarchs / Phil S. Dixon.
p.   cm.
Includes bibliographical references and index.

ISBN 978-0-7864-4425-0
softcover : 50# alkaline paper ∞

1. Rogan, Wilber, 1893–1967. 2. African American baseball players —
Biography   3. Baseball players — United States — Biography.
4. Kansas City Monarchs (Baseball team)   I. Title.
GV865.R635D59   2010   796.357092 — dc22 [B]   2010020182

British Library cataloguing data are available

©2010 Phil S. Dixon. All rights reserved

*No part of this book may be reproduced or transmitted in any form
or by any means, electronic or mechanical, including photocopying
or recording, or by any information storage and retrieval system,
without permission in writing from the publisher.*

Front cover: Wilber "Bullet" Rogan, 1913 (Fort Huachuca Museum);
1934 Monarchs team at the *Denver Post* Tournament

Manufactured in the United States of America

*McFarland & Company, Inc., Publishers
Box 611, Jefferson, North Carolina 28640
www.mcfarlandpub.com*

Table of Contents

Acknowledgments   vii
Preface   1

1. West-3541   5
2. Uncle Sam, Uncle Tom and Boss Wilkie   16
3. Birth of a Big League Star   31
4. A Most Valuable Asset   35
5. Salute to the Long Ball   49
6. The Man on the Bench   66
7. A Surge in Popularity   85
8. Going, Going, Not Gone Yet   96
9. A Lifetime in the Sun   122
10. The Reign of Error   139
11. A Hero's Farewell   161
12. The Supreme Monarch   181

Chapter Notes   195
Bibliography   207
Index   209

To the memory of
Carroll Ray Mothell,
Wilbur Rogan, Jr.,
and
Laurie Cobb

Acknowledgments

The following is only a brief listing of people whose assistance helped to make this book come alive. Without these individuals no well-rounded Monarchs history could have been written.

Most of all I would like to thank Wilbur "Little Bullet" Rogan, the son of Wilber "Bullet" Rogan, for his support and encouragement. Rogan was armed and ready with valuable stories, photographs and inspiration, for which I am forever appreciative. I would also like to thank Carl Rogan, Bullet's grandson.

The early years of Rogan's career might have been lost had it not been for Fred Langford, a player who actually began his career with Rogan on Fred Palace's Colts. Though Langford was well into his 90s, his recollections of Rogan as a teenager were simply amazing. Langford and I had many wonderful conversations about Bill Lindsay, Richard "Dick" Whitworth, Jack Marshall, Hurley McNair and the early years of Kansas City Monarchs baseball. Langford deeply inspired and motivated me to continue my baseball research. T. Roosevelt Butler of Kansas City, Kansas, was equally inspiring and forthcoming with documentation on his father-in-law, Tobe Smith. E. C. and Manville Boldridge, of Lexington, Missouri, were strong contributors with information on the Kansas City, Kansas, Giants, Bill Lindsay, Lexington's Tigers baseball team and semi-professional baseball in the upper Midwest.

Orrin Murray, a historian from Kansas City, Kansas, holds a special place in my life. We first met when I was in middle school. He showed up in our music class with his curved soprano saxophone and played a few songs with his band, and when I was an adult, he gave me the basic groundwork to become a historian. His astonishing memories and primary source accounts of Rogan's boyhood were remarkable and limitless. He was also a childhood friend of Willard Rogan, Bullet's younger brother, and knew Rogan's parents very well. It was through Murray that Rogan's childhood came alive once more.

William "Big C" Johnson was especially timely with his recollections of playing baseball in the famous 25th Infantry. His was a first-hand account of the men who formed the first generation of Kansas City Monarchs long before they arrived in Kansas City. Master Sergeant Bertram T. Beagle's paper on Rogan's army career was more helpful than words can describe.

Rogan's teammates supplied most of the background information about the Kansas City Monarchs teams. I was fortunate to interview many of them and to record the interesting stories about their lives. First and foremost, I would like to thank Carroll "Dink" Mothell, Chet Brewer, John "Buck" O'Neil, Maurice "Doolittle" Young, and James "Cool Papa" Bell. They adopted my research and helped formulate my identity in ways that aided in my development as a man. Among the other Monarchs who contributed mightily to this project were George Sweatt, Hilton Smith, Willard Brown, George Giles, Byron "Mex" Johnson, Curtis "Bingo" Lloyd, Connie Johnson, Mike "Tudie" Berry, Quincy Trouppe,

Fred McDaniel, Jesse Williams, Othello Renfroe, and Sammie Haynes. Throughout the league, Lou Dials, Willie Foster, Jimmy Crutchfield, Willie Powell, Ted "Double Duty" Radcliffe, Pat Patterson, Bobby Robinson, William "Judy" Johnson, Clint Thomas, William Lowe, and Dave Malarcher were also monumental sources of information.

Ernest Maun and Jimmy Zinn really opened my eyes to how the Monarchs were perceived by American and National Leaguers. Don Gutteridge of Pittsburg, Kansas, gave me valuable information about the Monarchs' visits to his hometown in the 1930s. James Gleason also provided his hometown perspective on the Monarchs. Al Piechota and Herman "Ham" Schulte tapped their memories on the Monarchs-Kansas City Blues series of 1937. Joe Bowman gave an account of playing against the Monarchs in the 1930s. Dorsey Moulder, a House of David player, verified games played against the Monarchs.

Harriet Wickstrom provided detailed accounts about her father, Thomas Younger Baird. Baird's brother Floyd was equally as resourceful. The same was true for Minnie Johnston Martin, who chronicled the life of her brother, Wade Johnston. Researcher Kevin Smith provided the intimate details of Johnston's boxing career. Newt Allen, Jr., and Myrtle Vanoy shared information about Newt Allen's celebrated Monarchs career. Dorothy Bell gave information about her father Clifford Bell and Donald Boyd supplied information about the life of his father Ollie Boyd. Hazel Foreman, the granddaughter of Zack Foreman, helped me to run down data about her family. Willa Simms gave detailed documentation about her brother Floyd Kranston. Ann Ward was equally forthcoming with stories about her two brothers, Thomas Jefferson Young (better known as T. J.) and Maurice "Doolittle" Young. Lorraine McGee was helpful with information on her grandfather, Nelson Dean. Maceo Brodnax, a former Monarchs batboy, gave first-hand accounts on the Monarchs in the 1920s. Eugene McFarland, a barber on Kansas City's Vine Street, supplied stories and background information that was simply amazing. Milton Payne supplied stories about the All-Nations and pitcher Jack Marshall, who played with Chicago's American Giants and Kansas City's Monarchs. Roger Whitworth, the son of Richard "Dick" Whitworth, embraced this project from the very beginning. In the early years of my research he was supportive and has continued to support this work some 20 years later. CeLois and Felix Street supplied background information about Carroll Ray "Dink" Mothell. Milton Morris told great tales about the night life of the individual players that befriended Julie Lee, Frank Duncan's first wife.

Ora O'Neil, the wife of John "Buck" O'Neil; Georgia Dwight, the wife of Eddie Dwight; Alberta Gilmore Penn, wife of Monarchs traveling secretary Quincy Gilmore; and Beatrice Joseph Garner, the wife of Newt Joseph, were among my early boosters. They teamed with Bernice Duncan, Frank Duncan's last wife, and Louise Smith, the wife of Hilton Smith, to tell the personal side of the ballplayers' lives. Sarah Barnes was equally encouraging with information about her husband, I. V. Barnes. This group of wonderful and inspiring ladies surrounded me with love and embraced my research long before anyone had ever read any of my work.

Thanks to authors John B. Holway and Jim Riley for their helpful publications on Negro baseball. William F. McNeil's book *The California Winter League* was also helpful. Pittsburg State University, Pittsburg, Kansas, supplied academic information on George Sweatt. Jay Sanford provided valuable assistance on games that were played in Denver, Colorado, along with the information on the *Denver Post* tournaments of the 1930s. Art Graham supplied some nice information about games played in Missoula, Montana. Dave Kemp, of Sioux Falls, South Dakota, was equally helpful on baseball information from the upper Midwest. And who can forget researcher-writer Normal "Tweed" Webb of St. Louis, Missouri? Webb's famous slogan "I saw them all" summarized an irreplaceable first-hand account that will be missed. Webb verified everything that happened in and around St. Louis, Missouri. I would also like to thank the researchers at SABR for digging into the microfilm for new information.

I was the recipient of a great deal of information on George Sweatt, which arrived with the blessing of Dick Davis. His efforts to keep Sweatt's memory alive in Humboldt, Kansas, are truly inspiring because Dick's health has not been the best. John W. Ward of Marshall, Missouri, was equally inspirational with information of his hometown hero John W. Donaldson.

The Reverend Charles Lucas was one of my early boosters. Two others who felt strongly about this work and encouraged me from the very beginning were Aaronetta and Louis Anderson of AA Production in Milwaukee, Wisconsin. They were a constant source of inspiration and support of my work on baseball in general, and especially the history which took place in Milwaukee.

I must also thank Don Motley, Ray Doswell and Bob Kendrick of the Negro Leagues Baseball Museum for keeping the history alive. Bill Livingston and Pam Ross of the Black Archives of Mid-America are also doing an outstanding job of preserving baseball history in Kansas City. I must thank the writers at the *Kansas City Call* newspaper for all of their support as well. In the final stages of any manuscript you need people with skill and experience.

Special consideration must be given to Timothy Rives, an exceptionally dedicated archivist in the National Archives and Records Administration-Central Plains Region in Kansas City. Timothy supplied information on the Booker Ts baseball team and Lemuel Hawkins' stay at the prison from the files of the federal penitentiary located in Leavenworth, Kansas.

I owe my mother, Margaret, a special debt of gratitude for her unwavering support of everything I do. My father Arthur Dixon, a longtime Kansas City Monarchs fan, was very proud of this endeavor and provided much inspiration and financial backing as did other members from my family of origin, especially my sister Wendolyn.

Finally, I would like to thank my wife, Kerry, and our three children. They had to listen to my rehashing of stories and accompany me on visits to libraries and visits to ballplayers' homes. Thank you for loving me when the going was tough. Kerry was equally as supportive in shaping this story.

And thanks to Steve Penn and other writers at the *Kansas City Star* for writing articles about Wilber "Bullet" Rogan and his Kansas City Monarchs teammates.

There were virtually hundreds of people that helped to make this project become a great success. Unfortunately time and space would not allow me to recognize all of them individually. I apologize to anyone whose contribution to this work has been overlooked or lost through many years. I thank you all from the bottom of my heart for all that you contributed. Together we made this project meaningful and so very worthwhile to complete.

Preface

As the year 1999 ended, there was a mad scramble to name the century's greatest baseball players. Babe Ruth seemed to top almost everyone's list. Occasionally, some writer would throw in an African American player from the Negro Leagues, but it was obvious that this politically correct exercise was simply an exhibition in name dropping. Few, if any at all, listed Wilber "Bullet" Rogan, an oversight of major league proportions. Rogan was perhaps the greatest all-around player ever.

Many may question my selection of Rogan as one of baseball's greatest ballplayers, and others will not be enthusiastic about my decision to write an entire book dedicated for the most part to his career. Why spend so much time researching one unrecognized player? After all, where are Rogan's lifetime totals, his previous biographies, his accolades? What appears to be a fairly outlandish claim at first is in reality only Rogan's due recognition. Rogan is interesting for many reasons, but there are at least two aspects of his life that lift him above many others.

First, Rogan's career demonstrates the deep-rooted influence of racism in American sports. Second, his career accomplishments speak for themselves, especially when we consider that equality for African Americans in baseball did not exist in his day.

This book, which was more than 25 years in development, is more than a biography of a baseball hero. It is a foundational account of one individual, the elements involved in his personal environment, his collective opportunity and most certainly his life as it was shaped by racism. Writing and researching this book was as much a labor of love as it was an effort to execute an accounting of a dream deferred for a very deserving athlete.

This work has its beginnings in 1980, although many years passed before I fully understood the ramifications of the project. In the ensuing years I published the *Kansas City Baseball Trivia Quiz Book* and *The Negro Baseball Leagues: A Photographic History, 1867–1955*. Although both books were well received, it was obvious that it would take a truly inspired effort to write a meaningful history of ball played behind the color line, especially one giving recognition to a player such as Wilber "Bullet" Rogan. I often wondered why no one else attempted such a work. Outside of Janet Bruce's *The Kansas City Monarchs: Champions of Black Baseball*, which was published in 1985, there were few efforts to chronicle this historic team or its best player.

Any number of individuals could have written a first-hand account of the Monarchs. The men who were actually on the team, the sportswriters of that era, perhaps even the local sports enthusiasts, admirers of the team for so many years, must have known more than they shared. However, by the mere fact of my environment and my early development in baseball, it seems that I was fated to write this story.

I was born in Kansas City, Kansas, in 1956, the youngest in a family of nine children. Our neighborhoods, our schools, and my church were segregated institutions. My first elementary school, Dunbar, was named after an African American, the legendary poet Paul Laurence Dunbar. Later I would attend Phillis Wheatley Elementary. Segregation was all that I had known in those early years. Coincidentally, our home was less than a mile from the neighborhood where Wilber "Bullet" Rogan was reared. And across the alley from our home—we had alleys in those old neighborhoods—stood the home of Eddie Dwight, a former Monarchs outfielder. Like segregation, baseball history also surrounded me.

In the mid–1960s my entire family moved to Kansas City, Missouri. Still residents of a segregated community, we lived within two blocks of where Leroy "Satchel" Paige resided with his family. Frank Duncan, the legendary Monarchs catcher, lived in our same neighborhood, and Newt Allen's home wasn't far away. John "Buck" O'Neil's home was also within walking distance. Living in the midst of all these well-known but unrecognized celebrities, I fell in love with baseball, and that love was reinforced by my first baseball coach, Sherman "Road Block" Jones, a former big league pitcher, and Reggie Smith, outfielder of the Boston Red Sox, who in 1967 became the first active player that I met.

By the summer of 1968, Kansas City's inner-city neighborhoods were in riotous turmoil. Our African American community was pressing at the seams of oppression and bursting for an opportunity to free itself from the angry grip of racism. Martin Luther King's death seemed to climax years of frustration. My family was in chaos as well, as my parents divorced that year. The new home my siblings and I moved into, with our mother, was within walking distance of Municipal Stadium, home of the Kansas City Athletics and Kansas City Chiefs. On many a hot and balmy summer's night, I was put to sleep by the noise of cheering crowds at the ball park. As the years passed my love for baseball blossomed. Within a short time, I began collecting baseball cards and soda pop tops of the local Kansas City Athletics. Nothing seemed to fascinate me more than sports, especially baseball.

In an effort to restore order within the city after the riots, local park department officials, with their portable entertainment trucks, set up on a playground across from our house, on the grounds of Phillis Wheatley Elementary. The truck was equipped to show movies. The feature one summer evening was *The Jackie Robinson Story.* This was my early introduction to baseball, and most importantly my first encounter with racism in sports. Although I was just 11 years old, Robinson's story left an indelible impression on my young mind. Instead of turning me away from baseball, racism drew me closer. Fascinated by the aura of it all, I read the local sports pages, checked books out of the library and watched baseball on television. Eventually, I became a walking encyclopedia of major league baseball information—a fanatic. To my disappointment, though, my wealth of knowledge only included major league baseball history. It would take some time before a full understanding of African American baseball would come into view.

Sometime during the 1970s, Fred Lieb of St. Petersburg, Florida, assembled what he considered to be the greatest team that could be assembled from the last 100 years of baseball. Lieb, 88 at the time, and an "objective observer" who had been chronicling the game for 68 years, was a respected member of the Hall of Fame Veterans Committee. Lieb failed to include a single African American on his select squad. His team selection conjured up some interesting discussions within the inner city, especially in my neighborhood, as I recall.

Many years passed, and my interest in baseball flourished through 3&2, City League,

Mickey Mantle League and high school play. I collected sports cards and devoured books and magazines, along with newspaper articles.

In 1980 a chance encounter in Topeka, Kansas, with Carroll Ray Mothell, a man his teammates referred to as "Dink," totally altered my vision of baseball history. Although I had read many books about major league baseball, Mothell talked of baseball that I had never known. He talked about baseball that was purposely omitted from the books that I had been reading. As if by magic, the missing pieces of the mysterious baseball equation became obvious, and for the first time ever, I began to think about African American athletes that performed before, with, and against Jackie Robinson. During one of my visits to St. Louis, Missouri, I was stopped cold by a statement that James "Cool Papa" Bell uttered. Bell said, "The greatest baseball players that ever lived were Black." I had never heard such a comment and it intrigued me. Bell's conversation sparked genuine thought. We talked often about Fred Lieb's selection of all-time greats as Bell attempted to fill in the blanks.

It was also in 1980 that Janet Bruce, a student at the University of Missouri-Kansas City, visited me for the first time. Bruce's project was to be a social history of the Kansas City Monarchs. I wondered what details her book would focus on, and knowing it was to be a social history I did not feel that it would contain enough of the actual on-field activities of the Monarchs, and thus I continued with my work. As it turned out my hunch about Bruce's book was correct. Although well-received, it included very little information on actual players' performances. Omission of the Monarchs' on-field achievements remains as common an occurrence today as it was in 1980.

All of the books I had read, which with only a few exceptions, were written prior to Jackie Robinson's arrival with the Brooklyn Dodgers in 1947, omitted details of games and colorful profiles of Negro League–era players. These often overlooked areas of detail now became my focus. Armed with this new vision, I set out to tell Mothell's story and the suppressed history of African American athletes in baseball. Ultimately, what started out to be a small pamphlet about Mothell's life ended up being the award-winning *Negro Baseball Leagues: A Photographic History, 1867–1955*.

Since Kansas City was my home, I naturally had acquired a strong admiration for the Kansas City Monarchs. In 1982, anticipating one of the greatest research projects of my youth, I set out to find every game played by the Monarchs. That same ambitious burst of effort was followed by an attempt to locate every man ever to wear a Monarchs uniform. The results were phenomenal. Without grants, or any help with funding whatsoever, my efforts eventually paid off. Much of what is in this work derived from that dedicated hunt for historical information.

This Monarchs project began with reconstructing the team's schedules from 1920 to 1955. As time passed, my research process was refined. Hundreds of interviews were conducted with former players, family members and loyal fans, and most of all librarians. Conversations with anyone and everyone who wanted to talk baseball—especially Monarchs baseball—continued for nearly 15 years. The hunt for information went way beyond interviews of players.

The Monarchs played hundreds of games in Kansas, Missouri, Texas, Oklahoma, Iowa, Nebraska and Minnesota, but they were not limited to the Midwest and Southwest. My search for games took me to more than 35 states and to two foreign countries: Canada and Mexico. A collection of several thousand box scores and hundreds of written accounts of

Monarchs games yielded all sorts of previously unrecorded information. There were players with thousands of hits, hundreds of home runs and countless extra-base hits. I found at least two pitchers who were reported to have struck out 500 batters in a season and several men that had stolen more than one thousand bases. I had also come to the realization that at least eight long-term Monarchs — Wilber "Bullet" Rogan, John W. Donaldson, José Méndez, Andy Cooper, Willard Brown, Newton Henry Allen, Hurley A. McNair and Chet Brewer — had Hall of Fame careers. And for once in my life, I had the information to validate this claim. A spirited debate could be waged for Charlie Beverly, T.J. Young, J. L. Wilkinson and Henry Milton. Some of the Monarchs were as illustrious off the field as they were on it. Take the case of Edgar "Blue" Washington. Prior to joining the Monarchs in 1920, Washington had made an appearance in the silent film *Rowdy Ann* in 1919. With the conclusion of the 1920 season, he returned to California and became an actor, appearing in many more movies, nearly 62 in all.

Unfortunately, after more than 25 years of searching, I can only conclude that many of these players do not get the respect they deserve. John W. Donaldson, for example, was denied entrance into the Baseball Hall of Fame in Cooperstown, New York, by a controversial panel of so-called Negro League experts.

For this work, with the help of many individuals, I have assembled what might be the most thoroughly documented history of the Kansas City Monarchs or any other minority baseball team. And even though this work is now completed, the research continues.

By the fall of 1997, after years of research in public libraries and historical societies, and after years of flying by the seat of my pants, it was time to summarize my research. Because of the enormous amount of available information it was only fitting to create two books. The first would cover the period from 1920 to 1938. Five chapters were written in one week in 1998. In that week, sequestered in a downtown Milwaukee Hilton hotel room, and with pen, paper and files, I dedicated myself to writing. The remaining chapters were written in Kansas City over a period of 90 days. By the spring of 1998, the manuscript was completed. Writing the book, however, was far easier than editing it. There were thousands of references to verify. When Wilber "Bullet" Rogan was selected to the Hall of Fame in February 1998, it was only natural that he be featured in the title of this publication.

Understandably, many of the stories contained within this book remain difficult for some to grasp. It may appear to others as if I am challenging the very foundation on which our national pastime was established. To all, I encourage you to read this work with an open mind, noting that references are given often and the ability to check the facts for yourself thus becomes a relatively simple task.

Interest in Negro League baseball history is far greater than it was when I originally started this project. And yet, there is much more to learn and uncover. With the publication of this work I am convinced that many of baseball's greatest players never played in the National and American Leagues. Today, I am positive that a great number of these outstanding and gifted individuals were in the Negro Leagues, performing for teams such as the Kansas City Monarchs. And in that illustrious history, Wilber "Bullet" Rogan was, perhaps, America's most magnificent all-around baseball player ever.

The statistics presented in this book come from research located by the author unless otherwise noted. League totals and exhibition totals are combined in an attempt to show a realistic seasonal contribution of the player in question.

1

West-3541

Rogan is rated by baseball experts as of full major league caliber and these same experts often have declared that if only he could get into one of the big circuits he would embellish his name in baseball history as have Rube Waddell, Eddie Plank, Grover Cleveland Alexander and others.—Joplin Globe, July 17, 1927

J. L. Wilkinson's Kansas City's Monarchs, organized in 1920 as charter members of the Negro National League, were one of the greatest attractions in baseball history. Between 1923 and 1929, the Monarchs won two World Series, and four league pennants. In the 1930s the winning continued, as Wilkinson's Monarchs barnstormed the nation, playing games against America's most renowned players and teams. In seven years of barnstorming, 1930–1936, the Monarchs won well over 800 games. In 1937 the Monarchs joined the newly formed Negro American League and won yet another pennant, their fifth in 12 years of league play. Though the Monarchs were a great team, one that had launched the careers of many outstanding athletes, some of their most monumental victories could be credited to a single talented performer named Wilber "Bullet" Rogan.

Ever since men began slamming balls with bats, there has been an ongoing argument as to who is actually the greatest baseball player of all time. Beginning with nineteenth century star Adrian "Cap" Anson and the legendary Ty Cobb, and eventually the immortal Babe Ruth, the question over baseball's greatest player seems to generate endless debate.[1]

Bullet Rogan is one baseball player that no serious argument should omit. He was a star pitcher, outfielder and slugger for the Kansas City Monarchs. His career totals from more than 25 years of celebrated play with a variety of military, semi-professional and Negro League teams more than qualify him for consideration in the debate.

He is seldom mentioned among the usual handful of players, however. Rogan's lack of exposure and his African American heritage are explanation enough for the oversight. African American athletes have long been omitted from the debate, and yet there are many, like Rogan, that deserve serious consideration.

Consider that Bullet Rogan won 350 games as a pitcher and on offense hit 350 home runs and stole 500 bases. Any one of those accomplishments might have been enough to make him a star. The fact that he achieved these remarkable feats under some of the most discriminatory conditions in baseball history only enhances the argument that he is one of baseball's all-around best.

To understand how Rogan could accomplish so much and remain so little known, we must revisit baseball's segregated past. From the founding of the National League in 1876 to 1947, when Jackie Robinson broke the color barrier, America's national pastime was rife with racism. African American players were excluded from white teams and discriminated against by the white media. In the years between the two great wars, African American athletes were forced to start their own leagues if they expected to continue playing America's national pastime. Despite their acknowledged equality as athletes, they were often forced to play in inferior ballparks, under inferior conditions. This brand of baseball denied opportunity to several generations of minority Americans — and weakened the game both on the field and at the gate.

Segregation made it fairly simple to isolate African Americans in the newspapers, and spotty coverage almost always clouded public opinion. Rogan's five hometown newspapers — the *Kansas City Kansan, Kansas City Star, Kansas City Times, Kansas City Journal* and *Kansas City Post*— offered many examples of how segregation in print media was successfully achieved.

During the 1920s, when Wilber Rogan was an acknowledged superstar in the black community, Kansas City's four daily newspapers regularly ran photographs of Babe Ruth, Ty Cobb, Lou Gehrig, Knute Rockne, Red Grange, Jack Dempsey, Gene Tunney and others on their sports pages. Rogan's photograph appeared in the local dailies only once during that period. Nearly 14,600 editions of the local press missed the opportunity to attach Rogan's image to an article in the 1920s.

Unlike many of the legendary names we have come to respect, Wilber "Bullet" Rogan's interest in baseball had very little to do with big league enchantment. Because of the insidious color line that prohibited African Americans from equal competition in all aspects of American life, reaching the so-called major leagues was an insignificant and meaningless goal. His was a simple rags-and-no-riches journey to excel at something he loved — baseball. To truly understand Rogan's great achievements, it would be beneficial to look back at how it all began.

Wilber "Bullet" Rogan was born Charles Wilbern Rogan on July 28, 1893, in Oklahoma City, Oklahoma.[2] It was shortly after his mother's premature death that Wilber, his brother Willard, and their father Richard migrated from Oklahoma to Kansas City, Kansas.[3] Wilber began visiting local ball diamonds, and during this same period he dropped his first name, Charles, and began calling himself by his now shortened middle name, Wilber.

Wilber's father, Richard, a former slave from Tennessee, was a tall, lanky man of immense pride. In an effort to stabilize the family's home, Richard married a lady named Ophelia Walstean. Richard was 12 years older than Ophelia.[4] When Ophelia moved into the Rogan household with her two children from a previous marriage, she brought a new element into the home with her outspoken and sassy comments.[5]

The years the two Rogan boys spent with the stepmother's two children, Leon and Beatrice, were arduous. Neither Wilber nor Willard, four to five years younger than his brother, seemed to make the adjustments needed as the newly enlarged family tried to come together.[6] Wilber eventually left home, still a teenager. Willard simply withdrew, and his life was later paved with personal despair and numerous run-ins with the law. Within a short time, Anna Rogan, Richard's sister, and a brother, John Rogan, also relocated to Kansas City, Kansas.

Long before Bullet Rogan's active interest in baseball, the sport had already grown wildly popular in Kansas City, Kansas. The city could thank "Topeka Jack" Johnson, a former Chicago Union Giants infielder, and a local businessman named Tobe Smith for this celebrated slice of regional baseball history. Johnson's original team, the 1905 Topeka

Richard Rogan (left) and Ophelia Rogan were the parents of Wilber "Bullet" Rogan. Richard was born in Tennessee in 1864.

Giants, were the first African American professional team organized in the state of Kansas.[7] In addition to baseball, Johnson had built a reputation as a prize fighter, starting in 1909. Before his fight career ended in 1925, Johnson had squared off against a host of legendary boxers, such as Jack Johnson, Joe Jeanette, Sam Langford, Tut Jackson and Bearcat Wright.[8]

In 1907, Johnson and Smith — spurred by some imaginative financing from a Kansas City, Missouri, numbers banker named Felix Payne — gave Kansas City its first professional baseball team with the creation of the Kansas City, Kansas, Giants. Payne's bustling numbers operation helped finance the erection of a new 7,000 seat enclosed park at Second and Franklin Avenues in Kansas City, Kansas. Built on the rich grass of the plains, the new ball field was named Riverside Park for its proximity to the Missouri River. The park was surrounded by factories and was highly accessible for the men who worked nearby.

On the river's other side, in Kansas City, Missouri, the powerful yet still semi-professional Kansas City Monarchs baseball team resided. Arthur "Chick" Pullam, a United States postal worker who moonlighted as a semi-pro catcher, managed the Monarchs. Pullam's team worked out an arrangement to lease Association Park whenever the Blues, Kansas City's newest entry in the American Association, were on the road. The straight-laced and college-educated Monarchs were determined to keep the mythical Negro baseball championship on the Missouri side of the river. That rivalry eventually led to the 1907 signing of the phenomenal William "Bill" Lindsay, the Monarchs' first paid player.[9] Lindsay's pitching

Tobe Smith with horses. Smith was the owner of Tobe Smith's Transfer Company. He simultaneously operated the Kansas City, Kansas, Giants and his transfer company. Smith left baseball in 1911 and died in Kansas City, Kansas, in 1926.

turned out to be precisely what the Monarchs needed to keep Topeka Jack Johnson's Giants continually moaning. In that first season, Lindsay beat the Kansas City Giants, 4–0, in one game, struck out 15 Giants in another, then returned to strikeout 16 Giants in the game after that.

After two seasons of intense battles, Lindsay bid a farewell to the Monarchs midway through the 1909 season and jumped to Johnson's Kansas City Giants for a more lucrative contract. That same summer, Johnson's Giants, behind Lindsay's stellar pitching, established one of baseball's truly remarkable records. They won 54 consecutive games.[10] The story surrounding the streak was more interesting than the streak itself.*

In late August of that memorable 1909 season, Andrew "Rube" Foster brought his powerful Chicago Leland Giants to Riverside Park for three games to decide the Negro World Championship. Foster's Leland Giants were among the most recognizable teams in baseball. With Foster, Pete Hill and Walter Ball, the Leland Giants boasted three of baseball's truly outstanding players, in fact, both Foster and Hill would eventually be enshrined at the National Baseball Hall of Fame in Cooperstown. Their wide recognition was a direct result of their on-field dominance against teams composed of National and American League stars.

The rest of the community shared the wonderment in young Rogan's eyes, in particular the men who gambled on the big series. Gamblers came from as far away as Topeka and Coffeyville, Kansas. From nearby Leavenworth, Kansas, soldiers flowed into Riverside Park to get a piece of the action. One Kansas City newspaper advertised the games as being for the "colored championship of the United States and a side purse of $1,000."[11] Many fans

Kansas City Monarchs, 1908. From left: William Houston, Bert Wakefield, Tully McAdoo, West Wilkins, Bill Lindsay, Thomas McCampbell, Arthur Pullam, Frank Evans, Tom Stearman, Ernest J. McCampbell, Fred Lee, Robert "Frog" Lindsay. The *Indianapolis Freeman* noted, "White people say that if Lindsay were white he could draw the salary that [Three Finger] Brown of the [Chicago] Cubs draws."

*My research has located 51 of the reported 54 games played during the streak. After the Giants left Kansas City they traveled to Nebraska and may have extended the streak to 57 consecutive games won.

arrived by streetcars and others boarded trains to get to the series. Youngsters lined the streets and others climbed trees for this, their once-in-a-lifetime chance to see the world-renowned Chicago Leland Giants. Baseball fans the whole city over were buzzing and a record crowd was expected.

The Leland Giants started as everyone expected, winning game one, 5–0, behind Walter Ball's masterful two-hit pitching.[12] After that, Foster's team ran into an unexpected phenomenon named Bill Lindsay. Out of the game with a broken leg, Foster watched helplessly as a record 16 of his Leland Giants struck out in Chicago's 3-to-1 loss.[13] The following afternoon, Kansas City managed a 5–4 win over the Leland Giants, winning the series.[14] Although attendance figures for the third game are missing, the first two games drew more than 1,100 people to Riverside Park. Seemingly, during the summer of 1909 there was nothing more popular in Kansas City, Kansas, than baseball.

As was customary in the era of pre-league baseball, the team that defeated the recognized champion laid claim to the crown. The Kansas City Giants declared themselves Negro world champions. Was it a legitimate claim? They had played 147 games and lost just 19 against the best teams — African American or otherwise — throughout Kansas, Missouri, Oklahoma, Nebraska, Iowa, Illinois, and Texas.[15]

For obvious reasons, the Kansas City Giants became the team that Rogan admired most. He visited Riverside Park frequently enough to beat the one-mile trek to the ball field into a path. The opportunity to see players like Bill Lindsay, Andrew Skinner, William Pettus, Robert Boone and Topeka Jack Johnson became the thrill of Rogan's youth. The Giants were far more than a team of locals gotten together to play baseball. One of the Giants' star players, Pettus, born August 13, 1884, in Goliah County, Texas, was recruited from Santa Fe, New Mexico. Prior to his career in baseball, he had been a prize fighter on the Pacific Coast, once fighting the legendary Jim Flynn. (Pettus lost to Flynn in Pueblo, Colorado, on September 22, 1909, in ten rounds.) Andrew "Big Red" Tenny came to the Giants from Little Rock, Arkansas. Eddie Douglass arrived from Fort Worth, Texas. Ashes Jackson, a native of Lexington, Missouri, and Topeka's Tully McAdoo* were also members of the Giants' formidable squad.

When Rogan decided to emulate his idols and become a professional baseball player himself, no one, including his own stepmother, took him seriously. Rogan had never demonstrated natural talent, and he didn't look much like a ballplayer. He possessed scrawny legs and an even narrower waist. The only part of his body that looked remotely athletic was his exceedingly broad shoulders. At 5-foot-7, it didn't appear that he was going to grow to be a very large man either.

Life at home went from bad to worse when Ophelia limited Rogan's ball playing in order to register him with the local high school for area African American children. Rogan, who had played baseball at his integrated middle school, refused to attend the new segregated school. He wasn't alone. Many of Wyandotte County's African American citizens were protesting the opening of the school, citing Kansas state law, which had provided for segregation "at the primary level only."[16]

The argument over school integration in Kansas City, Kansas, had been a heated one.

---

*Tully McAdoo, first baseman for the Kansas City, Kansas, Giants was married to "Topeka" Jack Johnson's sister. He later moved to the St. Louis Giants.

For many years, the city's upstanding white citizens openly objected to their children being educated with African Americans. The city fathers, strapped by state mandates on one hand and preoccupied with local complaints on the other, reluctantly overlooked the opposition. Finally, in the spring of 1904, an incident involving an 18-year-old African American boy named Louis Gregory, who had killed a local white teenager, gave the segregationists their ultimate weapon. Angry local whites attempted to lynch Gregory for the shooting, but a group of African American Spanish–American War veterans stepped in and restored peace. Shortly thereafter, the Kansas state legislature passed special laws exclusively for Kansas City. One of the laws promoted segregation of the races in all public schools. The bill was rushed through the Kansas legislature and rubber-stamped by the Kansas Supreme Court. And in the fall of 1905 eighty African American students reluctantly formed the first classes at the new segregated Sumner High School. For many in Rogan's community, the episode signaled an unforgivable return to second-class citizenship.[17]

Rogan eventually attended Sumner High School but did not graduate. He resented the school and segregation. Renowned historian, and friend of Rogan's family, Orrin Murray, who also attended Sumner, blamed the stepmother for Rogan's failure to graduate. "Rogan disliked his stepmother. She was a real battle-ax," Murray recalled; "Rogan moved his age up by several years, left school and joined the army."[18] However, many people, especially those involved in the day-to-day interest of baseball, knew Rogan's actual age because of his many appearances with the Palace Colts baseball team.

Kansas City, Kansas' Palace Colts were deemed the best teenage baseball team in the region. Catcher Fred Langford, who began his baseball career with the Palace Colts and later played with the St. Louis Giants, recalled how the Colts originated. "A gang of us boys hung out at Frank Lowe's Pool Hall on Fifth Street," Langford remembered, "and that's where Fred Palace [the owner of the team] found most of his young talent."[19] For Palace, born August 29, 1892, in Reno, Kansas, a worker at one of the city's many meat processing plants, baseball was a side hustle. It was a way of creating the sort of wealth that one could not acquire by simply working a job. Palace had gotten together with John N. Harris, and the two men began scheduling games from Palace's home. They proceeded to fill the Colts calendar with stops throughout Kansas and Missouri. These games gave the local youngsters an opportunity to hobnob with others of their own age and racial background living outside Kansas City.

While touring the surrounding area, the Colts witnessed other outstanding players within the same age division. Rube Tyree, a pitcher who later gained national prominence with Chicago's American Giants, was with the Liberty, Missouri, Tigers when the Colts visited that city, and George Sweatt, a future Kansas City Monarch, was with the Iola, Kansas, Go Devils. Locally, though, white teams supplied most of the opposition for the Colts. The Pastimes, Schmelzers Sporting Goods, the Beaver Athletics, the Browns, the Blowers, the Cubs, and Vassar Roofing Company were among the local teams that were easily beaten by Palace's Colts. James "Cot" Tierney, an infielder who played in the National League from 1920 to 1925, was a member of the Schmelzers team subdued by the Colts.

The Palace Colts were well covered by the local press. The *Kansas City Journal* newspaper noted, "The Palace Colts [are] the only 18- or 19-year-old team in the two cities having a reputation that stands next to the Kansas City, Kansas Giants."[20] Another issue of the same newspaper reported, "The Palace Colts are champions of the two cities and have won that title for four seasons."[21]

The Palace Colts' local games were well attended since many were played as preliminaries to Kansas City Giants games. Opening for the Saint Paul Gophers, the Pekin Tigers of Cleveland, the New Orleans Eagles and the Fort Worth Black Wonders of Texas gave Palace's Colts instant recognition.

Since the Palace Colts and the Kansas City Giants were receiving rave reviews, a game was scheduled for the two teams to meet. The game was played on April 23, 1911, and it resulted in a 4–0 Giants victory.[22]

Unsung and nearly anonymous, Palace's Colts continued to overwhelm their opposition for nearly four years before going undefeated in 1910.

But winning, as they soon discovered, provided no bed of roses, in fact, it was probably what caused the Palace Colts to disband. Nobody wanted to play them anymore. As a result, Fred Palace was left begging for games in the *Journal's* sports pages. Frustrated at his inability to secure dates, Palace listed his telephone number, West-3541, for easy contact. Though the Colts were champions on the field, much of the local press had labeled them as insignificant.

James "Cot" Tierney. A Kansas City native, Tierney had six successful seasons in the National League. He never forgot his experience of playing against African American teams as a semi-professional. Once Tierney reached the major leagues he returned to play many games against the Monarchs.

As good as the team had been in 1910, the 1911 Colts were better, largely because of the additions of Dick Whitworth, Rob Austin and Wilber Rogan to its roster.

Richard Henderson Whitworth, born August 28, 1894, in St. Louis and raised in Kansas City, Kansas, had been a third baseman before a timely incident forced him to the pitching mound. According to Fred Langford, "Whenever we were practicing, the ball players always worked out at other positions.... One day Whitworth went to deep center field in old Riverside Park and threw one to home plate without a bounce. Fred Palace's voice snapped, as his head spun around towards Whitworth. 'If you can throw like that,' said Palace, 'you ought to be pitching!'"[23]

Wilber Rogan had the privilege of catching Whitworth that season. It allowed him to observe every bend and break of Whitworth's pitches. It was information that would serve him many years later when Whitworth and he would do battle in the professional arena.

When referring to Rogan, Langford smiled and became preoccupied with the palm of his left hand. "That Rogan could really throw hard. So hard that everyone hated for him to throw the ball. On the Colts team, Rogan would catch and I would play second base, and then we'd switch around and I would catch and Rogan would play second," remembered Langford. "When Palace saw how hard Rogan could throw, he put him on the mound, but Rogan wasn't very good. He didn't improve until he went away to the army. After he returned Rogan was one of the greatest pitchers I ever saw."[24]

In Langford's opinion, Rogan was the Colts' best player — but not the team's best pitcher. Rob Austin was a better pitcher at the time: "Austin was Palace's nephew and you couldn't find a better pitcher anywhere, but Austin wouldn't leave home."[25] The *Kansas City Journal* even raved about Austin's "School Boy Pencil," a pitch he'd invented and named in 1911. That same newspaper's August 27, 1911, edition was among the first to mention Rogan's name in print. The article read, "The Kansas City, Kansas Palace Colts will play the Diamond Greys at Riverside Park at one o'clock today. O. Davis and W. Rogan report with the Colts."[26]

Fred Palace, who died on October 4, 1949,* silently footnoted himself into baseball history with the discovery of Rogan and Whitworth, two of baseball's finest pitchers. Palace surely would have discovered others if his Colts had not disbanded after the 1911 season, the number of bookings having sunk too far and for too long. In the fall of that 1911 season, one

Dick Whitworth. When he retired in 1936, Whitworth had won over 400 professional games. He had traveled so extensively that other ballplayers jokingly recalled, "Whitworth carried 54 pieces of luggage. His luggage consisted of a 52 piece deck of cards and a pair of baseball shoes."

---

*Fred Palace is buried in Kansas City, Kansas' Westlawn Cemetery, Section 23 Row 7, Plot 5. His burial date was October 8, 1949. His age was listed as 67 at the time of his death.

of the most anticipated local baseball series since the great Leland Giants battle of 1909 was scheduled to take place. It was a historic three-game series between the Kansas City, Kansas Giants, who had by then added the young Rogan, and the all-white Kansas City Blues of the American Association. The Blues lineup had eight men with major league experience.

The Blues were restricted from playing Negro teams without the prior permission of baseball's National Association, an organization united, on one hand, to promote baseball, and on the other hand to prohibit African Americans from professional play. Among their highest priorities was the banishment of inter-racial play. Thus Negro players were not allowed to join any of the National Association teams. In the history of the Association, the Chicago Leland Giants were the only African American team ever admitted.

In 1909, the Association stopped the Blues from meeting the Kansas City, Kansas Giants by refusing to sanction the series. But there was no stopping the 1911 series. The *Journal* informed its readers that "word was received yesterday from Secretary Fran Farrell of the National Association giving the Blues the privilege of playing the Kansas City, Kansas Giants, the best Negro team in American."[27]

For the series, tiny Hurley McNair, a left-handed pitcher from the Dallas Giants, was recruited and assigned the big task of whipping the Blues. McNair had pitched for the Marshall, Texas, Ned Ideas team before turning professional with Houston in the Texas Negro League. He would become a fixture in Kansas City baseball for the next 37 years.

Interest in the series increased as the games drew nearer. Kansas City's *Journal* estimated that each game would "draw 5,000 people."[28] The hotly contested opening game went to the Blues in ten innings. In that game's final frame, an error gave the Blues a 3–2 victory. In game two, McNair battled Harry Seibert in a scoreless seven-inning tie. The local *Journal* newspaper indicated that "in both games the Blues were out-hit and in the last affair but one scratch bingle by 'Spike' Shannon was all that was gleaned from the 'smoky' delivery of McNair."[29] In the eighth inning, the game was called because of darkness. McNair's splendid one-hit performance led many to believe the Giants would win game three, but the Giants lost that final contest by a score of 8–2.

By out-hitting the Blues in every contest, the Giants left little doubt as to the ability of minority athletes to play professional baseball. Evidently no one bothered to compare notes on the two different styles of play. An entirely different synopsis, published in one of the local dailies, duped the public into believing the Giants were only a bunch of lucky misfits performing far above their ability.

The local dailies published only one photograph of the Kansas City, Kansas Giants in the teams' first five years of existence. Rogan's hometown newspapers, the *Wyandotte Weekly Herald, Kansas City (Kansas) Globe* and the *Kansas City Kansan*, took little interest in the results of African American baseball games. It was as if these newspapers were oblivious to the Kansas City, Kansas Giants and other African American baseball teams, and the resulting absence of coverage created the illusion that very few people cared, thus encouraging fans to believe that black and integrated baseball didn't matter.

Nevertheless, African American athletes continued to excel, and a rare sampling of newspapers acknowledged their progress. The *St. Louis Post* offered, "We play it [baseball], to be sure, but the colored people play it so much better that the time is apparently coming when it shall be known as the great African game."[30]

During the summer of 1912, Langford, Whitworth, Mansfield, Austin and Harris were all promoted from the Colts to the Kansas City, Kansas Giants. Rogan never got the opportunity to play baseball for the Giants in 1912. He had made other plans, joining the United States Army. Evidently, the infusion of so much baseball and all of that military presence in the aftermath of the Gregory school segregation affair had made an indelible impression on young Rogan. Not surprisingly, the next time Rogan's name appeared in print, he was leading Uncle Sam's 25th Infantry baseball team to the championship of the Hawaiian Islands.

2

Uncle Sam, Uncle Tom and Boss Wilkie

Rogan easily demonstrated that he's the greatest pitcher white or black.—Kansas City Sun, October 15, 1921

At an age when white athletes were being scouted for minor and major league contracts, Wilber Rogan opted to join the United States Army. After all, he saw little chance to showcase his talents in professional baseball. America's armed service gave him the opportunity for a brighter future. It was his chance to shun the isolation that had denied so many of the great ballplayers he had known and admired. Within a short time, Rogan was shipped to the Philippine Islands for an extended tour of duty. While in the Philippines, the pontificating stopped and the bridge-building began.

Actually, Rogan's early introduction to the military had come by way of the baseball field. As early as 1907 numerous military teams had ventured to Riverside Park to play the Kansas City, Kansas, Giants. One of the Giants' most illustrious opponents was the famous 10th Cavalry team of Leavenworth, Kansas. Whenever the Cavalry team visited Kansas City, they brought soldiers and their idle wages into the city. Their dress, pride and commitment to the United States of America left an indelible memory. The 10th Cavalry was made up of African American men, and most people had never seen a full unit of African American soldiers.

In the years preceding World War I, the United States' African American armed forces were segregated into four traditional military units, and competition for new recruits was serious. In Rogan's hometown, the 10th Cavalry was actively recruiting new men from nearby Fort Leavenworth. Consequently, Army recruiters zoomed in on Rogan and found an interested candidate. Rogan pretended to be older than he actually was, having falsified his date of birth by four years. He was also being courted by the 24th Infantry.

Among the African American units in 1911, the 25th Infantry was stationed at Schofield Barracks, Honolulu, Territorial Hawaii; the 9th Cavalry, at Manila, Philippines; the 24th Infantry, at Fort Sam Houston, Texas; and the 10th Cavalry, at Leavenworth but would soon relocate to Fort Huachuca, Arizona. Master Sergeant Bertram T. Beagle wrote, "The regular army was a very close-knit service, especially the four colored regiments."[1]

Rogan eventually decided upon the 24th Infantry and enlisted on October 19, 1911. He would serve in Company M of the 24th Infantry until October 13, 1914, when he received a standard discharge. Bert Gholston, a solider who would later umpire in the Negro National League, wrote of Rogan, "During the year 1912, his [Rogan's] success as a leader and a player was well known throughout the [Philippine] Islands."[2] That reputation eventually forced him into an additional five years of military service with the 25th Infantry.

According to Beagle, "skullduggery" is what got Rogan into the 25th Infantry.[3] Beagle had served in Hawaii with Rogan and remembered the incident well. Beagle recalled how the 9th Cavalry's commanding officer grudgingly granted a three-month furlough to two members of the 9th Cavalry baseball team in order to induce Rogan into joining that unit. The two soldiers were successful in locating Rogan and getting him to reenlist with the Cavalry. Rogan and his two companions arrived in San Francisco in time to board an army transport ship at the Fort Macon dock for the long trip back to the Philippines. Army transports before World War I were all coal-burning ships with an average speed of ten knots an hour. It usually took ten days to reach the first port of call in Honolulu, Hawaii Territory.

By the time the ship reached Honolulu, the 25th Infantry's baseball team had been alerted to watch for Rogan and his 9th Cavalry escorts. Several of the 25th's soldiers were at the dock to greet them. They wined and dined Rogan and his two comrades until the wee hours of the morning. The following day, Rogan and these two gentlemen from the 9th Cavalry missed the transport ship to Guam. As punishment for the missed transport, the two 9th Cavalry ballplayers were given a summary court martial, and the three men were quickly transferred to the 25th Infantry, where each became members of the 25th's celebrated baseball team.

The 25th's baseball team was known as Uncle Sam's greatest. After their arrival at Schofield Barracks in January of 1913, they dominated baseball in the Hawaiian Islands. When the 25th first reached Hawaii, the entire regiment consisted of 29 officers and 801 enlisted men.[4] Reassignments and discharges usually kept the baseball teams in a constant state of change. Somehow, the regiment developed a knack for recruiting outstanding baseball players. Wilber Rogan, then serving in Company B, Oscar Johnson, Fred Goliah, Robert T. Fagan, Lemuel Hawkins, Walter "Doby" Moore and William "Big C" Johnson ultimately formed the nucleus of the regiment's baseball team. Johnson, a member of the 25th Infantry team from 1916 to 1919, cherished his memories of Army baseball. "Sergeant Jasper, Moore, Goliah, a pitcher named Linder, Hawkins and myself were all members of Company A," noted Johnson. "Rogan was in Company B, the machine gun company." Johnson added, "Fred Goliah, who was from Chicago, Illinois, was the only former professional athlete on the team. He had played second base with the famous Chicago Leland Giants in 1911."[5] Lieutenant Harbold was made manager of the elite squad.

A Post League was eventually organized among the First and 25th Infantries, the 4th Cavalry, and the 1st Field Artillery. A regular league schedule was arranged and played. At season's end, the 25th Infantry was declared Post League champions for 1913. A City League was also formed that same year in the city of Honolulu, consisting of the All-Chinese team, the Portuguese Athletic club, the Asians (the Mauis), and the 25th Infantry.[6] In 1913, the 25th Infantry won the Hawaiian Islands championship. About that same time, the infantry team nicknamed themselves the "Wreckers." The mighty 25th had destroyed nearly every Army and civilian team that visited their home field, Athletic Park, and the name "Wreckers" fit them perfectly.

Rogan proved to be a sensation at two positions, pitcher and catcher. His military buddies nicknamed him "Cap." "In the army, a captain was somebody," Beagle explained. "And on the ball field Rogan was somebody."[7]

If the Wreckers secured the lead in a ballgame, Rogan and his "mesmeric smile,"[8] as

Fred Goliah (far left) and William "Big C" Johnson (far right), shown with two unidentified men in 1919, in Nogales, Arizona. Both players were from Company A of the 25th Infantry. Goliah had a brief stay with the Leland Giants in 1911 and the Chicago Giants in 1920 but never prospered in league play. Johnson had an illustrious career in both the Negro National League and the Eastern Colored League.

it was described in the *Chicago Defender*, kept them there. In the heat of battle, Rogan nearly always got the ball. Apparently he knew what to do with it, as many big victories soon followed.

As a pitcher, Rogan's original no-windup delivery was by no means a cookie-cutter delivery. In addition, he developed a cocktail assortment of pitches too. Rogan threw two varieties of breaking ball. One was slow with a big circular break; the other was a sharp-breaking ball that, up to the last moment, resembled a fastball. All of Rogan's pitches were impossible to time because he had developed a change of pace pitch — the palmball. Hitters found him equally difficult to bunt against because Rogan covered his position like a shortstop. As a consequence of his great fielding, when he was not in front of home plate, he was behind it. Rogan was also the army's best catcher. Few men could match his versatility as a pitcher, catcher, hitter and base runner.

2. Uncle Sam, Uncle Tom and Boss Wilkie 19

The Company A, 25th Infantry baseball team: Sergeant Jasper stands in the back row, fourth from the left; Lemuel Hawkins (far left) and Fred Goliah (far right) kneel in front (Fort Huachuca Museum).

When it was announced that Rogan would pitch, ballpark crowds swelled to capacity seating. "During games," Beagle added, "the soldiers from the 25th Regiment, all in starched China Khaki, fill the first base bleachers. As Rogan strolled to bat, [we in] the first base bleachers would start a chant."[9] Fans were encouraging Rogan to be his very best and rarely were they disappointed.

In 1913, prior to Rogan's arrival, the 25th Wreckers "won twenty games and lost only one."[10] The Wreckers finished the 1914 season with another 20–1 record.[11] The next year was Rogan's first full year with the 25th Infantry's celebrated team.

Midway through 1914, a team of National, American, and Pacific Coast Leaguers, led by Happy Hogan, traveled to the island. A series of games was arranged and promoted by Herbert G. Lowry, sporting editor of the *Honolulu Advertiser*.[12] Lowry, formerly the sports editor of Oakland, California's *Tribune* newspaper, was the leading baseball promoter on the island. By terms of his contract with Hogan's team, they were to spend six weeks in Honolulu.

Hogan, manager of California's Venice Tigers, brought 16 players and an umpire, Jack McCarthy, and set up residence in Honolulu's Alexander Young Hotel.[13] A half-holiday was declared and a parade of both teams, led by the 25th Infantry band, preceded the game. The entire garrison turned out. That afternoon, Jim "Death Valley" Scott, a one-time Chicago White Sox pitcher, beat Corporal Willis, one of the 25th's best pitchers.[14] The Tigers' appearance was followed by a visit of National and American League players led by

Frank Bancroft and Connie Mack. While on the island the big leaguers did not play against the 25th Infantry.

For the remainder of 1914, the regimental baseball team continued its winning, crushing every team it played on the Hawaiian Islands. The next year, 1915, the 25th Infantry played 12 games and won 11 of them. Out of the 64 games the 25th Infantry played in their first three years in Honolulu, they had lost only three. They beat the best teams on the island, as well as visiting professional teams from the United States. They won both the Post League championship and the United States Army Series. In winning the army series, the Wreckers captured the silver trophy cup that was presented by the Honolulu Brewing and Malting Company, sponsors of the games.

In that great season of 1915, the Wreckers had played in a local league that included the P.A.C.s, All-Chinese, the All-Army team and the St. Louis University Saints. The Wreckers' reputation was a source of extreme pride among African Americans back in the United States. Starting in October of 1915, both the *Indianapolis Freeman* and *Chicago Defender* furnished regular reports on the team. One of the earliest articles was a report of the championship game between the 1st U.S. Infantry and the Wreckers. This game ended on a clutch home run by Oscar "Heavy" Johnson. In another game, the *Freeman* reported that, "Oscar Johnson knocked a home run so far that he hurtled around the diamond, sat down, fanned himself and had drunk a bottle of soda water before the ball had been found and thrown to the home plate."[15] That game was attended by 7,000 wildly rooting and yelling soldiers, backed by the regimental trumpet and drum corps. Sergeant Jasper was in the pitcher's box, and Rogan was behind the plate. In other games, Rogan simply stole the entire show by himself.

On October 18, 1915, Rogan, holding down the catcher's spot, and slotted third in the batting order, doubled, tripled, sacrificed and stole a pair of bases in the Wreckers' 11–0 win over the Saints.[16] He returned on November 8, still serving as catcher, to slam out three home runs and a double in four at-bats. The first home run was an initial-inning wallop into right field. Plow drive number two was a fifth inning blast to the same spot. In the eighth, Rogan's hit cleared the entire complex to climax a brilliant 13–1 win over the St. Louis University Saints.[17]

It was not until 1916, however, that the Wreckers gave Rogan more opportunities to showcase his skills. That year the Wreckers completed a string of 30 consecutive wins. During one of the team's big wins, on March 17, Rogan had pitched the Wreckers to a 2–1 victory over the Olympic Club team of San Francisco. In that game, Oscar Johnson aided the win with a massive home run in the last half of the ninth.[18] During a victory over the 1st Infantry on October 21, Rogan, as a second baseman and pitcher, went 2-for-4, scored two runs, stole two bases, then, in the seventh inning, he was called to the mound to preserve the victory. A November 24, 1916, clash between Rogan's 25th Infantry and the All-Stars was well documented in the *Chicago Defender* newspaper. The article stated, "The All-Stars scored on Rogan, which is the first time that a team has made a count against the Schofield twirler in 52 innings."[19] The Wreckers won that game by a 7–3 margin, and Rogan, by striking out 18 batters, which included nine consecutive to start the game, stole the headlines. Rogan's 18 strikeouts, an excessive number of strikeouts for most pitchers, proved to be an average day's workout for the Schofield twirler. An edition of the *Kansas City Call* informed readers of how Rogan, once struck out 25 men in a game.

Oscar Johnson in 1913. Johnson was one of the 25th Infantry's best hitters (Fort Huachuca Museum).

Walter "Doby" Moore, 1913. "Big C" Johnson, another member of the 25th Infantry, recalled, "Sergeant Jasper, [Doby] Moore, [Fred] Goliah, a pitcher named Linder [Lemuel] Hawkins and myself were all members of Company A" (Fort Huachuca Museum).

The real strength of the 1916 team was in its players. In addition to Rogan, Oscar Johnson, Bob Fagan, Fred Goliah, Lemuel Hawkins and Walter "Doby" Moore were outstandingly good.

The only known summary of Rogan's wins while with the Wreckers baseball team appeared in a *Chicago Whip* newspaper article that stated, "Rogan's Record, while in the service, will probably stand for some time to come, he winning 58 games and losing 2."[20] When the *Hawaiian Gazette* newspaper published an article entitled, "Who Is the Greatest of Ball Players?" Rogan eclipsed all of his competitors. "Out at Schofield Barracks, especially where the 25th Infantry holds forth, the vote would be all for Wilber Rogan. And a perusal of his record on the diamond and what he can do makes it a hard proposition to find any one his equal hereabout." The article continued, "All in all, if the question as to who is the best ball player in Hawaii was put to a vote, Rogan would get 99 percent of those votes. Verily Rogan looks to be the best ball player of them all."[21] Rogan had demonstrated his superior talent in performances against independent, military and local league teams, but the big league scouts were not interested in African American talent. They had, however, little problem in signing players of Asian origin.

William Tin Lai, signed as a shortstop by Charles Comiskey's Chicago White Sox in 1915, was touted as a "full-blooded Chinese."[22] Lai was spotted in exhibition games played in Honolulu while a member of the All-Chinese team. Another member of the All-Chinese team, Lang Akana, was signed to a Portland Beavers contract for 1915. Akana, a left-handed pitcher, was described as being "half Kanaka, half Chinese."[23] Rogan, the island's best right-handed pitcher, was never given a second look.

At least two of Rogan's wins came in 1916 when he played in the Oahu League, a multiracial minor league that provided the Hawaiian Islands with high-caliber baseball. A vote from the directors had admitted the 25th Infantry in March 1916.[24]

In the few league statistics that have been located, Rogan appeared in four Oahu League games, winning two, saving one and striking out 21 batters in 17 innings. On offense Rogan, who played five positions, was equally effective, batting .344 in nine games. He also hit two home runs, both coming in the same game on April 24, 1916. In that game, the Oahu League's season opener, Rogan collected four hits. The second home run, hit in the third inning, cleared the park and the roof of a nearby Chinese synagogue.[25] While dominating the Oahu League, the 25th was similarly leading the Post League. Master Sergeant Dalbert P. Green, one-time captain of the regiment's baseball team, when speaking of the team's greatest players noted, "First of all, then, there comes to mind Rogan, whose masterful pitching carried the regimental team to victory in many a tight game."[26]

Each February, from 1914 to 1918, the United States Army participated in general track and field meets during weeklong celebrations of George Washington's birthday. The celebrations preceded the Mid-Pacific Carnival, held in Honolulu. At the Mid-Pacific Carnival of 1914, the entire regiment of over 1,100 enlisted men proceeded to the city by rail and then marched through Honolulu's most populated business districts. Curious onlookers lined the streets in record numbers to cast an eye at the great Negro soldiers. It was during one of these Mid-Pacific Carnivals that Rogan was timed running the 100-yard dash in ten seconds. He finished third at the 25th Infantry's field day meet on January 25, 1916.[27] Finishing first and second in the 1916 event were Benjamin H. Mills of Company F and Clyde Gilbert of Company G. In winning, Mills had run the race in an unheard of time of nine and three-

Sergeant Jasper, 1913. Aside from Rogan, Jasper was the 25th Infantry's leading pitcher. Jasper, whose first name is unknown, did not follow his teammates into the Negro National League (Fort Huachuca Museum).

Wilber "Bullet" Rogan, 1913. When asked what he remembered most about the Kansas City Monarchs, William Lowe of the Memphis Red Sox yelled, "Rogan!" Lowe offered, 'Rogan was a control ball artist. Good curve ball and could throw it anywhere he wanted. He had full control. You didn't have to worry about him hitting you with the ball" (Fort Huachuca Museum).

fifth seconds.[28] Gilbert and Mills returned to set new Hawaiian A.A.U. records on March 13, in the Mid-Pacific Carnival. That day Gilbert set the Hawaiian 100-yard dash record with a run of ten seconds, and the 220 yard dash record of 22.6 seconds. In that same meet Mills established a Hawaiian A.A.U. record with a run of 52.6 seconds in the 440 yard dash.[29]

Between marching, baseball and his usual garrison duties, Rogan worked up a big league appetite. That appetite helped him to develop what was labeled "Rogan's All-American breakfast." Rogan's legendary meal consisted of three strips of bacon, two scrambled eggs, two pieces of toast, a slice of onion and a glass of milk. For Rogan, it was a morning ritual, particularly before important games.[30]

Rogan was also developing a reputation for physical toughness off the baseball field.

Bert Gholston remembered a fight that Rogan had with an ex-prize fighter named Bristoe. "The fight lasted fully 45 minutes," wrote Gholston. "Neither one gave an inch of ground. Rogan finally landed a terrific right hook to the stomach. It was fully ten minutes before Bristoe recovered consciousness."[31]

Rogan's physical toughness is what led many to speculate that he had received his noticeable facial feature, a deep scar across his right cheek, in a brawl. This of course was not how Rogan explained it. Rogan told Fred Langford, a teammate from the Palace Colts, "A mule kicked me in the face."[32]

While Rogan's pitching was wearing out baseball teams halfway around the world, Dick Whitworth's pitching was breaking down racial barriers in the United States. Since leaving the Palace Colts team, Richard "Dick" Whitworth had graduated to the Kansas City, Kansas Giants and to W.S. Peters' Chicago Union Giants (also known as "Peter's Chicago Union Giants"), which competed against white and black teams in the Windy City. In 1915, Whitworth's second season with Peter's Chicago Union Giants, he reportedly pitched in "thirty-seven games and [was] returned a winner in thirty of them," wrote *Chicago's Whip*. That impressive season eventually led to his signing with Rube Foster's famous American Giants in 1916.

In addition to Rogan and Whitworth, both right-handers, the Midwest was giving rise to a young left-handed pitcher named John W. Donaldson. When it came to strikeouts, Donaldson, born February 20, 1892, in Glasgow, Missouri, was the most phenomenal talent in the region, in addition to being the best pitcher to come from Missouri since the passing of Bill Lindsay. "Both [Charles] Comiskey of the White Sox, and [John] McGraw, of the Giants praised Donaldson for his ability," wrote the *Indianapolis News*.[33]

In 1915, while cruising to another 500-strikeout season — he had also done it in 1914 — Donaldson struck out no fewer than 133 batters in his first full month of play. At season's end, the *Kansas City Star* reported, "His [Donaldson's] strikeout average for the season [was] eighteen men a game." The next season, according to the September 23, 1916, *Chicago Defender*, Donaldson had struck out an incomprehensible 240 batters in only 12 games, adding to that at Sioux Falls he "whiffed 35 in an eighteen inning fray and ... a few days later [he] struck out 27 men in twelve innings."

Toward the end of the 1915 season, the All-Nations played seven games, all on neutral fields, against Peter's Chicago Union Giants for the championship of the Northwest. The series was advertised as a classic Whitworth against Donaldson matchup — finesse and poise versus speed and control. In Slayton, Minnesota, the *Murray County Herald* made a mockery out of the championship game played there between the Union Giants and All-Nations.

"Them niggers and all All-Nations did sure play a great game in the afternoon," spewed the *Herald*, "and the niggers beat the other fellows by a zero to two score." The Union Giants, behind the pitching of the legendary hurler Dick Whitworth, won the series four games to three.

Back in Kansas City, life had taken a tragic turn for Rogan's younger brother Willard. Arrested for burglary in Kansas City, Kansas, Willard had attempted to escape police while being transferred to Kansas City, Missouri, for questioning in another crime. In a futile dash for freedom, Willard leaped from the door of the vehicle in which he was being transported. In capturing Willard, a police officer shot him behind the ear, the bullet passing through the outer edge of his left eye. After his injuries healed, local authorities handed Rogan a two-year stint in the state prison in Jefferson City, Missouri. Willard was eventually pardoned on January 6, 1917. Wilber Rogan was too far away to help.

The 1916 Post League championship was not determined until January of 1917. That month, Wilber's bat put the 25th Infantry atop the league standings. Rogan's 5th-inning home run had given his team a 9–0 victory over the Artillery Brigade, elevating the 25th Infantry to a record of 9–2 and tying them with the 32nd Infantry for league honors. The big finish forced a special three-game playoff series for the title.[34]

Opening the series, Rogan, pitching one of the better games of his career, led the Wreckers to a 14–1 victory. One newspaper reported, "Rogan pitched in his usual good form, which is enough said."[35] The lone tally had come as the result of a ninth-inning passed ball. Rogan secured the Post League title a week later in front of 2,000, winning the second game of a planned three game series, 2–0. (The Wreckers having won the first game too, the series ended early.) Thirty-second Infantry batters got four hits off Rogan in the nine innings he fed them straights, curves and drops. The *Hawaiian Gazette* offered, "The Wreckers again demonstrated that they have not yet met their equals on the ball diamond in the line of winning pennants."[36]

Rogan's wins against Portland of the Pacific Coast League, a team that had scheduled their spring training in Honolulu, punctuated a great start to the 1917 season. Rogan beat Portland twice during their visit. In the first game he delighted fans by pitching a two-hit 3–0 win. He returned to strike out seven in a second game, a 4–1 win, in which he held Portland to four hits. The *Hawaiian Gazette* offered, "Rogan had a good head yesterday. Three times of four the first ball to the batter was straight as a string over the heart of the plate, and the Beavers, mistakenly waiting him out, found themselves in a hole. He had plenty of curves and worked the corners well."[37] In 18 innings, he allowed the Pacific Coast Leaguers just six hits and a run. His performance prompted Owen Merrick of the *Honolulu Star-Bulletin* to write, "In my opinion [Rogan] is one of the best ball players I have ever seen in action. He can hit, run bases and field his position in great shape."

After beating Portland's Beavers, Rogan requested a furlough and headed to Santa Clara, California, where newspapers announced the arrival of several 25th baseball players.[38] Leaving California he returned to Kansas City, Kansas, to see to family affairs. Things had really changed in his six-year absence. Riverside Park had closed down and his stepmother, Ophelia, and father, Richard, had divorced. Ophelia relocated to Kansas City, Missouri, eventually remarrying a man with the last name of Clark. "Topeka Jack" Johnson, the famed manager of the Kansas City, Kansas Giants, had become a policeman in Topeka, Kansas.[39] Fred Palace had given up baseball altogether and opened a fish market. The All-Nations, a team that relocated to Kansas City from Des Moines, Iowa, in 1915, had replaced the Kansas City Giants as the area's leading baseball attraction.

During his furlough, Rogan donned the uniforms of several Kansas City teams. On April 22, 1917, he fulfilled a boyhood dream when he suited up with the Kansas City, Kansas Giants and shut out the Chelsea Athletic Club, 1–0. In that game, he pitched seven innings of two-hit ball, striking out fourteen.[40] Rogan's next game was scheduled against John Donaldson and the All-Nations at Kansas City's Association Park. Donaldson told the *Kansas City Times* that he thought Rogan "[was] a worthy rival, having seen him on the coast."[41] Regrettably though, the game between Donaldson and Rogan was rained out and never rescheduled. J. L. Wilkinson was so impressed by Rogan's pitching, however, that he invited him to remain with the All-Nations for the remainder of his furlough.

Rogan suited up with the All-Nations for the first time on Saturday, May 5, 1917, in a scheduled two-game set against Green's Nebraska Indians, a team that was "organized in 1897 by Guy Green of Lincoln, Nebraska, [and had] been on the road each season since, playing the United States and Canada."[42] In the opener Donaldson held the Indians to four hits and whiffed a dozen batters for the win.[43] Rogan returned on May 6 to engage in another encounter with the Nebraska Indians. In that game, Wilkinson decided to play Rogan in left field rather than put him on the mound. That turned out to be a wise decision, as Rogan's only hit, a triple with a teammate on base, drove in a key run. Late in the game Rogan also stole home to give the All-Nations another score and a huge 5-to-4 win over the touring Native American team.[44]

Rogan remained with Wilkinson's All-Nations for road trips to St. Joseph, Topeka, Pleasanton, Fort Scott, and Lexington. In Topeka, the *Capital Journal* reported that Rogan "upheld his former record as a home run hitter, by clouting the ball far over the left-field fence, scoring a man ahead of him." Topeka Giants star infielder Carroll "Dink" Mothell, played second fiddle to the mighty Rogan in that game. In Fort Scott, Kansas, Rogan homered in a win over the local team. In Pleasanton, Kansas, Rogan had three hits, including a double. The All-Nations' lineup at Pleasanton included three future Cooperstown inductees: Cristóbal Torriente, José Méndez and Rogan. In responding to Torriente, the great Cuban outfielder, the local paper was quick to admit, "If he were a shade lighter in color, he might stand on the same pinnacle with [Tris] Speaker and [Ty] Cobb. His name is Torriente and he hails from Cuba. Every ball he hits is a bullet and among his other accomplishments, he can field, throw and run, but he can't speak understandable English."[45] In Lexington, Missouri, the All-Nations won, 2–0.

When Wilkinson's All-Nations returned to Kansas City, Rogan took the mound, losing a close 5–4 game to the St. Louis Giants. Not long after that, Rogan's name seemed to fade like yesterday's gossip. It was rumored that he had returned to his Army regiment.

A European war and troubles with Mexico forced Rogan's entire regiment to return stateside in August of 1918 to guard the Southwest border of the United States. In leaving Hawaii, the regiment had more than doubled in strength. There were now 72 officers and 2,264 enlisted men.[46] Most of the regiment eventually returned to camp Steven D. Little near Nogales, Arizona. "It took three trips to bring all the troops back to the States. After that, not much baseball was played,"[47] remembered "Big C" Johnson.

The 25th Infantry returned as a championship baseball team, having held the championship of Hawaii from 1914 to 1918. It was during this same period that J. L. Wilkinson's heavy use of Donaldson took a toll on the star pitcher's powerful arm.

2. Uncle Sam, Uncle Tom and Boss Wilkie

Tom Baird and J.L. Wilkinson. They were partners for more than 20 years but were rarely seen together. Here they pose before a Monarchs game on the prairie. Notice the Native American children in the background.

Starting in 1913, Donaldson had pitched four and five complete games a week, and he had kept that pace for over four years. One day, Donaldson's arm suddenly went numb, and soon he was struggling to pitch more than once a week. "Donaldson the Great" had become "Donaldson the Ordinary." It would take nearly five years of limited use before the left arm fully recovered. The All-Nations team limped aimlessly through two seasons. Then, late in 1918, Wilkinson's All-Nations, already decimated by the World War I draft, disbanded. Donaldson was picked up by C. I. Taylor's ABCs in an effort to keep his career alive until the war ended.

When World War I ended Wilkinson began contacting men for a new team he was organizing in Kansas City. Letters were sent to José Méndez, Sam Crawford and John Donaldson, all members of 1919's Detroit Stars. Next, Wilkinson contacted Rube Currie and Hurley McNair of Gilkerson's Union Giants. Rube Tyree, who was pitching for Kansas City's Allies, and Carroll "Dink" Mothell, of Topeka's Capital City Giants, were also contacted. Lightner, a Dallas, Texas, pitcher that originally came into the region with the Kansas City Giants in 1917, was recruited, as were Hugh Blackburn of Knobnoster, Missouri, and Lexington, Missouri's Otto "Jay Bird" Ray. Wilkinson followed with two letters to infielders George Carr and Edgar "Blue" Washington in Los Angeles. Wilkinson also sent contractual offers to Rogan, Moore, Johnson, Fagan and several others in the 25th Infantry.

In addition to the prospective ballplayers, Wilkinson hired Joe Rue, a white umpire who would later appear in the American League, to handle all of the new team's 1920 home games. James "Jew Baby" Floyd was employed as the team's personal trainer. And to seal the deal, Wilkinson formed a working relationship with Kansas City, Kansas' Thomas Younger Baird to assist booking and arranging events.

This flurry of activity is how the decade ended. In the Midwest, Kansas City's *Sun* had proclaimed Donaldson to be "The World's Greatest Pitcher." Another publication, the *Chicago Whip,* affirmed Dick Whitworth as its choice for "The Greatest Colored pitcher."[48] Both newspapers would have a sudden switch of loyalty after just a half season of watching Wilber Rogan in the new Negro National League.

3

Birth of a Big League Star

There are few pitchers in the game today, regardless of color, who look as good on the mound as Rogan. His stand is beautiful. His wind-up is perfect. He is a great twirler, we venture to say another Matty or Foster.—The Chicago Whip, July 1, 1922

The popularity of Rube Foster's Chicago American Giants, Tenny Blount's Detroit Stars and Charlie Mills' St. Louis Giants had sparked a vibrant movement toward the formation of a black major league, and in 1920, the Negro National League was born. The excitement surrounding the start of the long-awaited league, after years of pessimism and disappointment, was predictable. Newspaper publicity quadrupled, games increased, attendance swelled and owners finally saw returns on their investments. The organization of the new league had precipitated a major turn-around for professional baseball players and their owners.

The structure of the new league was not patterned after the National or American Leagues. It was structured to resemble Chicago's Park Owners Association. In that organization, some teams owned and played in their own parks while others, those that claimed no home field, traveled exclusively. Baseball in and around Chicago had flourished with this arrangement and the new Negro National League would too. The eight-team circuit, in addition to having two teams in Chicago, placed teams in Detroit, St. Louis, Indianapolis, Dayton and Kansas City. Wilkinson's Kansas City Monarchs, formed from the pick of the once-famous All-Nations, became the league's first expansion team. The Cuban Stars and Joe Green's Chicago Giants were both traveling teams and claimed no home park.

After much fanfare, May 2, 1920, signaled the historic start of the Negro National League. In the league's first game, Taylor's ABCs defeated Green's Chicago Giants by a 4–2 score at Indianapolis' Washington Park before a crowd of 6,000.[1] Within a week, the entire league was active. Members of Wilkinson's Monarchs team included Bartolo Portuando, José Méndez, Hurley McNair, George Carr, John Donaldson, Edgar "Blue" Washington, Otto "Jay Bird" Ray, Dink Mothell, Jose Rodriguez, Sam Crawford and Rube Currie.

The new circuit pressed into May and June, and as expected, Rube Foster's American Giants dominated. Kansas City's new Monarchs limped aimlessly along for the first two months of the 1920 season, as three of their regular men were out of the lineup with injuries. J. L. Wilkinson claimed to have signed new talent for his fledging team but relief was slow to arrive. The team fought honorably until the much anticipated Wilber Rogan and Walter "Doby" Moore arrived from Arizona and gave the team a hearty midseason boost.

Upon discharge from the 25th Infantry, Rogan and Moore caught up with the Monarchs in St. Louis, Missouri, where on July 4, each player participated in his first Negro National League game. Rogan, playing in left field, and Moore at shortstop, each went 1-for-4 in

From left: Elwood Knox, sports editor of the *Indianapolis Freeman*, Rube Foster, J.D. Howard, sports editor of the *Indianapolis Ledger*, and C.I. Taylor. During the 1921 league meeting Foster announced, "I will, with your assistance make the National Association of Colored Professional Baseball Players the ship, all other opposition the sea."

obtaining their first Negro League hits off St. Louis's John Finner in Kansas City's 4–2 victory.[2]

When Rogan reached the Monarchs he joined an organization that fielded several military men on the league's eight-teams rosters. In fact, he should have saluted his catcher, Sergeant Otto C. Ray, born May 19, 1894, in Lexington, Missouri. Ray served in France as a member of Company F in the 805th and played on the baseball team. Dayton Marcos pitcher Harlen Ragland, of Company L, and St. Louis's William P. Drake of Company B, the Monarchs' Hugh R. Blackburn, of Headquarters Company, had also served in the 805th and as members of the regiment's baseball team.

On July 5, Rogan pitched his first Negro National League game against Foster's American Giants. The American Giants were in the midst of a six-game winning streak when Rogan took the mound against them. Commenting on Rogan's arrival, the *Defender* wrote, "[Rogan] made a three night ride and jumped out with strange support, facing one of the best teams in the country and gave an exhibition of hurling that had 10,000 fans yelping and the American Giants standing on their heads."[3]

Rogan's initial appearance was one for the record books as the 27-year-old ace allowed just one hit, a triple by Elwood "Bingo" DeMoss, and struck out 11 for his first Negro League win. Back in Kansas City, Charles Starks of Kansas City's *Sun* was jubilant. "When the news came [of the American Giants' defeat] there was rejoicing," he wrote with glee.[4]

The way Rogan manhandled the American Giants, considering he had never pitched professionally, was phenomenal. The following afternoon the sensational performances continued, as Rogan, now a right fielder, collected two hits—the second and third of what would be his long Negro National League career.

After the Chicago series, Kansas City traveled to Detroit's Mack Park. In his turn on the mound, Rogan defeated Detroit's Stars by a 4–1 score. In that game, Rogan collected his first Negro National League extra base hit, a double off lefty Andy Cooper. In another game of that series, Rogan stole three bases. When Rogan and his Kansas City teammates showed up in Indianapolis, on July 18, Taylor's ABCs were introducing two future stars in catcher Raleigh "Bizz" Mackey, of Eagle Pass, Texas, and pitcher Robert McClure, of San Antonio, Texas. The new players however, weren't enough to stop Rogan from winning his third Negro National League game.

The Monarchs returned to Kansas City on July 24 to play three non-league encounters against a strong semi-professional team from Beloit, Kansas. In game one, Rogan went 3-for-4, with a double and scored three runs. The following afternoon Rogan pitched a five-hitter and struck out 12, winning, 1–0. After a rest in the series final game, he prepared himself for the biggest series of his young professional career. The stage was set for Kansas City's first six-game series against Foster's American Giants at Association Park. The results changed baseball history forever.

The big series between Chicago's American Giants and Kansas City's Monarchs opened in front of 2,000 passionate fans. Armed with cow bells and whistles, local fans were intent on cheering the home team to victory. Late in the game, John Donaldson collided with Leroy Grant, the American Giants first baseman, and a lively fistfight ensued between the two players. About that same time, 50 irate fans charged the field from the stands. It took a special detachment of officers, with guns raised, to quell the disturbance and chase fans off the ball field. The smaller Donaldson got the worst of the fight and Kansas City's Monarchs the worst of a 9–7 drubbing.[5]

Advance sales for the second encounter reached record proportions, as tickets were selling faster than they could be printed. It seemed that everyone wanted a pair. And if advanced estimates were correct, the Monarchs would break the Kansas City Blues single-season attendance record for 1920.

In game two, before what the *Kansas City Times* called the "largest gathering at Association Park this season," Rogan struck out 13 batters and pitched on even terms with American Giants ace Tom Williams for 11 innings.[6] Finally, in the twelfth, Rogan won his own game with a double that scored a runner to defeat the Giants, 5–4. To their discredit, Kansas City's four daily newspapers inappropriately downsized the crowd to 15,000. Starks, writing in the *Sun* newspaper, fervently challenge that total. "Fully 20,000 people were in attendance," Starks assured his readers. "We don't have to take the dailies' estimate of the number present, [for] we know that their conservativeness is not calculated to be so accurate as it is something else."[7]

The Monarchs won again the following afternoon. This time Rogan, back in right field after a day on the mound, collected two hits, one of which went for a triple. The following afternoon Kansas City made it three of four with another 6–5 win. Rogan lost game five when the American Giants came from behind to win, 4–2. Manager Sam Crawford's submarine chucking shut out the American Giants, 4–0, in the final game of the big series.

In an effort worth celebrating, the upstart Kansas City Monarchs had chastised Foster's veteran team. Most of the credit for winning was attributed to Rogan's on-field heroism. He had finished the series with 21 innings pitched and 21 batters struck out. At the plate he ripped American Giants pitching for a double, two triples and a stolen base. On defense he played errorless ball at three different positions.

When Rogan's obliteration of Chicago's American Giants became public, the new Negro National League had given rise to its first superstar. After that, whenever and wherever Rogan and the Kansas City Monarchs appeared, a crowd was almost certain to follow.

Such was the case when 1,100 showed up to see Rogan thrash Dayton's Marcos on August 8. He was going along in grand style until the fifth inning, when he injured his arm in receiving a throw and was forced to retire from the game.[8] The very next day Rogan celebrated his return to the lineup with two triples, one in the sixth and another in the ninth, and stole a base against this same Marcos team.[9] The outstanding play continued right into September, as Rogan polished off Nebraska's Omaha Armours, 9–0, at Omaha's Rourke Park.[10] Rogan returned to Kansas City on September 25, and ended his first Negro League season with a near perfect 13 strikeout performance over Taylor's Indianapolis ABCs.[11]

By season's end, Rogan had defeated the Detroit Stars three times, the American Giants and Indianapolis ABCs twice and the Dayton Marcos once. He finished that first-half with more than 119 strikeouts and a combined 11–6 record in 18 league and barnstorming contests. In all, Rogan had pitched two shutouts, along with five games of ten-or-more strikeouts. In four clutch performances against that season's Negro National League champion, Chicago's American Giants, Rogan had struck out 36 batters, an average of nine men per outing.

At Association Park, Rogan came to bat 96 times in league games, hitting .320 with seven triples. On the road, his batting record is much more difficult to compute, as Chicago's newspapers did not list at-bats and several games against Detroit and Indianapolis are missing box scores. Totals for Rogan's batting average in that first year, then, are non-existent, though the remaining box scores of Negro League and exhibition games credit Rogan with more than 50 hits for the 1920 season.

Led by Rogan's impressive finish, the Monarchs ended the 1920 season with a respectable 42–34–2 Negro National League record. At Kansas City's Association Park, the Monarchs won 28 league games and lost 16. An edition of the *Kansas City Times* reported that more than 125,000 of the loudest fans in baseball had attended Monarchs games at Association Park.[12] In league and exhibition games combined, the Monarchs played 114 games in 1920. When league attendance totals were made public, it was noted that "616,000 people had paid admissions to Negro National League games."[13]

Rogan's top-shelf performance had also won him a selection to the *Sun's* All-Negro League team. Other members of the *Sun's* elite All-Negro League squad were first baseman Ben Taylor, second baseman Elwood "Bingo" DeMoss, shortstop Walter "Doby" Moore, third baseman Bartolo Portuando, and outfielders Jimmy Lyons, Cristóbal Torriente, and Hurley McNair. George Dixon and John Beckwith were selected as the leagues' best catchers. Pitchers Bill "Plunk" Drake of St. Louis, John Taylor of the Chicago Giants, along with the mighty Bullet Rogan formed the nucleus of the *Sun's* top picks in 1920.

4

A Most Valuable Asset

Zack Wheat, Max Carey, Dutch Stengel, Bob Muesel, and many others who have faced the terrific speed of Bullet Rogan declare he is one of the greatest pitchers. — Leavenworth Times, April 15, 1921

Considering how Rogan performed during his first Negro League season, his stardom should have been certain. As a great-hitting pitcher, he had everyone taking notice. Rogan was carving a legacy for himself — one exceptional performance after another. Ultimately, it would take the actions of white sportswriters — who were, at best, patronizing — to keep Rogan from recognition as one of baseball's elite. The plan was ingeniously fulfilled in a nickname the writers devised — a name that would follow Rogan all the way to Cooperstown, New York.

It was rumored that Bullet's nickname originated because he threw exceptionally fast. Although his arm had the snap of a buggy whip, it is unconfirmed that his nickname originated in such a manner. In reality, there is no documentation as to how the nickname originated. Research does show, however, that Rogan was not called "Bullet" in any of the articles written about him during his entire nine-year stint in the U.S. Army. A December 11, 1920, edition of the *Chicago Whip* was among the first newspapers to refer to Rogan as "Bullet."[1] The first Kansas City newspaper to use the nickname was the April 30, 1921, edition of the *Kansas City Sun*.[2] The *Kansas City Times* and *Kansas City Journal* referred to Rogan as "Joe Rogan" in June of 1921. In 1922, the same year that "Bullet Joe" Bush went 26–7 for the New York Yankees, the (white) sportswriters for Kansas City's four daily newspapers began to refer to Kansas City's Bullet Rogan as "Bullet Joe." Kansas City's two African American weeklies, the *Sun* and the *Call*, refused to make Rogan a trendy version of a white leaguer and held fast to the nickname Bullet Rogan. (Comparisons of black players to white ones were in fact nothing new for white sportswriters, who tagged Pop Lloyd as "the Black Wagner," José Méndez as "Mathewson in the Black," and both Oscar Charleston and Spot Poles as "the Black Ty Cobb.") Without Rogan's permission, or the approval of the Kansas City Monarchs, Kansas City's four dailies transformed one of America's greatest athletes into an insignificant version of the white athlete named "Bullet Joe" Bush. Other dailies quickly adopted the moniker and as a consequence, confusion followed — and for years. As late as August 1930, when the Monarchs visited St. Joseph, Missouri, the local *St. Joseph Gazette* was still in an obvious state of understandable bewilderment. "No starting pitcher has been announced for the Monarchs," offered the *Gazette*, "the club having several from which to choose. It is probable, however, that Manager 'Bullet Joe' Bush, hard-hitting pitcher and outfielder, will start on the mound for the invaders."[3]

Rogan's nickname, chaotic coverage by the prominent daily newspapers, and other, larger issues kept the fledging Negro National League in constant confusion. With few exceptions, all of the prominent big city newspapers refused to print images of African American athletes. Others had chosen not to cover both home and away games, or to publish league standings. Whenever the official standings found their way into the media, they were more difficult than a Chinese puzzle to figure out.

Every city in the league, it seemed, was having some sort of problem. In Detroit, school board officials, owners of property adjacent to the Stars' home field on Mack and Fairview Avenues where Southeastern high school stood, failed in its attempt to condemn Mack Park, which stood on land valued at $92,188.80.[4]

The Dayton Marcos were among the first victims of this unjust state of financial affairs. The Marcos were dropped from the league after the 1920 season and replaced by the Columbus Buckeyes. In 1922, Joe Green's Chicago Giants and the Columbus Buckeyes were replaced by the Pittsburgh Keystones and the Cleveland Tate Stars, both of whom lasted just one season. In 1923, two teams named after animals, the Milwaukee Bears and the Toledo Tigers, joined the league. Through all of these changes, the leagues' five strongest teams—the American Giants, St. Louis Giants, Detroit Stars, Kansas City Monarchs and Cuban Stars—continued to flourish. Kansas City's Monarchs, largely because of the way they played roughhouse ball with Rube Foster's American Giants, were among the league's best-drawing teams.

Rogan was contributing daily to the Monarchs' mammoth stature. Though he would win more than 20 games in 1921, he also lost ten. Six of his losses were by one run. Whenever the Monarchs lost an important game they would gather in the clubhouse for hours afterward to rehash and strategize on various aspects of baseball. These skull sessions, as they were called by the players, were especially helpful when the Monarchs battled Foster's American Giants.

Rogan seemed to have an easy time with Rube Foster's Giants, who would win the 1921 Negro National League championship, beating them five times. One of Rogan's most storied wins against Chicago occurred on Independence Day 1921. Nearly 12,000 people jammed Schorling Park and witnessed Rogan's 10–1, eight-strikeout victory. In spite of the weather—the thermometer registered nearly 98 degrees in the shade—seven hits and six walks were all Foster's Giants could muster. "In inning eight," reported the *Defender*, "the Giants' saved themselves from a shutout when two walks and an error allowed them to score their only run."[5]

C. I. Taylor's Indianapolis ABCs were a much more difficult puzzle for Rogan to solve. In 1921, Rogan lost three games to the ABCs. "Rogan had a good everything," said Bobby Robinson, an infielder that played with the ABCs; "Rogan had a good screwball, a good curveball, and a change of pace. He had a great variety of pitches. You couldn't just go up there thinking you were going to take advantage of him."

At Kansas City's Association Park, Rogan's record for 1921 was an exceptional 8–3 against other league teams. In spite of his many remarkable improvements, most of Rogan's troubles were not in front of the plate but in the men behind it. None of the team's catchers were sufficient at harnessing his benders or breakers.

Against St. Louis, Otto "Jay Bird" Ray, the Monarchs' first-string catcher, cut loose a wild peg that deprived Rogan of a shutout. "For some reason Ray has not been able to stop the baserunners although on the Coast he stopped the big leaguers," said J. L. Wilkinson. "He may get to throwing better soon, which will be a big help to the great pitching Rogan and Currie are delivering."[6] Ray continued to falter, however, and the Monarchs decided to try somebody else behind the plate. George Carr was shifted from his usual first base position to become the team's new catcher. That experiment came to a screeching halt in Indianapolis when two passed balls gave the ABCs a come-from-behind 4–3 win and Rogan his first defeat of the summer. A third catcher, a youngster named Sylvester Foreman, did little to improve the situation. An article in the *Sun* summarized Rogan's plight, commenting, "Wilber Rogan, the Ace of the pitching staff of the National Negro League, is absolutely without a peer as a box artist."[7]

Rogan wasn't the only pitcher suffering from the Monarchs' string of unsteady receivers, so in between starts on the mound, Rogan would sometimes take a turn behind the plate. He turned out to be a better catcher than Ray, Carr or Foreman

There was much rejoicing in Kansas City when the *Sun* broke the news of a major trade for Chicago Giants catcher Frank Duncan. The two-for-one trade sent first baseman Lemuel Hawkins and catcher Jay Bird Ray to the Giants in exchange for Duncan.[8]

Frank Duncan was truly a live wire, and while he was not known as an outstanding hitter, he was an exceptional receiver, with a gun for an arm, and a likable personality. John "Buck" O'Neil, one of the premier players of the 1940s, recalled, "Frank could really catch and throw—a shotgun arm and a great memory. Before Frank died he would talk about a ballgame, he would tell you the inning, the pitch the guy hit and how the score ended. He had a wonderful memory." With his cannon arm, Duncan once threw out six American Giant runners in the same game.[9] The feat occurred in June of 1934 in Chicago, as Willie Foster and Chet Brewer engaged in a pitchers' battle, which the Monarchs eventually lost, 2–1.[10]

Duncan had the size and build of the legendary Bruce Petway, who at 155 pounds was one of the smallest and best catchers in professional baseball. Both Duncan and Petway were as thin as bamboo, and yet much stronger than they physically appeared.

Frank Duncan needed little introduction to local fans, because Kansas City was his hometown. His father, who was also named Frank Duncan, was a popular salesman of coal and block ice in the central city.[11] Frank Duncan the catcher was born in Kansas City, Missouri, on February 14, 1901. He attended Attucks Elementary School and Lincoln High School. At age 18, Duncan married Julia M. Lee, the younger sister of George Lee of the famous George E. Lee Jazz Orchestra. Julia, age 17, a native of Kansas City's west Italian section, was a prodigy and well on her way to becoming a Capitol Records recording artist. In addition to singing in English, she would often break into fluent Italian love songs.[12]

Duncan played with the local Kansas City Tigers prior to turning professional in 1921. The Tigers were a traveling team that played around Kansas City and other parts of the Midwest. Five of Duncan's Tiger teammates: Henry "Dimp" Miller, Ruben Currie, Herlen Ragland, Eddie "Pee Wee" Dwight and Roosevelt "Chappy" Gray, all graduated to successful Negro National League careers.

Owing to a variety of circumstances, among which was an allotment of exhibition games, an unexpected decline in attendance at both weekday and Sunday games, extended railroad trips, and difficulties of drawing up a schedule to avoid conflicts with other leagues using the same parks, many teams lost money in their second and third years in the Negro National League. The Monarchs were not one of them. Their earnings ballooned and so did the numbers of games on their schedule.

Lemuel Hawkins, 1913. A native of Macon, Georgia, Hawkins arrived in Kansas City during the 1921 season after many years in the 25th Infantry (Fort Huachuca Museum).

In league play, Kansas City ended 1921 with a 31–14 home record and a 19–24 record on the road. It was a record good enough for a third-place Negro National League finish, as the team finished behind only the league champion Chicago American Giants and second-place St. Louis.

During one of the games, George Carr won a horse with a hit. "It was in the ninth inning of a hard game and the Monarchs were on the short end of a 2–1 score," recalled Carr. "There were two outs and the tying run was on second. Just before [I] went to bat a fan yelled, 'I will bet my horse against a five dollar bill that you will not get a hit.' [I] yelled back, 'Your bet is called,'" Carr recalled jokingly. "I never wanted to hit a ball in my life as much as I wanted to hit then, but the pitcher kept cutting the corners on me and the umpire yelled strike two. So I said a short prayer."

Carr stepped back into the batter's box and the next ball came down the middle. Carr slugged the ball over the fence and it rolled out of sight. After the game the man who made the bet with Carr came over leading a big bay horse by the bridle. "'He's yours,' said the man, and he thanked me for hitting that ball."[13] Later, Wilkinson bought the horse from Carr and paid him in Liberty bonds. Evidently there was an abundance of horses to go around. In 1921 Charlie Rand, the Kansas City Blues vice-president, announced that "he would give a saddle horse to the Monarch player leading in home runs at the close of the season."[14]

Switch-hitting George Carr wasn't the only clutch hitter on the Monarchs. Rogan hit as well in the clutch as he pitched during the summer of 1921. In one ten-inning victory against Indianapolis' ABCs, Rogan walked, stole second and third and trotted home with the winning run when the catcher threw wild to third.[15]

Roosevelt "Chappy" Gray. Though he never made good in the Negro National League, Gray was a legendary baseball figure throughout the Midwest. He had brief stints with the Monarchs, Cleveland Tate Stars, Dayton Marcos and Toledo Tigers.

During one five game series against the Cubans, Rogan went 6 for 11, with a double, triple and a home run. In a homestand against Foster's American Giants, Rogan went 7 for 15 with three clutch triples. Against St. Louis' Giants, Rogan hit the only home run in the series, scored two runs and stole two bases in 17 at-bats. His 5 for 11 performance against the Columbus Buckeyes at Kansas City's Association Park was yet another peak performance. It was also in May of that same summer that Rube Foster, a man who is often referred to as baseball's greatest strategist, began to purposely walk Rogan instead of pitching to him with games on the line.

Rogan's defensive play was equally impressive. In mid–August, while playing right field at Detroit's Mack Park, Rogan walked away with a mitt full of memories after he robbed Detroit batters of at least three extra-base hits.

The season of 1921 also saw two college players join the Monarchs. They were pitcher Zack Foreman of the Oklahoma Normal School of Agriculture, which later changed its name to Langston University, and George Sweatt of Kansas' Pittsburg Normal College, now known as Pittsburg State University.

George Alexander Sweatt was born December 7, 1893, in Humboldt, Kansas. He was the grandson of slaves that migrated from Waxahachie, Texas, to Humboldt in 1881. Locally, George attended the city's integrated schools prior to spending a year at Emporia's Kansas State Normal College (now Emporia State University) in 1912 on an athletic scholarship. During the summers of 1911–1915 he played semi-professional baseball with the Iola, Kansas, Go Devils. In 1916 he was as a member of both the Go Devils and the Bartlesville, Oklahoma, baseball team. After serving two years in the army and seeing action in World War I, he returned stateside in 1919 and received yet another athletic scholarship from Kansas' Pittsburg Normal College. He had a tryout with the Kansas City Monarchs in 1920, but it took until June of 1921 for Sweatt to become a fulltime member of the team.

Kansas City closed their successful 1921 barnstorming schedule in Richmond, Missouri, where they played a picked aggregation of players from the Richmond Giants and the Lexington Athletics, at Bryan Park. Ray County, where Richmond was located, had an African American population of 1,025, which equaled five percent of the county's population, and yet the Monarchs usually drew well on their annual visits.[16]

George Alexander Sweatt. Sweatt lettered in three sports while attending Pittsburgh State Teachers College in Pittsburgh, Kansas. He joined the Monarchs in June of 1920. Sweatt, along with Harry Kenyon in 1928 and Byron Johnson in 1938, was always permitted to join the team in June because they were teaching school.

4. A Most Valuable Asset

With the great season of 1921 behind him, Rogan began to look toward 1922 with great optimism. He was determined to wrestle the world championship from Rube Foster's American Giants.

In 1922 Rogan improved his pitching record to 9–2 at Association Park. Overall, he was 13–6 against other Negro League teams and a 20-game winner for a second consecutive season when barnstorming games were added to his list of totals.* He was joined on that year's squad by pitching sensation William P. Drake.

Bill Drake, a former star pitcher for St. Louis' Negro National League Giants, came to the Monarchs in a trade that sent infielder Branch Russell to St. Louis. A native of Sedalia, Missouri, Drake was born on June 8, 1895. He turned out to be a valuable addition, and for the first time ever the Monarchs had the pennant well within their grasp.

One of the pleasant surprises of that year was Rogan's dramatic increase in home runs. In 1921 Rogan had hit just four home runs at Kansas City's Association Park. However, in 1922 his Association Park home run total jumped to nine. Two of the home runs had come off Cubans pitchers, Pedro Silva and Juan Padron. Three more home runs were hit off Jack Marshall, William Force and Bill Holland of Detroit's Stars. Another home run was credited to St. Louis' George Meyers. The home run Rogan hit off Indianapolis' Wayne Carr had won the game in the ninth. Rogan also blasted a pair of dingers off his old Palace Colts teammate, Dick Whitworth—and one of those hits was a grand slam.

Since joining the league in 1920, Rogan had been a thorn in Rube Foster's side. Rogan's play prompted the *Sun* to write, "Grand old Rogan. Without him, what would we do? Chicago fears him. He can make them eat out of his hand, lay down and roll over and then get up and say thank you." For those that had watched Rogan closely, his strong third year in the league could hardly have come as a shock.

In 1922, without any accolades from the prominent daily news services, and with very few white fans rallying to his cause, Rogan quietly established himself as one of baseball's greatest all-around players.

Few athletes—the legendary Babe Ruth among them—could rival Rogan's resourcefulness on the mound and at bat. Combining Negro National League and barnstorming games, Rogan finished 1922 with more than 20 games won, more than 100 batters struck out, more than 100 hits, more than 100 runs scored, more than 20 bases stolen and more than 20 home runs.† He ripped baseballs at a prodigious .457 clip in 116 at-bats at Kansas City's prestigious Association Park. Rogan's 1922 showing was one of baseball's greatest individual performances.

Al Monroe, of the *Chicago Whip*, selected Rogan as the Negro National League's best pitcher for that year, choosing him over Dave Brown, Harold Treadwell, Bill Holland and Jim Jeffries. "Rogan will show an equal form of effectiveness," penned Monroe, "and most assuredly out-hit the others, two to one. So summing it all up we are inclined to say that 'Bullet' Rogan should have the call."[17]

Though he was well rounded on the field, Rogan's personal life appeared a bit off balance. That changed, however, when Rogan started a courtship with Kathrine McWilliams,

---

*Negro League historian Gary Ashwill (Website http://agatetype.typepad.com) credits Rogan with 11 Negro League wins and 91 Negro National League strikeouts for 1922.

†Ashwill (who does not include exhibition games) credits Rogan with only 15 total Negro National League home runs, 49 runs scored and ten Negro National League stolen bases for 1922.

Montgomery Ward's Monitors, 1925. Among those pictured are Richard Whitworth (far left), Hugh Blackburn (sixth from left), Sterling Hall (fifth from right), and Otto "Jay Bird" Ray (third from right). Whitworth gained notoriety while pitching for the Chicago American Giants, Hilldale and Chicago's Union Giants. In 1922 Rogan hit two home runs off Whitworth, one of them a clutch grand slam that won a ballgame.

a farm girl from Colorado. Born in Cawker City, Kansas, she had grown up unaware of the chaos in urban America. Her family owned a farm in Hugo, Colorado, and she preferred the outdoors to life in the city. Not only was Kathrine beautiful — she was also an excellent fisherman. She was, in fact, everything that Rogan hoped and dreamed of in a lifelong companion. They were married October 22, 1922. Kathrine had taken on quite a responsibility too. She came into Rogan's life just when he needed to be replenished. She learned early how important it was to keep her husband encouraged. Due to the mounting social pressures of the time, she understood the spite endured by Rogan in his chosen profession.

Wilber and Kathrine became members of the Centennial Methodist Church in Kansas City, Missouri. A popular theme among African American ministers of this era was the message of the last becoming the first. Rogan's newfound religion was a great relief from the prejudices he faced as a professional baseball player. These were the kinds of inspiring messages that kept Rogan motivated both on and off the baseball field. Rogan's marriage and spirituality were among the many positive events happening in his life in 1922.

In 1923 Rogan's pitching showed substantial improvement, much to the bewilderment of the men he faced. One of the highlights of that season was an August 5, 1923, no-hitter

Rogan and José Méndez pitched against the Milwaukee Bears at Kansas City's new Muehlebach Field. Méndez pitched the first five innings, retiring 15 hitters in order before turning it over to Rogan, who went the distance without allowing another hit. In rendering the Bears hitless, "Rogan [had] allowed only one hit in his last 13 innings on the rubber, his streak [having started] against the Chicago Giants."[18] Added to the no-hitter was a game in Chicago, played July 5, when Rogan held the American Giants hitless until the ninth, only to lose, 1–0.

League and barnstorming games combined, Rogan won over twenty-five games and lost ten in 1923. Seven of the victories were shutouts.[19]

One of the contributing factors to Rogan's increased popularity was the barnstorming contests. When he was not beating the best teams of the Negro National League, he was constantly imposing a personal reign of terror on America's best semi-professional and minor league teams. Playing a schedule neatly arranged to accommodate barnstorming games, Wilkinson scheduled as many games as he could jam into six months of baseball. Every town had its own team, and without a doubt, there wasn't a good team anywhere that didn't go gunning for the Kansas City Monarchs. As expected, the Monarchs, with Bullet Rogan leading their way, pitched, hit and fielded their way into regional folklore, much to the misery of their opponents.

Kathrine McWilliams Rogan. She married Bullet Rogan in the fall of 1922.

Before a large crowd in Osawatomie, Kansas, Rogan shut out the locals on five hits and struck out eight, winning, 6–0, in 1921. At bat he went 2 for 3 with two runs scored. The *Osawatomie Graphic* reported, "Rogan hit one over the left field fence in the second frame to give the fans a sample of how they lay the wood on 'em in the big show."[20] In September Rogan's Monarchs returned to Osawatomie for a league game against St. Louis' Giants. Entering the game after St. Louis had scored a run and still had the bases full, Rogan fanned one batter to record the game's final out. According to Osawatomie's *Graphic* newspaper, "The Monarchs had one big inning, the second frame, scoring six runs. Rogan hit a long home run over the center field fence, with two on in this inning."[21] The following May, in 1922, Osawatomie hired Roy Sanders, a one-time pitcher for 1917's Cincinnati National League Reds, and assigned him the task of slaying the Monarchs. In addition to getting a cup of coffee in the big leagues, Sanders was famous for having struck out seventeen batters in a game against the Negro League All-Stars.[22] Against Rogan, Sanders could not turn the trick. Rogan, however, struck out seven batters and won, 5–0.[23] Osawatomie's local team never could beat the Monarchs but they kept on trying for some kind of a victory. When the Monarchs returned to Osawatomie late in 1922, it was requested that Rogan return to the mound. In that game Osawatomie's only hit, a single in the ninth, was obtained off Rube Currie after two were out. Rogan started the game and was virtually untouchable. Currie had taken the mound after Rogan's exit and pitched the final three innings.

In September of 1922, Rogan homered in Marysville, Kansas, while simultaneously throwing a seven-hitter at that town's best ballplayers. The local *Marysville Advocate Democrat* declared one of the home runs to be "about the longest drive ever made in the park."[24] In Topeka, Kansas, in August of 1923, Rogan, pitching in front of 2,800 fans, struck out seven and held the locals to one run. Doby Moore contributed mightily to Rogan's win with an "over the score board" home run.[25] That same month, the Burlington, Kansas, *Daily Republican*, after witnessing a well-pitched 14–2 win, reported, "Rogan, who pitched for the Monarchs, took it easy except when men were on bases, and when he did cut loose Burlington could do little with his delivery."[26] In that game the Monarchs got four singles, six doubles, three triples and three home runs. Unfortunately there was no printed box score and the players' statistics went without credit.

The same thing occurred at Junction City, Kansas, when the Monarchs beat the locals by what the newspaper described as "a score variously estimated at from 10 [or] 20 to 1."[27] Similarly, there was no box score or any mention of the players printed in Hartford, Kansas, when the Monarchs visited that city during Hartford's annual fair and won, 4–0.

Rogan was a master at working a semi-professional crowd into a frenzy for the home team—and yet, many times it was Rogan, the victor, after nine. Over-optimism is what Jackson, Michigan, experienced when the Monarchs visited that city in 1922. Rogan allowed a trio of safeties in the first inning, netting Jackson their only runs of the contest. "He looked easy and few thought he would last through the nine frames," wrote Jackson's *Citizen Patriot* newspaper. Several sentences later, the same newspaper concluded, "As the game progressed however, he [Rogan] improved and showed himself to be especially nasty just when hits would have meant much for the home boys."[28]

Against minor leaguers, Rogan's record was practically unblemished. One of his earliest minor league wins came in August of 1922, when he beat Sioux Falls of the Dakota League. In that game, Rogan struck out ten, pitched a five-hitter and hit a pair of home runs.[29] On the very next day, Rogan returned to the same park and victimized Willie Ludolph for yet another home run.[30] Ludolph was no slouch on the mound, either; in fact, he was good enough to perform for Detroit's American League Tigers in 1924. Rogan was just as successful the next month when the Monarchs mauled the Denver Bears, a Western League team. In that five-game series Rogan pitched the first and fifth games, winning, 4–1, in Sterling, Colorado, by tossing a four-hitter and losing, 5–2, in Denver. In that loss, the Monarchs made four critical errors behind him, one of which, "got thru Donaldson and rolled to the fence for a home run."[31] Rogan held the Bears to eight hits and struck out five batters in his losing bid. In the game Rogan won in Sterling, one of the Monarchs homered, but who it was remains an open question. "The Monarchs scored two runs in the first when a dusky player from Kansas City clouted the ball out of the field into the stock corral nearby," reported the *Rocky Mountain News*, adding, "No ground rules had been made on this as it never has been done before, and the batter and a man on base scored."[32] The name of the player hitting the home run is not given.

When the series visited Fort Morgan, Colorado, the local *Fort Morgan Evening Times* reported, "The Monarchs have the hardest-hitting club in the [Negro] league and the leading pitcher, Bullet Rogan, who also leads the league in batting. Rogan is not only a great pitcher but can play any position of the team and play it well. He is considered by many big league ballplayers as one of the greatest all-around players in baseball today."[33] The Monarchs won the Denver series, three games to two.

In October of 1923, the Monarchs split a series of six games against Wichita, a contender for the Western League title. Rogan pitched two games, winning both, the first was a 3–2 verdict in Fort Scott, Kansas, the second a 3–0 win in Kansas City. In game one Rogan upset Ernie Maun, the leading pitcher of the Western League. This was the same pitcher that John McGraw, the famous manager of the New York Giants, purchased from the Wichita club for $10,000.[34] If Maun was worth $10,000 — he won two and lost five in his big league career — what was Rogan worth?[35] McGraw had tagged Rogan with a "$100,000 price if the majors had not drawn a color line."[36] On yet another occasion, McGraw called Rogan "one of the best pitchers in the game."[37] J. L. Wilkinson tried unsuccessfully to settle any doubt about the date when Rogan and McGraw had met. "He's the one who stopped John McGraw's Giants cold in an exhibition game on the Philippine Islands in 1919, after which the New York manager said he'd gladly give $100,000 for Rogan if the man were white."[38] Maun was quick to add, "Rogan was the greatest nigger pitcher I ever saw."[39] In Kansas City, Rogan's three-hitter beat Wichita's Ed Hovlik, who had pitched for the American League's Washington Senators.

During the 1920s the American Association Kansas City Blues were one of the most famous minor league teams in America. The Monarchs played the Blues 12 times during the fall of 1921 and 1922 and were returned winners seven times.

Anthony "Bunny" Brief. He batted .351 and slugged 82 American Association home runs from 1921 to 1922. In twelve games against the Monarchs in 1921–22, Brief batted a disappointing .279 and hit one home run.

In 1921 the Kansas City Blues led the American Association in batting. In addition to leading the league in batting with a .313 team average, they paced the circuit in runs scored, doubles and walks. Gus Bono, the Blues' best pitcher, finished the summer with a 25–11 record. Pitcher Nick Carter had won 19 games and Leon Ames had won 17. Wilbur Good, the team's leading hitter, had led the league with 157 runs batted in.[40] Bunny Brief, the American Association's version of Babe Ruth, led the league with 42 home runs and 51 doubles.[41] To top it off, every member of the Blues was a former or future major league player.

The Monarchs and Blues battled in six memorable games to decide the city championship in 1921. Because of injuries to shortstop Doby Moore and third baseman Bartolo Portuando, the Monarchs reinforced their lineup with replacement players. The last minute reinforcements didn't help — the Blues won the series four games to two. Rogan was pressed into the lineup and batted a disappointing .188. He managed to hit one of the Monarchs' three home runs, a solo shot into the left-field bleachers off of Leon Ames in game six. Rogan looked better on the mound. He pitched to 63 batters and held the Blues to a .222 average, nearly 100 points off their league-leading total. The largest crowds, 10,000 and 7,200 were present at the games Rogan pitched. It wasn't until the following season, however, that the Monarchs got real revenge for the 1921 series loss.

When Bullet Rogan and his Monarchs met the Blues in the fall of 1922, they were primed and pumped for an upset. That year's version of the Kansas City Blues wasn't a motley collection of scrubs fronted by one or two "name" players; they were an All-Star cast of the American Associations' most talented men. Bunny Brief, Glenn Wright, Dutch Zwilling, Wilber Good and Jimmy Zinn were only a few of the well-known players on the Blues roster. And while it could be argued that Kansas City's adverse weather conditions — temperatures that dipped as low as 34 degrees at night and rose no higher than 69 degrees during the daytime — affected play, it certainly didn't seem to bother the Monarchs. The Blues were beaten five games to one, which included four straight wins for the Negro National League team.

Walter "Doby" Moore, 1924. He was considered the peer of any major league shortstop from 1920 to 1926. In a 1922 game against the Kansas City Blues, a pitched ball hit Moore above the heart and knocked him out. Some physicians at the game said that Moore was dangerously hurt. Against the advice of the players and the doctors Moore returned to the lineup and finished the game.

In that series Rogan hit .444. In his only appearance on the mound, which he won in front of 5,000 fans, Rogan struck out nine Blues batters.

There was no way to label the big victory over the Blues as inconsequential. The Monarchs and their star Bullet Rogan whipped the American Association team into total submission. George Muehlebach, the independently wealthy hotel proprietor who owned the Blues, stomped around as if he'd lost a major convention in the slow season. He swore never to play those Monarchs again — which he never did. Call it prejudice or plain old protectionism, the Blues weren't about to let the Monarchs create a yardstick by which to measure any league of the white players as inferior.

After the Monarchs' big win over the Blues, the *Associated Negro Press* distributed an article written by Charles A. Starks openly refuting the myth of white superiority in baseball. The article was entitled "Negro Baseball Breaking Down the Race Prejudice" and it appeared in the *St. Louis Argus*. It challenged the claim that "there is a psychology that implies always the superiority of the whites."[42] Starks concluded that three teams, "the St. Louis Stars, the Indianapolis ABCs and the Kansas City Monarchs, had killed the idea that colored players can not think fast enough to measure up to the standard of the major leagues." In an earnest response to the Monarchs' big victory Starks added that "in Kansas City where the racial lines are more in the ascendancy, there has been a disastrous setback. The Kansas City Monarchs, possibly the best Negro team in the country, out generaled and out played the Kansas City Blues of the American Association in every phase of the game. The Monarchs won five out of six games played, taking four straight. Most of the quick thinking and acting was displayed by the blacks. White psychology so far as applied to Negro baseball is a dead issue."

In an article in Kansas City's *Call* newspaper, Monarchs pitcher Rube Currie admitted, "It is true that the major leaguers have more of an abundance of developed players

Baseball Commissioner Kenesaw Mountain Landis. Landis, who'd been hired to restore baseball's good name in the wake of the 1919 Black Sox scandal, always insisted, "There is no rule against major leagues clubs hiring Negro baseball players. Negroes are not barred from organized baseball by the commissioner and never have been. There is no rule in organized baseball prohibiting their participation and never has been to my knowledge."

than our league, but in looking over their material we find that they only have a larger number than we have, but this does not signify that their players will be of better quality than the players of our race. This point is emphasized even in prize fighting."[43] Wilkinson's printed remarks supported Currie's. "There aren't as many Negro ball players as there are white," he pointed out; "but when a colored boy is a good athlete, a good baseball player, he's very apt to be mighty good."[44] Currie commented further on the intelligence of African American ballplayers: "Just like the white man studies baseball night and day, so some of us study it. I think we are just as fit mentally and physically as the whites are. Also it might settle their worried minds to know some of us study our opponent's weaknesses and are capable of making our observations mean something toward their defeat."

With that big series against the Blues tucked safely in the win column, the Monarchs started advertising themselves as "The team that beat the Kansas City Blues." Next to Wilber "Bullet" Rogan, it was the most effective form of advertisement in the Monarchs' arsenal.

5

Salute to the Long Ball

Because of the failure of Bullet Joe Rogan, the Monarchs' star hurler, to catch a train out of Kansas City the admission price was cut to 50 cents.—Pittsburg Kansas Daily Headlight, 1926

After the Monarchs' big win over the American Association Kansas City Blues, it hardly shocked anyone when Kansas City surpassed Rube Foster's celebrated American Giants to win their first Negro National League pennant in 1923. Kansas City's first pennant signaled the end of Foster's bunt-and-run offense and started the era of the long ball—the reign of the Monarchs. In the years that followed, Kansas City's Monarchs became one of the best at winning games with a single stroke of the bat. The season of 1923 also signaled the end of white umpires in virtually every Negro League contest.

With the start of the Negro National League's fourth season, there was a very different look at all league diamonds, one that was especially obvious in Kansas City, where Negro umpires finally graced Muehlebach Field. After a long and heated debate, the league, by way of president Andrew "Rube" Foster, announced the signing of seven colored umpires to be used in league games. Charles D. Marshall, a writer for Indianapolis' *Freeman* newspaper, had been an advocate of African American umpires since the league's formation in 1920. "In either the major or minor leagues they had not found room for us, not even as mascots," stated Marshall. "Why can't we manage and play the game ourselves without the aid of the other race, for certainly we know how."[1] The signing of Billy Donaldson came first. Donaldson was recommended by businessmen in California, as well as managers of colored and white clubs. He went immediately to work and umpired his first game in the opening series between the Monarchs and American Giants. Speaking of Donaldson, the *California Eagle* noted, "Though small of stature Donaldson was a giant on the diamond and his keen knowledge of the game made Bill a respected citizen among the players as well as the fans. It would not surprise us to see the big league reach out and take Donaldson East next spring as he is a valuable indicator man."[2]

Working with Donaldson was Bert E. Gholston of Oakland, California, who had been officiating in a white league in Arizona. Among the other umpires that took employment in the Negro National League were Leon Augustine and Lucian Snaer of New Orleans, who worked Bear's games in Milwaukee. Caesar Jamison of New York and William Embry of Vincennes, Indiana, opened the 1923 season in Indianapolis, where Detroit's Stars battled the ABCs. Tom Johnson, a former pitcher for Foster's American Giants and a former officer in the 365th Infantry in France, was held as a reserve umpire.

The *Kansas City Sun* was sure the Monarchs would win the 1923 pennant. "We have the best pitching staff, we have the best catching staff, we have the best shortstop in the

Wilber "Bullet" Rogan, 1924. Rogan was 27 years old when he joined the Monarchs in 1920. After that first season the *Kansas City Call* declared that "Rogan was the best pitcher in the league because he could get up for the big games."

country, we have the greatest hitting team in the country, we have an outfield that compares with any in the league, we have three of the most promising youngsters in Joseph, Anderson and Allen that ever broke into this league, we have a manager second only to Rube Foster."[3]

After some strenuous spring training — a trip that took them into parts of Texas, Oklahoma and Kansas — the Monarchs opened 1923's regular season with a string of victories. They won three of five from the American Giants, swept five straight from St. Louis' Stars, three straight from the Milwaukee Bears, and then four of five from Detroit's Stars. The winning went uninterrupted throughout the summer and overflowed right into September. If it had not been for Foster's troublesome American Giants, Wilkinson's Kansas City Monarchs would have won the pennant virtually uncontested.

No other Negro National League team played the Kansas City Monarchs any harder than the American Giants. Whenever the two teams met, fisticuffs were as good at winning ballgames as singles, doubles, triples or stolen bases. Even the normally mild-mannered "Gentleman" Dave Malarcher became rowdy in games against the Monarchs. In 1923, Kansas City won only ten of the 23 games. Five of the wins and three of the losses belonged to Rogan. A noteworthy example of these teams' contempt for each other occurred in a 1924 game.

> The contest was marred by several squabbles, one of which resulted in Buck Hewitt, Giants first baseman, and Rogan, Monarchs pitcher, being sent to the showers. A later argument caused Hawkins, Monarchs first baseman, to be banished. Hawkins was fined $25 and suspended five days for his part, the suspension to become effective after the series was over; Rogan was fined $5, and Hewitt, the instigator of the first brawl, escaped without a fine. The man who really should have been suspended was Malarcher, who, in an effort to frighten Duncan into backing away from the plate, slid in with his spikes fanning the breeze, a habit of his that should be outlawed.[4]

With all of the difficulties between the Monarchs and American Giants, there were few men who could infuse more life into a game than Rube Foster. "I have often remembered him, standing in front of Street's Hotel in Kansas City," recalled George Sweatt, "telling his listeners how his team was going to beat the Monarchs."[5] When Rogan was on the mound Foster's predictions often went wide of the mark.

Starting with the one-hitter he'd pitched against Galveston's Sand Crabs in early April, Rogan was incomparable in 1923. "Bullet Rogan, the King of Kings," wrote Billy Donaldson, a new Negro National League umpire, "was certainly a wonder. He pitched several shutout games in which he allowed from two to four hits a contest. His one big feat was when he pitched a no-hit, no-run game against Milwaukee in Kansas City before 8,000 wild fans. He was robbed of another no-hit game against the ABCs when [Oscar] Charleston hit a safety in the ninth after two were down."[6]

Kansas City finished the 1923 season with a 60–36 Negro National League record. Preseason and barnstorming games included, the team's overall record was an astonishing 111–41. Included among the wins were more than 50 exhibition victories against five losses. Three of the exhibition losses had come against Western League opponent Wichita in early October. Rogan finished with more than 20 wins, and, six of those wins were shutouts. He led his team in appearances, and, in addition to starting three games a week on the mound, he was an everyday outfielder whose home run totals eventually surpassed those of Oscar "Heavy" Johnson, the Monarchs outstanding power hitter — and that was no minor feat.

Oscar "Heavy" Johnson was rated among baseball's most intriguing left-handed long ball threats. His nickname hinted at what you could expect when you met him in person. Johnson's neck bulged and his chest was massive. His biceps matched most men's thighs. Johnson's Herculean mass had made him one of the biggest sensations ever to originate from Atchison, Kansas. (Amelia Earhart was another.) On the baseball field Johnson's list of unforgettable home runs had included tape measure shots off Babe Ruth, Carl Mays, Gus Bono, Ray Caldwell and a host of lesser-known big league stars. His ability to drive the cowhide a country mile had become a factor in winning big games. As Rogan's teammate on the famous 25th Infantry ball team, Johnson blasted drives that had kept military men buzzing long after the team returned to the United States.

In jest, William "Big C" Johnson recalled, "Oscar Johnson would get in trouble and they would put him in the guard house and they would only let him out to play baseball, and back to the guard house he went. I remember a time when Johnson was asleep on the bench and he was called to pinch hit. He didn't even tie his shoes, and he hit a home run and walked around the bases."[7]

In 1922, Johnson's first season in the Negro National League, he batted a remarkable .427 at Kansas City's Association Park where his 12 home runs had surpassed George Carr's record of ten at the same park in 1921. Only seven of Johnson's record-setting home runs occurred in league play, the others were hit in barnstorming games. Rogan's nine home runs at Association Park, an incredibly high total for a man almost half the size of Johnson, led the team in league play. Rogan also led the team in batting at Association Park with a .457 average in 1922.

Johnson, Moore and McNair were all members of Rogan's slugging cast. In Rogan, who was driving them from the right, and McNair, who was pounding them from the left, Kansas City had two of the most powerful little men ever to play big league ball. Neither cared for individual averages, they utilized the corporate approach to winning big games.

Since joining the Monarchs in 1920, Rogan had hit two home runs in a game five times. The feat was achieved early on against the Detroit Stars in 1922. He had also hit two in another game in Detroit on May 20, 1923, while simultaneously pitching a three-hitter and winning, 6–0.[8] Among the most notable of Rogan's multi-homerun games was one against the Sioux Falls team of the Dakota League, and one in which he hit a pair of homers off of Jesse Barnes, a star pitcher for the Boston Braves, in a post-season game in Topeka, Kansas.[9]

Though Rogan was leading the team in multi-home run games, Oscar Johnson remained the team's best slugger. Johnson became the first Monarchs batter to belt three home runs in a single game, a feat he had achieved in June of 1923 against the Milwaukee Bears. He had also slammed two home runs in a game in Marysville, Kansas, on August 14, 1923, and another pair during an exhibition game in Waco, Texas, when the Monarchs defeated Paul Quinn College.[10] Hurley McNair compiled an equally impressive list of multi-home run games. In addition to hitting the first home run in the history of the Monarchs, he became the first of his teammates to have a multi-home run game at Kansas City's spacious Muehlebach Field. Walter "Doby" Moore's slugging was equally plentiful. In 1920 and 1921, Moore hit grand slams off the Detroit Stars and Indianapolis ABCs. In Fort Scott, Kansas, two of Moore's tape measure home runs were etched into local folklore. The *Fort Scott Daily Tribune Monitor* claimed that one "went fifty feet on the other side of the center field score board." In Benedict, Kansas, Moore drove a pair of home runs so deep into the cornfields that local farmers had to wait until harvest time to recover the souvenirs. He had similarly victimized cornfields in Fredonia, Kansas.[11]

Moore was equally adept at impacting games with his glove. "Moore is one of the fleetest shorts seen at Rickwood [Field] this year," wrote the *Birmingham Herald*, "and covers all the ground around the keystone and short."[12] Another writer added, "Moore, the big Monarch shortstop, was one of the features of the game. He got everything hit between second and third and once ran far out into left field to rob Gordon of a hit."[13] Chet Brewer, who played with Moore for two seasons, 1925 and 1926, added, "Moore, way on the edge of the grass, would scoop that ball up and throw strikes from deep shortstop."[14]

Kansas City's Association Park appeared custom made for home runs, but the opening of Muehlebach Field in July of 1923 took Kansas City from a modest home run city to one of the most difficult on the entire Negro League circuit. The design of the massive park cut Monarchs' home runs from an all-time home high of 42 in 1922 — their last full season at Association Park — to seven in 1924 — their first full season at Muehlebach Field. On the road the Monarchs continued to terrorize pitchers, especially at Detroit's Mack Park and St. Louis' Stars Park. Had the Monarchs played in those parks as often as they had played in Muehlebach Field, it would have taken a computer to tabulate the home run totals. For instance, in a July 1924 four-game series at Detroit's Mack Park the Monarchs' nine home runs exceeded the total they hit in an entire season at Muehlebach.

Constantly on the hunt for pitching, the Monarchs signed former American Giants pitcher Jack Marshall and Centralia, Missouri's James Homer "Hop" Bartley. Bartley, born on February 29, 1900, was the younger of the duo. The older Marshall was born May 11, 1895, in Carrolton, Missouri, and had started his career with Kansas City's Royal Americans in 1913. John Donaldson's exit in the spring of 1924 made Bartley the Monarchs' only left-handed pitcher during both the 1924 and 1925 seasons.

5. Salute to the Long Ball

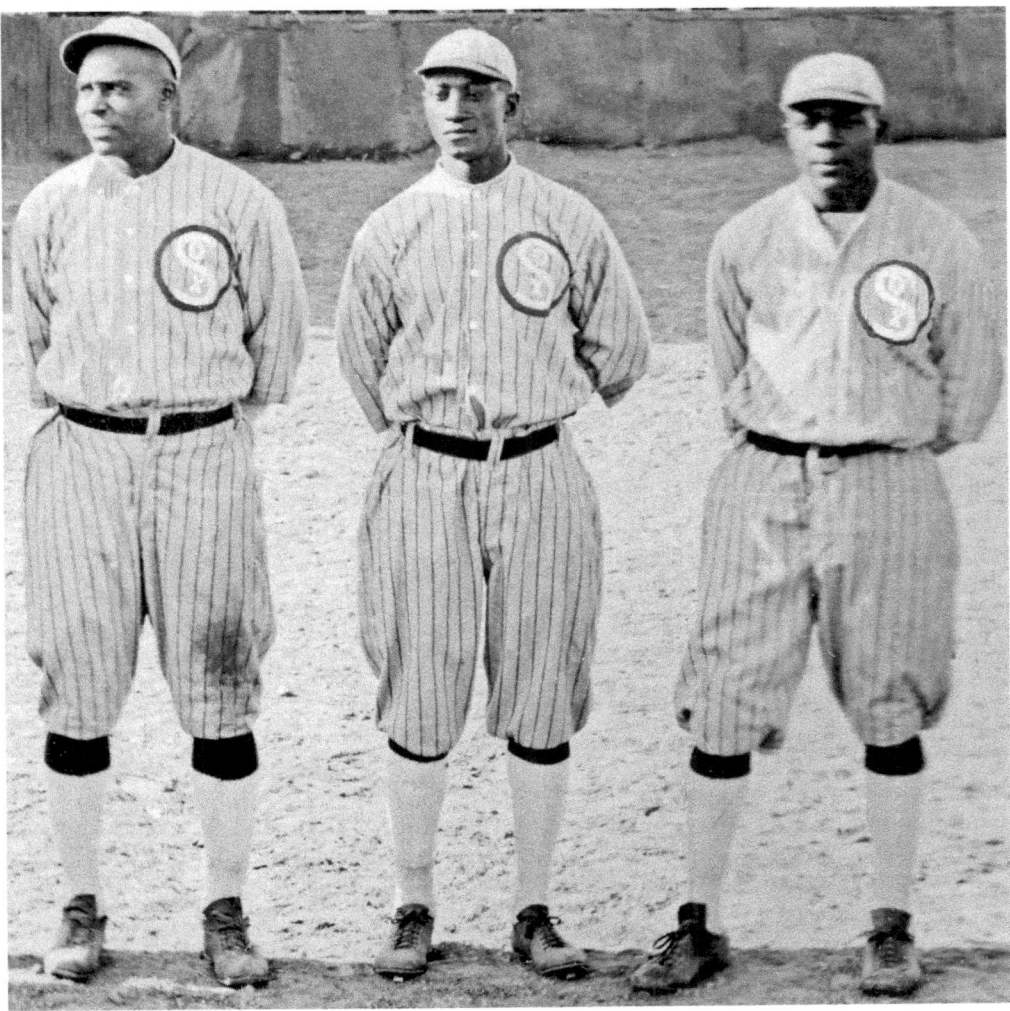

From left: George Carr, Unknown, Walter "Doby" Moore. Carr, commenting on his legendary teammate, said, "Rogan was the greatest pitcher that ever threw a ball. He had not only an arm to pitch with but a head to think with. Rogan was a smart pitcher with a wonderful memory. Once he pitched to a batter he never forgot that batter's weaknesses and strong points." Moore was described as a 400-foot line drive hitter.

In 1924 the Negro National League added two new teams, Birmingham and Memphis, as replacements for the defunct Milwaukee and Toledo teams. In an attempt to cover this vast new territory, Wilkinson sliced a chunk of exhibition games from the schedule. As a result, the well-rested Monarchs cruised to an easy 55–22 league record and their second consecutive Negro National League pennant. Overall, including games won in the World Series, the Monarchs finished the season at 83–28–1. Along the way Rogan put up his usual number of outstanding performances.

Rogan opened the summer with an 8–4 win over the Western League's Topeka Senators. He beat the Birmingham Black Barons for his fifth win, and his tenth win was a 13–2 blowout of the Detroit Stars. Rogan's 20th victory was a splendid 14–0 whitewash in Fort Scott, Kansas. In league play, Rogan lost just three games: A 3–2 contest to the Detroit Stars on June 8, a 13–11 game on July 6 and a 9–2 game on September 2, both times to Rube Foster's American Giants. That's the record Rogan took to Philadelphia's Shibe Park for a planned nine-game World Series against Hilldale, champions of the Eastern Colored League.

What looked to be the baseball battle of the century could have easily been the battle for baseball's most colorful nicknames. The Monarchs featured Bullet, Doby, Newt, Plunk, Heavy and Yellow Horse. Hilldale had nicknames like Judy, Bizz, Top, Nip, Hawk, Sleepy and Scrip. When it came time to play the two teams approached their play with even more colorfulness.

No one seemed surprised when Rogan beat Pete Cockrell in the opener, 6–2. Game Two went to Hilldale, as southpaw Jesse "Nip" Winters bullied Kansas City in an 11–0 win. Game Three, played in Baltimore, Maryland, ended in a 6–6, 13-inning tie. Game Four, a playoff of the previous day's tie game, ended in a 4–3 Hilldale win. The series promptly jumped to Kansas City for games on October 11, 12 and 14. Wilkinson hadn't realized it yet, but Babe Ruth was about to dramatically undermine the Negro World Series.

Rogan's win in the east necessitated his appearance in the home opener at Kansas City, which he lost by a 5–2 score on Judy Johnson's clutch two-run, inside-the-park home run in the ninth. Up to that inning Rogan had pitched excellent ball. Hilldale's shortstop Paul "Jake" Stevens explained, "Rogan was tough. He had a good hard one and just enough meanness in him to keep you honest up there at home plate. If you dig in, you make him wild."

The result of the middle game, one the Monarchs won by a 6–5 score in front of 8,000 screaming Kansas City fans, was another clutch win for the Westerners. Kansas City was gaining momentum, and then, with less than a few days' notice, they were forced to step aside for Babe Ruth, the most publicized athlete in baseball history. Ruth's appearance denied 30 of the nation's best Negro League ballplayers for the sake of glorifying one white one. The delay cost that year's Negro World Series a bundle of money.

Of all the cities in America, why Ruth showed-up in Kansas City, right in the middle of the Negro World Series, was anybody's guess. The game in which he appeared was appropriately titled the "Babe Ruth–Mercy Hospital benefit game." No civic-minded fan could have been against it, but it left the Monarchs crying uncle. Bob Meusel, also of the New York Yankees, most of the Kansas City Blues, and the biggest names in Kansas City semi-professional baseball formed the two teams that participated in the game. That afternoon, Ruth's poke of a Roy Sanders pitch over Muehlebach's right field fence gave Ruth's All-Stars' a 5–2 win.

The following afternoon Ruth moved on and the Kansas City Monarchs returned to Muehlebach Field for a close 4–3 win behind Rogan's splendid 3 for 5 batting performance. Rogan's last hit, a single that sent William Bell across the plate, drove home the game's winning run. As predicted, most of Kansas City's expendable funds were depleted. Only 3,000 people paid their way into the World Series' final game at Kansas City. The series was tied at three wins for each team when it moved to Chicago.

The last three games of the World Series were played at Chicago's Schorling Park, where Rogan won the first game on Duncan's dramatic single in the ninth. Duncan's single had sparked a Monarchs three-run burst and a 3–2 come-from-behind victory. Hilldale rebounded the following afternoon to tie the series at four wins apiece, with one game remaining to be played.

George Sweatt recalled, "Rube Foster advised Méndez to pitch [the series' final game] and he made Méndez promise to get a good night's sleep. Méndez told me [this], as I was his roommate. I [had] wondered why he went to bed so early. Generally he was a night owl."[15]

Méndez, a Cuban whose full name was José de la Caridad Méndez, had pitched in many outstanding games throughout his lengthy professional career. Born March 19, 1887, in Cárdenas, Matanzas, he had become a hero to the entire island. His 1–0, one-hit victory over the Cincinnati Reds in November of 1908 turned him into an overnight sensation. The sensational pitcher, however, lasted for nearly two generations, and his list of monumental victories seemed to never end.

Méndez had pitched many memorable battles against Rube Foster's teams, starting in 1909 when he arrived in the United States. Listed among their many clashes was a July 1, 1909, game that ended in a 1–0 win for Foster. An 11-inning game on July 21, 1910, also went to Foster, who won 3–1. There were two historic tie games in which Méndez and Foster appeared. The first occurred on July 29, 1910, and it ended in a 4–4 tie after eleven innings. The second was a 2–2 game in 1912 that was ended by darkness after twelve innings. In that contest Foster struck out seven to Méndez's five. Recalling that image of Méndez in his youth conjured up many memories for Arthur W. Hardy. "The first time I met Méndez was in Chicago," recalled Hardy of the old Kansas City, Kansas, Giants, "and boy could he throw a ball! He had developed tremendous shoulders and biceps from chopping sugar cane. That ball was hopping. It looked like a pea coming up there."[16] Foster had likely taken these epic battles into consideration when making Méndez his selection for the 1924 Series' final game.

In 1920, Méndez had been one of several Cubans on the Kansas City roster. Portuando was another. "Portuando roomed at Effie Saunders boarding house," recalled Langford, "and he could speak better English than Méndez."[17]

In the final Series game of 1924, Méndez, in perhaps the most celebrated outing of his long career, pitched Kansas City to the world championship with a brilliant, 5–0, win. The victory gave Kansas City a five-to-four advantage games won and its first World Series title.

The ten-game Series, in spite of the Bambino's interruption, had drawn upwards of 45,000 people. Rogan, one of six Monarchs to appear in all ten games, led his team with a .317 batting average. He had won two games and lost one on the mound, holding Hilldale to 23 hits in 28 innings. If there was such a thing as a series Most Valuable Player it positively belonged to Rogan. On the other hand, one of the series' most disappointing performances belonged to Oscar "Heavy" Johnson, who collected only three extra-base hits.

After the Series ended, the Monarchs returned to Kansas City and displayed their trophies and keepsakes from the historic season at Stark's Shoeshine Parlor. Two months later someone broke into the back room at Stark's, where the Monarchs stored their sweaters, uniforms and other equipment. When the stolen items showed up in a local pawnshop, an investigation led police to Oscar "Heavy" Johnson.[18] Rather than face public humiliation Johnson was traded to the Baltimore Black Sox of the Eastern Colored League.

The Monarchs were doing their part to totally change the landscape, both physically and financially, of metropolitan Kansas City. Lemuel Hawkins, Herland Ragland, Wade

Johnston, Eldridge E. "Chili" Mayweather, Newt Allen and Newt Joseph all married young ladies from Kansas City. Newt Joseph started the Monarch Cab Company and Wade Johnston opened a barbecue restaurant.

Rogan was one of the first to enter the marketplace when he threw open the doors to the new Monarchs Billiard and Recreation Parlor in 1921. When it opened, one local newspaper boasted that it was "the finest Billiard Parlor in America for Negroes." The same article added, "None of the parlors in the country, Chicago and New York included, can boast of anything near the equal of the Monarchs' establishment. The place will be conducted on high plans and there will be no singing, whistling, dancing or mysterious noise, nor gambling allowed."[19] Rogan formed a partnership with Quincy Gilmore, the Monarchs' traveling secretary, to operate the establishment. Rogan's parlor was equipped with a soda fountain, cigar case, large electric signs, carpet and newsstand where all of the leading newspapers and magazines could be purchased.

Gilmore, Rogan's partner, was a real entrepreneur. Born June 29, 1892, in Gary, Indiana, he was an unrecognized force behind the organization of Negro professional baseball. Gilmore, an Oberlin College–educated promoter dedicated himself to Wilkinson and Baird as the third most important figure in the Monarchs' management. At all times activity minded, "he participated in eight-day bike rides in his youth," said wife Alberta.[20] Gilmore had been a policeman in Gary, Indiana, and had once owned a private detective agency, before the Watkins Brothers funeral parlors requested in 1914 that he relocate to Kansas City to assist in running their business.

Tom Baird and his wife, Frances, on their wedding day. Tom was partners with J. L. Wilkinson from the very beginning of the Negro National League in 1920 and would eventually take over sole ownership of the Monarchs in 1948.

According to one source, "Gilmore had for a number of years been in the undertaking business in the cities of Chicago and Denver."²¹ In 1928 Gilmore served as the Negro National League's secretary, treasurer and the director of publicity. In 1929, he would operate the Texas–Oklahoma–Louisiana League from offices at 2549 Elm Street in Dallas. When adding his praise to the Gilmore legacy, Bert Gholston stated, "Ask him sensible questions concerning baseball, and he becomes not only instructive, but illuminating. He tells you things you did not know and will not forget. During an interview, he speaks in a loud tone which is full of meaning and action. His only real hobby is baseball. He eats, dreams and talks baseball morning, noon and night."²²

When the 1925 season opened Heavy Johnson was nothing more than a relic of the Monarchs past. So were the annual pennant races. Wade Johnston, who replaced Heavy Johnson, was positioned in the outfield. The season was now split into two halves, with the winner of the first half playing the winner of the second half for the Negro National League pennant and the honor of appearing in the World Series. Kansas City, despite opening as a team in transition, won the first half of the divided pennant race.

Thomas Jefferson "T. J." Young joined the Monarchs in 1925. Having come on recommendation from Gilkerson's Union Giants, he remained with the Monarchs in various capacities until 1941. In that first season he was a backup catcher for Frank Duncan. Young was a native of Tatums, Oklahoma, being born on September 6, 1902. His prominent cheekbones suggested a Native American heritage, and according to one source he was "three-fourths Choctaw."²³

Rogan was cutting his pitching losses annually. By the end of 1925 he had lost only two games, and both of those, a 3–2 sit-back to the American Giants and a 4–3 loss to Detroit's Stars, occurred in May. After that, Rogan didn't lose another game all season. Included among his more celebrated performances were the 1–0 and 17–0 wins over the American Giants and 13–0 and 3–0 wins over Birmingham's Black Barons. The wins were mere icing on Rogan's sixth consecutive season of 20 or more victories.

The 1925 season ended with the Monarchs, winners of the first half, and St. Louis' Stars, winners of the second half, meeting in the playoffs. During the regular season Kansas City had dominated St. Louis, winning 12 of the 15 games played.

Quincy Gilmore. He was one of baseball's greatest organizers and also the Monarchs' traveling secretary. He had gone to Wilberforce College to be an undertaker but ended up on the police force in Gary, Indiana. In 1913 he came to Kansas City to work for Watkins Funeral Home. Gilmore was with the Monarchs from 1920 to 1935. In 1929 Gilmore served as president of the Texas-Oklahoma-Louisiana League.

Rogan had beaten them three times. The addition of several new men improved the Stars overall play. In the playoffs St. Louis was blessed with a glitch in the schedule that forced the entire series of nine games to be played in St. Louis and Chicago.

Wilkinson set up offices in St. Louis' West End Hotel and prepared for a great battle. Stars manager "Candy" Jim Taylor, when asked for his opinion, stated, "In the series with the Monarchs the Stars could win. My club is not a great club when you compare the players man for man, but the fighting spirit of the club and the team play should win for them." José Méndez, the Monarchs manager, would only say, "We always play to win."[24]

In the opener, a Saturday afternoon crowd that numbered more than 9,000 fans poured into tiny Stars Park. Rogan mowed them down that day. He retired the first seven batters before allowing a single. In the fourth Rogan picked Willie Bobo off first base to kill an apparent St. Louis rally. Rogan's breaking ball was nicking the corners too. Four of his five strikeouts were called third strikes. On the other side of the box score, the Monarchs had three home runs; Allen's solo shot that landed on top of the car barn in inning three; Moore's two run blast over the car barn in the eighth and Duncan's solo shot to the car barn in the ninth. The game went in the books as an 8–6 Rogan win.[25]

St. Louis got fighting mad and won the next two games. When the series moved to Chicago for games four, five, six and seven, Rogan was called to pitch two more times. Although he started out poorly in game four, allowing four hits, one a double and four runs in the first inning, Rogan finally settled down. After that, the Stars hit safely just three more times, and nobody came close to walking. On offense, Rogan went 4-for-5, scored a run, stole a base and collected one RBI. Needless to say, Rogan took the larger portion of a 5–4 victory. The Monarchs lost game five and St. Louis took a three games to two advantage in contests won. When rain interrupted play, the series was reduced to seven games.

A second rainstorm forced the series into one final doubleheader. In game one, William Bell held St. Louis to seven hits, giving Kansas City a 9–3 win to tie the series. Rogan came back in the twilight game and shut out St. Louis, 4–0, on seven hits to assure Kansas City's second trip to the World Series.[26]

Rogan was easily the star of the entire playoffs. He batted an amazing .450 in the series, and fielded flawlessly. As a pitcher he faced 95 batters and held St. Louis to a .253 average and won three games.

Times couldn't have been more jubilant. Expectations couldn't have been higher. Like the beauty of a rose, Rogan's 1925 season was ephemeral. Only the World Series remained, but when the series started Rogan was not in the lineup. He was scratched from the World Series because of an injury that was one of the oddest in baseball history. And, it couldn't have happened at a worse time.

Following the St. Louis series, Kansas City's Monarchs returned home where the World Series was scheduled to start on October 1. Rogan was playing with his infant son, Wilbur Rogan, Jr. Young Rogan was not quite a year old, having been born just after the previous year's World Series. In the frolicking on his living room floor, Rogan's right knee landed on a needle that wedged into the skin. Foolishly, he attempted to take it out himself and the needle, being much deeper than anticipated, broke off. He was rushed to General Hospital #2, a segregated hospital in midtown, where doctors tried to draw out the remainder of the needle with a magnet capable of lifting 500 pounds.

The series opened without Rogan, and yet it took twelve innings to settle, as Hilldale won, 5–3, with a three run rally in the top of the last frame.[27] The Monarchs countered in game two and tied the series at one win for each team. The slim victory had given hope of another Monarchs comeback. When reporting on the Monarchs' 3–1, 10-inning loss in game three, Kansas City's *Journal* remained optimistic. "Bullet Rogan, Monarchs hurling ace, may pitch the fourth and final game of the series here today. Rogan has been out of the game, having had a needle lodge in his right kneecap, but it is believed he will be able to work today."[28]

Weary from their constant efforts to extract the needle with magnets and worried about infections, doctors decided to make an incision just above the knee, forcing Rogan out of the series for good.

Without the aid of two key men, Bullet Rogan and Dink Mothell, who was forced to leave because of injuries sustained in the last playoff game against St. Louis in Chicago, the Monarchs lost the next game by a 7–3 score. Trailing three games to one, and after time off for travel, play resumed in Philadelphia.[29] That's when the *Call* broke the sad news. "The Monarchs baseball players who are out of the World Series because of injuries Wilber Bullet Rogan, pitcher and Dink Mothell, utility," explained the writer, "it is absolutely certain now that neither of them will get in the post-season classic this year."[30]

Needing only one victory for the title, Hilldale capture game five by a 5–2 score to take the Series and World Series title. The Series was over and Kansas City had lost, four games to one. Kansas City's only victory, a 5–3 win by rookie pitcher Nelson Dean, came

Raleigh "Bizz" Mackey, 1924. Though he played against Rogan as a member of the Indianapolis ABCs and Hilldale Club, Mackey caught some of Rogan's greatest games in both the Cuban and the California Winter leagues.

in game two.[31] "'Smiling Charlie' is what we called Dean," Chet Brewer recalled. "He [Dean] had a good fastball, curveball, control and he kept 'em low." Dean was discovered by the Monarchs in 1923, when they battled the Monrovians in Wichita, Kansas. That game, one which the Monarchs won 4-to-2, Dean pitched a seven-hitter at Wichita's Island Park.[32] He was a native of Muskogee, Oklahoma, born February 18, 1899. Dean was famous in Monarchs history for having pitched a 1926 five-hitter in Lenora, Kansas, in scorching 107 degree weather, after which time he became known as the hot weather pitcher.[33]

In the Series, Hilldale batted .301, out-hitting the slumping Monarchs, whose team batted a depressing .221. Switch-hitter Bizz Mackey and left-handed slugging George Carr both homered for Hilldale. The Monarchs didn't hit a home run in the entire Series. Without Rogan the attendance shrunk to 20,067, nearly half of the total that attended the 1924 World Series.[34] Fay Young, writing in the *Chicago Defender*, agreed. "The series was disastrous as far as finances were concerned," penned Young. "Thursday's crowd in Kansas City was small on October 1. Not anywhere near what it should have been, and Friday's was smaller. Sunday and Saturday the crowd was kept down by the fact that Rogan's injury kept him out of the game."[35]

Could one man really make that much difference? The *Call* sure thought so. "While no ball club is or should be a one-man organization," the newspaper admitted, "when as good an all-round player as Rogan is taken out of the lineup, it has its effect." The *Defender* concluded, "Kansas City was weakened 20 percent by the loss of Rogan. Two of the games lost, one in the ninth, Rogan could have won.[36]

After the Series concluded, the Monarchs participated in an exhibition game in Baltimore, Maryland, where a funny thing happened. "Big Bill [Drake] liked to laugh," recalled George Sweatt. "He'd laugh at anything. He was comical. He'd be sitting on the bench, you'd tell a story and he'd just fall out laughing. He'd stop the ball games lots of times he was laughing so loud. We were playing a World Series game in Philadelphia and stopped by Baltimore to play an exhibition game. Big Bill wasn't pitching that day, he was sitting on the bench. Now he and [Lem] Hawkins were good buddies. Hawkins went to steal second, and when he went to slide, the catcher threw the ball and hit him [on the] right side of the head. It bounced about 15 feet in the air, and big Bill was sitting on the bench, and he laughed: 'Ha ha ha!' Hawkins started toward the bench after him and big Bill cut out. I laughed. I never will forget that! They were good buddies, but Hawkins was going to get him."[37]

In closing the 1925 season and the World Series, the *Call* added, "No, the gonfalon won't fly from the centerfield flagpole next season. It will be high on a stick in the little town of Darby, Pa., amongst strangers, and instead of absorbing perfume from the packing houses, its blue will grow black with an accumulation of smoke. So be it — the game is even with the rubber yet to be played. On that day — well, just wait until that day. Selah."[38]

In the home league portion of the 1925 season, not counting the playoffs and World Series, Moore paced the team in at-bats with 188 and hits with 57. Mothell led in doubles with 11 and stolen bases with 10, Rogan in triples with 9 and Allen in runs with 42.

Hoping to recapture some of their previous good fortune, Kansas City traded for the left-handed hitting Cristóbal Torriente of Chicago's American Giants. The trade looked like one of baseball's most ridiculous — a player destined for the Hall of Fame for a utility outfielder named George "Never" Sweatt. In time the deal would prove legitimate.

"I was traded to the Chicago American Giants for Torriente, an excellent outfielder and hitter," recalled Sweatt. "I reported to Foster in the spring of 1926. He had made arrangements for my lodging, with Mr. and Mrs. James Johnson, an elderly couple. They rented the second floor of Rube's building at 4131 S. Michigan Avenue. Rube's wife Sarah, his son Earl, and a half-brother, William, occupied the first floor. When [Pythias] Russ, a young catcher from [Sam Houston] college came, he and I were roommates and we became fast friends. The Johnsons treated us as if we were their own. When school at Pittsburg, [Kansas] was out, my wife joined me. A week later Russ' wife, Mary Richard, arrived. All of us camped [out] with the Johnsons. Mr. Johnson taught us how to play a card game called 500."[39]

While Sweatt was making a well-adjusted blend with Foster's American Giants, Torriente was taking his lumps in Kansas City. Shortly after arriving in Kansas City, Torriente sued trainer Jew Baby Floyd for losing an expensive diamond ring after he requested the trainer hold it for safekeeping during a game. The legal proceedings only added to Torriente's frustration at his already slow start at the plate.

A stocky Cuban with more flash in his presentation than a cheap suit, Torriente wore chain-link gold bracelets around his neck and bulky diamond rings on his huge fingers, years before it was fashionable. But oh, how he could play. In Willie Foster's opinion, "You weren't going to find anybody that could play more outfield than Torriente." Known for his intrepid play, in November of 1920 he had hit three home runs in a game against the New York Giants. Babe Ruth pitched and held down first base for the Giants on that eventful afternoon.

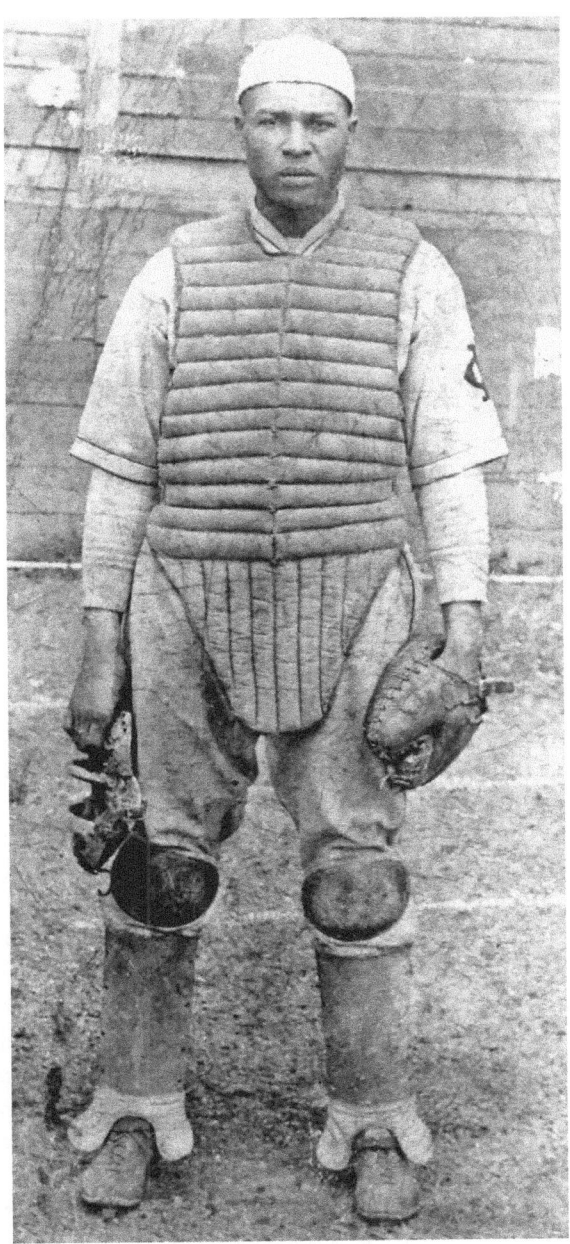

Carroll Ray "Dink" Mothell. Discovered by Topeka Jack Johnson, in 1920, Mothell caught the eye of Rube Foster and saw limited action as a catcher with the Monarchs and the Chicago American Giants. Mothell resurfaced with Wilkinson's All-Nations in 1923, and in 1924 he returned to the Monarchs. During his 14 years in baseball Mothell was considered baseball's super substitute.

Evidently, 1926 was a tough year for new players because another new acquisition, pitcher Randolph Prim of Prescott, Arkansas, who came to the Monarchs from Salina, Kansas, also failed to endure the season.

The 1926 Negro National League pennant race was even hotter than the year before. Prior to the start of the season, though, the Monarchs sweep a three game series at Topeka, Kansas. The Monarchs dominated the series winning, 3–1, 7–2, and, 9–2. Torriente, who was slotted between McNair and Moore in the number four spot, disappointingly produced little. Torriente went 3-for-13 with a double, a stolen base and a pair of runs scored. Moore, batting in the number five spot, went 6-for-11, with a double, five stolen bases and five runs scored. Moore out-hit Torriente in an earlier three-game series in Salina, Kansas, when he went 7-for-12, with a home run and a double while Torriente finished with a 4-for-9 performance and added a home run, double and a stolen base.

Kansas City opened by winning 13 of their first 15 games. The victory celebrations were all too regular. After beating the Cuban Stars in a 15-inning game, some of the boys ended up at Elsie Brown's residence on the city's East Side. The get-together turned tragic when Brown shot Doby Moore. The impact of the blast took Moore's feet out from under him. Doctors confirmed the worst. The shortstop's right leg had bones that were broken into six pieces. He suffered a compound fracture of the tibia, the large bone in the lower leg, and the fibula, the smaller bone, was fractured also. His season, and perhaps his career, came to a shocking halt.

In a statement to local law enforcement authorities Elsie Brown alleged that "she and Moore had quarreled and that he had struck her three times, [once] in the face, the eye and the back of the head," reported the *Kansas City Call*. Brown added, "[I] slammed the door in Moore's face and as he went away he saw [me] in the window and threw something. [I] jumped back from the window and came back with a pistol firing once." Fearing for her personal safety, Brown, according to Newt Allen, "moved to Anthony, Kansas, right after she shot Moore."

Looking upon Moore's injury as an opening for other teams, the Chicago *Defender* predicted, "With Moore out of Kansas City's lineup for the balance of the season the Monarchs will be lucky if they finished in third place."[40] Shaken by the loss of their prize shortstop, the Monarchs stumbled into Indianapolis and lost three of five to the ABCs. After that, Kansas City faltered. The Monarchs temporarily resumed their conquering ways, winning 16 of their next 21, and the first half championship. In the second half, Kansas City didn't adjust nearly as well, especially against Chicago's American Giants, who beat the Monarchs three of five in late August. As luck would have it, the Monarchs were forced to depend on Torriente much more than anyone expected, and without Moore it cost them the pennant.

When the Monarchs faced Chicago's American Giants, Rube Foster failed to make an appearance because of his ailing health. In his absence David J. Malarcher, known far and wide as "Gentleman Dave" because he "never smoked a cigarette or [had] taken a drink of alcohol," took over the reins of the club.[41] A 1918 graduate of New Orleans University, which later changed its name to Dillard, had catapulted Malarcher to a successful Negro League career. He formerly performed with the New Orleans Eagles, the Indianapolis ABCs and the Detroit Stars, prior to joining Foster's American Giants in 1920. As the new manager of the American Giants, one of his greatest projects was the development of young Willie "Bill" Foster.

5. Salute to the Long Ball

William Hendrick Foster, the American Giants' best pitcher, was Rube Foster's baby brother. Unlike his older brother, Willie was a southpaw. In 1926 Willie had taken over as the ace of the American Giants. He had formerly played with Memphis, a city that idolized him. The leading citizens of the city had offered to raise a fund for the purpose of defraying his expenses in school and paying his scholarship during the next year, if he would only remain in Memphis to play for the Red Sox. Rube Foster upset Memphis' plan and Willie joined Chicago's American Giants in 1926.

Willie Foster was especially miserly in games against the Monarchs. "The only team that would come in there to [Schorling Park] and try to hit us out was Kansas City," recalled Foster. "They would come slugging and still get beat one to nothing because pitchers in those days believed in [the] change of pace — change ups [to] keep em off stride."[42] Consequently it was Chicago that walked away as second half champions in 1926.

Since the Monarchs had won the first half of the split schedule and Chicago's American Giants the second, the playoffs would decide which team would represent the league in the World Series against the Bacharach Giants, champions of the Eastern Colored League.

The playoffs opened in Kansas City, where the Monarchs won three of four. Rogan won his game by holding Chicago to eight hits. The Monarchs came to Chicago needing just one win to take the series. But they lost the next two games by 2–1 and 4–3 scores. The season was down to its final day and another doubleheader was played to settle the pennant.

In game one, Chicago chose its ace, Willie Foster, to face Rogan. The game was a pitchers' duel, in which Rogan had the upper hand through eight innings. In the ninth, however, the Giants scratched out a run on an infield hit, a sacrifice, and a timely single to beat Rogan, 1–0. The American Giants had tied the series and there was only one game left to play.

Chet Brewer was warmed up and prepared to pitch, but José Méndez suggested that Rogan return to the mound. He wanted Rogan to have the ball — that same chance to win the pennant that Rube Foster had given him in the final game of the 1924 World Series. Willie Powell was supposed to pitch for the American Giants but Willie Foster approached him and there was a change in plans. Foster, too, would pitch both halves of the doubleheader.

After a few preliminaries, the Kansas City fans that were huddled together in Chicago's Schorling Park fell silent as Chicago scored three quick runs in inning one on four consecutive hits. The Monarchs' struggle to recover those runs ended when the umpire stepped in and called the contest after the fifth inning. The game was over, the playoffs had ended, and Chicago captured both ends of the twin bill, winning, 1–0 and 5–0 — and the pennant too.

The return trip to Kansas City was excessively quiet and then all hell broke loose. Clifford Bell, a right-hander from Kildare, Texas, cut loose a howl and shot his pistol right through the roof of the Pullman train. Bell was angry for two reasons. He was a single parent supporting a daughter that had been abandoned by her young mother. The extra World Series money was needed to raise his child. Like all of the Monarchs, Bell hated to lose a ballgame, especially when losing cheated him out of World Series play. Once Bell was physically restrained, bemoaning over that day's activities continued.

Members of the American Giants team that dethroned the Monarchs in 1926 included George Sweatt, William "Nat" Rogers, Floyd "Jelly" Gardner, Dave Malarcher, Sanford

Jackson, Charlie Williams, Walter "Steel Arm" Davis, Jim Brown, John Hines, Pythias Russ, Buck Miller, Rube Currie, Webster McDonald, George Harney and of course Willie Foster.

Still in a whirlwind because of the loss to the American Giants, the Monarchs lost the final exhibition game of the season in Pittsburg, Kansas, on October 10, against Nonnie Baker's Pittsburg (Kansas) Pirates. When Rogan missed the train out of Kansas City, what had been advertised as a hurlers' duel between Jimmy Zinn of the Kansas City Blues ended up with William Bell taking the pitching chores. Facing a lineup that was packed with minor league stars, Bell pitched a six-hitter and Zinn a four-hitter. Zinn's two triples ultimately led to a 4–1 thumping of the Monarchs.[43]

Though the 1926 season had ended on a sour note, Rogan couldn't complain. It had been one of his best years ever. He had more than 20 wins, and only six losses — and four of those losses had come in games against the American Giants. To conclude their 1926 campaign, the Monarchs traded Torriente, in spite of his having batted .411 (58–141) at Kansas City's Muehlebach Field. He also hit well in the Monarchs' many exhibition games. In a big 7–1 win in Oberlin, Kansas, Torriente had gone 3 for 4 with a pair of runs, helping Rogan, who pitched three innings, to a win.[44] Torriente was a force to be reckoned with even without his bat. In Wymore, Nebraska, in a mid–July game, Torriente succeeded in making five putouts and six assists from center field.[45]

In the end the temperamental Cuban had gone hitless far too often, and missed too many games to justify his excessive contract. After Torriente missed exhibition games in Wichita, Clinton, Great Bend and Anthony during the Monarchs' mid–August barnstorming tour, Wilkinson decided to move the veteran while he could still command a reasonable price. It was obvious to Wilkinson that Torriente, once one of the most feared long-ball threats in baseball, was on the back side of a celebrated career, his power having diminished to an alarmingly low level. Bert Gholston went as far as to snub Torriente in his annual list of All-Stars, selecting instead St. Louis's James "Cool Papa" Bell in center, George "Mule" Suttles in left and Norman "Turkey" Stearnes in right as the Negro National League's best outfielders.[46] Rogan and William Bell as pitchers, Frank Duncan as catcher, Hawkins at first base, Allen at second, Newt Joseph at third base and Dink Mothell at utility were the other Monarchs selected.

Detroit jumped at the offer to sign Torriente, just as the Monarchs had done a year earlier. In return the Monarchs received pitcher Harry Kenyon, but Kenyon failed to make good in 1927 and was sent to Birmingham's Black Barons. A school teacher by profession, Kenyon, a graduate of Arkansas Baptist College, spent several of his winters teaching at Luther, Oklahoma's Washington High School. He rejoined the Monarchs in 1928.

The Monarchs' four-year run had been one of baseball's most successful — three pennants, two appearances in the playoffs, two trips to the World Series and a world championship. But the winning was about to come to an unexpected halt. That year, 1926, would go on record as a transition year for the entire Negro National League. Rube Foster's failing health had forced his resignation as Negro National League president and manager of Chicago's American Giants. George Sweatt, a former Kansas City Monarch who was rooming on the second floor of Foster's apartment, said,

> Two or three times when I was returning to our apartment, I would catch up with Rube Foster and we would walk home together. I noticed that he would be walking all right, when all

of a sudden he would start to run and I would have to catch him. I told Mr. Johnson of this, and he said that he had heard, by way of the grapevine, rumors that Rube was a sick man. About a week later, as we were sitting down to our card game, we heard Mrs. Foster scream. I don't remember whether she came to our door or [if] one of the boys [came down], and said they had called the police. They took Rube away in one police wagon. That was a terrible thing to witness; here was a brilliant man, being removed from his own home. He was put in the hospital and finally removed to an insane asylum.[47]

Foster's massive shoes were eventually filled by attorney William Clarence Hueston, a graduate of Kansas University's law school. Hueston would carry the league into the 1930s.

José Méndez was also hanging up his spikes, and it was a well-worn rumor that Bullet Rogan would be the next Monarchs manager. Though Rogan was essentially taking on an aging team, a team sorely in need of a legitimate power-hitter, and an infield that was literally shot to pieces, he was ready for the challenge.

6

The Man on the Bench

Rogan, manager of the Monarchs, is more of a player-manager than a bench manager. On the field he is an inspiring leader, who leads his men rather by his own example than by his advice. When he manages from the bench he is not quite so successful. He has the ability to develop team play of the highest order, which is one of the outstanding features of his position as manager. Where Rogan shines most, I think, is in his ability to keep his men satisfied and pulling together. — Umpire Bert E. Gholston, *Kansas City American*, September 6, 1928

Wilber Rogan was his team's best hitter, best pitcher, best reliever and best pinch-hitter. Now Rogan was also going to be the manager. Had the burdensome tasks of managing resulted in a drop off in his on-field performance, it would have been understandable. But it didn't and in part because of reliable play the Monarchs would only narrowly miss the league pennant in his first three seasons as manager. By his fourth they were back on top of the Negro National League.

A March 12, 1926, edition of the *Kansas City Call* broke the news about Rogan's new job as player-manager, a position that was a virtual minefield of hazards. The writer explained, "Manager's duties are not new to Rogan. There have been times in the last two seasons when the club was practically under his control."[1] Players who also became player-managers recognized that a successful player-manager could only be useful as long as he remained a successful player. If he could not demonstrate by his own play what he wanted the players to do, the players would not respond.

José Méndez, one of baseball's best player-managers, had hung around to mentor Rogan in that maiden year, which saw Kansas City finish at 54–29, a game behind the American Giants. Méndez retired after the end of that first season.

Always willing to take a chance on a young recruit, Rogan signed six new pitchers in 1927: Maurice "Doolittle" Young, Bazz Owen Smaulding, Admiral "Deacon" Walker, George Mitchell, Carl "Lefty" Glass and William "Steel Arm" Tyler. George Giles, a teenage infielder fresh from Manhattan, Kansas, also joined the team. Giles, who batted left-handed but threw right-handed, had fallen in love with the Monarchs several years earlier, after witnessing them beat Manhattan's Trident team by a 3–1 score in 1923, behind Bill Drake's six-hit, ten-strikeout pitching.[2]

Born March 2, 1909, in Junction City, Kansas, Giles first tried out with the Monarchs in 1925 when he was 16 years old. "I put on my uniform, [an] old Manhattan uniform — probably looked like a farmer," said Giles. "They let me take batting practice, always could hit the ball. That catches those big league boys' eyes. You can hit the ball — they looking at you a second time!"[3]

6. The Man on the Bench

In Giles' first full year, Rogan was particularly tough, probably because Giles was young and aloof as well as gifted. At practice, and even in games, for instance, water was withheld from the young player. But it wasn't only Giles who suffered; the veterans were every bit as cold toward the other rookies on the team. When Smaulding took the field wearing eyeglasses, he became the butt of every joke imaginable. Doolittle Young, another rookie, recalled, "I was a country boy, and, boy, don't you know what Kansas City was to a country boy. Seventeen years old and gonna play for the Monarchs. I was on top of the world."[4] But being a teenager on the Monarchs, as Young soon discovered, was a very costly proposition.

"On the days that I had to pitch," Young offered, "I set up three guys. I paid Frank Duncan's way in the cab to Muehlebach Field, brought Newt Allen a half pint of whiskey and paid 25 cents to have Hurley McNair's shoes shined."

The relationship between Young and catcher Duncan soon became strained. "I was pitching side arm and I was cutting the ball, putting emery on it. Duncan liked to look good catching," remarked Young. "And if a guy swung at a fastball [and missed], for Duncan it was like taking candy from a baby. But if you threw him one of those emery balls up there he didn't like that. He was afraid to hurt them cute fingers. He kept them polished up all the time."

One afternoon, Duncan, worn out from catching one too many of Young's emery balls, lumbered from behind home plate for a lively discourse with the youthful Monarch about his pitch selection.

"I want you to throw me a fast ball with nothing on it," demanded Duncan. "I ain't got one," Young fired back, "I don't have it. Every ball that I throw is going to have something on it if you catch it or not."[5]

After that Young and Duncan remained at odds and it produced a negative effect on a team that wasn't playing all that well anyway. Just the same, Rogan's hitting and pitching appeared to be unaffected.

Of that new crop, George Mitchell would remain in the game the longest, playing until 1948. He also had a twin brother, Robert, who played in the Negro National League with Birmingham and St. Louis. Born on March 31, 1900, George attended Sparta high school and played with the Sparta Stars, a widely-known amateur team, as a pitcher and first baseman.[6]

Rogan's on-field presence was as steady as a metronome. He opened the season in Tennessee, where his three-hit shutout beat the Memphis Red Sox. Next, he beat the Stars in St. Louis on nine hits. After that Rogan held the Detroit Stars to four hits in a 15–2 Kansas City ambush. That game was followed by yet another shutout of Birmingham's Black Barons. By the time Rogan's Monarchs reached Kansas City, the team was leading the league with 11 victories — and four of the wins belonged to Rogan. If the Monarchs had sustained that pace they would have won the first-half pennant. But the pace began to slow, and by the time the team rolled into Chicago's Schorling Park, on July 2, Kansas City needed to win four of the five games played to take the first half pennant.

Kansas City won the first two games by identical 3–1 scores. In the first game William Bell beat Willie Foster. Rogan's five-hitter got the best of George Harney in game two. Chicago took game three by a 7–6 score, and then the Monarchs won, 3–0, in game four. In game five, Rogan took the mound with his team needing one more victory for the first half championship. Foster was Chicago's choice as pitcher. As it turned out Foster's hook was twisting and turning like well-lubricated machinery. Behind the plate, umpire Eddie Stack, who once pitched for the Chicago Cubs, was calling them to perfection. Rogan pitched one whale of a game too — ten hits, two walks, and five very big strikeouts — but Foster, the man of the moment, won, 4–0.

Losing the pennant to a team, Chicago, that played eight fewer games was perhaps unfair but not uncommon in Negro National League scheduling. This time the freaky schedule left Kansas City on the minus side of the championship ledger. The first-half pennant went to the American Giants by fewer than thirty percentage points, as Chicago finished at 32–14 (.696), the Monarchs at 36–18 (.667). Kansas City exploded to start the league's second half, behind the potent bat of Hurley McNair. In that first game, McNair hit for the cycle in Detroit, going 5-for-6 with a single, double, triple, two home runs — one coming with the bases full — and a stolen base. Too bad his performance could not have been stored for replay; the Monarchs went into a batting slump and were unable to break out. Rogan's team tumbled to a disappointing 19–14 second-half record.

Tabulated results for 1927 showed Kansas City with a 32–12 home record. The 12 losses were the largest number of home defeats since 1923, when the Monarchs lost 18.

One of the reasons for Kansas City's lackluster showing was the startling play of Birm-

Emma McNair (center), the wife of Monarchs outfielder Hurley McNair. She is pictured here with unidentified friends at a local Kansas City photography studio.

ingham's Black Barons. In three series with the Barons, Kansas City went 2–3, 0–5 and 1–4 in games won and lost. In early June the Barons' sweep of the Monarchs was the first five-game sweep in Monarchs team history. Birmingham's pitching staff of Harry Salmon, Sam Streeter and a young strikeout artist just up from Chattanooga, Tennessee, named Leroy "Satchel" Paige, were more than the Monarchs expected.

Another factor in the Monarchs' downfall was Rogan's attitude. Having tried to emulate the two previous managers, Sam Crawford and José Méndez, Rogan became unapproachable, creating difficulties with rookies and veterans alike.

Crawford and Méndez were the only men to manage Kansas City's Monarchs before Rogan, who respected them both because they were excellent teachers. Crawford was a large, dark-skinned pitcher from Dallas, Texas, and like so many from that state attempted to imitate Rube Foster's style of managing. "Crawford made the ballplayers keep the hours and kept you out of the ballgame as punishment," stated Newt Allen. "He was strict on drinking and you could only stay up late if you were playing cards or dominos."[7] Sportswriter A.D. Williams once said of manager Sam Crawford, "He was always a stickler for strict training rules obeyance. He never let up in a game even though the game might seem safely tucked away in the win column. He was something after the old C.I. Taylor and the Andrew Foster style, the go-get 'em type."[8]

Better yet, Crawford was a tremendous strategist. One of his most controversial pieces of strategy was the use of multiple pinch-runners. On one such occasion, following a Newt Joseph single, Crawford put John Donaldson in to pinch-run for Joseph. The next batter sacrificed Donaldson to second. When Donaldson reached second base safely, Crawford stopped the game long enough to substitute Dink Mothell as a pinch-runner for Donaldson. Mothell eventually scored when the next batter singled—three runners to score one run. Crawford's explanation: Donaldson was used because he was a faster runner. Mothell, because he was smarter. "Three runners to score one run ought to interest Ripley," wrote the *Denver Post*.[9] There was also a funny side to Crawford. During a 1923 game, Méndez was playing third base, and the local batter began to irritate Crawford, who was pitching. When the batter sent a high pop fly towards third, Crawford yelled loudly, "Doan' catch that! I want to strike this man out."[10]

After Crawford's tenure as Monarchs manager ended, he found employment with the St. Louis Stars in 1924. He also managed Cleveland's Negro League entry in 1924 and coached the American Giants in 1928.

Crawford's style of managing proved too combative for the oldtimers on the Monarchs' roster. Complaints about Crawford nearly started a player rebellion and Wilkinson was forced to give Crawford's job to José Méndez mid-way through the 1923 season.

"Méndez was a player's manager and he won the respect of his men" because, as Newt Allen put it, "he was one of the smartest managers we ever had." Méndez would train, teach and reinforce everything he wanted his players to remember. "Often he would make a statement, quickly turn to a player and blurt out, 'What did I just say?'" said Chet Brewer. "If you were not listening you were totally thrown off by the question." Méndez was a strategist too. He never hesitated to use pinch-hitters, relief pitchers or late-inning replacements in the outfield. He would pinch-hit for a veteran just as quick as he would pinch-hit for a rookie. In Rogan's first few years as manager he was reluctant to pinch-hit for many of the veterans on his roster because they were his friends. When Rogan did pinch-hit, it was usually for rookies like George Giles. One such occasion occurred in June, when Rogan pinch-hit for Giles in the ninth and homered to beat Birmingham's Black Barons.

As a reliever, Rogan was constantly rescuing Young, Smaulding, Mitchell and occasionally William Bell. All totaled, Rogan made over 40 appearances in 1927 — at least 12 of them in relief. On two occasions, once against Memphis and another time against Chicago, Rogan faced only one batter, thus preserving a Kansas City win. Other times, he was called upon to pitch in long relief.

As a starter, Rogan continued to excel. He closed the season with a record of more than 20 wins and six of them were shutouts. It was Rogan's seventh consecutive 20-win season.

Kansas City's substandard finish hadn't stopped umpire Bert Gholston from honoring Rogan, Frank Duncan, Dink Mothell and Lemuel Hawkins as members of his 1927 Negro National League All-Star team.[11] But Gholston was among those who felt Rogan had taken on an excessive amount of responsibility, saying in a lengthy *Kansas City Call* article that "Rogan tried to play entirely too many positions; regular and relief pitching, outfield, pinch-hitting and coaching." Nevertheless, the article concluded with this assessment: "He [Rogan] was practically half the team's playing strength, and at that the club only missed the play-offs by a half game."[12]

José Méndez. Known as "The Black Diamond," Méndez was manager of the Monarchs in 1920, for part of 1923 and from 1924 to 1926. A Cuban who was too dark for the majors; nevertheless, he beat many major league teams. He had wins over the Cincinnati Reds, the Philadelphia A's, and the Detroit Tigers. Méndez was also the first Monarch to receive a fine from the Negro National League. It was a $5.00 fine for refusing to leave the field following his banishment from a 1924 game against the American Giants.

When Rogan was in the everyday lineup, he was among baseball's top hitters. That's why Wilkinson sent outfielders Hurley McNair, Wade Johnston and Cristóbal Torriente, along with first basemen Lemuel Hawkins and pitchers Clifford Bell and Nelson Dean packing. After Wilkinson released Hawkins, Giles received a letter stating, "You are the man, had to let Hawkins go." Now that first base was his for the taking, Giles told Rogan, "I'm going to drink water this year, referring to the rough treatment he received as a rookie." Rogan said to Giles, "I only wanted to see if you had guts."[13]

To start the 1928 season, Rogan seemed to find his own path as manager. He began to interact with his players, on and off the field. He posed

6. The Man on the Bench

Carroll "Dink" Mothell (left) and Dewey Creacy. In 1924, Kansas City offered seven players in a trade for Cool Papa Bell of the St. Louis Stars. When St. Louis demanded that Mothell be one of the seven men included in the deal, Kansas City was forced to refuse the trade. Creacy was later traded to St. Louis where he became a solid-fielding third basemen.

for their pictures, laughed at their jokes and took more interest in their off-field activities. The team he fielded that year was younger, though no less talented. Larry "Goo Goo" Livingston, a big 200-pounder from Texas; slick-fielding Leroy Taylor, the outfielder with the trick knee; speedster Eddie Dwight of Kansas City, Kansas; and Reginald Hopwood of Milwaukee, Wisconsin, were the Monarchs' new outfield.

Taylor, born August 11, 1902, was a native of Marshall, Texas, and "a left-handed batter."[14] He had a system for doing things which helped him remember when they occurred. For instance, he had married Elizabeth Eckley in Alexandria, Louisiana, on his birthday, the same year he broke into professional ball.

First recruited by Rube Foster in 1925, Taylor was highly recommended by umpire James McCary. McCary, a great judge of baseball talent, also recommended such men as Bobo Miller, Johnnie Hynes, Willie Ware and John Shackleford to the league and all had made good except for Taylor. "At the time he

William Wade Johnston, 1923. He was born in Columbus, Ohio, in 1897, but grew up in Steubenville, Ohio. After playing locally, Johnston joined the Pittsburgh Giants in 1920 as an outfielder, pitcher and first baseman. Next he went to the Homestead Grays and then the Tate Stars in Cleveland. As a member of the Tate Stars in 1922, Johnston became the first batter to get four hits in a game off Rogan. The fourth hit won the ballgame and defeated Rogan.

was a little hot-headed," stated McCary, "[so] Rube traded him to Birmingham and there he quit and came home. When [Bingo] Demoss took hold of Indianapolis in 1926 he sent for [Taylor]. He [Taylor] fell out with the owners of that club."[15] Toward the end of 1927 Wilkinson began inquiring about a natural-born outfielder that could hit, and Taylor's name came up in the conversation.

Two left-handers, one from Kansas City, Kansas, named Alfred "Army" Cooper, and Andy "Lefty" Cooper, who was acquired in trade from the Detroit Stars, were also signed by the team. To acquire Cooper, Wilkinson traded three players, Hurley McNair, George Mitchell and Grady Orange.

Andrew "Andy" L. Cooper was well-connected to the region, as was "Army" Cooper. One newspaper noted, "[Andy] Cooper [had] lived in Wichita for ten years before going into professional baseball [eight] years ago at Detroit. While here, 'Lefty' started his baseball career, being an employee at Cudahy's when he played his first game. Cooper later pitched for the Monrovians when that team had on its roster two other Monarchs players, 'Pep' Joseph and [T. J.] Young."[16] When Cooper pitched for Detroit it was rumored that Henry Ford said, "he would give a new automobile if they beat Cooper on a Sunday."[17]

The team's other Cooper, "Army," was given his nickname because he came to the Monarchs after an eight-year military career in the 25th Infantry. Born on April 1, 1900, in Kansas City, Kansas, he was 5'10".[18]

Herbert "Tack" Wil-

Leroy "Ben" Taylor. A left-handed hitter, Taylor came to the Monarchs in 1928 from Wiley College in Texas, the school from which the Monarchs recruited more great players than all others combined. Among the Wiley alumni on the Monarchs were Grady Orange, L. D. "Goo Goo" Livingston, Hallie Harding, Pat Patterson, Henry Milton, Packinghouse Adams and Byron Johnson.

James Starks. A native of Springfield, Missouri, he broke into professional baseball with the Monarchs in 1928. Starks eventually became an outstanding first baseman with the New York Black Yankees in the 1940s.

son, a rookie right-hander secured from Texas' Tyler College, also joined that year's pitching staff. At shortstop, the Monarchs were experimenting with a well-traveled college football quarterback named Hallie Harding. Highly versatile, Harding had excelled at football, baseball and basketball for several African American institutions of higher learning. Harding was selected as the quarterback on Fred Long's All-Southwestern Football Eleven of 1928, after having led Wiley College to the league championship. John Fan, writing in a 1933 issue of the *Chicago Defender*, described Harding as "one of the best athletes Wilberforce has ever had."[19]

That Dwight and "Army" Cooper were both recruited from Kansas City, Kansas, came as no astonishing fact. The local sandlots had produced many of baseball's most recognized stars. Rube Currie, Jack Marshall, Frank Duncan, Henry "Dimp" Miller, Harold Vaughn, Dick Withworth and many others had taken the same route into Negro Baseball. Without question, though, the best prospect to have come out of Kansas City during the 1920s was Newton Henry Allen.

Born in Austin, Texas, and partially raised in Cincinnati, Ohio, Allen's temporary arrival in Kansas City, to visit an aunt whose young son had recently died, turned into a lifelong experience. Young Newt's age was the same as his aunt's deceased son, so she asked, and was granted permission, to keep Newt in Kansas City where she raised him as her own child. He attended Bruce Elementary and Lincoln High School.

Allen's first ball team was the Kansas City Tigers, but he could never break into their outstanding starting lineup. That's why he moved to the Paseo Rats team. He also played for Swift's in a local packinghouse league before turning professional with Omaha's Nebraska Federals in 1921. In 1922 Allen signed with the All-Nations, a barnstorming team J. L. Wilkinson operated in addition to the Monarchs. At season's end, Allen was promoted to the Kansas City Monarchs.

When Allen first arrived in the Negro National League, Elwood "Bingo" DeMoss was the best of all second basemen. Allen studied DeMoss' every move and emulated many of his hero's outstanding stunts, one of which was throwing to first without looking at the base. Another of DeMoss' specialties was his patented low release on throws to first base, developed to keep runners from wiping him out on double plays. Allen saw it, practiced it, and worked it to perfection.

Throughout the 1920s, Allen's hitting improved. "A line-drive hitter, with occa-

Newton Henry Allen, 1925. Newt Allen topped all players by hitting seven doubles in the 1924 World Series. He played second base and shortstop for the Monarchs from 1922 to 1945. His 23 seasons with the Monarchs are the most in club history. He was born May 19, 1901, in Austin Texas.

sional power" is how John "Buck" O'Neil classified Allen. In the 1924 World Series, Allen batted .281, collecting a Series-leading seven doubles. That same fall Allen made his first trip to Cuba to perform in the Winter League. While battling his way to a .313 average, Allen became a celebrity and was affectionately tagged by the Cuban press as the "Black Diamond." In appreciation, Allen had one of his front teeth capped in gold and a diamond placed in the center.

"As far as I'm concerned," responded pitcher Doolittle Young, "Colt — we called Newt Colt — was about the best second baseman the two years that I played in Kansas City that I had ever seen. He wasn't such a good hitter and he didn't steal many bases, but he caught all the balls hit down that way. He knew how to play second base very well."[20] Buck O'Neil thought the secret to Allen's success was his "wrist." "He could throw as hard from there," O'Neil illustrated from a slightly bent-over position, "as I could rare up and throw. Lots on the ball and a strike."[21] Jesse Williams, an infielder that played many games beside Allen, concluded, "Allen looked better missing a ball than most people looked catching it. And I never saw him make a bad throw to first."[22] Owner J. L. Wilkinson's praise was direct and point-black. "In his prime he [Allen] never had an equal."[23]

Allen performed brilliantly in Doby Moore's absence. And yet, the story of how Allen, the best second baseman in baseball, became one of the best shortstops ever, was largely a credit to Rogan's coaching. Harding's signing in 1928, Allen envisioned, would allow for his return to second base. After a brief examination Allen surmised, "Harding was only a fair shortstop who couldn't make the long throw from behind third base. So I remained at shortstop to start the season."[24]

As one newspaper wrote, "Allen's unassuming and quiet ways on the diamond also helped to make him one of the most popular players with the fans."[25] Frank Duncan was known to have said, "I used to get a thrill just knowing he was putting on a Monarchs' uniform."[26] Reflecting back to his celebrity status, Allen added, "The women, they were lovely everywhere we went. If they didn't recognize me in my regular clothes, then I'd go up to them and tell them who I was. But sometimes they could be a worrisome deal."[27]

If 1927 had been an all-star year for Rogan, it was a laugher compared to his performance in 1928. Giles concluded, "It seemed Rogan had a reason, a purpose and a spot for every pitch."[28]

In June, Rogan's six-hitter beat the St. Louis Stars. In another game, pitching in relief of Army Cooper, Rogan showed physical toughness when Mule Suttles plowed a hot one through the box that nearly tore off Rogan's shoulder. Rogan recovered, picked up the ball, threw out the runner, then came back the next inning and struck out the side. In July he pitched a 5–4 win over the Birmingham Black Barons, beating the legendary Leroy "Satchel" Paige.

Rogan's hitting was just as impressive as his pitching. When the Monarchs and Detroit's Stars met in Clinton, Missouri, Rogan was intentionally walked three times and yet he managed to drill three home runs — the first three-homer game of his Negro National League career. In another game, substituting himself for Eddie Dwight in center field, Rogan paced his Monarchs with two doubles and a triple. In an additional five-game series against Chicago's American Giants, Rogan pounded the ball at a merry 12-for-19 clip and scored nine runs.

The fact that Rogan wasn't spending much time on the bench was obvious and few

6. The Man on the Bench

Transportation advertisement: Opening day 1928, from the *Kansas City Call*.

Monarchs fans seemed to complain. He was learning — and doing it as well as Méndez and Crawford ever had — when to substitute himself off the bench. Rogan's timely substitutions made him the league's top pinch-hitter too.

Rogan's batting was the quickest way to turn an opposing manager's grin upside down. Jim Taylor, manager of the St. Louis Stars, tried to take the bat from Rogan's hands in game-winning situations. He would rather be beaten by someone else — anyone else — but Rogan. One such occasion occurred during a game in 1926. A batter doubled to start an inning, and after two men were out, Rogan came in to pinch-hit. Taylor waltzed out of the dugout, and in full view of the packed grandstand, ordered Rogan purposely walked. When the next batter whaled a double and two runs scored, Taylor fell into a virtual depression. He couldn't believe his eyes. "That Rogan can beat you even when you pitch around him," Taylor exclaimed.

In 1927, Rogan's pinch-hitting almost spoiled the Fourth of July for 8,000 people at Chicago's Schorling Park. In that game, manager Dave Malarcher made the mistake of pitching to Rogan instead of purposely walking him. Fay Young of the *Chicago Defender* was shocked. "Everyone thought the Giants would walk Rogan, filling the sacks and then take their chances on a double play," he wrote. "But [Malarcher] didn't and Rogan smacked one to right, scoring Wade Johnston and Newt Joseph."[29] The Giants managed to hang on to get the victory, thus avoiding the embarrassment of being beaten by Rogan's bat.

Rogan had dozens of ways to beat you and nobody understood that better than his old nemesis Willie Foster, and Foster had learned his lesson the hard way — through experience.

In June of the 1928 season, Chicago's American Giants, with Foster on the mound, were leading, 2–0, in the sixth when they attempted to walk Rogan. Foster's first three pitches were wide of the plate. The fourth ball was also thrown wide, but Rogan extemporaneously reached out and walloped it to deep center field. A very surprised Floyd "Jelly" Gardner, the famous Arkansas Baptist College outfielder, stood flat-footed and apparently content in centerfield as the ball sailed over his head. Rogan galloped around the bases, dead on the heels of two very astonished baserunners, with the game's winning run.

Other teams had devised less dramatic ways to stop Rogan from beating them. Ted "Double Duty" Radcliffe was with the Detroit Stars when he was first told how to pitch Rogan. Manager DeMoss said to pitch him "inside and tight," Radcliffe remembered. "Rogan hit most everything to right center. You couldn't throw him a curve because it would break across the plate. If you were going to get him out you had to throw fast balls, inside and tight."[30]

That year's pennant race was another fight to the finish. The way the St. Louis Stars jumped out front, with a record of 14 wins and one loss, made them impossible to catch. The Monarchs settled for second place. Toward the end of the second half, which was more competitive, St. Louis and Kansas City met in a series of five games with both teams tied for second place. Rogan pitched a clutch one-hit win in game one. Ted Trent came back the following day and St. Louis won. Eggie Hensley's 5–4 win gave St. Louis another victory, but Kansas City won games four and five by 13–2 and 12–1 scores, taking the series. And after beating the Cubans four straight, Kansas City was back on top of the Negro National League. Chicago was a close second. The season had come down to yet another Kansas City–Chicago fight to the finish — another classic Rogan against Foster pitching battle.

Emotions were running high as the season funneled down to its final series. Kansas City needed to win four of five from the American Giants, a team that had beaten the Monarchs in every important series since 1926.

Game one was a clutch, 6–3, win by Willie Powell, with the aid of Willie Foster's one and two-thirds innings of relief. Games two and three were part of a Sunday doubleheader. The first was advertised as a classic battle of nerves that pitted Rogan against Foster. The game started with both pitchers living up to their advanced billing. Neither pitcher faltered, and the game hung in suspense through four innings. Chicago broke through with two runs in the fifth, and the Monarchs came back with three to take the lead. Chicago finally tied it up in the seventh when Russ' lazy single got past an outfielder and went for a homer. "Rogan proceeded to fall apart after that," noted the *Kansas City American*, "the Monarch hurler being hit freely but refusing to take himself out of the game."[31] Chicago broke the tie in the eighth and went on to put away an easy 8–4 win. In winning, the American Giants collected 19 hits, the most Rogan had ever allowed in nine innings.

The second half ended with Chicago at 30–13 and a .698 winning percentage, and Kansas City at 26–14 and a .650 percentage of games won. In the playoffs, St. Louis beat Chicago, four games to three, to take the Negro National League championship. Many years later Malarcher admitted that his secret against Kansas City was his concentrated attack, something he'd learned from Rube Foster.

With the conclusion of the 1928 season, Rogan's streak of seven consecutive 20-win seasons was over. That season he pitched ten complete-game victories and made more than nine appearances in relief. Though Rogan had won more than 200 league and barnstorming contests since joining the Monarchs, lefty Andy Cooper, whom the Monarchs acquired in

Touring, 1928. Standing behind car, from left: Newt Allen, Newt Joseph, Goo Goo Livingston, J.L. Wilkinson. The team had stopped to help a farmer and his daughter with a flat tire.

trade from Detroit, was now the Monarchs' pitching ace. At the plate Rogan remained one of the premier players in baseball. As a manager, he and his team showed considerable progress.

Although they were not the powerhouse teams of 1922–1926, Rogan's young Monarchs won many spectacular games. In early April they defeated two Western Association teams in Springfield and Joplin. Among the other features of the 1928 season were exhibition games in Russell, Atchison and Wichita, Kansas. In the late August encounter in Russell, T. J. Young and L. D. Livingston hit mammoth home runs as the Monarchs won, 9–3.[32] In an encounter in Atchison, Kansas, they edged out a good Boosters team, 2–0, on only four hits.[33] During a doubleheader in Wichita, Livingston homered in both ends of the twin bill. "Several hundred colored fans rooted enthusiastically for their heroes," wrote the *Wichita Eagle*. "The Monarchs showed all of their old time skill, although several new faces were on the club."[34]

In yet another 12–3 win in Tonkawa, Oklahoma, George Giles homered and William Bell pitched a six-hitter.[35] The Monarchs' new infield caught everyone's attention. "A major-league baseball owner has said that if the Monarchs infield was whitewashed it would bring $500,000 at current quotations," wrote the *Arkansas City Daily Traveler*.[36]

Retired player William "Dizzy" Dismukes, writing a Hot Stove League column in the *St. Louis Argus*, picked Rogan as center fielder on his 1928 All-Star Negro National League team. George Giles at first, Newt Allen at third, Frank Duncan behind the plate and William Bell were the other Monarchs named to this elite group of stars.[37]

The summer of 1928 closed with the entire team grieving. José Méndez, the Monarchs' first manager, died of pneumonia at age 41 in his native Cuba. His official date of death was October 31.

By the start of the 1929 season, it didn't seem to matter that the league had cut rosters to 14 players, that the team had released Eddie Dwight, their fastest outfielder, or that George Giles, the Monarchs' promising first baseman, had jumped to the Gilkerson Union Giants. Dwight was released to cut expenses but Giles was allowed to jump because he wanted a

Eddie "Pee Wee" Dwight. Dwight, who had two stints (1925–1929 and 1933–1937) with the Monarchs, was one of the fastest runners in baseball.

small raise.³⁸ Giles had planned on getting married that year and politely asked for a $25 per month raise. Wilkinson said no to Giles' request and said, "I could go down to Louisiana and get three ball players for what you are asking."³⁹ The determined Giles promptly jumped to the Union Giants. To make matters worst, Brewer told Giles that Wilkinson "would never have you back on the team. When Wilkinson reorganized in 1931, however, one of the first players he contacted was Giles."⁴⁰

Utilizing the remaining men, Rogan devised his own managerial strategy. In some positions he platooned his younger talent. The rest of the time Rogan took the weakest spot in the batting order, and the most important position on the field, and promptly inserted himself. Nobody gave the Monarchs an outside chance at winning the pennant.

Rogan opened the season by hitting the first home run at Kansas City's Muehlebach Field. "There are home runs of many kinds," reported the *Kansas City Call*. "Some are winning home runs; other just plain home runs with nothing gained by it except an extra tally which was not needed, or which came after the game was lost. Then there are the home runs that count for more than is seen on the surface. That's the kind of home run Rogan poled last Sunday afternoon at the ball park."⁴¹

Summer 1929 was grand for fans who visited Kansas City's Muehlebach Field, as the Monarchs played .900 baseball, winning 36 games while losing only four at home. It was the best home record in Monarchs history, easily surpassing 1925's record of 39–6. The team hit an amazing .340 in 40 games at home, with T. J. Young at .443, Taylor at .386, Rogan at .382, Harding at .366, Allen at .357, Livingston at .326, Duncan at .325 and Mothell at .298.

Mrs. Scottie Mothell, the mother of Carroll Ray "Dink" Mothell. In this photograph, Scottie is holding the child of the family for which she did day work. She arrived in Topeka, Kansas, from Tennessee.

Even the pitchers, who finished with a combined .272 average, were pounding the old pill into powder.

On August 6, against the Detroit Stars, Harding, Mothell, Allen and Rogan each made two hits in one inning. In early July, Army Cooper and Chet Brewer combined to pitch a 4–0 no-hitter against Chicago's American Giants. T. J. Young hit for the cycle in another game. Young's .394 batting percentage also led the league in hitting.

Rogan pitched only two Negro National League games in 1929 — one at home and one on the road. In Kansas City, he pitched three and one-third innings of relief. When 7,000 people showed up at Chicago's Schorling Park on July 4, Rogan, always the focus of a big crowd, pitched a few innings before giving way to a relief pitcher. An August 2 edition of the *Kansas City Times* reported, "Manager Rogan has been playing the outfield all season, but says, if the race gets too hot he is ready to take his turn on the mound." Once the Monarchs warmed up the race never got hot. The Monarchs won both halves of the Negro National League pennant, thereby avoiding yet another Monarchs–American Giants playoff at season's end. It was the Monarchs' fourth Negro National League pennant in ten seasons.

The year 1929 firmly established Rogan as one of the league's best outfielders, as his play took the admiring public by storm. As early as April 12, Rogan showed signs of what was to come when his home run beat the Shreveport, Louisiana, Sports. Ironically, Willard Brown, a future Monarchs outfielder, was the bat boy during that game. Brown remembered, "I was about twelve when I started to be the batboy for the Monarchs. They used to come and train down there in Shreveport. I'd let one of the other batboys go to the visiting team. And I'd go to the Monarchs. That was my team. I didn't let anybody take the Monarchs."[42]

On May 27, Rogan's 3-for-4 day, which included two home runs, helped to cream Memphis. Another home run downed Chicago's American Giants right in the heart of the pennant race. In June, Rogan's triple, with two on, led to another late-inning win. For a good-natured taste of revenge, Rogan's two hits — one of them a timely home run — treated Willie Foster to an early shower in another game. On September 3, the very day the Monarchs clinched the second-half pennant, Rogan went 3-for-5, scored three runs and added yet another home run.

On the home portion of Rogan's season, Rogan had played 39 games and made only three errors at his home park in Kansas City. He had gone to bat 144 times, collected 55 hits, of which nine were doubles, six were triples and five were home runs. Rogan's 21 stolen bases, which established a Monarchs home record, was among that season's pleasant surprises.

Even with the weight of all his tasks, Rogan remained a leader by example, not just the manager on the bench. The collapse of the Eastern Colored League left the Negro National League and the Texas–Oklahoma–Louisiana League as the only two African American professional leagues in existence during the summer of 1929. There were strong teams in the east that the Monarchs should have played for the title, but a previous agreement was broken when the eastern circuit started tampering with some of the western's leading stars. So in late September the Monarchs traveled to Houston for a seven-game World Series against the Black Buffalos, champions of the Texas–Oklahoma–Louisiana League. They took one of their own umpires, Bert Gholston, along with them to Texas.

Houston's Black Buffalos were owned by J. B. Grigsby and featured former Negro National League stars in center fielder Roy "Red" Parnell and catcher Eppie Hampton, formerly of Memphis' Negro National League Red Sox. Pitchers Henry McHenry and left-hander Charlie Beverly were the Buffalos' top pitchers.

As it turned out, the team that had run away with the Texas–Oklahoma–Louisiana League proved little competition for Rogan's powerful Monarchs. The big seven-game series was over in four. In the ninth inning of the last game, Rogan cleared the center field fence with one of his famous tape-measure home runs. It was game three, however, that ended up being one for the ages. In that game, Houston's third and second basemen viciously attacked umpire Bert Gholston over a protested call. "In a flash, it seemed to me, scores of police rushed onto the playing field and took charge of the situation," stated L. D. Livingston. "They did a very neat job of it, too. They were very nice about it. But — they took charge of the Kansas City players who had nothing whatever to do with the row. They told the Missourians a lot of things, mostly uncomplimentary, about northern Negroes. They were impressive with their words ... I've never seen so many police at one ballgame before in my life, and the guns — well, it looked like the return of the boys from 'over there.'"[43]

After the victory in Houston, Monarchs' outfielder Livingston visited his home in Fort Worth and was to rejoin the club in Dallas for the trip back to Kansas City. "Arriving in Dallas in the early morning, about 12:55 o'clock on the interurban," said Livingston, "I looked up and down the street in search for a taxi cab — a Negro taxi. Blacks do not ride in other than Negro cabs in Dallas." Finding none in sight, he was about to pick up his bags and move on when he heard two white men calling him: "Hey, big boy, come over here." Livingston said, "When white men in Dallas speak to you, regardless of the manner in which they accost you — well, I went ... and discovered that they were policemen. They wanted to know what I wanted in Dallas, why I stopped in Dallas, where I came from and why." After a bit of small talk, Livingston explained, "I told them I was a member of the Kansas City Monarchs baseball club and was returning to Dallas to join the club for the trip back to Kansas City." As the two police men thought for a moment one replied, "Oh, yes, you are one of these northern boys who beat the Houston club in that series. Well you can just set in the wagon and come along with us. The chief will enjoy talking to you." Searched and ushered off to jail, Livingston was relieved of some $62.00 in cash. A lawyer came in and said he could get the player out of this, and "cheap." When Livingston asked the lawyer about the charges against him, the reply was, "Charge against you! Hell, boy, you are in Texas!" After paying the crooked chief of police $20.00, Livingston was permitted to leave. "He counted out the sum remaining," added Livingston, "and told me to make it snappy and keep my black mouth shut."[44]

There was at least one more noteworthy victory that season. It was the game against the Professional All-Stars, a team made up of several well-known players, in Muskogee, Oklahoma. "Five of the local players are veterans of professional baseball," wrote a local newspaper. "Willie Goodell, southpaw pitcher, was with the Chicago White Sox for a time last season and later in the Cotton States and Three-I League. Jack Raper, outfielder, played in the Lone Star League as a pitcher; 'Gyp' Haley, shortstop, is an old Western Association star; O'Malley, outfielder was in the Virginia League in 1928 and with the Muskogee Chiefs for a time this year, and Willie Wishkeno, second sacker, was recently released by the Chiefs."[45]

That the Monarchs finished the decade in a blaze of glory can be taken as a literal fact. On July 7, prior to a Sunday doubleheader at Detroit's Mack Park, a portion of the stadium went up in flames. "We were sitting in the dugout while Kansas City was taking batting practice," remembered Bobby Robinson. "We heard all this screaming, all this noise, and we thought maybe a fight was going on in the stands. We jumped out and looked and the stands were in a blaze. Man, I never will forget that."[46] The *Detroit News* reported, "The fire, a burst of flame that flashed through the floor of the stands, reached the seats with a suddenness that caused the people in the stands to scramble in all directions. In the meantime, the fire spread so rapidly that the roof [of the grand stand] fell in and the stand collapsed, injuring many who still were attempting to escape through the exits below."[47] "A quantity of gasoline, stored under the main stands, for use in drying off the diamond after a rain ignited when a match or lighted cigar was dropped down," added the *Kansas City Call*, "and panic followed the cry of fire."[48] Miraculously, no one was killed, although hundreds of panic-stricken spectators were injured.

Though records for the Monarchs road games during the 1920s are inconclusive, what the team achieved in the home portion of their schedule is well documented. During the 1920s the Monarchs played 507 games in Kansas City and won 381 of them while losing only 122 and tying 4.

Sadly, Ophelia Rogan also died in 1929. She was quietly laid to rest in Kansas City, Kansas' Westlawn cemetery.*

The Roaring Twenties had essentially burned itself out. But the Kansas City Monarchs, one of baseball's most dominant teams, were still league champions. Better yet, Wilber "Bullet" Rogan, baseball's greatest all-around player, was still playing the most celebrated ball of his career.

---

*Ophelia Rogan is buried in Kansas City, Kansas' Westlawn Cemetery; Section 14 or 15, Row 14. Her monument stone gives her life span as 1876–1929.

7

A Surge in Popularity

Mr. Rogan will live on and on and on — he is like the proverbial bad money, so to speak, always where he must be encountered, and his presence is ever known. — Walter Scott, Chicago sportswriter

Any baseball team that was a recognized champion among African American teams was guaranteed to be an excellent draw on the barnstorming circuit. And barnstorming is what helped teams like the famous Cuban Giants, Philadelphia Giants and Chicago Leland Giants to become brand name products. Both Philadelphia and Chicago had at least one player that fascinated the crowds. The Philadelphia Giants featured the slugging genius of Bill Monroe and the Chicago Leland Giants boasted pitching great Rube Foster. Kansas City's star attraction was Bullet Rogan. Wherever Rogan and his Kansas City Monarchs teammates appeared, the commotion they created was as festive as a three-day weekend. Some towns closed business districts while others declared half-holidays. The record crowds were clamoring for a peep at Rogan, baseball's greatest crossover attraction.

The Negro National League drew well on weekends but through the middle of the week the league struggled to fill empty seats. Owners tried all sorts of promotions to get the fans out on weekdays. League-wide, Tuesdays were proclaimed as Ladies Day. Other teams tried Texan Day and Tennessee Day in an attempt to lure the crowds. To combat its sagging attendance, the league reduced the big six-game series, which were very prominent in 1920 and 1921, to four-game series starting in 1922. The reduction in league games opened the middle of the week for barnstorming. Chicago's American Giants, the Indianapolis ABCs and Wilkinson's Kansas City Monarchs took full advantage of the open dates and barnstormed rigorously. It was through these efforts that black-ball barnstorming became an American sports institution.

In the Negro National League, Rogan's popularity was a given — an ultimate money-maker, especially so in Chicago's Schorling Park. In a 1923 game at Schorling, Rogan attracted one of the largest crowds ever to witness a Negro League contest. Hours before the game sold-out signs were strung all over the advance ticket booth. When all the seats were filled, standing room only tickets were sold. By game time the crowd numbered 17,000. The swelling crowd collapsed a portion of the temporary stands in left field. Bruised, scratched and still hoping to get a peek at the great Rogan in action, the rabid fans re-erected the bleachers, only to go down in a second crash of the stands. They would have tried to climb back again if the police had not made them vacate. Fay Young, writing in Chicago's *Defender*, called the gathering "the largest in the history of the park and the largest crowd that had ever seen two colored teams perform in the history of the national pastime." That afternoon Rogan beat the American Giants, 5–4, and Wilkinson pocketed $2,222.90 as his team's share of the gate.[1]

Chicago was also one of the league cities were it was unpopular to pull Rogan off the mound. When Rogan pulled himself out of a game in 1927, he was booed and cursed by the Chicago fans and a slew of local gamblers. Rogan had just returned from Kansas City, where his newborn daughter had died and his wife was seriously ill. The *Kansas City Call* acknowledged, "His grief and worry had their effects on his chances to win, however, and he was batted from the mound in the fifth." The Chicago gamblers weren't the only ones profiting off Rogan's talent. Rogan's pitching charmed Kansas City's gamblers too. Regarding a 1921 game, the *Kansas City Sun* offered, "All eyes are centered on the pitching ace of Negro baseball Wilber 'Bullet' Rogan and bets are being freely made on 12th and 18th Streets that he'll win the game he pitches. $10.000 is likely to change hands on this one game."[2] Against every team in the league Wilkinson was making money each time Rogan toed the rubber.

Rogan's celebrated arm was owner J. L. Wilkinson's ultimate wager. Dating back to July 5, 1920, when Rogan first appeared at Chicago's Schorling Park, Wilkinson had netted a cool $1,048.74[3] in gate receipts. Chump change compared to the $2,364.20[4] Wilkinson deposited when Rogan beat the American Giants at Kansas City's Association Park on August 1 of that same year.

On June 12, 1921, Wilkinson collected $2,101.76[5] for his share of the gate when Rogan defeated the Cincinnati Cubans. In July of that same year, Wilkinson bagged another $2,060.08[6] when Rogan beat the Detroit Stars in Kansas City. Two months later, on September 4, 1921, when the American Giants came to Kansas City's Association Park, Wilkinson pocketed an additional $1,720.46[7] off Rogan's astonishing arm.

George Sweatt lightheartedly recalled the first time that his wife visited a Monarchs game. "My wife [Evelyn Groomer] came to Kansas City only when the Monarchs were in town," recalled Sweatt. "The first game she attended I don't think she saw any of the game. She had never seen that many colored people assembled together or drinking beer openly as Kansas our home state was a dry state."[8] The Monarchs were drawing well and their agreement required that a portion of all the proceeds went to Andrew "Rube" Foster — but that too was about to change.

Wilkinson had also become the only owner to avoid paying Foster five percent of all his gate receipts. By reorganizing his All-Nations as a strictly barnstorming unit in 1922, Wilkinson found a source of revenue that Foster couldn't touch. The plan worked well enough for Wilkinson to take the All-Nations out on a second barnstorming tour in 1923. To bolster the All-Nations lineup, players were shifted from the Monarchs. John Donaldson, Theodore Anderson, Dink Mothell, Newt Allen and José Méndez remained with the All-Nations for extended stays. And there were others.

William "Plunk" Drake and "Bullet" Rogan also made periodic appearances with the All-Nations. With the aid of the Negro National League's best talent, the 1923 All-Nations put together a streak of 44 consecutive wins and concluded the season with more than 120 games won while barnstorming through North Dakota, South Dakota and Minnesota.

Even though Rogan was drawing well, league attendance overall, at home and abroad, decreased. In Kansas City many were content to blame the smaller crowds on the opening of Muehlebach Field, which threw open its gates in July of 1923. Wilkinson wasn't taking many chances with the expensive new park and he continued to slim down the number of home games he scheduled. His shuffling took the team from an all-time high of 57 home games in 1923 to 39 in 1924. The rest of the time, Wilkinson opened the schedule to barnstorming.

The Monarchs plowed their way through the late 1920s as profitable as any team in Negro baseball. To assure that they remained that way, Wilkinson's barnstorming agreement called for a lopsided 75–25 split. Because they won so often, seldom if ever did the Monarchs fail to take the larger winner's share of the gate. It forced entire communities to pull together to make Monarchs visits profitable. The excitement surrounding the Monarchs' visits changed peaceful little towns into swelling fortresses of anticipation.

Bus travel and all its unique flexibility made barnstorming a more socialized event. Large crowds would form wherever the Monarchs stopped for gas. In some cities players would disperse for an afternoon at a local billiards hall. On other occasions local residents would take Monarchs players to their farms for a morning of fishing or hunting before the game. Regardless of the pregame activity, everyone knew when the Kansas City Monarchs came to town, and most everywhere they appeared they were treated as honored guests. Frank Duncan recalled, "They once said Picher, Oklahoma, was a tough, rowdy town where we'd find trouble. We went in as men expecting the best and we got the best. I got pretty badly hurt there but the Picher people took care of me like I was one of their own."[9]

Many of the Monarchs' wins were just as one-sided as Wilkinson's take at the gate. In Hiawatha, Kansas, after the locals were beaten, 21–0, a local newspaper surmised, "Perhaps they [the local team] were as anxious to see how their opponents play as some of the spectators were." In Great Bend, Kansas, the locals lost by an 18–11 drubbing, with Rogan and George Mitchell sharing the mound chores. Mitchell started the game, but Rogan pulled him and inserted himself in the third after the home club had made six hits and seven runs. The following afternoon the *Great Bend Tribune* bragged, "The 11 runs we made against the big league stars established a new record. It was the first time an amateur team had ever done such a thing on the Monarchs [in] six years of barnstorming. It is common for an opposing side to make one, two, three, or maybe four runs against the Monarchs, but 11 runs — well, that was just a little more than they expected."[10] In speaking of the Rogan and Duncan battery, the same newspaper offered, "In 'Bullet' Joe Rogan, manager of the colored champions and Duncan, his catcher, the assembly saw the finest battery in colored baseball. A super pitcher and a catcher just as good. Rogan served a screaming fastball, curves of varying speeds and his change of pace with a sweeping motion as easy and unaffected as though sitting in a rocking chair."

While not usually publicized, trouble over the special living accommodations remained at issue. "Accommodations were bad. Very bad," recalled George Giles. "We [would] come to Manhattan to play and two had to stay in your house — two had to stay over there. Sometimes they'd fix meals for us at the Baptist church, or we'd go to the grocery store, cause we couldn't go to town to eat."[11]

Whenever the Monarchs traveled to nearby St. Joseph or Topeka they packed meals called "Dutch lunches" and usually returned to Kansas City without having to stay overnight. Lunches usually consisted of a sandwich, a soda pop and a pastry. On longer trips the team faced harsh discrimination at hotels and restaurants.

African American men were prohibited as customers in white-owned hotels, motel and restaurants, and as a consequence the Monarchs were forced to seek alternative accommodations. The politically correct way to refuse African American clientele from hotels and motels in the North was to post the no vacancy sign. Minority owned boarding houses supplied most of the lodging. The team stayed in many large houses as well. "We [would] stay in a lot of rooming houses," stated George Giles, "You had to leave the light on while you slept. Bedbugs wouldn't move in light."[12]

In other cases it took a series of residential homes to lodge the entire team. For meals, most restaurants opened their doors after hours to feed the Monarchs. If the restaurants were open for business, African Americans had to go in the back door. If the restaurants were closed, and all of the white customers had left, African Americans were allowed to walk through the door with some half-baked dignity. If there were no minority-owned boarding houses to be found, the team just kept traveling — sleeping and eating on the bus.

From left: Frank Duncan and Wilber "Bullet" Rogan. With more than 200 wins to their credit, Duncan and Rogan are one of the most successful batteries in baseball history (Negro League Baseball Museum).

7. A Surge in Popularity

Using the men's room was equally as challenging. More often than not, when the Monarchs showed up in their team bus the "Out of Order" sign on all local restrooms went up. Though he was white, Wilkinson won the respect of his players by enduring the hardships of travel with them. Wilkinson found life equally interesting when traveling with the team. "They [the Monarchs] never permit things to become dull, keeping the party lively with their spontaneous humor and wise cracks."[13] George Giles simply stated, "Wilkinson was a prince of a man." In 1934 Wilkinson reportedly "mortgaged his home" to pay his ballplayers."[14]

The Monarchs were everything that advance notices said they would be. As a result, they lost very few of the barnstorming contests, especially so when Rogan was on the mound. By 1926, however, Rogan was making fewer and fewer appearances outside of league play. When he did take the field, it was usually somewhere other than the pitcher's mound. On the few occasions when he did grace the mound, it was in relief of another struggling hurler. In such situations Rogan rarely faltered and was seldom turned back.

In 1926, Rogan pitched the last three innings of a game in Topeka, Kansas, and didn't allow a runner to reach first base. One of his best barnstorming outings of that year, however, occurred in Hutchinson, Kansas. That afternoon 1,500 jammed into Carey Lake Field, and those who couldn't get into the park hurried to park their cars along the left field line, necessitating ground rules. That afternoon Rogan, who was stationed in center field, went 5-for-6, with three doubles, and scored four runs. Rogan added several outstanding games throughout that summer.

In Pittsburg, Kansas, Rogan pitched and beat the locals, 11–0. In mid–August of 1926, in Clinton, Missouri, Rogan demonstrated his versatility to a crowd of nearly 1,800. Clinton had employed pitcher "Chub" Songer, a veteran minor leaguer, a brother of big-leaguer Don Songer, to stop Rogan's Monarchs. While the Monarchs were bumping Songer for 11

Monarchs team bus: "Some of Mr. Wilkinson's most interesting accounts [of the Monarchs] related to trips," wrote the *Kansas City Call*. "'Many occasions we frequently had to get out and push over miles of muddy roads in order to keep engagements,' said Wilkinson."

hits, Rogan handily struck out three from the mound, in four-innings, and added a 2-for-2 day at the plate, with a run scored. With the aid of a Hurley McNair home run, Kansas City beat Clinton by a 6–2 score.[15] Rogan performed a newsworthy feat in Larned, Kansas, when he got credit for a 16–0 win on the mound while batting 2-for-5 at the plate, with a home run.[16] In beating the Concordia Travelers 16–3 in 1927, Rogan allowed a pair of runs and six hits, while simultaneously slamming a home run.[17] That same year, when the Monarchs made their first visited to Enid, Oklahoma, Rogan celebrated the arrival by allowing three hits and no runs in five innings in gaining the victory, while at the same time batting 2-for-3 at bat with a stolen base. In a bit of showmanship, "Two times when the batter hit a roller to the pitcher, Rogan snapped the ball to the catcher [Duncan] who tossed the runner out at first."[18] In Arkansas City, Kansas, Rogan struck out three and then homered in a 10–3 Monarchs win over the Local Kanotex–Roxana team in 1928.[19]

Residents of Trenton, Missouri, had the pleasure of seeing Rogan perform in consecutive years. During a 1927 game in Trenton, after picking up a hit as a batter, he pitched five innings of two-hit ball and fanned five batters. A local enthusiast of baseball was quick to note, "Bullet Joe Rogan was apparently at his best."[20] In a return to Trenton, in 1928, Rogan pitched two splendid innings. The local newspaper fervently proclaimed, "Rogan was worth the price of admission. His easy delivery, with a world of speed, places him in a class with the best pitchers, white or black of all time, if he were not handicapped by age."[21] Of all the cities out West, Wichita, Kansas, is where Rogan pitched some of his most classic ball games.

During the 1926 season Rogan pitched a seven-hitter and defeated the local Advertisers ball team at Island Park.[22] In Wichita, during the 1927 season, the All-Professionals put former St. Louis Cardinal Clyde "Pea Ridge" Day on the mound and Rogan shut them out 4–0 on two hits and six strikeouts while going 1-for-4 at the plate against Day.[23] Rogan returned to Wichita in 1928 and struck out seven, allowed seven hits, walked none and toppled Wichita's Henry Clothiers team 10–4. In August of 1929, Rogan had a big offensive game there when he played four positions and hit a pair of home runs. In 1930, when the Monarchs introduced night baseball to Wichita, Rogan hit two additional home runs on consecutive nights.[24] According to one source, prior to the start of the 1935 season, the Monarchs were defeated only twice, in 35 games played in Wichita.[25]

Rogan could make the minor leaguers bow down any day of the week — and barnstorming gave him the chance to prove it. On April 18, 1926, Rogan allowed one run and four-hits in six innings and struck out five in the Monarchs' 14–1 win over the Salina Millers of Kansas' Southwestern League.[26] On September 11, 1927, Rogan pitched part of the game against the Western Association's Joplin Miners. That day he struck out nine and slammed a home run in the Monarchs' 19–12 victory.[27] In still another game against this same Miners team, Rogan, playing third base, went 3-for-4 with a triple. Considering that Joplin, during a 1903 race riot, had driven out half of its 770 African Americans population living in the city and lynched Thomas Gilyard, it was remarkable that Rogan and his Monarchs teammates even remained in the city for multiple games.[28]

Over in Springfield, Missouri, Rogan went 1-for-3, stole a base and participated in a sparkling double play as a second baseman in the Monarchs' 5–4 win over the Western Association's Springfield Midgets.[29] The year prior, Rogan, pinch-hitting for Wade Johnston, tripled to center in the Monarchs' 8–7 loss.[30] Then again, there was that famous game in

1927 when Rogan battled the legendary veteran Babe Adams in Springfield. Born Charles Benjamin Adams, in 1882, he was a winner of 194 big league games and the first rookie to win three games in a World Series, a feat he'd accomplished in 1909.

In a game that was widely advertised, Adams was pitted against the Monarchs' ace, Rogan, and the mere anticipation of the event attracted a crowd of over 2,000 to the festivities. Rogan, "breezed through four easy innings without a mishap."[31] In the fifth, however, "with one out, [Springfield's Carl] Davis smacked a long triple to the left field sheds and scored when Allen threw the relay wild to third base and the ball went into the Midget dugout."[32] Rogan protested, as he thought it was a double and the runner should have held at third. When overruled, the Monarchs pitcher let out such a howl over the play an umpire ordered him to leave the field. The crowd demanded, however, that Rogan return to finish the game. "When the fans yelled for him to come back and pitch he wouldn't do it."[33] Unfortunately, Adams remained in the game and the Monarchs bashed him for 14 hits, four of them going for doubles. The final score was 9-to-1.

Rogan's versatility was always a bonus. In Atchison, Kansas, the *Kansas Daily Globe* reported that Rogan played first base and pitched. On the mound he threw a one-hitter for two-innings, and at-bat he was 1-for-3 with a run scored. Against Concordia, Kansas, Rogan played center field, batted 1-for-4 and swiped a base. In Moberly, Missouri, Rogan was stationed in right field and also pitched. In spectacular celebration of his arrival in the Missouri town, Rogan struck out three batters from the mound, then as a batter added three hits, two runs, a pair of stolen bases and a home run.[34]

Year by year, throughout the 1920s, the barnstorming crowds remained consistently large — and there was plenty of documentation to support that fact. When the Monarchs visited Morland, Kansas, the *Morland Monitor* reported, "This was the best patronized single game ever played in this part of the country."[35] During a visit to Concordia, the *Blade Empire* called its crowd of 2,100 "The largest crowd ever accommodated at a ball game here."[36] That night Rogan, pinch-hitting for Leroy Taylor in the twelfth inning, tripled to the cars surrounding the park, scoring William Bell. Hallie Harding drove the next pitch through the box to score Rogan, in a stinging come-from-behind 5–3 win.

Wilkinson was in awe of Rogan's ability to draw a crowd. And whenever the formula for drawing crowds was mentioned Rogan's name was always in the mix. In 1928, Wilkinson gave his explanation to the *Wichita Eagle* in an attempt to help everyone understand the Monarchs' unique popularity. "Many teams give themselves a name similar to the Monarchs in an attempt to draw huge crowds by misleading the public. There are barnstorming clubs now playing under Monarchials, Monarivons and similar names, which have no meaning whatsoever. Two year ago I was glancing over the sports page of the *Los Angeles Times* when I read that the Kansas City Monarchs won a game in a small Arizona town 'Bullet' Rogan turning in the victory. As a matter of fact, Rogan was sick in bed and my club was playing a National Colored League contest in St. Louis."[37]

Still, the real Monarchs and their famous pitcher Rogan were advertised with vigor every place the team appeared. In Newton, Kansas, the local *Newton Evening Republican* wrote, "Bullet Rogan, the greatest Negro pitcher to grace a mound, also playing-manager of the Monarchs, is having one of his best years in his career, both on the mound and in the field. He is considered one of the greatest all around ball players in baseball. His hitting is superior to any colored ball player in the country." Joplin, Missouri's *News Herald* priced

Rogan's worth at $100,000 if only he were white. When Great Bend scheduled their annual game in 1928, local newspapers advertised the game as "Big League Base Ball."[38]

As lucrative as barnstorming might have been, it was not without its complications. Negro League baseball and baseball played in the National and American Leagues were worlds apart — one was blessed with opportunities, the other choked with obstacles. The trips to visit cities, no matter how short or scenic, were not easy. African Americans were not permitted to stop for food or rest in most surrounding areas.

If there was one thing to which every player agreed, it was to avoid mixing with the women in the audiences. To do so caused nothing but trouble between the races and the last thing a traveling team needed was altercations with the public. And as veterans of the highways, they were ever alert to Missouri's infamous tradition of lynching. "Between 1900 and 1931, mobs in the state lynched 22 men, 17 of whom were black."[39] Rogan could intimately relate to many confrontations on, as well as off, the ball field.

In 1923 the Monarchs were scheduled to play in Columbia, Missouri, the same year that local citizens grotesquely hung James T. Scott, one of its colored citizens. On April 29, 1923, a mob in Columbia lynched Scott, a 35-year-old African American janitor, employed by the University of Missouri, from Stewart Bridge, an automobile overpass located a quarter of a mile from the school's campus.[40] Scott was being held in Boone County jail, charged with assaulting the 14-year-old daughter of the University's foreign language professor. The Monarchs won the ballgame, but it must have been difficult to play with one eye focused on the ball and the other on the audience. There were other cities, some well-known for their heritages of violence against African Americans, that the Monarchs chose to avoid altogether. One such place was Maryville, Missouri. As late as the 1980s Monarchs players could actively recall the story of Raymond Gunn, a 27-year-old African American who had reportedly confessed to the murder of Velma Colter in January of 1931. A mob overpowered the local sheriff and his deputies and took Gunn. Three miles south of Maryville, the mob chained the prisoner to the roof of the schoolhouse, where the murder had been committed, doused the structure with gasoline and set it on fire. Over 3,000 angry whites watched Gunn burn alive.[41] The author was told different versions of the same story by Chet Brewer, George Giles and John "Buck" O'Neil.

Likewise to be avoided was Coffeyville, Kansas. There had been a race riot in that city on March 18, 1927. On that occasion, after two white high school students claimed rape, "angry whites, mad for revenge on the attackers of their women," pursued Negroes to their homes, and made attempts to storm the jail where three suspects were being held. The attack story proved to be false and white men were arrested for the crime although a great injustice had already occurred.[42]

Though Rogan's entire life had been influenced negatively by racism he refused to surrender to its oppression. As a child it had limited his education and now as a professional ballplayer it was limiting his ability to provide income for his family. In his own patriotic way, Rogan was doing his part to end that apartheid. In many cases, Rogan's apartheid fighting tendencies were physically targeted at cheating umpires.

In October of 1922, during a game in Iola, Kansas, Rogan was forced to battle a cheating umpire with his fists. The Monarchs first appeared in Iola in late August and shut out Jack Griffin's Oilers, 6–0, behind Currie's three-hit pitching.[43] For the return engagement, local promoters acquired Ernest Maun, a New York Giants recruit, in an attempt to beat the Monarchs, who selected Rogan to pitch. Iola also acquired a new umpire to call balls and strikes for the pre-arranged two game set.

As promised, Rogan took the mound. He struggled through five scoreless innings, not on his own account, but because of egregious calls made by the umpire. Before taking yet another exception to the umpire's questionable calls, Rogan chose to chat with the controversial arbiter. When the umpire resorted to racial slurs, Rogan slugged the slanderous arbiter, knocking him to the ground. There are two different accounts of what followed. "That one punch agitated several groups of white men that were seated nearby in the grandstand and several charged the field in anger and began chasing Rogan, but Rogan had already planned ahead," stated Maun. "He ran to the outfield fence, went over the top and fled off in a waiting vehicle." During a chance meeting some years later, Maun said that Rogan told him, "Man, I didn't stop until I reached Kansas City."[44] Maun should have left the game when Rogan left. He didn't, and the Monarchs ripped him for 16 hits and a 7–2 win. In the *Daily Register's* account of the controversy: "Manager Crawford immediately responded to the demand to 'jerk' Rogan, and Méndez finished the game."[45] Luckily, there were only 400 people at the park.

Then again, there was that famous commotion with Casey Stengel's All-Stars in 1920. There were 10,000 people in Kansas City's Association Park to see Stengel's team of big leaguers play the Monarchs. Stengel's All-Star team featured Cot Tierney and Walter Schmidt, from the Pirates, Gene Paulette and Lee Meadows, of the Phillies, Speed Martin, of the Cubs, and both Meusel brothers, Bob and Irish. Stengel had batted .292 in 129 games for the Philadelphia Phillies and Tierney had made his rookie debut with the Pittsburgh Pirates in 1920. For eight innings the score was deadlocked at zero. It was a real pitchers' battle between Rogan and Meadows, who had won 16 games for the Phillies in 1920. Both pitchers had allowed a mere four hits through eight innings. In spite of the plate umpire's bad calls, Rogan somehow managed to strike out eight of Stengel's big league stars. In the top of the ninth inning, fed up with the favoritism after what should have been a called third strike to Bob Meusel, but was called a ball, Rogan decided to take matters into his own hands. The umpire and Rogan had a few choice words and reportedly Rogan said something like, "So that's how it's going to be." Rogan went back to the mound and intentionally lobbed a gift pitch that Meusel pounded over the center-field bleachers to give his team a 1–0 win.[46]

As the slugger was cheerfully completing his home run trot, Rogan was slipping into his street clothes and angrily leaving the park. The *Kansas City Sun* acknowledged in its coverage of that game, "Most fans are of the opinion that the spoils went, not to the victors but rather to recipients of Anglo Saxon favor from the white gent who arbitrates the contest."[47]

Chet Brewer could recall many such stories, some humorous and others down-right life threatening, that had taken place during barnstorming tours. During his many years with the Monarchs, he pitched hundreds of league and barnstorming games. One of his more memorable outings was in 1928, when he and Rogan held the Atchison, Kansas, Boosters to one hit, winning 10–0. Brewer faced 18 men in the first seven innings, and Rogan pitched the last two innings and gave up the game's only hit. Only 29 men faced the two Monarchs hurlers that day.[48] Next to Rogan, Brewer had become a front-line starting pitcher. It wasn't always that way. Once upon a time, manager José Méndez considered sending Brewer packing forever, and he had good reason for making that decision.

Chet Brewer (left) and Maurice "Doolittle" Young, 1927. They were pitchers in manager Rogan's youth movement in the late 1920s.

In his first season with the Monarchs, 1925, it was evident that Chet Brewer and Frank Duncan didn't get along. One night Brewer started a fight, and Duncan pulled out a pin knife in self-defense. In the commotion, Duncan stabbed Brewer in his pitching arm. Manager José Méndez banished Brewer to the bench for most of the season, and as further punishment Brewer was not permitted to pitch in that year's World Series. Knowing that the two ballplayers might never forget the affair, Wilkinson's decided to hire T. J. Young as Brewer's personal catcher. As time passed, Brewer and Young became more than batterymates; they became best friends. Duncan eventually made up with Brewer and the two remained on the Monarchs roster for many season.

Barnstorming was big business. For African American teams it was a summer tradition and it helped to keep baseball alive and prospering in towns and cities all over America. J. L. Wilkinson liked to tell the story of how the Kansas City Monarchs once drew 7,000 people to two games in Oxford, Nebraska, a town with a population of 1,100.

Of all that was written and said about them, no reference to the Kansas City Monarchs seems more revealing than the straightforward commentary that appeared in the *Dodge City Journal*. The newspaper wrote, "The Negroes played a fast game of ball here and left little doubt in the minds of local fans that they were of big league caliber, barred only because of a certain ruling of the major organizations."[49]

8

Going, Going, Not Gone Yet

In Bullet Rogan the Monarchs have who is generally termed the greatest Negro pitcher in the game. He often is ranked with Walter Johnson and Grover [Cleveland] Alexander as one of the three greatest twirlers in baseball.—Joplin Globe, April 13, 1928

Bullet Rogan entered the 1930 season more or less a triple threat—the greatest living hitting/pitching/base-running threat in baseball. Picking up from where he left off in 1929, Rogan started that season with a flurry of offensive outbursts. Then strange things started to happen. Three months into the season Rogan was permanently forced out of the lineup with an injury. This serious injury, as it turned out, was career threatening. It was serious enough to bring Rogan's illustrious career, and possibly his life, to a sudden and scary end. Eventually, Rogan made a 100 percent recovery. His recovery, and his eventual return to baseball, began the most illustrious chapter in his storybook rise to baseball immortality.

Bullet Rogan turned 37 in 1930. Though he was still hustling like a rookie trying to break into his team's starting lineup, it was obvious that he couldn't keep this pace forever. Nobody understood that more than J. L. Wilkinson, who in an effort to keep the crowds at an all-time high, began experimenting with night baseball. Considering what happened to Rogan, Wilkinson's timing couldn't have been more perfect.

The Monarchs employed virtually the same team that won both halves of the 1929 Negro National League pennant and the World Series to start the 1930 season. As was always the case, Rogan couldn't resist picking up two new pitchers. He signed a left-hander named Johnny Markham and a right-hander named Henry McHenry.

Wilkinson's night baseball was kicked off in big headlines in a March 27 edition of the *Kansas City American*, which proclaimed, "Monarchs First Team to Play Ball by Floodlight." The article that followed outlined Wilkinson's new plan: "The Monarchs will carry with them this year, their giant portable lighting equipment on wheels, which consists of a 110 kilowatt generator and a 250 horsepower, six cylinder marine gas engine, which will furnish the power to illuminate the entire baseball park using giant flood lights carrying one hundred thousand watts."

An article that appeared in Hannibal's *Courier Post* added, "The giant electric floodlights, which encircle the park, are supported by a series of poles and towers that are similar in construction to a jack knife or fire department equipment with its extension ladders. The telescoped poles and towers extend forty to fifty feet into the air, making every play as easily seen as if it were in the afternoon."[1]

Night baseball may have been the rage in 1930, but for Wilkinson it was old news. He had first attempted it with the All-Nations in 1914. During that season his team played night games with tremendous success. Night games were played in New Ulm, Owantonna,

Night baseball, 1930. Five years before the Cincinnati Reds brought nighttime play to the major leagues, the Monarchs took to the road with portable lights and packed in the crowds.

and Austin, Minnesota. In promoting the game in Austin, the local newspaper noted, "The All-Nation management carries a special lighting system for the night games and offers to refund the admission if the fans cannot see every play. This is a novelty and ought to pack the stands."[2] By 1930 Wilkinson had refined the process and it was about to become a paying proposition.

The 1930 season started in Houston, Texas, where the Monarchs slaughtered the Black Buffalos by a 16–7 score in early April. The Monarchs went to Galveston, Texas, next. In Galveston it was like pioneer days for Newt Joseph, a former member of the Galveston Sand Crabs. He slammed three home runs against his former team in a Monarchs 17–4 blowout. From the sixth inning on the Monarchs played without an infield.

Making an excursion to San Antonio, Texas, the Monarchs battled the San Luis Cuban All-Stars in four exciting games. After losing the opener, 3–2, Kansas City stormed back and won three consecutive games behind the pitching of William Bell, 9–2; Chet Brewer, 5–3; and Andy Cooper, 4–3. Newt Joseph and Frank Duncan both homered in the series.[3]

After the San Antonio series the Monarchs stopped in Crescent, Oklahoma. They were there just long enough to hit ten home runs in yet another smashing 18–0 win. Outwardly shaken by the whole affair, Roy Waller, a member of the flustered Crescent team, testified, "If you would have been there you would have thought it was more than ten!"[4]

Finally, the Monarchs pulled up in Arkansas City, Kansas, to play their first night game. The *Chicago Defender* reported that "10,000 fans brought ducats for the game but old Jupiter Pluvius said no. The game had to be canceled on account of rain."[5] The *Arkansas City Daily Traveler*, commenting on the missed opportunity, noted, "Twice this season the Refiners have booked a night game with the famous Kansas City colored team, and each time his honor Jupiter Pluvius has blessed the countryside with a generous downpour of aqua pura."[6]

On Monday, April 28, in Enid, Oklahoma, the Monarchs finally squeezed in that first night game against Phillips University. More than 3,000 curious onlookers were on hand at Enid's Alton Stadium as Kansas City won, 12–4. The *Enid Morning News* reported that Rogan had gone 2-for-4, with a double and two runs scored that night.[7] "Boy," said Chet Brewer, "they'd kick that thing over and the flood lights would light up that park like day. And people would come from miles around to see that baseball could be played at night! In Enid, Oklahoma, you never saw so many people."[8]

More history was yet to be made when Johnny Markham placed his name into the annals of the immortals by becoming the first pitcher to toss a perfect game under the lights. That night, May 6, 1930, the Monarchs beat the Waco, Texas Cardinals, a rival African American opponent, 8–0, at that city's Katy Park. The *Waco Times-Herald* reported that a crowd of "2,000 fans looked on." Another newspaper's description of the game noted, "In the nine innings he [Markham] allowed only twenty-seven men to face him. He did not allow a run, nor a hit, and he did not let a Waco runner reach first base during the entire game."[9] And while the opposition was struggling with the new night baseball, the Monarchs continued to make steady adjustment. "It was hard at first," offered Newt Allen, "but when you began to play under them regularly, the only hard part was when a fly ball was hit. You'd have to wait for it to come out of the dark to catch it. Sometimes a fellow would hit it clear out of sight of the lights, then you had to try to find it. But we got used to it later and developed a pretty good judgment of where the ball was."[10]

When the team reached Wichita, Kansas, on June 2, the Monarchs introduced night baseball games on two consecutive nights. A crowd of 3,000 flocked to the opener of the two-game set.

June 13, 1930, was another historic date. That night the Monarchs trashed Tom Wilson's Nashville Elite Giants in the first-ever night game at Kansas City's Muehlebach Field. More than 12,000 people were on hand to see Rogan go 2-for-5 with a stolen base and a double, as Kansas City prevailed, 15–8.

While the Monarchs were devoting an overabundance of attention to night baseball, St. Louis' Stars were cruising to an easy Negro National League pennant. Wilkinson didn't seem to care. Night baseball's enormous potential had become the Monarchs' savior. Attendance figures were rapidly erasing the importance of the actual scores, and every crowd reflected that fact. In Dallas, Texas, 7,000 braved the night air to see the Monarchs beat the Black Giants. That same month 8,000 witnessed another game in Memphis, Tennessee. In St. Louis 9,000 jammed the Stars' park to see that city's first nocturnal contest.

On June, 28, Detroit's first game under the lights was played before a crowd of motor city sports enthusiasts. "It was very exciting," said Bobby Robinson, a Detroit infielder; "It was the first time I'd played under the lights. But it was kind of rough. The generators would go down and the lights would start to dim, and then they'd start back up and the lights would get bright again."[11] That night, Goo Goo Livingston slammed three home runs in another impressive 17–4 win.

Night baseball's prosperity in the West prompted Wilkinson to introduce it to the East. Placing their league schedule on hold, the Monarchs took a two-week hiatus to play a nine-game series with Cum Posey's Homestead Grays. Big crowds followed the two teams everywhere they played.

The opening game against the Grays, at Cleveland's Hooper Field, drew 6,000 curious onlookers.[12] By far, the largest crowd of the entire series was the 12,000 fans that showed up at Pittsburgh's Forbes Field for that city's first-ever night game on July 18.[13] The final game of the series was played in Columbus, Ohio, in front of a crowd that numbered 7,500.

As late as August of 1930, the Monarchs and their portable floodlights were still packing parks. In the first-ever night game in St. Joseph, Missouri, the Monarchs helped to fill up the city's stadium fund with Brewer's 4–1 win over the Sunday League All-Stars. The *St. Joseph Gazette* offered, "It probably would be safe to wager [that] the Saints [minor league team] will play to twice as many persons next year should the club install lights Not especially because a large crowd turned out for the first night game here, that being expected, but due to the favorable sentiments expressed by those who did attend the melee."[14] In reference to the massive crowd, another local newspaper added, "Although it seemed that 'thousands' were on hand, the Chamber of Commerce, backers of the game, reported today there were 2,605 paid admissions. Children under twelve were admitted free, bringing the total attendance near 3,000."[15]

When the Monarchs visited Hannibal, Missouri, on August 15, they could have added a new chapter to Tom Sawyer's adventures. That night the Monarchs, with Harding's three doubles, and doubles by Young, Duncan, Mothell and Livingston, knocked paint off the walls in a 16–1 win and nearly whitewashed the local Hansox ball team. The local *Hannibal Courier Post* called the more than 1,800 fans that attended the event "the largest crowd of the season."[16] In tiny Brookfield, Missouri, the Monarchs attracted a big crowd in the first night game ever played in that city. Home runs by Mothell and Markham figured largely in a 10–8 Monarchs victory. Later that month, 5,000 enjoyed night baseball in Chicago, Illinois.

The 1930 season concluded with a string of night games across Western Kansas. Great superiority on the part of the Kansas City Monarchs allowed them to simply toy with that region's best competition. In one of the games, one which was played on September 15, in Manhattan, Kansas, the Monarchs triumphed over the Manhattan All-Stars, 7–2. T. J. Young starred at bat with two doubles and a single in five times up. On the mound, Henry McHenry pitched the first five innings, Leroy Taylor, the sixth and seventh and Halley Harding the eighth and ninth.[17] Harding had already played left field, third base, shortstop and first base in this game prior to his taking the mound. In one of the more spectacular plays of the season, a Manhattan player almost simultaneously tagged two Monarch runners at home, both attempting to score on what looked like a home run off Duncan's bat. "Cochrane took Cross' peg," wrote Manhattan's *Republic* newspaper, "tagged out Harding as he slid on one side of the plate, then turned to get Duncan who was right behind him" sliding on the other side of the plate.[18] "More than 1,000 fans (not counting the nearly 100 which were holding a two-hour tree-sitting endurance contest in anything that was tall enough to prevent the paying of the six bits admission) saw the game."[19]

The Monarchs also captured victories in Concordia where another good-size crowd of 1,300 was in attendance. Brewer struck out 13 batters, while his teammates were chopping out 16 safe blows in a 14–0 blowout. In Liberal, the Monarchs beat a select team formed of the best players from southwest Kansas, 10–5. Following that encounter the Monarchs lambasted Garden City, 10–2, behind Cooper's seven-hit pitching and 14 hits by the Monarchs.

The 1930 season had been a gigantic success for everyone except Rogan. Early on, he was playing well in both league and exhibition games. Center field felt comfortable and the old power was still manifesting itself. During an April 10 game in Texas, Rogan contributed a home run in Kansas City's 16–4 win over Galveston's Sandcrabs.[20] On June 2, in Wichita, Kansas, one of Rogan's hits had landed far beyond the fence. He returned the next night to smash yet another home run in a Monarchs 10–8 win. The ball Rogan homered on in Detroit was good for another Monarchs victory. In league play Rogan's average was a splendid .311 for 28 games. He had played 13 games in Kansas City, batting .353. But it was just after the Nashville series that Rogan became ill.

At first it looked as if Rogan would be out for several weeks. When he attempted to direct his squad from the bench, the pace was too furious for his ailing body. The doctor advised rest. In Rogan's absence Dink Mothell took over as manager of the team.

Rogan's condition was rumored to be lockjaw. Others speculated that he had caught a virus. Charley Hancock, an old-time catcher, said that Rogan had had an operation on his eye.[21] No one, except Rogan's doctors, knew for sure. And it was a mystery why the doctors weren't talking. Historians still don't know all of the reasons for Rogan's absence. Whatever the illness was, it kept Rogan out of baseball for more than a season. When visited by teammates, Rogan promised he'd be back, and he was a man of his word, but days turned into weeks and weeks into months.

As Rogan recuperated at his home, he was informed that one of his childhood baseball idols had passed. On June 9, 1930, Andrew "Lefty" Skinner was shot and killed by police in Leavenworth, Kansas, while bootlegging liquor during prohibition.* Famous in baseball circles, Skinner, an Atchison, Kansas, native, had emerged as a renowned pitcher with the Kansas City, Kansas, Giants as early as 1908. He played a prominent role in the Giants' 54-game winning streak of 1909. Tough and hard-nosed, Skinner also served time in the Missouri State Penitentiary for stabbing his wife with a pair of scissors. At the peak of his professional career, Skinner conquered the Stars of Cuba, New Orleans' Eagles, the Buxton, Iowa, Wonders, San Antonio's Black Broncos, original Kansas City's Monarchs and the Lexington Tigers. Among his most celebrated outings was an August 10, 1909, shutout of the Cuban Stars. As a member of the ill-fated Texas Colored League's Oklahoma Monarchs of 1910, Skinner toured Illinois and pitched against the legendary Chicago Leland Giants. He retired from baseball in 1915, following a season with the Kansas City All-Stars. One of the last times Rogan saw Skinner was when the Monarchs played the state prison team in Jefferson City, Missouri, in 1922.[22]

On a more upbeat note there was Grady Orange. When Grady Orange graduated from Meharry Medical College, on May 28, 1931, the Monarchs produced their first doctor.

---

*Andrew Skinner is buried in Kansas City, Kansas at Westlawn Cemetery, Section 7, Row 1, Plot 3. His burial date was 6/14/1930. His age was listed as 46 at the time of his death.

He completed that season with the Monarchs, his last as a professional ball player, and relocated to Port Arthur, Texas. Orange built a thriving practice before his premature death in a house fire many years later.

The 1931 season was historic for many reasons. For the first time ever, the Monarchs started a season late. Forecasting a bleak financial situation, Wilkinson decided to sit out the season but reluctantly changed his mind and reorganized his Monarchs on July 4, after which time he assembled one of the greatest teams in Monarchs history.

Getting off to such a late start should have hampered the Monarchs, but somehow they survived. Playing without their star, Rogan, who was out with an injury, the team was also devoid of several other regulars. Frank Duncan, L. D. Livingston, Henry McHenry and William Bell had joined the New York Harlem Stars. Hally Harding had joined the Baltimore Black Sox. In regrouping, the Monarchs fielded a representative squad of new faces. First time Monarchs outfielder Nat Rogers, infielder Curtis Harris and pitchers Charlie Beverly of Houston along with Samuel Thompson of Wiley College and Big Bill Lane of Cincinnati brought new life to the besieged franchise. Turkey Stearnes, who jumped the Detroit Stars for the Bacharach Giants, and Willie Foster, who was plucked from the Homestead Grays along with Frank Duncan and Henry McHenry, and Chet Brewer who had been playing for Crookston, Minnesota, arrived at different intervals as the season progressed.

Legendary pitcher-outfielder John Donaldson, who had not worn a Monarchs uniform since 1924, returned to take a berth in the outfield after starting the season with the Colored House of David team. A year earlier, in 1930, while pitching for St. Cloud, Minnesota, Donaldson finished with a 13–6 record and batted .341 in 24 games, proving that he could still contribute.

His return prompted one newspaper to write, "John McGraw once said that if he [Donaldson] had been white he would willingly have paid $50,000 to get him on the Giants, and that was back in the days when a price of $11,000 for a battery including pitcher and catcher set the baseball world to wondering what the game was coming to."[23]

Wilkinson soon discovered that playing an exclusive schedule of barnstorming games, without the restriction of a league schedule, could significantly change a team's economic perspective, especially so during a depressed economy.

After losing, 4–3, to Chicago's Duffy Florals on July 5, the Monarchs reeled off 20 straight wins. During win number 17, played in Sioux Falls, South Dakota, Newt Allen slammed two home runs. He had duplicated a feat achieved by T. J. Young, who slammed two home runs in a July 10, game in Wisconsin Rapids, Wisconsin, in the Monarchs' 5–2 win over that city's best team.[24]

Consecutive win number 14 had been a 6–0 shutout of the Crookston, Minnesota, Red Sox. Pitching for Crookston was Chet Brewer. Battling on the mound, Charlie Beverly tossed a five-hitter and Brewer a six-hitter, but nine errors by his Red Sox teammates kept the former Kansas City ace from defeating his buddies on the Monarchs.[25] T. J. Young, with two of the Monarchs hits, laced a triple. Other batters were equally as productive, as the wins continued to pile up.

Hard-hitting Curtis Harris' lusty wallops were a feature. In Burlington, Wisconsin, he slammed, "probably the longest hit ever made in [Athletic] park."[26] He had also struck a decisive home run to defeat the Cuban House of Davids in Council Bluffs, Iowa. Harris slammed a two-run shot in Marysville, Kansas, in still another electrifying performance. In one of the Monarchs' most celebrated home run performances, Harris was not a factor. In that game, played in Wymore, Nebraska, the Monarchs hit seven home runs, two each by Newt Allen and T. J. Young and three others by Powell, Duncan and McHenry, in a 13–4 final. Both of Allen's home runs had come with the bases loaded.[27]

Pitcher Charlie Beverly was just as splendid throughout the 1931 season. Beverly, a native of Houston, Texas, and a former member of the Houston Black Buffalos, was by this time one of baseball's premier left-handed strikeout pitchers. He won the first Monarchs game of the 1931 season, a victory over Chicago Mills on July 4. Evidently he was already in midseason form, as he quickly followed that performance with a nine strikeout outing in Wisconsin. Beverly's performance prompted one newspaper to expound, "If Lefty Grove of the Athletics were turned loose on the Wisconsin Rapids ball club, he couldn't dazzle the local willow wielders much more effectively than did Beverly, dark skinned southpaw mound ace of the Kansas City Monarchs."[28]

Against the Sioux Falls Canaries on July 22, Beverly allowed five hits and struck out eight batters in seven and two-thirds innings. He also managed to strike out ten in the Monarchs' 9–0 win over the Union Pacific club in Kansas City, Kansas. That night, which happened to be the only night game played in Kansas City, Kansas, for the 1931 season, Beverly allowed three hits and left the game in the fifth inning.[29] Beverly's list of victims included Omaha's Western League team, against whom he pitched a four-hitter, and two important games against the Homestead Grays, one in Akron, Ohio, when he struck out six,[30] and a nine-hitter at Cleveland's new Municipal Stadium.[31] Though Beverly would lead the staff in wins and strikeouts, it was "Big" Bill Lane's no-hitter in Alliance, Ohio, that reigned supreme until Willie Foster joined the team in mid–September.

Carroll "Dink" Mothell, (far left) his longtime girlfriend Roma Street (next to Mothell), and three unidentified friends. In a 1931 game at Pittsburgh's Forbes Field, Mothell tagged Willie Foster for four hits, which included two doubles. Street died in 1947 in Utah.

Willie Foster's good fortune started with the Homestead Grays, and he had already won 20 games by the time he caught on with the Monarchs. He proceeded to beat the Cuban House of Davids, 3–1, on a three-hitter and 12 strikeouts in Council Bluffs, Iowa, leading the Monarchs to victory in the Arlington, Nebraska, baseball tournament.[32] Foster added yet another double-digit strikeout performance against the Sioux Falls Canaries. His crowning victory, though, was the 4–3 win over the Major League All-Stars in Kansas City. The Monarchs pitching staff of 1931, Chet Brewer, Army Cooper, Sam Thompson, Henry McHenry, Charlie Beverly, Bill Lane and Willie Foster, finished with more than 20 shutouts in spite of the late start.

Probably the best pitching performance witnessed by the Monarchs was pitched against them. In that game the St. Louis Stars' ace, Ted Trent, beat the Monarchs, 6–5, in twelve innings, striking out 16 Monarchs batters, a total that was second only to Joe Williams' famous 27 strikeout game against the Monarchs in 1930. A local newspaper added, "Stearns whiff[ed] five times and every other Monarch but Allen and Mothell at least once. Only seven scattered bingles were garnered off his [Trent's] tantalizing curves and slow balls in the long tilt."[33]

The series against the Sioux Falls Canaries team was one of the highlights of the Monarchs' 1931 season. The Canaries featured Swede Riseberg, a player made famous by the "Black Sox" scandal of 1919, which involved throwing major league baseball's World Series. The Canaries and Monarchs met in a series of four games in 1931. Game one, played in front of 1,400 at Elmwood Park, was captured by the Monarchs in what eventually became a free-slugging 12–5 affair. That night, the Monarchs pounded two doubles, a triple and three home runs as part of their 16-hit attack.[34] Charlie Beverly got credit for the win.

Sioux Falls got revenge in Sioux City, Iowa, winning, 11–7, as pitcher Sam Thompson allowed 12 hits. Newt Allen, John Donaldson, Nat Rogers and Thompson led with two hits each for the Monarchs off the Canaries' Claude Bradford.[35] The series concluded with a September 20 doubleheader. The Monarchs lost the opener, 2–1, in spite of Willie Foster's eight-hit, ten strikeout performance from the mound. Newt Joseph added a perfect 4-for-4 performance at-bat. Game four, the series' final encounter, was won by a 2–1 score, when Brewer's seven-hitter and a pair of hits by Allen gave the Monarchs an even split of the four games.

During Rogan's absence in 1930 and 1931, the Monarchs also played four big series against the powerful Homestead Grays of Pittsburgh, Pennsylvania. Two of the series were played in the West and two in the East. Nearly all of the contests were night games that started around 8:30 to 8:45 P.M. The series matched two of baseball's best-known units, and the crowds packed ballparks virtually everywhere games were played. It was during this series, in Kansas City, on August 2, 1930, that Grays pitcher "Smokey" Joe Williams struck out 27 batters and allowed one hit in the same game that Chet Brewer struck out 19 batters in an intensely contested twelve-inning clash.[36]

Of the 21 games played in the two years, the Grays won 16 times. The team the Grays paraded out in 1931 was one of baseball's greatest teams ever, and yet Kansas City, even without Rogan, managed to defeat them three times. Grays owner "Cum" Posey rated the Monarchs of 1931 as the third best team in baseball, behind his Homestead Grays and Hilldale of Darby, Pennsylvania.[37] Posey also selected pitcher Beverly, second baseman Newt Allen and right fielder Dink Mothell to his "All-America Ball Club."[38]

Four members of the Chicago Palmer House Hotel team, 1940. From left: Nat Rogers, Curtis "Bingo" Lloyd, Jack "Bosie" Marshall and Sandy Thompson. Rogers and Lloyd had played with the Monarchs in 1931 and 1932, respectively. Rogers, one of baseball's best hitters, was the replacement outfielder that the Monarchs employed in Rogan's absence.

Posey's estimation that Kansas City was the third best African American team of 1931 probably hit a bull's eye. In addition to suffering a setback in the Grays series, Kansas City's Monarchs lost other games that they should have won. One such loss had occurred in Topeka, Kansas.

Battling Frank Isbell's Topeka club, the Monarchs were knocked off, 4–3, with their ace Charlie Beverly on the mound. Beverly pitched a three-hitter and struck out five, but walks and four errors by the Monarchs caused the reversal—their first ever in Topeka.[39] Likewise, the Monarchs were manhandled at Marysville, Kansas, being upstaged, 11–4, by the locals. It was the Monarchs first ever loss in Marysville.[40] A day earlier, the Kansas City team had lost a 5–1 game to big league bound Eldon Auker in Manhattan, Kansas. The team would suffer additional losses in Chicago to the Mills and Duffy Florals teams.

Shortly after conclusion of that final Grays series in 1931, Rogan fulfilled his promise to actively return to baseball. Though it had taken a year-and-a-half, Rogan's return was widely anticipated.

8. Going, Going, Not Gone Yet

Rogan's return to the field on September 28, 1931, was truly an inspiring event. The fact that it occurred at Kansas City's Muehlebach Field, against Grover Cleveland Alexander's barnstorming House of Davids, only added to the dynamics.

Alexander had joined the whiskered crew in 1931, and he was drawing crowds everywhere the club appeared. One of 13 boys born to William and Martha Alexander in Elba, Nebraska, he had finished his major league career with, "373 wins, 90 shutouts, 20 or more wins ten times, and 30 or more three times."[41] Alexander finished the 1930 season with Dallas in the Texas League.

In Trenton, Missouri, the 5,000 that flocked to see Alexander outdrew the mob that saw Babe Ruth in Trenton a few seasons earlier. "Alexander," wrote Kansas City's *Star* newspaper, "was receiving $150 a month, to manage and pitch for the House of David team. In addition there was a special condition that he didn't have to grow whiskers."

That year's version of the House of David team played from coast to coast, winning a reported 110 out of 155 games played. About 134 of the games were played at night. It was little wonder, then, that 10,000 showed up to see Alexander and the Monarchs go head-to-head when the two teams battled in Kansas City.

Rogan's appearance against Alexander's House of Davids was simply for exhibition purposes. Even at that, Rogan could reflect on a lengthy list of celebrated figures he'd once beaten, and many of those wins had also come in front of Kansas City crowds. In those years Rogan won so regularly that it seemed as if there was a tacit agreement with the white professionals to throw the games.

One of the local games that seemed locked in most everyone's mind was the 1922 game when Babe Ruth's All-Stars came to Kansas City. That afternoon in the pre-game workout, Ruth, dressed in his Yankee road uniform, planted four balls over the fence in right field. One of the

Chet Brewer. On August 7, 1930, at Kansas City's Muehlebach Field, Smokey Joe Williams of the Homestead Grays and Chet Brewer of the Monarchs toiled in one of baseball's legendary pitching duels. When the game ended, 1–0, in favor of the Grays 12 innings later, Williams had 27 strikeouts and Brewer 19. Though Brewer lost that game, he finished his career with more than 100 shutouts.

drives cleared two houses south of the park on Wabash Avenue. It didn't matter how many home runs Ruth hit in practice, that hitting exhibition stopped when Rogan took the mound. For nine innings the legendary Yankee slugger did everything that was expected of him except hit a home run. Ruth, a .315 hitter with thirty-five home runs, could claim only two lazy singles off Rogan in tiny Association Park.

There was also a barnstorming game in 1923 when Rogan beat Cot Tierney's All-Stars. Rogan struck out 11 that day and bested Roy Meeker of the Philadelphia Athletics. That lineup had included Hall of Famer Zack Wheat.

In his 1931 comeback, Rogan and Alexander did not start the game. Alexander was first to enter when he pitched one inning, the eighth. Evidently there was no Tony Lazzeri to be subdued, as Alexander was greeted by a single, a double and a triple off the respective bats of Duncan, Allen and Young. Of all these hits, only one run scored, as Duncan was trapped off first and run down. Alexander then struck out Newt Joseph to retire the side.

Watching Alexander getting shelled, before that massive crowd — well, it was too much for Rogan. Out of the dugout he rose to pitch his first game in Kansas City since June 16, 1929. Rogan proudly took the mound and retired the side one, two, three and the game was over. The final out was a feathery tapped ball off the bat of Alexander. Rogan's cynical smile, as Alexander wobbled down to first, expressed things few reporters dared to imagine, let alone write. At the last minute the ball was buggy-whipped across the diamond for the last out of an 11–2 Monarchs win.

The remainder of Rogan's season was torturous. There were few extra-base hits, and home runs were a rarity. Advancing age and sluggish limbs had alienated Rogan from his colorful past. Having already proved he could still pitch, he had to impatiently wait until 1932 to know if he could still rip that apple to all corners of the lot.

Because of the depression and low attendance a year earlier, the Negro

Grover Cleveland Alexander. Alexander appeared in more games against the Monarchs than any other major league pitcher.

National League did not organize in 1932. In the South, Nashville's Tom Wilson organized the Negro Southern League. Out East, Cumberland Posey, owner of the Homestead Grays, was organizing the East-West League. A March 17, 1932, edition of the *Baltimore Afro-American* hinted that Rogan would take over the league's new Cleveland, Ohio entry. "Out at Cleveland the question of leadership has not yet been decided," wrote the *Afro-American*, "but, those in the know class that rumors are getting pretty persistent that 'Bullet' Rogan of Kansas City Monarchs fame will pitch his tent on the shores of Lake Erie and guide the destinies of the Cleveland team in the Posey loop." Evidently Rogan never set foot in Cleveland. He had made other plans to play ball in Jamestown, North Dakota.

Charlie Hancock, the great semi-professional catcher from Lexington, Missouri, was wintering in Kansas City and heard rumors that Wilkinson wasn't going to organize a Monarchs team in 1932. Hancock approached Rogan about playing in Jamestown, North Dakota, and Rogan accepted.

Negro batteries were all the rage in the Northwest. John Donaldson had started the most recent trend in Bertha, Minnesota, when he combined with Sylvester Foreman to put that city on the map. Foreman ended up at Little Falls, Minnesota, where he and Webster McDonald formed a tandem in the early 1930s. Cold Springs, Minnesota strutted out Bill Freeman and Edgar Jackson as their team's battery. Over in Crookston, Minnesota, it was Chet Brewer and Johnny Van in 1931.

In 1932, Rogan started one of the most impressive comebacks in modern sports history. Nearly all of it was recorded in the *Jamestown North Dakota Sun* newspaper. An April 21 edition of this publication first informed readers that Charles W. Hancock and Bullet Rogan were hired by the board as Jamestown's Negro battery. "Rogan, the pitcher, is from the Kansas City Monarchs and has been recommended," the *Sun* insisted. "Hancock, the big colored catcher who was here with Lone Rock, Iowa, last year and with Gilkerson's Union Giants the year before, will do the back-stopping for Jamestown."[42]

In reality, Hancock had formerly played with the Negro League St. Louis Giants in 1921. He went back to the mines—his hometown's major industry—because the $90 St. Louis was paying him monthly was hardly enough. At some point he discovered he could go on the road playing baseball and get $150 a month, with room and board included, and so, in 1932 he headed to Jamestown.

Rogan's six-hit, seven-strikeout win over the Fargo Moorhead Twins triggered one of Jamestown's best season openers ever.[43] The next time Rogan pitched he struck out six and walked one.[44] Against New Rockford, North Dakota, on May 24, Rogan hit his first home run for Jamestown.[45] On May 30, Alexander's House of David team arrived in Jamestown for two games over the Memorial Day holiday. In the first contest Rogan pitched, and won, allowing only seven hits. In the second game, Rogan walked, singled and hit two home runs. Rogan followed that game by tossing a one-hitter in Beulah, North Dakota.[46]

When Corwith visited Jamestown on July 4, they had a Negro slugger with them named Red Haley. In that game Haley accomplished something no batter had ever done before—he hit three home runs in one game off Rogan. "In his first two times up he sent balls clear over the fence," the account in the *Sun* reiterated. "The third time up Rogan struck him out and after he had two strikes in the eighth he [Haley] sent another over the fence." Not to be outdone, in that same game, Rogan blasted two home runs and a triple and was intentionally walked.[47]

Meanwhile, Wilkinson had changed his mind about not having a team and began reorganizing the Monarchs. He had said early in the season that he would wait for 1933 before attempting a comeback unless his players demanded his re-organizing. "For me to return would mean the breaking up of several eastern league clubs, and I do not wish that to happen," the K. C. Skipper said. "But," he continued, "should the East fail to pay the men, then I shall return to the front and see that they make enough money to tide them over the winter."[48]

Lo and behold, the Homestead Grays had not paid their players a full salary in over a month. Wilkinson moved in and lured Newt Allen and Frank Duncan, along with James "Cool Papa" Bell, T. J. Young, Willie Wells, Curtis Harris, Bertum Hunter and Quincy Trouppe from the Grays. Trouppe remembered, "One day an older player who had been with the Kansas City Monarchs asked Hunter and [me] if we would like to join that team."

"Should we do it?" I asked Hunter.

"No, I think we might as well stay here. Half the season is gone now and if we stay we have a better chance of getting our money," judged Hunter.

"We stayed with the Grays for another two weeks and then I decided to go with the Monarchs. I was so short of cash I had to borrow from Hunter to wire Chicago so we both left to join the Monarchs," Trouppe recalled.[49]

Hunter had come to the Negro Leagues highly recommended. At age 22, Hunter, a native of Phoenix, Arizona — the same hometown as Willie Bobo legendary St. Louis Stars first baseman — had worked himself into a promising pitching career. Hunter formerly pitched for the Phoenix Giants. The summer of 1928 had found him with the Milwaukee Giants, where he was "credited with pitching 26 games and winning 24."[50] He also played with Los Angeles' Philadelphia Royal Giants in the winter of 1930-1931. In 1931 Hunter joined the St. Louis Stars. Other ballplayers were jumping to the Monarchs too. George Giles returned to the Monarchs from Manhattan, Kansas, where he was filling his idle time with a team called the Monitors. Wilkinson found Giles, and talked him into re-signing a contract, just as he had done to get Chet Brewer from D.C.'s Washington Pilots, along with Charlie Beverly and Dink Mothell from Cleveland.

In the acquisition of James "Cool Papa" Bell, the Monarchs picked up one of the most colorful players in baseball. Born James Thomas Nichols, in Starkville, Mississippi, on May 17, 1903, he later adopted the last name of his father, Bell. After a brief semi-professional career with St. Louis' Compton Cubs and the East St. Louis Cubs, Bell joined the St. Louis Stars in 1922 where he was utilized as a pitcher. His first Negro National League win was a six-hit victory over Chicago's American Giants, defeating Giants great Richard Whitworth. Weighing only 140 pounds, and a left-handed thrower, he learned to switch-hit and started to play more in the outfield by 1923.

When Andrew "Rube" Foster, manager of Chicago's American Giants, saw that Bell was a hoofer he set up a race for the youngster against the legendary speed merchant Jimmy Lyons. When Bell won the race, Foster suggested a switch for Bell to the outfield. In addition, Foster requested that he toss away his $1.25 shoes and wear some new $22 featherweight shoes, which Foster gladly offered to buy. Bell switched to center field and remained with the Stars through the 1931 season.[51]

Speaking of Bell, Paul Waner, star outfielder of the Pittsburgh Pirates, who had seen many of the greatest ballplayers in the big circuit, told the world that the fastest man he ever saw on the diamond was James "Cool Papa" Bell. "He was on first base and the next batter hit a single to center," explained Waner. "This fellow Bell by that time was rounding second base and watching me as he ran. He never stopped. I made a motion, thinking to get him at third. As I started to throw I saw I was going to be too late, so I stopped. But he didn't. He kept on for home plate. By the time I could get the ball away he had slid in there, was dusting himself off and walking calmly away."[52]

Just as a cat plays with a mouse, Wilkinson's revamped Monarchs toyed with teams all over the Midwest. In Holdrege, Nebraska, the Monarchs listed among the team's 14 hits three home runs, two by Mothell and one by Cool Papa Bell. In Oxford, Nebraska, Harris hit not just one, but two inside-the-park home runs. Bell also hit a home run that afternoon. "Folks said that it was the longest home run ever hit in Oxford," recalled Bell. "It was a night game and the ball was hit so far out of the park, and into the corn field, that kids on the fence were afraid to go get the ball." In Manhattan, Kansas, the Monarchs hit safely 14 times, collecting seven doubles, and Bell had another big 3-for-4 afternoon at the plate. In Kansas City's 8–5, 13-hit smothering of Sioux Falls, South Dakota, Bell went 2-for-4, stole three bases and scored a trio of runs.[53] In Grand Forks, North Dakota, batting against Bill Wilson, formerly a pitcher for Minneapolis' American Association Millers, Monarchs batters collected 12 hits and stole 11 bases. When the Monarchs collected 14 hits in a 7–0 rout of Crookston, Minnesota, with Brewer and Beverly holding the locals to a single hit, that city's *Daily Times* admitted, "Somebody said this year's Kansas City Monarchs had the best baseball team in the history of that colored championship organization. They were right. The Monarchs team which beat the Crookston Red Sox 7 to 0 before a huge crowd in Highland park here yesterday is the best team seen in this city in the last ten years, according to baseball experts who have seen all games here in that period. Fans say no aggregation of major league stars and no American Association team playing here has shown the class exhibited by the colored stars."[54] Against Crookston, Brewer allowed no-hits in seven-innings before yielding to Beverly who issued just one hit to finish the contest.

After that, the Monarchs whirled into Winnipeg and took a trio of games from the Winnipeg All-Stars by 14–1, 5–1, and 3–1 scores. In the opener 3,500 fans witnessed the Monarchs' 14-hit assault that was punctuated by a Willie Wells "titanic clout"[55] that cleared the fence near the center field scoreboard.

Before leaving the region, the Monarchs took yet another victory from Crookston, Brewer pitching a two-hitter and getting an 8–0 victory.[56] The team continued to triumph with a 13-hit lambasting of Alexander's House of David in an 11–4 win at Milwaukee's Borchert field, before a crowd of 2,000.[57] When the Monarchs reached North Dakota, they arrived in Jamestown boasting a streak of 20 games won without a loss. It was a streak of consecutive victories that was not in jeopardy of ending anytime soon, as one newspaper explained, "The club has no equal, having lost but a single game the entire year, running up 44 consecutive victories to date."[58]

In a game replete with fantastic plays by the Kansas City Monarchs, Rogan watched in envy. For the first time in his professional career he was playing against the Monarchs instead of for them. Every time a Monarch got on base—Rogan was holding down first base that day—he would start up a conversation interesting enough to hold Kansas City to three stolen base attempts. After seeing blanks for six innings, Hancock reached first for Jamestown on a hit to deep right field. Next, Rogan stepped in, and with one down, one strike and two balls,

James "Cool Papa" Bell. The 1932 season was the only time that he played for the Monarchs. In 1923 Bell had made the mistake of playing winter ball on a team that did not feature Rogan or any of the Kansas City Monarchs. "The ballpark where we played was named Good Year Park. It was a converted racetrack. It was so far out of town hardly anyone came. We played anyway and I got paid a nickel for my share of the gate."

he sent a Hunter offering far over the fence. The *Jamestown Sun* reported, "Bullet Rogan's home run saved the Jamestown team from a shutout." The *Sun* newspaper went on to proclaim the Monarchs as "One of the fastest teams ever to step on [its] local diamond."[59] After that, the Monarchs continued winning until the total reached 44 consecutive wins.

On August 14, Rogan pitched his last game as a member of the Jamestown team. Hurling in vintage form, he allowed three hits, struck out five batters and walked two. At-bat, he drove the ball over the high fence in center field for a bases loaded home run, capping off the afternoon with a splendid 3-for-4 performance at the plate.[60]

With Rogan's assistance, Jamestown won 32 out of 39 games played in 1932. When the *Sun* published individual batting averages, Rogan's totals sparkled. The line read: Games 39, at bats 149, runs 42, hits 47, doubles 3, triples 4, homeruns 11, stolen bases 11, runs batted in 51, batting percentage .315. Rogan's pitching had reached that magic number of 20 wins and only three losses.[61] Hancock remembered, "Rogan was a grand old man. They [Jamestown] just fell in love with him. He could really pitch and hit."[62]

Rogan rejoined the Monarchs for the balance of the summer, and his return was very big news. A September 2 edition of Kansas City's *Call* reported, "When the Missouri boys took the field for a workout, 'Bullet' Rogan, the middlewest's most famous pitcher and Newt Joseph, sensational third sacker, were given a rousing cheer. Neither participated in the contest, but both attracted much attention during their capers on the coaching lines."

Rogan's return prompted the *Wichita Eagle* to reminisce. "Bullet Joe is well known in Wichita as he pitched games several seasons ago at Island Park which were spectacular. His unusual ability to hurl his offerings with blinding speed has been equaled only by Walter Johnson and Rogan certainly made use of it."

In Wichita, the Monarchs beat yet another tough team of All-Stars by an 11–0 score in late September. That All-Star team included Lefty Holmes, Lefty Graham, Charley Wood, Howard Lindimore, Herb Asman and other Wichita and St. Joseph Western League stars playing in the lineup of the Kansas Stage Lines state championship team. The three Western League players went hitless. Brewer showed plenty of class, finishing with a six-hitter and eight All-Stars struck out.[63] The win in Wichita was followed with a 6–0 win in El Dorado, Kansas, behind Hunter's three-hitter and Harris' home run.[64]

Late in the season, September 23, Rogan appeared in his first starting pitching assignment in Kansas City since 1928. It was reported that nearly 1,000 people lined up for tickets to see Rogan. Well rewarded for their loyalty, for nine innings Rogan pitched as if he was the master of old. He allowed just nine hits, four of which came in the ninth inning, and ended with eight strikeouts. At-bat Rogan's only hit, a liner off the left field wall, went in the books as a triple. The old bat was back, the arm was in old-time form and the Monarchs took a close 5–4 game from Alexander's House of David team.

In closing the 1932 season, the Monarchs, with Rogan and Beverly on the mound, whipped Joplin's Tournament All-Stars in a 17–7 rout at that city's Childress Field League Park. Joe Blackwell of Kansas City's American Association Blues was bumped for four runs in the first and for several of the Monarchs' 15 hits. Don Gutteridge, of Pittsburg, Kansas, a member of the losing Joplin team, reached the big leagues several years later with the St. Louis Cardinals.[65] A day prior, the Monarchs whipped Oswego, Kansas' Midland Life club, 10–3, on back-to-back home runs by Mothell and Harris.

Dominating town teams all over the Midwest, the 1932 Monarchs looked unbeatable.

Against two of that year's top teams, Chicago's American Giants and the Cuban Stars, the Monarchs won eight of the 13 from Chicago and went undefeated against the Cuban Stars in three encounters. In one game, the Monarchs stomped the American Giants, 17–0. When the Giants defeated the Monarchs on August 27, it ended the Monarchs' winning streak at 44 games.[66] In a return game at Crookston, Minnesota, the locals had hired former Minneapolis American Association pitcher Bill Wilson to battle the Monarchs' Chet Brewer. In winning that game, 8–0, Brewer pitched a two-hitter, while Wilson was rapped for 11 safe blows — two each by Bell, Allen, Trouppe and Harris.

At season's end, when the Monarchs swept a doubleheader from John Donaldson's All-Stars at Kansas City's Muehlebach Field, one newspaper acknowledged, "The Monarchs' season record now stands at 73 victories and three defeats in their last 76 engagements."[67] This record did not take into consideration three additional losses and another game won when the Monarchs opened the season in Chicago on July 9, and thus, Kansas City's record was 74-6 for the season. After that Kansas City proceeded to reel off at least six more victories, capping off the season with a big game against a team of major league All-Stars to complete the United States portion of their season. One of the season-ending wins occurred in Fort Scott, Kansas, where Charlie Beverly struck out 15 batters and let the locals down on a five-hitter. Of the five hits, two were picked up by Don Gutteridge, a big league recruit. After these wins, the Monarchs headed to Mexico.

The big victory over the major league All-Stars, in Wichita, Kansas, took place in early October. In that game, which was won, 6–2, by the Monarchs Chet Brewer started in a storm of controversy. Prior to the teams arriving at that city, Joe Kuhel, Washington Senators first baseman, and a .291 hitter on the season with four home runs, insulted the Monarchs with his prejudiced remarks. "The Monarchs have a pretty good ball club, all right," declared Kuhel, "but they can't be compared to a major league organization. They haven't got the hitting power. The only way they could ever beat a club like ours is to have enough pitching to hold us scoreless."[68] Oddly enough, future Hall of Famer Paul Waner, a .341 hitter on the season, collected only one hit during the affair. His brother Lloyd, also a future member of baseball's Hall of Fame, and a .333 hitter in 1932, cracked out three hits, including a double, but he was called out for not touching first base. Brewer finished with 13 impressive strikeouts while his opponent, pitcher Ralph Weingarner of the majors' Cleveland Indians, struck out seven Monarchs. Willie Wells hit his usual home run, a shot over the right-field fence, with a mate on to silence the critics. And Joe Kuhel — the man who was so talkative before the game — went 0-for-3.[69]

By ending the season in Mexico, and having also played in the United States and Canada, the Monarchs performed in three countries in 1932. After losing their first game to the Aztecas club in Mexico City, they proceeded to win five straight. "Bullet Rogan hurled one of the games and should have credit with a shutout," wrote the *Call*, "an error in the ninth paving the way to a score for the Mexican club."[70] Hotel Cosmos was where the club was headquartered. Appearing as popular as any team that ever visited the country, traffic cops were placed out in front of the hotel in order to keep the crowds moving. The Monarchs left Mexico with a record of 14 wins and two losses.

Quincy Trouppe wrote, "The season ended in Kansas City and all I had in cash to take home was seventy-five dollars. When I received that last pay, the owner [Wilkinson] told me, 'I want you to come back next year and hit a thousand.'"[71]

1932 Kansas City Monarchs. Standing, from left: Quincy Gilmore, T.J. Young, George Giles, Turkey Stearnes, Frank Duncan, Popcycle Harris, Dink Mothell, Cool Papa Bell, Newt Allen, Willie Wells, J.L. Wilkinson. Kneeling, from left: Chet Brewer, Bertum Hunter, "Bullet" Rogan, Charlie Beverly. This photograph was taken in Mexico when the Monarchs visited that country.

When the 1933 season opened, Trouppe, Hunter, Bell and Wells were gone, but Rogan returned. Better yet, Rogan was back at his old position as the Monarchs' team manager. In returning to his former job, he proceeded to do the only thing he knew — win baseball games.

That season, in addition to himself, Rogan's pitching staff consisted of Chet Brewer, Charlie Beverly, Andy Cooper and Ollie Boyd, a rookie that had formerly pitched for the Quindaro Athletic club in Rogan's home town. Unfortunate for Boyd, he broke his arm in an early September game against the Nashville Elites. In spite of losing Boyd, 1933 was certainly an unforgettable season, perhaps Rogan's best ever as a manager and one of his greatest as a hitter. The season of 1933 also signaled the last great season of the first generation of Monarchs.

After opening the season in Shawnee, Kansas, the Monarchs jumped over to St. Joseph, Missouri, before going into Muskogee, Oklahoma, for a five-game series against the Muskogee Hustlers, a rival African American opponent. The Monarchs made a sweep of the three games in Muskogee, tied one and won another in Fort Smith, Arkansas, against this same team. In the two games played in Fort Smith, the Monarchs tied the Muskogee Hustlers on May 23, in a 2–2 game at that city's Andrews field. The Monarchs returned to Fort Smith for another encounter with the Hustlers on May 25, and captured the game, 14–0. In that game, "The Monarchs did about everything they pleased and piled up 14 runs with little effort."[72] It was obvious that the depression had reached the Midwest as the Monarchs could command only a 35 cents admission fee.

The team returned to Kansas City, Kansas, in early June and beat Jim Thorpe's barnstorming Oklahoma Indians at Union Pacific Park.* That was on June 4. Thorpe's Indians

---

*No score has been located for the June 4, game that was played against Jim Thorpe's Indians.

had upstaged the Monarchs on May 27, taking a 9–3 win in Joplin. The loss was the Monarchs' first of the 1933 season. About 800 fans showed at Joplin's Miners Park to witness the historic affair. "The Indians, not content with getting Rogan himself off the mound in the third inning, continued with a lusty attack against Andy Cooper and had 21 safe hits at the end."[73] Thorpe entered the game as an eighth-inning pinch-hitter and smote a double to left field, the drive almost carrying to the fence. His speed having diminished with age, he managed to pull up at second and then went out courtesy of a pinch-runner. Ticket prices were increased in Joplin, where general admission seats went for 40 cents. Women were admitted for 25 cents.

The Monarchs left Kansas City, again, and this time they didn't return until July 23. In between, Rogan's team won nearly every time they took the field. While away, they went North, then South, and crossed back into the upper Midwest where they engaged the Northern Pacifics of St. Paul, Minnesota.

On June 23, Rogan's Monarchs stopped in Fargo for an exhibition game against the Fargo-Moorehead team, members of the Northern League. Kansas City won easily on Rogan's ninth-inning blast over the left-field fence. Rogan's late-inning heroics gave Kansas City a 4–2 victory. The win signaled the start of a string of many monumental victories. The winning continued into Winnipeg, Canada, where the Monarchs disposed of St. Paul's Northern Pacifics in a 6–1 win, behind Brewer's three-hit pitching and ten batters struck out. A total of 2,500 fans attended the contest. The following day 3,000 were in attendance when Andy Cooper defeated the Northern Pacifics by a 5–2 score.

The Monarchs' win in Grand Forks, North Dakota, on July 4, brought Kansas City's record to an amazing 42 and four.[74] The very next night, in Jamestown, North Dakota, Brewer shut out the locals, 6–0, and after that the Monarchs defeated Red Lake Falls, 14–2, to add to their impressive streak of victories. Another win was added in Omaha, Nebraska, where Kansas City edged the local Western League club, 5–2. Rogan's Monarchs won again in Duluth, Minnesota, when Newt Joseph homered to give them a 6–5 victory.[75]

In Wisconsin Rapids, they swiped two encounters from the locals, winning, 16–2, and, 8–0, on July 13 and 14. In game one, the Monarchs opened fire on two local pitchers for 21 hits,[76] while Brewer completely outclassed the locals in game two with a three-hitter.[77] Before returning West, the Monarchs won big in Winona, Minnesota, and Sparta, Wisconsin. When they reached Chicago on July 16, for two games against Chicago Mills, they were boasting a record of 27 consecutive wins — and they continued the streak with 3–1 and 9–6 wins. On June 20, in Mason City, Iowa, Rogan, playing in left field, went 3-for-5, with a run and two doubles in Kansas City's 16–5 win over the Sioux Falls Canaries, members of the Nebraska State League. In that game Charlie Beverly finished with 11 strikeouts.

That's the kind of record they brought back to Kansas City when they returned for two games against Syd Pollock's Cuban Stars on July 23. Pollock's Cubans ended the Monarchs' winning streak with a 5–1 win in the opener. Following the two game series with Pollock's Cubans, the Monarchs headed into Kansas and Nebraska for another series of barnstorming games. On July 26, Rogan had two hits in a 4–3 win over the Wareham Ice team in Manhattan, Kansas. When the *Jewell County Monitor* advertised the game in Mankato, Kansas, on July 28, it noted, "The club [Monarchs] has played 64 games, winning 57 and losing seven."[78] During their visit to Oxford, Nebraska, on July 29 and July 30, the locals rolled out Clarence Mitchell, former spitball pitcher of the New York Giants, and

Beryl Land, formerly of Nebraska University. The Monarchs won both games, 19–11 and 12–11. The Monarchs returned on July 31 and captured another 13–3 victory.

After Cooper's 11–1 win in Concordia, on August 2, the *Kansas City Times* reported, "The Monarchs have won thirty-one out of their last thirty-two games." The streak continued as the Monarchs rolled into Linn, Kansas. The crowd that greeted the Monarchs in Linn was "the largest crowd ever assembled to witness a ball game in Linn."[79] In spite of the "approximately $800" taken in by the ticket-sellers at the gate, the Monarchs blasted the locals, 13–5.

The Monarchs' victorious romp continued in Des Moines, Iowa, where their appearance prompted a reporter to write, "It [the Des Moines Demons] will face a Negro team that has played 82 games this year and has lost only five. It has lost only one contest out of the last 34 played."[80] True to their winning ways the Monarchs thumped the minor leaguers, 14–3. Brewer, pitching in front of his hometown fans, elicited the following in one local newspaper. "Seldom are the Demons called on to face a twirler with more stuff than Brewer, who showed the large crowd of 3,100 persons why he ranks as one of the best pitchers among the Negro players."[81] Brewer finished with a seven-hit, eight strikeout performance. Newt Joseph's timely placed drive over the center-field fence drove in four runs, as the bases were full when he came to bat. Dink Mothell also added a home run.

The Monarchs then rolled into Wichita's Island Park and waylaid the Kansas Baseball tournament All-Stars in another 15–1 drubbing. The white All-Stars picked up one-time Monarch Alfred "Army" Cooper in an attempt to halt the Monarchs' torrid onslaught. Cooper was disposed of early when Rogan took the liberty of hitting a home run off his old teammate.[82]

Some of 1933's most profitable games, from both a monetary and a social standing, were played against Western League teams and Grover Cleveland Alexander's House of David squad. The Monarchs, having alienated themselves from the Negro National League, forced the *Chicago Defender* to offer, "[The Monarchs] are playing through Nebraska and other western points at a very high rate of profit and laughing merrily as the associated clubs wallow in the confines of a red ledger."[83]

Among the first Western League teams to face the Monarchs were Edward "Dutch" Zwilling's St. Joseph Saints. Brewer lost that game by a close 5–4 score. In Omaha, a pair of doubles, and a triple by Rogan helped defeat the Omaha Packers in mid–July. On August 7, when the Monarchs beat the Western League's Des Moines, Iowa, team the *Kansas City Call* fired back with a few unkind slurs of its own, boasting that Brewer "had the white boys eating out of his hand."[84] Kansas City tucked that victory away on a nine-run uprising in the fifth. On August 23, Brewer defeated Topeka's Western League team by a 9–2 score, with the aid of Rogan's hit and a stolen base.[85]

Grover Cleveland Alexander's barnstorming House of David team treated Rogan's Monarchs to many nip-and-tuck battles during the summer of 1933. In August the two teams met in Winnipeg, Canada, in a four-game series. The opener was played when the Winnipeg Maroons were one game out of first place in the race for the Northern League pennant. Wilkinson had originally inquired for dates that would not conflict with the Northern League schedule, but was arrogantly advised to consider his own team first, as the games he was trying to schedule would in no way affect the Maroons.

In the opener, the Monarchs captured a big 1–0 win at that city's Wesley Park. Sensational pitching and brilliant fielding kept the paying crowd of approximately 3,000, plus more than a thousand unaccounted for, on edge throughout an eleven-inning errorless win over Alexander's House of David. Charlie Beverly was the star of the exhibition. He was nicked for only one hit, a single in the ninth by the House of David's Dewey Hill, before winning the game in the eleventh-inning. "Beverly's performance was as close to being perfect as possible to be without performing the rare feat of a no-hit, no-run game," wrote the *Kansas City Call*.[86]

"Grover Cleveland Alexander just hurled the first round," wrote Winnipeg's *Evening Tribune*, "forcing three batters to hit to the infield."[87] Beverly finished with 13 batters struck out and of these 11 came in the first six innings. He also issued two walks. The House of David evened the series with a 2–1 win in game two, while playing before a crowd of 5,000 paid, with Frank "Spike" Hunter capturing the victory. As was the case in game one, many saw the game for free.

In the series finale, a doubleheader at Wesley Park, a crowd of 6,000 paid watched Chet Brewer lose a 4–3 three-hitter in the opener and a Charlie Beverly ten strikeout performance take a 9–5 advantage in the nightcap, after he relieved Ollie Boyd in the second frame. All totaled, the four-game series drew an estimated 20,000 fans, while the hometown Maroons played to a measly 640 in paid attendance for their series — an average of 160 people a game.

Left to right: Tom Baird, C.A. Franklin, J. L. Wilkinson. Franklin's *Kansas City Call* newspaper, which began in 1919, grew up with the Negro National League. Clara Franklin wrote of her husband, "The firm and courageous stand [he] took against things that were not right has left behind a heritage greatly cherished and one which will serve as a strong bulwark to us in making decisions today."

The Monarchs and Grover Cleveland Alexander's House of David team had also done battle in the Midwestern cities of Wichita, Topeka, Dodge City and Bartlesville prior to returning to Kansas City in mid September. In Topeka, the House of David team was defeated 8–4 after Alexander opened as a pitcher, holding the Monarchs hitless and scoreless.[88] In Wichita the two teams engaged in two winner-take-all games with the victor getting the right to meet a team of major league All-Stars in an October series in that same city.

The Monarchs won the first encounter, 6–2, getting to Spike Hunter for 11 hits in five innings. Although advertised to pitch, Alexander did not make an appearance on the mound, stating, "The weather was hardly suitable for his pitching." In addition to Newt Joseph's home run, Rogan added a double in the contest.[89] When the Monarchs and House of David reappeared in Kansas City, for a September 19, game, a local newspaper reported the African American team as having "won 132 and lost 11 so far during the season, while Davids have won 149 and lost 23."[90]

A second encounter, which was played on September 24, ended in yet another Monarchs win. Rogan went 2-for-4 at bat, and home runs by Brewer, Joseph and Young brought the score to 9–7 in favor of the Monarchs. Alexander pitched the first two innings and was scored upon once. More than 6,000 fans witnessed the Monarchs' second win.[91]

The two teams concluded seasonal play on the first day of October, 1933, in Carthage, Missouri, as some 2,000 fans watched Alexander pitch the first two innings. The Monarchs won with ease, as Chet Brewer and Andy Cooper combined for an 8–0 whitewash of the bearded fellows from Benton Harbor. Rogan was at his best, collecting three hits in five trips to the plate and a pair of runs batted in.[92]

One of the more spectacularly played games against the House of David took place at Kansas City's Muehlebach Field on September 30, where 4,000 fans looked on as the Monarchs posted a 6–1 win under the lights. The Monarchs' triumph over Alexander's House of David set the stage at Kansas City's Muehlebach Field, where an even larger attraction was set for October 3, when Pepper Martin and Dizzy Dean brought an All-Star team to town.

Dizzy Dean's and Pepper Martin's smug remarks to the press had pumped a bit of New York's Madison Avenue into Kansas City's local baseball economy. "Every place we played last fall we can go back," boasted Martin to a *Kansas City Times* reporter. "That's because it's not play for us, we battle just as hard as we can."[93]

Dean bragged, "If I've got a sore arm I'll only strike out five in the first three innings. If the arm ain't sore we'll make it six. It's no exhibition."[94] Dean didn't appear to have much respect for the Monarchs prior to his first appearance against them. After all, in St. Louis, "the big league [park] was segregated. We [African Americans] could only sit in the pavilion or the bleachers," remembered James "Cool Papa" Bell. "We couldn't sit in the stands."[95]

Dean's arrogance was effective enough to draw 8,000 fans. In the pregame warmup, Rogan peered from the dugout to see for himself why Dean and Martin were creating such a ruckus. Rogan could only shake his head in disgust as he watched nonsense of the highest order. Obvious to many was the press' role in maintaining the confusion. An edition of the *Wichita Evening Eagle* illustrated how the puzzlement had gone on for years. "After every appearance of the Kansas City Monarchs here, Wichita fans spend several days speculating on the real strength of the colored team," reported the *Eagle*. "Some fans declare the Monarchs are the equal of any class AA team in the country, and others assert the dark-skinned athletes couldn't beat a good Western Association club. The critics of the Monarchs base their claims on the alleged inability of the Kansas City team to hit classy pitching."[96] When Wilkinson was asked to gauge the Monarchs' level of play by the standards of so-called organized baseball, he replied, "Better than the Western League, about on a par with the American Association."[97]

With all of the controversy about the level of play, it came as no surprise that integration into the white leagues stood at a standstill. One reason for the public's confusion was the negative attitudes of the white ballplayers. When New York's *Daily News*, in a column entitled *Photographer Asked the Question*, asked a ballplayer named Teetsel, "Have you any objection to seeing colored players on the big league baseball?" he responded with a familiar refrain. "Yes, from a player's viewpoint." Teetsel went on to say, "I was signed with the Giants for three years while playing for Toledo. I know from talking to many other players that you can't mix white and colored players so closely. Players in every league would not stand for it."[98]

Dean seemed to be an exception to the rule, and made good his boast striking out five on one hit during his three innings on the slab. He turned the job over to Lou Garland, of the Kansas City Blues, at the top of the fourth, leading by three runs. Garland worked in fine style until the eighth, when a walk to Rogan started a Monarchs rally. Joseph singled and Dwight was passed. Rogan then scored on a wild pitch, and Joseph and Dwight followed him home on errors. Three runs, on one hit, had put the Monarchs in the game, and in the ninth they staged another rally. The *Kansas City Call* caught the action: "Rogan was up. But Rogan had been up three official times before and hadn't belted the ball out of the infield. His fourth time up he got a walk ... Garland slipped a strike over on Rogan. Bullet fouled off two and then took two balls. The Monarchs fans were praying for 'Bullet' to send a long fly to the outfield so that Giles could score after the catch. Nary a soul moved for the exits. People were standing. Some were cheering. Cowbells rang. Army whistles blew. Even the old staid fans that never got excited lost their equilibrium and could not restrain themselves. Rogan slashed one to right. It fell 15 feet in front of Connastser. The right fielder lost sight of the ball as it fell down through the haze to the green grass. Giles scooted home with the tying run. The Monarchs fans were jubilant. There was Young racing to third base with Duncan waving him on home. On he came like a thundering locomotive getting up full steam. He crossed the plate as the Monarchs fans went crazy. Even the portion of the white fans who were for the All-Stars joined in to give praise where it was due."[99]

In spite of Dean's appearance, Charlie Beverly's 13 strikeouts were the big highlight in the Monarchs' 5–4 win. "Pepper" Martin accounted for three of Beverly's strikeouts. The *Call* added, "It was one more ball game never to be forgotten. And the fans up and down Eighteenth, Twelfth, the Paseo, [and] all of Kansas City's streets have been playing that eighth and ninth inning over and over again all week long."

The Deans engaged the Monarchs in another historic encounter in Oxford, Nebraska, shortly thereafter. It was here that Dizzy was first beaned. Wilkinson related the story to the *Wichita Eagle*. "[Chet] Brewer, powerful Monarchs right-hander, was pitching when Dizzy came to bat," explained Wilkinson. "Brewer got one of his fast ones too close and beaned the older Dean. Dizzy dropped like [he was] shot." There was wild confusion. The local manager rushed to a phone and called an ambulance. They carried Dizzy to the bench.

They applied towels and whatnot. In the meantime Wilkinson, extremely anxious about the great pitcher, and of course the success of the rest of the tour financially, rushed out to get a doctor. In the excitement, the Oxford manager and Wilkinson were busied around the front gate and in about ten minutes the ambulance arrived.

When they went to get Dizzy, he was nowhere to be found. They searched frantically and finally someone said Dizzy had gotten to his feet and stumbled away. In the meantime, the game had gone on. Wilkinson and his friend looked for Dizzy everywhere, in the dressing rooms and the box office and finally wandered back into the park. To their amazement, Dizzy came trotting in from the outfield. He had recovered and insisted on playing ball. Wilkinson commented, "If that blow didn't wreck him I guess nothing could."[100]

On October 8, Rogan's Monarchs faced yet another group of major league All-Stars. This time the team featured Glenn Wright, Paul Waner, Forest Jensen, Larry French and Hollis Thurston, all members of either the Pittsburgh or Brooklyn National League teams. Fritz Nicolai, Jimmy Horn, Lefty Cotter and other well-known minor league players joined them. And there was a schedule of five games this time. Waner had twice finished as the leading hitter in the National League. French, awarded ten votes as the National League's most valuable player for the 1933 season, was eclipsed by only one other big league hurler, Carl Hubbell, the famed southpaw of the New York Giants.

In Kansas City, "Paul Waner had to raise his cap as he went to the plate, so great was the applause," noted the *Times*, "He wore the same uniform that he wore when the National League battled the American League in Chicago this summer."[101] The mighty Waner did little at the plate, batting 1-for-5 as well as being struck out by Brewer. On the other hand, Rogan went 2-for-4 off French and Thurston. The Monarchs won, 6–3. Brewer, who struck out nine and held the All-Stars to seven hits, got the victory.

After Kansas City, the two teams met in Joplin, and it was here that the All-Stars got their first taste of victory. Waner added three additional stars to bolster his already stellar squad of French, Thurston, Jensen and Wright. Don Gutteridge of the Nebraska State League, Ray Mueller of the New York–Penn League and Cliff Geer of the Western League were all added at Joplin. The All-Stars ran off with the victory, getting 18 hits, good for 35 total bases against two Monarchs pitchers, Andy Cooper and Sam Thompson and captured a 14–2 win. Larry French effectively halted the Monarchs, but was nicked for a home run by "Bullet" Rogan in the second inning.

Paul Waner was bragging all along the route. "Right now I believe we have the fastest barnstorming team on tour," said Waner. "Usually the big shots in the major leagues divide up into trios and tour the country. Our drawing cards are Wright, French and I suppose, myself. But we've added others that are under contract at present or have been stars in the past in the major leagues to round up a first class team."[102]

When the tour arrived in Oklahoma City for game three of the series, Jack Fitzpatrick and Liza Funk, both of the Pacific Coast League, were added to the squad. Bruce Sloan, a future major leaguer, and minor leaguers Jesse Welch and Leonard Sedbrook were also added. On this night, though, it would be all Charlie Beverly, as the Monarchs ace left-hander struck out 14 of the major league All-Stars. "Beverly might have run his strikeout total to 16 or 17 had not a sudden rain and wind storm washed out the last half of the ninth inning," noted one local newspaper.[103]

Every man in the all-star lineup but French, who batted only once, fanned at least once, and Wright, Sedbrook, Sloan and Welch went down twice each. Beverly finished with a two-hitter, as only Jenson and Waner could connect safely, and won a 3–0 victory. Allen was the big offensive force in the game, as he went 3-for-4 with a run scored, a triple and a stolen base. A total of 2,500 people attended the contest.

On October 12, the Monarchs and major league All-Stars took their show to Wichita, Kansas' Island Park. Once in town, Waner added Tank Horton, former Wichita catcher, to further enhance his team. Frigid weather kept the crowd size low for this historic clash.

The long Wichita winning streak by the Kansas City Monarchs was finally smashed at 30 consecutive games, as the major league All-Stars took a decisive 11–6 win before 1,500 fans. French hurled for the All-Stars and Brewer for the Monarchs. The All-Stars' pitcher lasted eight innings before he was relieved by Waner. The Monarchs led for the better part of the game, but brilliant late-inning rallies, in the seventh and eighth frames, brought about the Monarchs' defeat. George Giles was the only player to hit French with any regularity on this night, as he went 5-for-5 at the plate. Waner went 3-for-5, with two runs scored, and Jensen 3-for-4, with four runs. The Monarchs finished with 11 hits, the All-Stars 14.[104] It came as no surprise that Giles hit the major leaguers well. In commenting on how well he hit Dizzy Dean, one Negro Leaguer remarked, "He hit Dizzy like he was pitching soft ball."[105]

Wichita took great pride having seen Kansas City defeated. In games throughout Kansas the Monarchs dominated for years. "The club has lost but one exhibition game in Kansas, Nebraska and Missouri in the past seven years," reported one publication.[106]

For the series' final game, both teams returned to Kansas City. Waner and Wright were still with the club but the remainder of the All-Stars roster changed considerably. Johnny Kerr and Joe Kuhel of the Washington Senators, Jim Mosolf of the Chicago Cubs, Roy Caldwell, Dutch Seibold of the Reading, Pennsylvania, club, Jimmy Gleason of the Cleveland Indians and Buzz Arlett of Baltimore's International League team. Joe Bowman, the game's starting pitcher, had been a, "sensational young right hander who won 23 games in the Coast League [that] summer."[107]

This time the All-Stars took a quick 2–1 lead. The Monarchs waited until the eighth to tie the score. In the ninth Giles got a break when he hit to deep short, behind third, and beat Wright's throw to first. Young hit to the infield but both runners were safe when Wright muffed the third baseman's toss at second. Rogan was next to bat and he ran the count to three and two. Rogan called time, then stepped out of the batter's box to signal for the hit and run play. The hit and run play was put on and it worked! Rogan singled to center, and Giles slid home with the winning run.

Charlie Beverly, the Monarchs' winning pitcher, struck out 13 batters, including every man in the All-Stars' lineup. Arlett was a strikeout victim three times. Joe Bowman was the losing pitcher. Admittedly, in their collective big league careers, very few of the white leaguers could remember seeing a player call his own hit and run, with the count full, and then pull it off.

At season's end, Kansas City's *Times* newspaper tabulated the results of the 1933 season. "A review of the Kansas City Monarchs' activities during the season just closed shows a remarkable record of victories. In a schedule of exhibition games, including AA teams as well as others of lesser organized rating, the strongest independent nines and combinations of players from the National and American leagues, the Monarchs have emerged with the outstanding record of 134 games won and 14 lost."[108] Rogan's team finished an amazing 60 games over .500.

For Rogan, 1933 was one of the best seasons of his career. Though he had pitched very little, he was still up to the task of finishing any games he started. His hitting had demonstrated that he could still be counted on in the clutch. And while it was assumed that Rogan had lost a step here, a step there, taking into consideration his accomplishments of the season just past, he was still two steps ahead of nearly everyone else.

9

A Lifetime in the Sun

Just why a mosquito couldn't bite Rogan and render him hors du combat is truly the fortunes of fate, but it didn't and for the third time in two weeks we found ourselves face to face with the greatest figure in baseball with the possible exception of Andrew Rube Foster—and Foster doesn't pitch any more.—A Chicago newspaper, 1920s

It was not uncommon for Bullet Rogan to pitch year-round. And yet, regardless of how often he pitched, seldom did he suffer a sore arm or long periods of inconsistency. Amazingly, year-round pitching affected him very little. His arm essentially remained one of the more durable in baseball. The countless numbers of big leaguers he embarrassed in the blistering sun of California's Pacific Coast only made this fact more obvious. And while newspaper writers were doing their best to convince their readers that the best players in the world were white, Rogan was defying this lie with every pop of the catcher's cowhide and with every swing of his mighty bat in winter league play.

One of the earliest records of Rogan's winter league play occurred in Los Angeles during the fall of 1917. That winter, Rogan appeared in several games for the Los Angeles White Sox on the Pacific Coast. The White Sox's roster featured such legendary players as José Méndez, Dave Malarcher, John Donaldson and George Carr. "The colored teams used to play against these fellows in the major leagues in the winter, like a winter league," Malarcher stated. "And in the fall of 1917, they asked me with John Donaldson; John had been going out there before. John was a great left-hander, Méndez was a great right-hander. They had been playing, and they played against my team in Indianapolis, and they knew me then as a player, and they asked me to go out with them. They wanted to bring out three men to boost these White Sox. I went to California and played that winter baseball and I went back to school along about the mid-winter of the year, but I played with the White Sox against these major leaguers out there."[1]

Although records are sketchy for that first Winter League campaign, the *Kansas City Times* gave a glimpse of how many games were played by documenting, "Donaldson just arrived from Los Angeles, where it is said, he pitched 22 games and lost only three of them."[2]

Rogan's return to California in the fall of 1920 was widely publicized by the California press. That winter Rogan, along with seven of his Kansas City Monarchs teammates, returned to California and suited up with the Los Angeles White Sox.

The White Sox were part of an incorporated organization named, "*The White Base Ball and Amusement Association*." Each of the Association's four stockholders was of a different background. President Frank Howard was a prosperous junk dealer; Secretary J. E. Walton was a very successful butcher; Treasurer J. H. Graham was an auto-express man; and General Manager James P. White, a popular concessionaire, was the only individual in the Association with prior baseball promotion experience.³ White had brought Rube Foster and his world famous American Giants to California in 1916. Alonza Alfred "Lonnie" Goodwin was the longtime field manager of the White Sox. White's association approached interracial baseball in ways that wouldn't be matched by Branch Rickey's celebrated Brooklyn Dodgers for at least two more decades.

The California Winter League played games in and around Los Angeles, at Long Beach and at San Diego, on weekends and holidays. Most of the games were played at White Sox Park, a park that many considered the California home of Negro League baseball. White Sox Park stood on a remote location at East Fourth and Anderson streets. The park was famous for its interracial baseball and its brawling.

Ironically, it was the white players that had given the park such a poor reputation for fighting. One of the more famous fights was between former big league umpire Beans Reardon and Irish Meusel of the Philadelphia Phillies. On that occasion Meusel cursed and complained about being thrown out at the plate in a close game against the White Sox. Umpire Reardon pulled off his mask and chest protector and did a "Jack Dempsey on Meusel."⁴ More than 25 cops were needed to restore the peace prior to a restart of the game.

There was, however, a fight in 1928 that involved National Leaguer Eddie Pick and the Monarchs' Chet Brewer. According to Brewer, "I was trying to pitch him inside and the ball hit him."⁵ The *Kansas City Call* wrote, "The tall, good-natured youngster who has been the pitching ace this year, said nothing until Pick blurted out, 'You black blankety blank! You hit me purposely.' Brewer threw down the ball and rushed the big blond who advanced to meet him. Fists flew; those of Brewer's darting in and out like a trained boxer's, and raising a big lump on Pick's left eye, showing they had found their mark."⁶ "A near riot ensued," Brewer stated, "when the fans began to agitate the matter by yelling 'beef stake' directed at Pick."

In the winter of 1920 Joe Pirrone lured many players to California. Irish and Bob Meusel, Lu Blue, Frank Shellenback, Chet Thomas, Speed Martin, Max Carey, Ducky Jones and Nick Altrock were among the more recognizable of the National and American League players on the Coast. Bob Meusel, a member of the New York Yankees' famous "Murderers Row" was considered by many to be the best outfielder in the American League. The *Los Angeles Times* noted that Yankee manager Miller Huggins put Bob Meusel's worth at "$250,000."⁷

Whenever Meusel batted against Rogan, his value dropped dramatically, largely because of his inability to drive the curveball — a Rogan specialty. Ed Barrow, owner of the New York Yankees, for whom Meusel performed, was once quoted as saying, "Anyone who has a 20–1 record anywhere is worth taking a look at." Unfortunately he was only referring to white players, and the results of the games played in California illustrated the real tragedy of Barrow's prejudice.

All totaled there must have been 40 or more National and American Leaguers parading their talents in and around Los Angeles in 1920. To even the odds, Monarchs George Carr, Hurley McNair, Walter "Doby" Moore, Lemuel Hawkins, Jay Bird Ray and Rube Currie joined the Los Angeles White Sox. With over two dozen big league pitchers in the city, Rogan, a pitcher that no National or American League team would sign, materialized into California's sensation.

Rogan's 1920 California arrival was spectacular from the very onset. In losing a 5–4 five-hitter in his October 24 debut to Detroit's "Red" Oldham, Rogan starred on the mound and at bat, doubling to drive in two runners on two hits.[8] He returned on October 31, to slam a homer off pitcher Joe Pirrone and lead his White Sox to a 5–4 victory.[9] It would become the first of more than 30 home runs that Rogan would hit during his illustrious winter league career. Pitching on November 14, Rogan notched his first Winter League win with a 5–4 thumping of Casey Stengel's All-Stars. Bob and Irish Meusel, two of Stengel's big stars, batted eight times and neither secured a hit. Irish had batted .309 for the National League Phillies in 1920, and younger brother Bob had smashed American League pitching for a .328 average and 40 doubles as a member of the Yankees. On the mound Rogan completely upstaged Philadelphia's Lee "Specs" Meadows. All totaled, the White Sox pounded poor Meadows for 13 safe hits, while Rogan was allowing just three hits. Though there was no printed box score, the *Los Angeles Times* noted, "Besides pitching superb ball, Rogan connected with the pill for a brace of hits."[10]

Surprised by the superior play of the African Americans, Pirrone sought reinforcements. That move, though, did little to stop Rogan from having dozens of big games, on the mound and at the plate, against the big leaguers in 1920. Slightly encouraged, after National Leaguer Max Carey had been signed, the *Times* pondered, "Carey should also be a big factor in stopping the winning streak of the Sox, if such a thing is possible."[11]

In another game Rogan ripped Wheezer Dell, a pitcher with 231 minor wins, for three hits. In yet another contest Rogan added a two-run home run off Dell. In a November 21 game, both Rogan and McNair hit home runs to defeat Walter "The Great" Mails, the famous Cleveland Indians pitcher who had been a big winner in that year's World Series.[12] On December 12, Rogan humbled Mails once more, but this time he bettered the big-leaguer from the pitcher's rubber by striking out ten batters and tossing a two-hitter. Although Mails would finish his major league career with more than 200 career strikeouts, four strikeouts was the best he could do against the so-called inferior athletes of the Negro National League on that eventful afternoon.[13]

Sensing the devastation wreaked by the African Americans, the *Times* concluded, "These Los Angeles White Sox black birds seem to have a happy faculty of messing up any old kind of a white team that has the courage to fling a challenge at them."[14]

Rogan concluded the winter of 1920-21 with victories over Detroit's Red Oldham, Speed Martin and Bill Pertica of the Chicago Cubs, and three Pacific Coast League stars in Ray Keating of Los Angeles, John "Sloppy" Thurston of Salt Lake City and Carl Holling of Oakland. In a January 23 game with Martin on the mound, Rogan defeated Dutch Ralls' All-Stars on a four-hit, 2–0, shutout.[15]

Rogan departed California with at least 84 additional strikeouts and a minimum of eight dominating wins. The men that he defeated played in the best baseball leagues in America.

At-bat Rogan collected over 40 hits and blasted at least four home runs, among the most by any player on the coast.[16] To show his durability as baseball's greatest all-around player, Rogan had played center field on November 21, second base on November 25, third base on February 5, left field on March 5 and right field on March 27.

Rogan's dynamics transformed the tiny *California Eagle,* an insignificant minority weekly, from a community and religious newspaper into a true sports page. Unfortunately, most of the 1920-1921 editions are missing. There are, however, many written accounts of that year in Rogan's scrapbook and other Los Angeles newspapers.

One Los Angeles newspaper wrote, "If Brooklyn, champions of the National baseball league, had the team of colored players which played the American and National League stars at White Sox Park on last Sunday they would have won hand[s] down, the championship of the world."[17] At least two players, George Carr and Hurley McNair, gave similarly first-hand accounts of what Rogan achieved in the winter of 1920-1921. Carr reported to the *Kansas City Sun* newspaper that, "Up to date Rogan had won 13 games and lost only four."[18] A letter received at the *Sun,* from Hurley McNair, supported Carr's comments. "Rogan seems to have the Golden West gone loco about his pitching. Neither National or American Leaguers can touch him," wrote McNair.[19]

In a dramatic conclusion to the winter of 1920-1921, Rogan's White Sox played four games against W. W. McCredie's Portland Beavers of the Pacific Coast League in Santa Maria, California, and two games against Alexander's Giants, Los Angeles' other African American All-Stars. In the four documented games against Portland, the White Sox split the series. Rogan lost his game, 3–2, when three runs were scored on four bunts in the second. With a great chance for a rally, Portland's Sam Ross struck out the final White Sox batter with the bases loaded in the ninth.[20] Against Alexander's Giants, Rogan, while stationed in centerfield, went 4-for-5, scoring two runs. Included among his hits were a pair of triples, a pair of singles and a stolen base.[21] The White Sox beat the Giants 4–1 in game two to capture the series.

In the winters of 1921-22, 1922-23 and 1923-24, Rogan did not return to California. He remained in Kansas City to look after his billiards hall and to get married. There was some speculation about his going to Cuba in 1923-1924 that never materialized. Rogan finally returned to winter play in 1924-25, when he appeared in the Cuban Winter League.

Cuba's harmonious association with America's Negro baseball players was openly publicized. According to Clint Thomas, a long time Cuban Winter League participant, "Inviting white athletes to play winter ball in Cuba was generally discouraged. It was common knowledge that they spent more time on the beaches than the baseball field. They were also overvalued in price."[22]

To fill Cuban winter league rosters, African American athletes were a highly desirable alternative. The birth of the Negro National League in 1920 had rekindled the demand for African American talent. By 1922, African American athletes had grown so enormously popular that bonuses were used to lure the league's top stars. The island's leading manufacturers paid stipends of $500 to players on pennant-winning teams, along with bonuses of $500 to the league's best pitchers and top hitters. The honorariums attracted many of the Negro Leagues best — and that included Wilber "Bullet" Rogan.

The Cuban Winter League was composed of four teams: Almendares, Santa Clara, Havana and Marianio. In November of 1924, Rogan joined the Almendares team, which was managed by Adolfo Luque, a Cuban pitcher and member of the Cincinnati Reds.

In Cuba, the broad features of the African American Kansas City Monarchs were just as familiar as those of Babe Ruth. In 1923, inserted into every box of Billiken cigars or candy was a small baseball photograph of a Winter League player. Photographs of the 1923-24 Santa Clara team, which were featured on Tomas Gutierrez and Fabrica de Cigarros tobacco premium pages, became prized collectables. The *Santa Clara Sun* had considered the Santa Clara team of 1923-24 as the greatest in the island's history. This team featured five of Rogan's Kansas City Monarchs teammates: José Méndez, Walter "Doby" Moore, Rube Currie, Frank Duncan and Oscar "Heavy" Johnson.

Though African Americans were members of Cuba's championship teams, there were signs of a rising tide against them. "This is not to the liking of the fair [skin] Havanans

Entrance of White Sox Park, Los Angeles, California. In 1927 the 7,500 people that showed up to watch Rogan's Royal Giants exceeded the 5,000 that showed up at Wrigley Field (of Los Angeles) to watch major league All-Stars and the Pacific Coast League championship game a week prior. The All-Star lineup featured Babe Herman, Bob Meusel, Fred Haney, Johnny Rawlings and others.

Bullet Rogan in Cuba, 1924. Rogan spent only one winter in Cuba, leading the league in wins for 1924. In total, Rogan played six years of winter league baseball and won nearly 50 games as a pitcher.

who have to a certain extent, become inoculated with the prejudice germ so prevalent in this country," noted the *Kansas City Call*. "[They] do not care to see their idols demolished by boys who may or may not be Cubans, but who are undoubtedly black."

In October of 1924, former Monarchs catcher Jose Rodriguez recruited "Bullet" Rogan and Newt Allen as mid-winter additions for the Almendares team. Rogan appeared in his first game on December 2, 1924, as a pinch-hitter.

On December 6, Rogan went to the mound and lost a tight 3–2 game to Santa Clara. Rogan won his next outing against Santa Clara by pitching a three-hit, 6–0 shutout. Rogan lost yet another game to Havana when his team was held to five hits. In that contest he walked seven men. Plagued by a late start and a 2–2 record, Rogan finally began to piece together a season that was more indicative of his ability.

In the big Christmas celebration game, Rogan pitched a six-hitter against Santa Clara and won, 7–2. In that same game he struck out six men and hit a home run. Another big 4–0 shutout over Martin Dihigo's Havana team followed that outing. In that game Rogan struck out five and hit a triple. Rogan won his next game, a 4–3 nip-and-tuck battle against Santa Clara, when he drove in his own winning runs on two doubles. In that game Rogan struck out six. Rogan also won his next outing against Havana, when he pitched a seven-hitter in his team's 6–4 win.

Chet Brewer remembered hearing about an event that Rogan's teammates used to rave about. It occurred in the 1924-25 Cuban Winter League championship game against Havana. The battery for Almendares that afternoon was Bullet Rogan and Bizz Mackey. In one particular inning, Alejandro Oms, a third-place batter whose league-leading .393 batting average paced the Winter League, came to the plate with the game on the line. "Oms was a left-handed hitter that was known to hit curve balls well," Brewer recalled. "Mackey gave Rogan a fastball and Rogan shook him off. Rogan wanted to throw his curve drop. Mackey called for the fastball a second time and once again Rogan shook him off. That's when Mackey called time to talk the situation over."

"What's wrong with you, are you crazy?" Mackey asked. "Everybody knows this man can hit a curveball. He's one of the best curveball hitters in baseball and you want to throw him a curve!"

Rogan fired back, "He can't hit mine."

Mackey went over to talk with the manager.

"Rogan has got to be crazy! He wants to throw Oms a curveball and you know he can hit a curveball, he hits everybody's curveball," Mackey proclaimed. The manager threw his hands up, shook his head and fired back, "It's his money just like it is ours. If he wants to throw it away, let him throw it."

Mackey returned to his position and reluctantly gave the signal for a curveball. Rogan threw a big looping drop ball and Oms left the ground swinging, but he didn't come within a foot of hitting that ball. Rogan proceeded to throw two more curveballs to Oms who missed them both—he didn't even foul tip one. Rogan walked off the mound staring all the time at Mackey. "I told you he couldn't hit mine," Rogan confirmed, "I told you he couldn't hit mine."[23]

Rogan's pitching was as newsworthy in Cuba as it had been everywhere else he appeared. Play-by-play accounts of all his games appeared in the *La Lucha* newspaper and the stories told by these play-by-play accounts were familiar to everyone who had ever witnessed Rogan on the mound. And thanks to Rogan, Augustin Molina's great Santa Clara team did not repeat their reign as champions of the Cuban Winter League in 1924-1925. Almendares won the Cuban Winter League title with a 36–16–1 record.[24]

In spite of a late start, Rogan's nine victories, which tied him with Oscar Levis for the most games won, made him one of Cuba's most valuable pitchers.[25] His nine wins paced the entire Cuban Winter League. Rogan also finished with a .692 winning percentage in 18 appearances. It was an outstanding showing for Rogan in his only appearance in Cuba. After that winter, Rogan never returned to Cuba again. He enjoyed California much more than Cuba.

Rogan's injuries delayed his arrival in California during the winter of 1925-26. In his four year absence, California Winter League attendance totals had dropped to record lows, partially because the Los Angeles White Sox totally dominated the league and won pennants in runaway fashion. So, after four years Rogan was back in California.

When Rogan arrived in California for the 1925–1926 Winter League campaign, he was accompanied by only one Monarchs player — Newt Allen. Allen formed the double play combination with Indianapolis' Connie Day.

Both the Los Angeles White Sox and the Philadelphia Giants had teams on the coast. Rogan and Allen, the two Monarchs, joined the Philadelphia Royal Giants, a team managed by Lonnie Goodwin. Goodwin had recruited green-eyed Crush Holloway, George Carr, Bizz Mackey, Herbert "Rap" Dixon, Jess Hubbard, Rube Currie, Neal Pullen and High Pockets Hudspeth to complete his roster. Within a short time Rogan was playing as well as he had prior to missing the 1925 World Series.

In addition to Rogan's return, Pirrone's All-Stars, Shell Oil and the White Kings had stockpiled their rosters with big league stars. Casey Stengel was a member of Pirrone's All-Stars. Ferdie Schupp, a one-time 20-game winner for the New York Giants, was a member of the league, as was Babe Herman of the Brooklyn Dodgers, who would hit .319 in his rookie season the following year. Herman was joined by his soon-to-be Brooklyn teammate Dick Cox, an outfielder who had batted .329 in 434 at-bats during the 1925 season. The league also featured Jigger Statz, who had collected an astounding 291 hits in the 1925 Pacific Coast League season, and Clyde Barfoot, who led that same league in games won with 26 victories.

Rogan's first win was an 11–5 decision over Barfoot of the White Kings. Carr starred with three hits and Rogan had two in the Royal Giants' 15 hit bombardment. The Winter League schedule was split into two halves. In the first half Rogan won at least six games, but his team failed to take the first half title, which was won by the Los Angeles White Kings. Behind Rogan's pitching, the Royal Giants rallied in the second half and won the championship. In a January 17 game, which Rogan won, 8–7, over Pirrone's All-Stars, Stengel laced Rogan for two hits.[26]

In the three-game championship series, played in late February, Rogan pitched a six-hitter and took a 5–1 positive verdict in the opener. Rogan's presence was the dominating factor in the Philadelphia Giants run to the title.* Rogan also had more than 28 hits and a pair of home runs.

In the winter of 1926–27, Rogan returned to the West Coast as a member of the Los Angeles Royal Giants. This time he was selected to manage the team, as well as pitch and play the outfield.

Rogan's Royal Giants were part of a better organized league than in previous years. The four-team league also included the Shell Oilers team, the White Kings, and Joe Pirrone's Major League All-Stars. The season was broken into two halves with the winner of the first half playing the winner of the second half for the league championship. That winter, Babe Herman, Bob Meusel, Johnny Rawlings, Hughie McMullen and Fred Haney were some of the popular big league stars that participated in California Winter League play.

---

*Researcher William F. McNeil credited Rogan with 18 appearances, 16 complete games, 14 victories, 153 innings and 82 strikeouts. He also credited Rogan with hitting a solid .326.

Los Angeles Royal Giants, 1929. Standing, from left: Lonnie Goodwin, Andy Cooper, Crush Holloway, Neil Pullen, L.D. Livingston, T.J. Young, Raleigh "Biz" Mackey. Kneeling, from left: Dink Mothell, Bullet Rogan, Porter Charleston, Newt Allen, Newt Joseph. Players made more money participating in winter ball because they were paid by the game. The larger the crowd, the greater the pay.

For his Royal Giants roster, Rogan recruited some of the biggest names from the Negro National League. He recruited Crush Holloway, Willie Wells, Bizz Mackey, Herbert "Rap" Dixon, Andy Cooper, Norman "Turkey" Stearnes, Willie Foster and George Harney. From Kansas City's Monarchs, Rogan recruited Dink Mothell, Frank Duncan, Newt Joseph and Newt Allen.

Out west, thousands gathered on splintered bleachers, sitting in such close proximity that they could feel the heat from one another's breath, to savor the excitement of watching "Bullet" Rogan's new team. They packed in and protected their spaces and then wedged themselves in tightly with their sons, buddies or significant others, waiting eagerly beside people of all races for that chance to see an African American all-star team in action.

More than 4,000 screaming fans packed into White Sox Park for the season opener. In that game, George Harney, with the aid of Dink Mothell's five RBIs, bested Red Oldham of the Pittsburgh Pirates by a 9–0 score. The next day 7,500 people crowded into White Sox Park to see their hero Rogan pitch his first Winter League game in several seasons.

Rogan's pitching was the highlight of the season. In one game he pitched a splendid nine-hitter and beat pitcher Lou Koupal's major league All-Stars by a convincing 9–1 score. Rogan practically won this game at the plate too, when he went 3-for-4 with three runs driven in. New York Yankees outfielder Bob Meusel, a player that had struck out only 32 times in 413 official American League at bats, fanned twice. Rogan had struck out Meusel so often that he clipped Meusel's photograph out of the newspaper, cut out the articles around it for proof, and made them a part of his personal scrapbook.

Rogan's bat also won the game on October 31, when the Royal Giants beat the White Kings by a 4–3 score. Rogan came into the game in the eighth inning as a relief pitcher. When he came to bat in the ninth, the tying run was standing on second base. Rogan singled to right to score the runner and win the game. In their joyous celebration the fans pelted the field with seat cushions. Jimmy Smith reporting to the *Pacific Coast News Bureau* noted, "It was the most thrilling win imaginable."[27]

Rogan's arm won yet another game when he allowed just six hit in his team's 4–1 win over the White Kings. In that game, Rogan electrified the crowd when he stole home with the bases loaded to give his team the lead in the game and an ultimate victory. In still another special afternoon, the *Pacific Coast News Bureau* boasted of how Rogan's marvelous throw from right field had cut down a runner at the plate.

When Rogan's Royal Giants went on a four-game losing skid, the Shell Oilers edged them out for the first half pennant by a half game. Rogan rallied his troops for the second half and led his Royal Giants to an uncontested Winter League title.

Rogan's Royal Giants opened the second half of the 1926-27 Winter League campaign with a big 4–3 win. In that game, George Harney pitched nine full innings before Rogan came into the game as a pinch-hitter in the bottom of the ninth. The game remained tied and Rogan stayed in the game to pitch. In the eleventh inning, Rogan came to bat with the bases loaded. He promptly singled across the winning run for his team's victory. After that wonderful start the Royal Giants were well on their way to winning the second half title — and no

Clipping from the *Los Angeles Daily Times*, October 1926.

one would stop them. After December 16, the Royal Giants won 13 games and lost only two.

The Royal Giants were set to battle several Pacific Coast League teams in a series of spring exhibition games when Bizz Mackey, Frank Duncan, Herbert "Rap" Dixon and Andy Cooper unexpectedly disappeared. When they resurfaced they were part of a tour that was headed for Japan.

Rogan finished the winter of 1926-27 with a record of six wins and only one game lost.*[28] It was his pinch-hitting however, which caught the attention of the public. As a pinch-hitter, Rogan had come to bat on seven different occasions and hit safely four times—and three of the hits had won ballgames. Luckily for the teams in the California Winter League, Rogan did not play Winter League baseball in 1927-28. Among the Monarchs who did visit California to play Winter League baseball were Dink Mothell, Frank Duncan and Newt Allen. While on the coast they joined the Cleveland Giants. Hilldale, of the Eastern Colored League, also had a team playing in Los Angeles that winter.

During the winter of 1928-29, Rogan returned to California and joined the Cleveland Giants. That year's Cleveland Giants lineup was practically the same as the Royal Giants lineup from previous years. The new lineup was bolstered with the additions of John Beckwith, Carl "Lefty" Glass, Connie Day, and George "Tank" Carr.

When it was announced that Rogan had arrived, more than 6,000 overflowed White Sox Park. The game ended in a 7–7 tie, and Rogan, the left fielder that afternoon, went 1-for-4 at the plate. On January 13, the Giants, with Brewer starting and Rogan pitching in relief, beat Joe Pirrone's All-Stars by a 12–10 score. In another battle, Shell batters had gotten to Rogan for ten runs in a wild fourth inning and were leading the game by nine runs. Rogan toughened up from that point forward and the scoring ceased. At the same time, Rogan's team knocked Ferdie Schupp, a veteran of ten major league seasons, off the mound, collecting 19 hits and nine runs to tie the game that was called on account of darkness at the end of the ninth.

On February 24, in that year's deciding game for the championship against the Shell Oilers in Long Beach, California, Rogan got the pitching assignment for the Giants and Roy Wilkinson went to the mound for Shell Oil. Those who put their faith in the all-white Shell Oil team saw their team humbled, on offense and defense too. John Beckwith knocked out two home runs for the Giants, and Rogan went 2-for-5, stole a base and scored a run. On the mound, Rogan struck out four and allowed nine hits in his team's 10–5 win.

The Cleveland Giants team that won the 1928-29 California Winter League title was one of the most powerful teams to ever visit California.† Members of that year's Giants team were Newt Allen, Connie Day, Bizz Mackey, Herbert "Rap" Dixon, Turkey Stearnes, John Beckwith, Dink Mothell, Carl "Lefty" Glass and Neil Pullen.

The Cleveland Giants needed to capture the final series from the Shell Oil team to claim the Winter League title. In the series' final game, Shell suited up Roy Wilkinson, a former American League pitcher, and ordered him to beat Rogan. Things went decidedly against Shell early, as John Beckwith bashed two home runs. Rogan pitched his usual good

---

*William McNeil credited Rogan with two losses as a pitcher and 20 hits for the 1926-1927 season.
†William McNeil credited Rogan with 43 hits, of which five went for doubles, one for a triple and four for home runs. On the mound, Rogan is credited with a 9–1 won-lost record.

game and held the opposition to nine hits and struck out four. At-bat he went 2-for-5 and stole a base.²⁹

At season's end, Chet Brewer was the leading coast pitcher for the 1928-1929 season, having won 12 out of the 16 games in which he appeared.³⁰

In 1929-30, Rogan returned to California with an equally interesting roster that featured

From left: Frank Duncan, Hoss Walker and Andy Cooper in Japan, 1927. Duncan added, "We played in all the great cities of the Orient — Tokyo, Yokohama, Manila. We played in Rio, New York, everywhere. But we liked playing in our own little American towns best." In 1937 Cooper pitched the longest game in Monarchs history. It was a 17-inning affair against the Chicago American Giants.

Dink Mothell, Newt Allen, Crush Holloway, Bizz Mackey, Larry "Goo Goo" Livingston, T. J. Young, Chet Brewer, Leroy Taylor, Newt Joseph and Andy Cooper. That year the team's name was changed from the Cleveland Giants to the Philadelphia Royal Giants.

The California Winter League opened on October 21, 1929, with a big 12–9 Royal Giant win. Bob Meusel, Irish Meusel, Gus Suhr, Fred Haney and Tony Lazzeri were in Joe Pironne's starting lineup. Hollis Thurston, of the Brooklyn Dodgers, was on the mound, while the Royal Giants countered with lefty Andy Cooper. The game featured five Royal Giants home runs off the respective bats of Bullet Rogan, Bizz Mackey, Dink Mothell, Newt Joseph and Goo Goo Livingston. The game-clincher was Joseph's home run with the bases

Three Monarchs on the California Coast, 1929. From left: Newt Joseph, Bullet Rogan, Newt Allen. "Joseph had brains with his fielding," recalled Hall of Fame third baseman William Judy Johnson. Rogan was as adept as Joseph at shooting jackrabbits from the window of the Monarchs' touring bus.

loaded. The next afternoon, Brewer beat the same team by an 8–7 score in front of 7,000. In that game, Newt Joseph doubled in the first frame with the bases full, and Bullet Rogan also doubled in a run and led his team with a pair of hits.[31] Chet Brewer finished with 12 strikeouts.

On October 31, manager Pirrone put Jimmie Foxx and Al Simmons in his lineup in a supposed attempt to upset Rogan. Pironne's plan to beat Rogan failed, but in the process fans were treated to a unique bit of baseball lore. That afternoon Foxx went three for three, with two triples, against Rogan, but Simmons had no hits in five times at the plate. "Rogan was requested," wrote the *Call*, "to let Foxx and Simmons hit out of turn for the benefit of the cheering fans in the stands. Much to the fans' delight, Rogan upstaged them both by striking them out."[32] In that game Bullet Rogan struck out eight batters. Rogan also collected two hits of his own in three times at the plate, one being a double, the other a triple, to give the Philadelphia Royal Giants a 10–3 win.

One Los Angeles newspaper pondered, "The Philadelphia Royal Giants are composed of mostly Kansas City Monarchs players and the fans are now wondering just what the Monarchs would do to the average big league ball club in a series of games or if they played in the same league in regular competition."

The Winter League season of 1929-1930 was a virtual highlight film of outstanding plays. In mid–November, in Long Beach, California, Chet Brewer let the Shell Oil team down with five hits and the Royal Giants copped the fray, 4–2. Newt Joseph added a long triple for his share of the day's work, while Rogan, Young, and Joseph batted in runs.

In late November, Rogan came to the mound as a relief pitcher for Cooper. Lefty Andy Cooper had started the game, but was hit to all corners of the lot. Bullet Rogan relieved the southpaw and held the Oilers to two hits, but the damage had been done. The *Kansas City Call* noted that Rogan was "pitching like the Bullet of olden days when batsmen trembled as they approached the plate and wobbled away after the third strike."[33] That afternoon Mickey Heath, a player that finished his career with over 2,000 minor league hits, faced Rogan four times and wobbled back to the dugout hitless four times.

On December 11, Rogan went 4-for-5 with two home runs that accounted for six runs in the Royal Giants big win over Joe Pirrone's All-Stars. The following day Rogan beat the San Luis team from the mound. One of Rogan's biggest games resulted in a 7–5 win over Charley Root, pitcher for the White Kings. Root, although he won 201 National League games, was out-pitched by Rogan, a man that had not won a single National League encounter. Against Root's team, Rogan allowed ten hits, struck out eight and walked two. At bat, Rogan banged out two hits, in three times at the plate, including a home run. The winter of 1929-30 was perhaps the finest Winter League season of Rogan's long career.*

Injuries hampered Rogan's return to the Winter League in 1930-1931. And in the fall of 1932-33 he opted to remain with the Kansas City Monarchs team that went to Mexico as part of a second 16 game tour that visited Mexico City. During the tour, the Monarchs beat the famous Gallos and Aztecas baseball teams of Mexico City. Quincy Gilmore wrote in the *Kansas City Call*, "Each member of the Monarch club should be given credit for the great baseball he played here. The boys look fine in their new uniforms with the American flag on their sleeves. When we leave our hotel for the ballpark, several policeman and soldiers

---

*William F. McNeil credited Rogan with 28 hits, four home runs and a 5–1 pitching record.

have to be employed in order to keep the crowd moving. If we stop any place, the whole traffic is blocked. They are real hero-worshippers here."[34] The Monarchs left Mexico with a record of 14 wins and two losses.

For six winters, Rogan pitched, hit and fielded with an all-round versatility that was rarely matched. Dave Wyatt noted in the *Indianapolis Ledger* that "Oscar Charleston's name will always loom to the foreground when speaking of any sort of an all-round player." But even Wyatt was quick to note that "Wilber Rogan is my ideal of the make-up of a great all-round ball player."

There is however, a distinct line to be drawn between an all-round player and a utility player. The utility player can be depended upon to take care of various positions upon the playing field. Dave Malarcher, Frank Warfield and Bingo DeMoss were some of the best utility players that baseball ever produced. In Carroll Ray "Dink" Mothell the Monarchs had the most versatile utility man in baseball history. Infield, outfield, behind the plate, you name it, Mothell could play them all — and play them well. James "Cool Papa" Bell insisted, "Mothell was the only player he knew that could fill in for a superstar defensively and you would never miss that other player."

Born in Topeka, Kansas, in 1897, Mothell turned professional when "Topeka" Jack Johnson signed him to a Topeka Giants contract in 1916. In March of 1920, Mothell corresponded with J. L. Wilkinson about joining the newly formed Monarchs. Weeks later he received a contract for $120 a month. The $120 was a big disappointment since Mothell was gainfully employed in the construction business, but off he went to Kansas City. When several of the old-timers suggested that $120 wasn't enough money, Mothell went to Wilkinson and asked for an increase. "Well you ain't hardly made the ball club," stated Wilkinson, "I can't afford to pay you no more than $120."[35] So after the game Mothell went to the clubhouse, packed his bags, and went home to Topeka. When Rube Foster received word that Mothell had quit the Monarchs, the American Giants owner expressed personal interest in the former Monarch. Realizing that this might be his last chance at playing in the league, Mothell jumped at "Rube's" offer. Much to his dissatisfaction however, Foster's top offer was $125 a month. Foster's final words were easily understood, "take it or leave it, the train is leaving Union Station at 10:30 in the morning."[36]

Mothell joined the American Giants as a catcher, but the team already had Tubby Dixon and Jim Brown, two of the best receivers in baseball. As a consequence, Mothell didn't see much action with the American Giants. He caught a couple of games, pinch-hit every now and then, but mostly he rode the bench from the middle of June right into October.

His bewildering experience led to his departure from baseball in 1921 and 1922, at which time he found gainful employment for the Santa Fe railroad. By 1923, baseball had lured him back, and he took a job with J. L. Wilkinson's All-Nations team, which was a kind of minor league operation for the Kansas City Monarchs. In 1924 he rejoined the Kansas City Monarchs and remained with the team for the next ten seasons. In an article that was first published in the *Philadelphia Tribune* and republished in the *Kansas City American*, Ralph H. Barber acknowledged, "This boy Mothell in my opinion, is just as great as [Bizz] Mackey. He has also played every position and played each one well. I can go back over my scrap book and dig up some great ball players, but I'd rather send Mothell to bat when a run is needed than any player I know."[37]

Though Mothell was known primarily for his defense, it was a mistake to take his hitting for granted. He had excellent speed and on occasion he could, and would, hit for power. He was a switch-hitter. Mothell once stated, "When I first started playing, they fed me so many curveballs from the right side that I knew I had to do something to stay in the league, so I switched over. As a kid I was a cross-handed hitter. I had more power from the right side but I struck out a lot from the left side, it looked like I could see the ball better."[38]

One very memorable demonstration of his seeing the ball better occurred in Salina, Kansas, where he once hit three home runs in a game against the Concordia Travelers.[39] Later in the season Mothell performed an almost similar feat in Arkansas City, Kansas, when he blasted two home runs in the same game.[40]

In the winter of 1933-34, Mothell and Bullet Rogan took the longest trip of their entire professional careers. As members of the Los Angeles Royal Giants, Rogan's team returned to the Philippines and Honolulu. It was his first opportunity to visit that region of the world since 1917. Upon arrival Rogan was very surprised to discover that he had not been forgotten in Honolulu.

The tour that Rogan took to the Far East in the fall of 1933 and spring of 1934 also visited Japan and China. Though details of the trip remain sketchy, photographs and passports support the historical fact that Rogan's African American All-Stars were well-received as recognized champions of baseball. It was a more than fitting conclusion to Rogan's many years of winter league play.

During his eight years of winter league play, Rogan won more than 60 games as

Carroll Ray "Dink" Mothell. The best switch-hitter that ever wore a Monarchs uniform, Mothell was also versatile in the field, where he could play nearly every position.

a pitcher and collected over 300 hits as a batter. At least 30 of the hits were home runs. In the process, Rogan and his Kansas City teammates turned back many of the National and American League's best and brightest stars. Researcher William F. McNeil has credited Rogan with 52 complete games and over 516 innings pitched in California. He also credited Rogan with 42 victories.[41] McNeil, though, missed many games that have since been located.*

Having known segregation more personally than he ever cared to admit, Rogan must have found winter-league play, and in particular his success, sweet indeed.

---

*A three game series against the Portland Beavers, played in Santa Maria, California, in mid–March of 1921 is an example of winter league contests that were not reported in McNeil's career totals for Rogan.

10

The Reign of Error

Yes, he's a great player, the greatest in the league. He could make any major league club and would be a star. Every where we go they want to see Rogan.—J. L. Wilkinson, 1926

As the rest of America staggered through the mid–1930s, African Americans in baseball finally breathed a sigh of relief—a long awaited relief that resulted from sluggish National and American League attendance. National and American League attendance was down—way down. Across the board, big leaguers' salaries were being cut to deplorable levels. Many of baseball's well-known stars were forced to live on wages similar to those that Negro Leaguers had received for generations. And for most, that was just a bit too low.

The low attendance eventually resulted in an increased number of barnstorming games. The excitement surrounding the interracial games, ever so crucial to the popularity of baseball for generations, had returned. Out west, National and American League stars scrambled for postseason games against the Kansas City Monarchs. In the east, the big leaguers found a profitable foe in the Pittsburgh Crawfords. This mad rush for games didn't seem to affect the national press, though; they remained one of the few organizations that snarled at the proposition of true interracial play. "Funny thing what depression will do," wrote the *Kansas City Call*. "Make an All-Star big league team come 'south' and play a professional colored team. Then, too, everybody sits any place they can find a seat. Oh boy! For just a little more of [that] depression."[1]

In that era of subtle and misleading references towards race, comparisons based on prejudiced opinion, regardless of how illogical, were seemingly embraced with open arms. With the exception of the derogatory names writers were forever conjuring up, the negative messages that the public received about African American athletes were often subliminal. These subtle messages were buried beneath generations of negative stereotypes about African Americans. Essentially, the media was perpetuating the lie that segregated baseball was the best brand of baseball in the world, and America swallowed the bait, hook, line and sinker.

In 1934, Wilkinson brought Sam Crawford out of retirement to manage his Monarchs. Crawford proceeded to rehire veterans John Donaldson and Hurley McNair, two stars from the team's glorious past. The Monarchs then departed in three Ford touring cars for the southern states, up to the Dakotas, across to the Pacific Northwest and into Canada. It was obvious, though, that this was an aging Monarchs team desperately in need of some young blood. As a result, many games that were once automatic victories became losses, as the team of veterans struggled through the extreme travel and an exhaustive string of one and two-night stands. Rarely appearing at home, the Monarchs played more games in Winnipeg, Canada, where they appeared eight times, than they did Kansas City where they played four games. They would also appear in Chicago for eight games and in Denver for six games.

Monarchs team bus from another angle, 1934.

10. The Reign of Error

As a player of much renown, Rogan was still contributing mightily. At La Crosse, Wisconsin, Rogan pounded out three hits in four at bats with a double.[2] In Kansas City's 7–3 win in Madison, Wisconsin, Rogan banged out a pair of hits, one a double, and stole a base.[3] And the hits kept on coming. The summer of 1934 would be Giles' last with the Monarchs, and it was oh so evident that it would be one of his best seasons yet.

In Madison, Wisconsin on May 31, George Giles's bat rang out three hits, which included two doubles and a triple. He also had a pair of stolen bases.[4] During a visit to La Crosse, Wisconsin, Giles hit two home runs and a triple.[5] Against Chicago Mills, his four hits had given Kansas City a 5–3 win.[6]

By mid–June the Monarchs were in the upper Midwest, in Jamestown and Bismarck. In Bismarck, they encountered Barney Morris, who was the throwing end of the new African American battery that featured Quincy Trouppe on the receiving end. "Red" Haley and Roosevelt Davis were the other African Americans on the Bismarck team that trounced the Monarchs 7–0.[7] Moving onto Jamestown, the Monarchs didn't fare much better, losing, 5–1, to that town's African American battery of Ted Radcliffe and Bill Perkins.[8] The Monarchs' next stop would be the highly publicized Denver Post Tournament.

Prior to reaching Denver, the Monarchs had beaten the House of David, 5–4, in Missoula, Montana, on July 14. While in that city, Art Murphy and Mel Ingram of the Kellogg Miners caught on with the House of David.[9] They had also beaten the House of David in Spokane, Washington, 4–0, on July 12. In that game Brewer limited the bearded men to four hits.[10] Grover Alexander's House of David had also felt the wrath of the mighty Monarchs in Canada, where they were trounced, 4–0, in Virden, 1–0, in Regina and, 7–4, during a visit to Moose Jaw.[11] The Monarchs totally stunned the Davids in Winnipeg by capturing a complete five-game series. Brewer took that series' opener with a 4–2, nine strikeout performance. Beverly followed with a 4–3, 13 strikeout outing. In game three, the aging Monarchs had to overcome a six-run deficit to win, 11–9, with Andy Cooper getting credit for the victory. In the series remaining two encounters, games which were played as part of a doubleheader on July 29, Bullet Rogan pitched the Monarchs to a 7–6 win in the opener, an appearance that was followed by John Donaldson's 3–1 win in the nightcap.

On Monday, July 16, in Lethbridge Canada, the House of David team got even by handing Kansas City's Monarchs one of their worst beatings of the year — a 15–1 lambasting. That night David batters pummeled pitcher Chet Brewer for 18 hits.[12]

Lefty Charlie Beverly, one of Kansas City's best pitchers, was having a mediocre year with only sporadic bursts of his one-time brilliance. On May 30, Beverly had struck out seven of the Chicago Mills team in a 12–2 win.[13] In a 2–1 loss to Bismarck, North Dakota, Beverly managed to strike out only two batters.[14] He returned to form in Winnipeg, Canada, and defeated the House of David with 13 strikeouts. With two days' rest he returned to win, 1–0, and logged a four-hit, 13 strikeout game in Regina, Saskatchewan.[15] Beverly struck out five in another 10–4 win over the House of David.[16] It was evident, though, by looking at his strikeout totals that Beverly's three-year reign as a strikeout king was coming to a close. In the previous three seasons, as one of the premier strikeout pitchers in baseball, he had run up an astronomical number of strikeouts and wins.

With Beverly ailing from an injured arm, when the Monarchs reached Denver, lefty Willie Foster, one of Negro baseball's best pitchers, joined the team as they prepared for the biggest tournament in the Midwest.

In Denver, Colorado, the local *Post* newspaper had been sponsoring a "for whites only" baseball tournament for 19 years. Finally, in 1934, after a long history of Northern Jim Crowism, the Kansas City Monarchs became the first African American entry in the tournament's history. A purse of $5,000 was to be awarded to the winner, an influence powerful enough — in the middle of the depression — to lure teams from all over America. Grover Cleveland Alexander, who was backed by promoter Ray L. Done of Muscatine, Iowa, entered the House of David crew.

Taking into consideration that Kansas City's Monarchs had recently taken a five game series from them, and in spite of the new men they had picked up, Alexander went looking for additional reinforcements. He found them in pitcher Leroy "Satchel" Paige and catcher William Perkins, an African American battery. When the Monarchs heard what Alexander had done, they wired for Chicago's Norman "Turkey" Stearnes and Willie Foster, and also recruited Nashville's shortstop Sam Bankhead.[17]

The *Denver Post* tournament opened on August 2, 1934. As was the custom at most tournaments, African American teams battled in the opening rounds, thereby leaving the white teams in line to capture the lion's share of the money and prizes after they had been bumped off. That night Brewer struck out 19 batters and downed the Greeley Advertisers, a rival African American club, by a 12–1 score.

The 2,500 fans that showed up for game one set a tournament record for the largest opening day attendance. The *Post*, by writing, "Yes, siree, neighbors, these colored lads, representing the finest ebony talent in the land, have a ball club," had seemingly picked the

House of David team photograph. The House of David colony operated several teams at once. One club worked the East, another the Midwest and Upper Northwest, and still another remained home in Benton Harbor, Michigan.

10. The Reign of Error

1934 Monarchs team at the *Denver Post* Tournament. The Monarchs were the first all-black team to play in the tournament. Cumberland Posey wrote in the *Pittsburgh Courier* that "Giles was [the] best ground-ball man and the fastest man in baseball going to first base, with all due credit to [Cool Papa] Bell and 'Fats' Jenkins."

Monarchs as the tournament's big winner, but this was not the case. The same article had referred to the Monarchs base runners—they had pilfered ten bases that night—as "scared rabbits."[18] As the tournament went forward the *Post's* indignant personality began to show throughout the articles.

Andy Cooper beat the Denver Athletic Club by a run under threatening skies in game two. The final score was 4 to 3. In spite of the threatening weather, that Sunday's crowd numbered some 6,983. Rogan practically won this game all by himself. In the sixth, he raced over into right center, reached down and made a knee-high grab of a line drive, backhanded, too. The *Post* called Rogan's catch as "spectacular a catch as anybody ever saw."[19] Rogan also scored what eventually became the game's winning run when he and Bankhead engineered a double steal.

The next morning, the *Post's* bigoted editorial referred to the Monarchs' Sam Crawford as "King Fish." The name "King Fish" made reference to a seedy African American character, whose rank dialect voice was performed by a white actor in the popular *Amos 'n' Andy* radio program. The newspaper's negative comment, a throw back to the media's *Amos 'n' Andy* mentality toward African Americans, was nothing new to the Monarchs. Another section of the same article spewed, "The dark day gave them [the Monarchs] the upper hand."[20] The ballplayers had learned many years prior to this tournament to ignore the white media, and when Brewer won game three by one run, the Monarchs remained undefeated.

The *Post* wasn't any more generous toward Paige. After he beat Overton, Texas' Humble

Oilers, this same newspaper referred to Paige's pitching as "black magic."[21] Acting as if Paige's nickname of "Satchel" wasn't good enough, the newspaper invented a new one— "The Chocolate Whizbang." Thank God the nickname never stuck.

When the Monarchs met Alexander's House of David on Friday night, August 11, a crowd of 11,120, another tournament record, poured into the park. A 19-year *Post* tournament record was smashed by the overflow crowd that crammed its way into Merchants Park to see the big battle.[22]

Rogan excelled at the plate that night but failed to hit in the clutch. Against Paige, Rogan went 2-for-4 with a double and a stolen base. In the sixth inning, Rogan had a chance to break the game wide open. Allen and Giles had singled and a pair of stolen bases put runners on second and third. Paige, taking plenty of time, struck out Rogan with three outstanding pitches. That at-bat ended the Monarchs last opportunity to grasp some additional scores, and Alexander's House of David captured a 2–1 victory.[23]

The Monarchs came back the next night and whipped the Eason Oilers of Enid, Oklahoma, by a 5–4 score, and prepared themselves for the championship game, a rematch with Alexander's House of David.[24]

The House of David put "Spike" Hunter on the mound, instead of Paige, in the *Post's* championship game. The Monarchs knew Hunter well. In fact, on July 26, Rogan had turned back Hunter in a pitchers' battle at Portage la Prairie, Manitoba, Canada, where the Monarchs won, 3–2, before a crowd of 1,500 fans. The Monarchs, however, decided to stay with their ace, Chet Brewer.

Exciting things began to happen in the second stanza when Rogan and Bankhead singled, but Duncan grounded out and Mothell lined to the shortstop for a double play. In the third, Joseph and Brewer led off with singles, but Hunter struck out Allen, Giles and Stearnes on nine pitches. After that inning, though, the Monarchs' scoring opportunities began to dwindle. The game ended with Alexander's House of David beating the Monarchs, 2–0.[25]

"The happiest person in the park after the game," wrote the *Post*, "appeared to be manager Grover Cleveland Alexander. He was shaking hands with everybody and apparently enjoying himself more than anytime since his relief pitching saved the World Series for the Cardinals in 1926."[26]

Paige was selected as the tournament's

Andy Cooper, 1938. Cooper joined the Monarchs in 1928 after a great career with the Detroit Stars. Rogan's first Negro League extra-base hit had come off Cooper. On July 23, 1922, Rogan's first multiple home run game was off Cooper too.

best pitcher. He was the whole show on the mound, striking out 44 batters in only 28 innings, and 41 percent of the batters who faced him. "Turkey" Stearnes, the tournament's big hitting star, finished with a .444 batting average and three doubles. He also won recognition as the tournament's most outstanding player, leading outfielder, and an award for the most sensational play. Newt Allen won acknowledgment as the tournament's leading base stealer.

Brewer, the Monarchs' ace, finished the tournament with 41 strikeouts in 30 innings pitched — 16 of his strikeouts had come in the two House of David games. Rogan had appeared in all six games, batting .261, with a double, two bases stolen, and three multi-hit games. Monarchs pitchers, in 55 total innings, walked just five batters. The total attendance that saw the Monarchs in that tournament was 40,344, an average of 6,724 per game.

Showing one last bit of biting irritation, the biased author of the *Post's* article, representing the so-called opinion of the "American public," wrote, "House of David, the people's choice, wins!"[27]

Many years later Monarchs first baseman George Giles hinted that the series' final game had been fixed so that Alexander's House of David team would win. He did not indicate exactly how or why that victory was handed over.[28] An edition of Benton Harbor's *News Palladium* also alluded to something funny in the tournament's results when it wrote,

Norman "Turkey" Stearnes. Originally a member of the Detroit Stars, Stearnes appeared with the Monarchs on four occasions. He was a member of the team in 1931, toured with them to Mexico in 1932, played on their *Denver Post* Tournament squad in 1934 and spent the final three seasons of his playing career (1938–1940) as a Monarch.

A handful of Monarchs at the *Denver Post* tournament. From left: Newt Allen, T.J. Young, Norman "Turkey" Stearnes, Eddie Dwight, Dink Mothell, Wilber Rogan (Black Archives Mid America).

"Federal government officers in the postal department, it was said, launched a probe today to trace an unsigned letter from Benton Harbor addressed to [Spike] Hunter that [read], 'for his own good, he should 'lay down' and 'throw' the final game to the Monarchs."[29] For their share of the winnings, Alexander's House of David team made the colony $5,800 richer.[30]

The Monarchs were also beaten by the House of David, 2–1, in ten innings in Colorado Springs.[31] Working with a shuffled lineup the Monarchs lost on a single batted ball, reported a local publication. "Rogan, Negro second-baseman, went back after it but muffed [it]," recorded the writer, "and crashed into [Andy] Cooper, his right-fielding mate. Both men rolled to the turf and Hill [of the House of David] went over the plate with the winning score."[32]

No one could have been more disappointed at the outcome of the game than Rogan. His aunt, Eva Deason, was in attendance with family and well-wishers who had wanted to see the Monarchs cash in on the big day of activities. Their appearance at Wichita, directly following the *Denver Post* Tournament, was really hyped by J. L. Wilkinson and Ray L. Doane, the Davids' publicity manager.

"We don't care a whole lot about playing those Monarchs in Wichita," declared Doane. "Last year when they beat us, they capitalized off the publicity all season. We have the best baseball club this season, however, and feel certain of beating them again in Wichita."[33] Wilkinson declared, "My colored boys have been gunning for the Davids ever since we were beaten out of the Denver Post tournament championship. There was only one thing for me to do to please the boys, and that was to arrange another game with the Davids."

Illustrating their immense popularity, the Monarchs rolled into Wichita with hopes of drawing the largest crowd in the city's sporting history—and history was certainly on their side. They had "won 30 games and lost but one in Wichita in 11 years," said Wilkinson.[34]

Getting into the publicity, Alexander added, "The Monarchs used to have the best ball club but they haven't now. There's not a team in the country that can best us in a series of games. The majors have been after our players for the past month, but the boys have agreed to stick it out at least until the season is over. Benson, one of the pitchers, left the colony team recently and pitched for Cleveland. In his first game he blanked the Washington Senators, allowing but three hits."[35]

The preliminary darts were more than enough to draw thousands of fans to Lawrence Stadium where the Monarchs dashed any hope of David's domination, with an 8–5 victory. The massive crowd was so large that ground rules were necessary and several hits which were labeled for triples were cut down to doubles. Fans overflowed the temporary bleachers and were seated on the field as well as along the foul lines. The big eighth, which saw the Monarchs scoring a pair of runs on singles by Mothell and Dwight and a Rogan double to the center-field fence, gave Kansas City the victory, as pitcher Charlie Beverly was nearly untouchable in the late innings.

Unfortunately, the Monarchs had not broken the single game attendance record for Wichita. The all-time high was 8,900, set in 1921 in a game between Wichita and Tulsa. By drawing crowds of 8,147 against the Davids in 1934 and 6,300 at Wichita, in 1933, the Monarchs were clearly the best attraction ever to visit the Midwestern city.[36] On September 27, the Monarchs returned to Wichita and shaved the House of David in a close 7–6 win. Chet Brewer and John Donaldson combined for ten strikeouts, and Newt Joseph added a home run for the victorious Monarchs. The two teams fought to a tie encounter too.

In La Crosse, Wisconsin, the teams battled to an 8–8 deadlock at Tronick Park. This game, although played against the House of David, was the colony's team that had traveled to the eastern states and into Canada. Dorsey Moulder of Kansas City, Kansas, and Poncho Traynor, kid brother of the Pirates manager, Pie, were members of this squad.[37]

The following night, Elmer Ambrose, who had pitched for the Tulsa Oilers in their Western League days, helped the House of David beat Kansas City, 6–4, in Tulsa. Earl "Oil" Smith, veteran National League catcher, joined Alexander's team to conclude their series of games against the legendary Monarchs from Kansas City.[38]

The Dizzy Dean tour, which took place after the World Series, was 1934's other highlight. And just as it had done in the *Denver Post* Tournament, the media never gave the Monarchs a fighting chance. The big leaguers were favored mightily.

The Deans, Dizzy and Daffy, were riding high in 1934. As members of the St. Louis Cardinals, they had combined for 49 wins. Their success had catapulted them to national prominence. Though they were at the height of their popularity, they weren't getting paid well, and it was the middle of the Depression. That eagerness to cash in on their success, during one of the most difficult periods of economic woes in the nation's history, is why the Deans started barnstorming against African American teams. So, directly after the conclusion of the 1934 World Series against the Detroit Tigers, the Deans, assisted by Dizzy's wife, and Tom Baird, manager of the tour, assembled a series of All-Star teams and began a schedule of six barnstorming games against the Kansas City Monarchs. At every opportunity that presented itself, the Deans were bragging and boasting of what they were going to do to the Monarchs and how they had defeated the Detroit Tigers.

The series opened in Oklahoma City, Oklahoma, where Dean's All-Stars won, 4–0. Although the Deans had captured the win, the Monarchs had dominated the game. Every player in the Monarchs lineup had hit safely. All totaled, they collected nine hits and eight of these safe blows were off Paul "Daffy" Dean.

The *Daily Oklahoman* attempted to downplay Kansas City's offensive onslaught. "Most of them would have been easy outs under normal conditions," grumbled a local reporter. Kansas City's ninth hit, one that was obtained off "Dizzy," the more famous of the brothers, was labeled a "scratch hit" by the same newspaper. In contrast, the *Oklahoman* identified each of the ten hits made by Dean's All-Stars off the Monarchs' pitching as "stinging singles."[39] Afterward, the Monarchs were left to wonder if Chet Brewer would have made the game more positive in their favor.

Monarchs ace Brewer was absent, as he was traveling back from Jamestown, North Dakota, where he had participated in a series versus another group of major league All-Stars a week earlier. On Sunday, October 7, at Jamestown, Brewer had shut out an All-Stars team, 11–0, that featured Jimmie Foxx and Dick Porter of the Boston Red Sox, Marty Hopkins and Ted Lyons of the White Sox, Roger Cramer and Pinky Higgins of the Philadelphia Athletics, Ralph Kress, Heinie Manush, Alfonse Thomas and Luke Sewell of the Washington Senators. Brewer let the All-Stars down on four hits and struck out five.[40] At Valley City, North Dakota, on October 6, Brewer had combined with Barney Brown to defeat the All-Stars, 6–5, in the series opener. Brewer allowed four hits with three batters struck out during his three innings of relief.[41] Brewer was making short work of his opponents just when the Monarchs needed him to beat Dean's All-Stars.

At Wichita, in game two of the tour, Dean's All-Stars won by an 8–3 score. Dizzy pitched three innings and the Monarchs got three hits and a run off him. The *Wichita Eagle* tried to explain away the performance by writing, "[Dizzy] showed the strain of his grueling performances in the clos-

Jay "Dizzy" Dean. The ace of the St. Louis Cardinals barnstormed with Paige in the 1930s, and the public came out in droves to see the two face off.

ing days of the National League campaign and in the World Series." In referring to the Monarchs, the *Eagle* termed their play "erratic." Commenting further, the *Eagle* wrote that the Kansas City team had "functioned with only fair success."[42]

Game three was played in Kansas City, where the Monarchs' hometown newspaper should have given its blessing, but the *Kansas City Times* chose otherwise and refused to grant the Monarchs equal billing. "The Deans, Paul and Dizzy, playing in a lineup with Kansas City professionals and semi-professionals, were unable to stop Young, the Monarchs' catcher," lamented the *Times*.[43] Blaming the weak performance on "Kansas City's professionals and semi-professionals" didn't stop Rogan from going 2-for-4, nor did it stop T. J. Young from going 4-for-5 in the Monarchs' immense 7–0 win over the Deans. Frank Frisch, manager of the St. Louis Cardinals, was among the spectators at the game. When asked what he thought of the postseason tour, he called it "unwise."[44]

On October 13, the two clubs met in Des Moines, Iowa, and the Monarchs won another lopsided 9–0 game. While the *Des Moines Register* raved about the Deans, evidently their journalistic credibility was not as important. The newspaper totally ignored Charlie Beverly's throw-back performance of nine innings and five hits and 15 strikeouts. As a further insult, the *Register* failed to mention Beverly's name in the entire article.[45] The newspaper did not mention Rogan either, but he went 2-for-5 that night.

While in Des Moines the Deans refuted the published statement that manager Frankie Frisch had advised them not to make the exhibition tour. The statement, which appeared in the *Des Moines Register*, was made by Dizzy, the spokesman of the talkative pair. "Frisch told us to clean up while we are hot. He never did tell us not to pitch," Dean reveled. "He knows we'll come through next year and that exhibitions ain't gonna hurt no good pitcher. With the emphasis on good."[46]

Chicago, Illinois, was host to the series' fifth game, which took place at Chicago's Mills Stadium. The Dean All-Stars won this game by a 13–3 score. One local news writer penned, "The Dean brothers came to Mills Stadium, on the West Side, and they left with the wild applause of 20,000 ringing in their ears and $5,000 jingling in their pockets."[47] The newswriter added, "Lots of toes were stepped on; one big fellow up in front blocked the view of little Johnny in the row behind; about 3,000 'rail birds,' that made for an extra shelf of humanity on the railroad tracks, yearned for a closer view."[48]

Game six, the Monarchs' final game with the Deans, was an 8–8 tie at Milwaukee's Borchert Field. In that game, Dizzy pitched the first two innings, allowing a run on two walks, and a single, then retired to left field for four more innings.[49]

The six games between the Deans and Monarchs had drawn upwards of 64,500 cash-paying customers and covered thousands of miles in territory. In Kansas they had drawn "The largest gate that ever was paid to see a baseball attraction in Wichita."[50] One newspaper listed the Deans' take of the postseason series at $14,000.[51] Another newspaper said that the Deans were to "receive a guarantee of $2,500 for playing against the Monarchs, with a privilege of 50 percent of the gross gate receipts."

Throughout the tour the Deans chartered airline flights to every city, sometimes requiring one plane for luggage and another for the players. The Monarchs weren't nearly as coddled. Their transportation consisted of two trailers pulled by Ford motor cars. Eddie Dwight and Bullet Rogan were two of the players forced to drive day and night and then play baseball the following evening. They also weren't allowed to stay in any of the first class

Lemuel Hawkins and unknown batboy. Hawkins spent eight seasons with the Monarchs. Hawkins was a maverick on and off the field. "Hawkins was known as the hardest loser on the team," wrote Quincy Gilmore in the *Kansas City Sun*. "When the Monarchs lost it was said that Hawkins shed tears."

hotels or eat at any of the fine restaurants that hosted the Deans for free.

Although they had many reasons to moan and complain, the Monarchs chose not to make their feelings known. Some of the major leaguers chose otherwise. Elden Auker, for instance, still boiling over his team's loss to the Deans in the World Series, noted that "Babe Ruth, Walter Johnson, Lefty Grove and the other great stars of baseball got their publicity from what they did. The Deans get most of theirs from what they say about themselves."[52]

Immediately following the Monarchs segment of the historic tour, the Deans proceeded to exasperate the media while playing games against three other African American teams: the Pittsburgh Crawfords, New York's Black Yankees and the Philadelphia Stars, before ending what could well be considered one of the greatest barnstorming tours in baseball history.

The Monarchs, in spite of the aging squad they placed on the field, ended one of the most profitable campaigns in their history, and their record was still impressive. The *Kansas City Times* noted, "The Monarchs played 143 games winning 127." Both the *Denver Post* Tournament and the "Dizzy" Dean tour affirmed the Monarchs' unique popularity among baseball enthusiasts.

On a more somber note, Lemuel Hawkins, a former Monarchs first baseman, was shot and killed during an apparent holdup in Chicago on August 10, 1934. As fate would dictate, it was one of his own buddies that fired the fatal shot, during an attempted holdup of a beer truck gone bad.[53] Hawkins, a member of the Monarchs'

1923 to 1925 championship teams, was cut by the Monarchs in 1928 and chose a life of crime after his professional career abruptly ended in 1930. One local newspaper offered, "Lem Hawkins who for the past several season had played first base for the Monarchs, joined the Chicago club at Kansas City last week. Old Hawk has not played much this season but just as soon as he gets into condition he will be a tower of strength to the American Giants. He is a smart player and a good hitter."[54]

When Hawkins failed to make good with Chicago's American Giants, he caught on with a host of semi-professional clubs. Hawkins also performed a brief stint as a Negro League umpire. He participated in a bit of history in 1930 when he umpired the famous pitchers' battle of August 7, 1930, between "Smoky" Joe Williams of Pittsburgh's Homestead Grays and the Monarchs' Chet Brewer. In that game Williams struck out 27 batters, Brewer 19. Mostly, though, Hawkins moonlighted as a chauffeur for wealthy whites in metropolitan Kansas City.

A player that was inexplicably private, he had married Opal Johnson, age 21, on June 7, 1923, when he was 27. Opal became involved with drugs and considering the sudden change in Hawkins' lifestyle, it is a good bet that he had become a user too. His first serious altercation with the law occurred on the morning of May 5, 1931, when he shot and killed one Lon Campbell as the two men squabbled over five cents worth of change. The two were engaged in a card game and Hawkins is said to have changed a dollar for Campbell and taken out a nickel, which was due the game. "Campbell," it was reported by Kansas's *City Call*, "became enraged at having the nickel taken in advance and threw the change across the room." Witnesses told police that Campbell had gone outside and returned with a gun and after some more words were exchanged, began shooting at Hawkins. Taking cover, Hawkins returned fire with a .38 caliber revolver and shot Campbell in the back three times. Arrested on manslaughter charges, Hawkins claimed self-defense. The case was later dismissed because Hawkins' assailant had pulled his pistol and fired first. In the exchange of bullets, another man, Louis Taylor, age 33, was killed by a stray bullet to the abdomen.

After that frightful experience Hawkins should have straightened up — he did not. Several months after the shooting, Hawkins was sentenced to two years in the United States Penitentiary at Leavenworth, Kansas, following his arrest in July of 1931 for auto theft and an attempted holdup in Chanute, Kansas. His police file stated that he and another individual, Leroy Worten, had stolen a vehicle and driven it from Missouri into Kansas, which was a violation of the Dyer Act. The pair ended up in Chanute, Kansas, where an attempted robbery of a gas station led to their capture. Hawkins served time for the crimes and was released from the federal penitentiary in June of 1933.[55] At the time of his death, police in Kansas City were on the lookout for Hawkins for a holdup of an investment company. Seven witnesses to the stickup had identified Hawkins' mug shot as one of the bandits.

Still, the name of the game is winning baseball, not editorials. And in 1935 that's exactly what the Monarchs performed, even though five of their top stars had jumped to other teams or retired. George Giles had gone east with the Brooklyn Royal Giants, Frank Duncan had jumped to the Pittsburgh Crawfords, John Donaldson left to form his own barnstorming team and Dink Mothell had retired because of problems in his right shoulder. Hurley McNair's career, one that should surely stamp him as a Hall of Fame candidate, succumbed to old age.

Quincy Troupe, after a year in Bismarck, was back with the Monarchs, but for only a brief period. Wilkinson had provided him with some advance money over the winter and he had used most of it to purchase a new 1935 Ford. Sam Crawford and Henry Milton had all ridden to Texas in Trouppe's new vehicle, where they met the Monarchs. "Crawford and Trouppe fell out when Trouppe refused to have the controlling Monarchs' manager call pitching signals from the bench. After the opening barnstorming series, which started in Wichita against the Chicago American Giants, Trouppe jumped to Bismarck."[56] With so many of their former players gone, new men were hired and the Monarchs became a totally different team.

Sam Crawford returned to manage one final season. Among his first moves was to take Bullet Rogan out of the everyday outfield, leaving him more available for the pinch-hitting and the utility roles that Mothell formerly filled. In Chet Brewer, Charlie Beverly and Andy Cooper, manager Crawford had three of baseball's premier strikeout pitchers. First year players Willard Brown, Eldridge E. "Chili" Mayweather and Floyd Kranson joined the team from Louisiana's Monroe Monarchs. Bob Madison, another first-year player, came over from El Dorado, Arkansas. Henry Milton, a speed merchant in the outfield, had been heavily recruited from Wiley College. Milton, a native of East Chicago, Indiana, had received national attention when Oscar Charleston tagged him as a coming prospect. Milton, the regular second baseman of the college nine, played halfback on the football team and forward for the basketball team. It was as an amateur track and field runner, though, where he really excelled.[57]

In 1931, while performing in the Tuskegee Relays for Wiley College, Milton ran the 100-yard dash in 9.9 seconds. His time was only slightly behind that of Edward Tolan, holder of the World's Record at 9.5 seconds. When Milton joined Dwight in the outfield, it gave the Monarchs two of baseball's fastest runners. In 1935 and 1936, the duo peaked with a combined 200-plus stolen bases, leaving little doubt that this tandem was probably the best base-stealing duo in baseball. Batting one-two in the lineup, one of their specialties was the double steal. So smoothly was it executed that one newspaper offered, "some of them [their opponents] think it's all done with mirrors."[58]

A native of Dalton, Georgia, Dwight was already labeled as one of the fastest runners in baseball. "In Dwight, an outfielder," wrote William Dismukes, "the Kansas City Monarchs have just about the fastest thing on foot in baseball. J. [Cool Papa] Bell of the St. Louis Stars, too, is somewhat of a hoofer, which brings about the general discussion as to which is faster. Whomever you choose between [the two] you will have select[ed] [a] single piece of baseball machinery."[59] Dwight was also one of baseball's most colorful stars. During a 1928 game, he had played centerfield while having a five inning conference with some small boy on a Shetland pony.[60]

Eddie Dwight arrived in Kansas City, Kansas, in 1917, after his father was forced to leave their home town by a local white sheriff because he could not pay $2 he owed on a payment for a mule.[61] Edward, born February 25, 1905, was immediately enrolled into Sumner High School. In 1924 he spent an entire season with Brown's famous Tennessee Rats and the next year was promoted to the Indianapolis ABCs. Nicknamed "Pee Wee," he stood only 5-foot-5 tall. He was farmed to the Gilkerson Union Giants for the 1926-27 seasons and joined the Kansas City Monarchs in 1928. In 1929-30, he returned to Gilkerson's Union Giants, and in 1931 he did not play ball. In 1932 he stayed home and played with Kansas City's Board of Trade team. Dwight spent the balance of his career, 1933 to 1937, with Kansas City's famous Monarchs.

Eddie "Pee Wee" Dwight (left) and Hurley McNair, 1930. Both men are wearing Gilkerson Union Giants uniforms. McNair was with the Monarchs from 1920 to 1927 and returned in 1934. Dwight was with the Monarchs in 1928–29 and returned for a second tenure in 1933–1937. Dwight's career started with Brown's Tennessee Rats in 1924. At season's end he asked the owner for the balance of his salary, and the owner said, "Didn't you know? You ate up your salary!"

Mayweather, born November 26, 1909, in Shreveport, Louisiana, came to the Monarchs as the owner of one of the best long ball swings in baseball. Although he was only 5-foot-7 and 188 pounds, he appeared much larger at first glance.

Though Rogan was no longer expected to have big days at the plate, running the bases, or pitching on the mound, he nevertheless filled the utility role well.

Kranson, one of the Monarchs' new pitchers, was the product of a biracial union — his father was white and his mother African American. He had turned professional after graduating from Natchitoches High school in the city of his birth. Though he was only age 18, he was an excellent complement to the Monarchs' already outstanding staff of pitchers. He would continue in that role until 1940, at which time yet another mixed-race player, Fred Youngblood McDaniel, an outfielder that had grown up in Athens, Texas, joined the squad.[62]

In Willard Brown, the Monarchs had discovered an unpolished gem. In Brown's first season he was producing hits at a remarkable pace. Originally recommended to the Monarchs as a shortstop, he eventually developed into one of baseball's truly outstanding outfielders, and after a steady diet of curveballs from Chet Brewer began to hit many home runs.

"They could get me out on the curveball when I came to the Monarchs," recalled Brown. "Chet Brewer, he was one of the best curveball pitchers in the league. Every day he would throw me nothing but curveballs. He'd throw a fastball to move me back and then throw the curveball. He'd say, 'that's the way they [are] going to pitch you. They know you're going to hit the fastball. The only thing you're weak on is the curveball.' He had one of the best curveballs so when I learned how to hit it that made me a finished ballplayer."[63]

Shreveport, Louisiana, was Brown's home. He was born there on June 26, 1913.[64] He was 5 feet 11½ inches of pure exhilaration. Though blessed with tremendous natural ability, Brown had prospered early in his career because he took instruction well. Chet Brewer taught Brown how to hit curveballs, and it was "Candy Jim" Taylor who had encouraged Brown to use a heavier 36-inch, 40-ounce bat. Brown eventually settled into a patented 36-36 medium handle rod. "Oscar Charleston was Brown's favorite hitter and the man Brown tried to pattern himself after."[65] On the Monarchs team only Dwight and Milton ran faster than Willard Brown. Brown, however, was almost never recognized for his speed. He personally blamed his damaged ankle for his less than colorful base running.

In Alexandria, Brown had broken his ankle sliding into a base. Doctors advised, "you will never play with that ankle."[66] The healing was slow and arduous, but Brown wanted to get back into his team's lineup anyway. When the impatience reached a climax, he simply ignored the doctor's advice, removed the wrappings, and proceeded to rub the ankle with some Sloan's liniment until it healed. Within a short time he was back on the field. After that though, he developed a phobia against sliding.

During the winter of 1934, "Wilkinson," Brown recalled, "came down and offered me $250 and a contract of $125 a month. And a dollar a day to eat on. I wasn't making but $10 in a week, so you know I'm going to take that."[67] Brown took that little bit of money and made it pay long-term dividends. In just his first season, according to one source, Brown led in long balls, "hitting 43 home runs."[68] Another source credited Brown with "54 home runs in 160 games" in 1935.[69]

Kansas City didn't see much of Brown in 1935. In the nine games the Monarchs played at Kansas City's Muehlebach Field, Brown hit .355 with four doubles, a triple and a home run. Like all of the Monarchs, he excelled on the road.

In 1935, Sam Crawford's last season as manager, the Monarchs were strictly a road club, and for good reason. In nine home games, two in May, one in August, four in September and two in October, they drew approximately 18,000 fans to Muehlebach Field in nine home games.[70] With the Depression breathing down their necks, they had to live on the road to survive. And still, they "played 162 games and lost only 18 of them."[71]

In April, the Monarchs spent most of the month in Texas and Oklahoma, whipping-up on the Waco Cardinals, Houston Black Buffalos, Dallas Black Giants and Chicago's American Giants. From there they traveled to Denver, over to Chicago, and back into Kansas and Oklahoma. Some of the Monarchs' staunchest competition had come from the American Giants, whom they had battled to a 2–1 advantage in games won in Muskogee, Oklahoma City and Tulsa. The series continued on into Wichita, where the clubs were scheduled to play two additional games.

Wichita, in preparing for the large crowd, set up a special reserved section for the "colored fans" in the east wing of Lawrence Stadium. When interviewed, Chicago's Willie Foster, who had reportedly gone 31–3 the previous year, made the following comments. "Those Monarchs play nothing but semi-pro clubs and we hope to run up the score against them," said Foster. "They've been advertising themselves as the leading Negro club in baseball ever since they withdrew from the national colored league. The truth of the matter is that they haven't had a good enough club to finish in first place in our league in the last three years."[72]

The Monarchs took the opener, 13–8, shelling Willie Foster early. Kansas City touched up the offerings of a trio of Chicago's hurlers for 18 hits. Foster started on the mound but was relieved when the Monarchs pushed over a pair of runs in the second, added another in the third and then uncorked eight runs in the fourth. Rogan, playing in left field, went 1-for-4 at-bat, with a double. Willard Brown homered.

The following night, the Monarchs returned to Lawrence Stadium and took a 10–8 verdict from the American Giants. Rogan's sacrifice hit, when he batted for Kranson in the ninth, tied the game. Mayweather's single in the tenth, sending two men home, capped the Monarchs' ten-inning victory. The game was a wild one from the start, with four players, Norman "Turkey" Stearnes, George "Mule" Suttles, and Jack Marshall for Chicago and Trouppe of the Monarchs, hitting four-ply blasts.[73] On the following night, in Emporia, Kansas, the Monarchs captured another game, 11–9, in a home run derby. That night, Alex Radcliffe hit three home runs, Chili Mayweather two, Willard Brown one, Jack Marshall one and T. J. Young one.[74] Altogether it was a bad day for pitchers, Chicago getting 13 hits and Kansas City 15.

After pounding the Boosters by a 3–1 score in a water-soaked affair in Burlington, Kansas, the Monarchs jumped over to Emporia to battle the Hawaiian All-Stars. Charlie Beverly proceeded to pitch an eight-hitter and struck out five in the Monarchs' 4–3 win.[75]

In late May, the Monarchs were in Denver's Merchant Park, downing the White Elephants and Denver Athletic Club in a doubleheader. Eddie Dwight starred in the two games with a 6-for-11 day at-bat and eight stolen bases.[76] From Denver, the team worked its way into North Dakota.

When the Monarchs returned to the upper Midwest, the *Devils Lake Journal* displayed a rare photograph of Rogan in its newspaper, with the following caption. "Rogan is one of the greatest all-around players in colored baseball, and formerly a stellar hurler. [He] performs in the outfield for the Kansas City Monarchs, where the veteran's hitting power can be utilized."[77]

Leroy "Satchel" Paige, 1935. While pitching in the 1934 *Denver Post* Tournament, Paige was selected as the tournament's best pitcher. He was the whole show on the mound, striking out 44 batters in only 28 innings — 41 percent of the batters who faced him.

On June 9, the Monarchs trimmed the Devils Lake team, 5–2, before what the *Journal* called "the largest crowd in years."[78] Rogan played first base and had 12 putouts. In capturing the victory, the Monarchs defeated Paul Kardow, a pitcher that would go to the Cleveland Indians in 1936. In Valley City, North Dakota, the *Valley City Times-Recorder* noted of Rogan, "Bullet Joe Rogan, one of the greatest pitchers ever in colored baseball, is still able to take his turn in the box, and is also used as utility man on the club. Rogan has been one of the great all around players ever in baseball."[79] Brewer went on to defeat Valley City by an 8–3 score. Rogan played first base, went 1-for-4, and scored two runs. The following afternoon the team crowned Jamestown in a 21 hit, 16–6 blitz.[80]

Some of the Monarchs' best games that year were played against the mixed race team at Bismarck, North Dakota, where Leroy "Satchel" Paige was virtually unbeatable on the mound. In 1935, Paige was fast, very fast. An edition of the *Kansas City Journal* acknowledged "Whether or not Paul Dean is faster [than Dizzy] is a question that has not been settled by National League batsmen. However, Jimmy Zinn, former star pitcher of the Blues, and Max Thomas, who was number one man of the Blues' staff in 1929, both vote for Satchel Paige as the fastest in the game."[81] Newt Allen, in discussing his good friend's fun-loving attitude to all these accolades, concluded, "He could laugh, and dance, and sing. He was a man who just loved life itself."[82]

Paige, Quincy Troupe, Hilton Smith, Barney Morris, Ted "Double Duty" Radcliffe and Red Haley were all members of that Bismarck team.

Trouppe had jumped the Monarchs in early June to catch Paige in Bismarck.[83] Radcliffe had exited the Claybrook Tigers to get his shot with Bismarck. Paige had joined from the Pittsburgh Crawfords.

The first time the two teams met was at Winnipeg's Osborne Stadium on June 6. That game, a scoreless pitchers' battle between Paige and Brewer, was called after nine innings on account of the cool temperatures. When it ended, the two pitchers had 30 strikeouts between them, 17 for Paige and 13 for Brewer.[84] The *Winnipeg Evening Tribune* noted that Paige "display[ed] more smoke than Winnipeg fans ha[d] seen since Lefty Grove pitched here in the fall of 1933."[85]

Paige nearly lost the game in the sixth when Leroy Taylor beat out a bunt to start Kansas City's half. After the next two batters were retired, T. J. Young came through with a scratch single, Taylor being held at third. Paige purposely passed big Mayweather, filling the bases, and then wasted Willard Brown on three pitched balls to end the threat.

Both pitchers received brilliant support, the only error of the game coming in the third when Newt Allen let a grounder go through his legs. Paige held the Monarchs to seven hits while Brewer allowed five. The following day, Kansas City edged Bismarck by a 2–1 score, as Floyd Kranson struck out ten Bismarck batters and limited them to four hits. "A double by [Willard] Brown followed by [Newt] Joseph's triple gave the Monarchs a run in the second and they added another on a hit by Taylor, a sacrifice and [Bullet] Rogan's slash to center."[86]

On Saturday, June 9, the two teams split a doubleheader, Paige beating Charlie Beverly in the opener, 11–4, and Kansas City winning the nightcap, 3–1. The two teams met for a second series beginning on June 10. In game one, the Monarchs bunched 18 hits and won, 14–3, in East Grand Forks, Minnesota. The series then moved to Bismarck for a doubleheader, on June 16, where Kansas City won a 2–1 opener behind Charlie Beverly's three-hit, eight strikeout pitching. Paige won the nightcap on a 12 strikeout, five-hit effort. Brewer, although giving up six hits, suffered the Monarchs' 2–0 loss.[87] After their battles with Bismarck the Monarchs headed further west.

By late June, the Monarchs were in Portland, Oregon. They visited Seattle, Vancouver, Bellingham and other major Northwest cities. Rogan was promoted heavily throughout the region. "'Bullet Joe' Rogan, one of the greatest Negro stars of all time," wrote one newspaper, "is still carried by the team, though he is well along in years, and he can still turn in a creditable performance at any position on the diamond."[88]

Most of July found them around Seattle, Yakima and Tacoma, Washington. In Yakima,

LeRoy Taylor. Taylor, after retiring from the Monarchs, became a 33rd Degree mason.

they slaughtered the Indians of the Northwest League, 19–1.[89] After the Monarchs beat Tacoma's Northwest League team, 7–1, Tacoma's *News Tribune* reported, "The game last night was the 27th straight [win] for the Negro club and the 61st in 66 games played this season."[90] In a return game in Yakima, the Monarchs were victorious by a 10–3 score, as Newt Joseph, Chili Mayweather, Bob Madison and T. J. Young crowned the victory with home runs.[91] The home runs had equaled the Monarchs' mark of four, hit in the same city during a 1934 game by Dink Mothell, Newt Allen, and two by Bullet Rogan.[92]

As the 1935 season raged, the Monarchs continued to pound the ball lively. In Missoula, Montana, during a July 20 game against the House of David, Rogan blasted three home runs.[93] By mid–July, the Monarchs were winning with alarming regularity. The *Kansas City Call* proclaimed, "The club has played 79 games to date, losing four."[94] The same article acknowledged that Mayweather "hit 20 home runs in 50 games." Mayweather's numbers were put up in spite of missing 20 games with a sprained knee. All along their way the Monarchs brought attention to the need for realistic travel accommodations for African Americans.

When traveling, African Americans were prohibited from using public restrooms or anything else that was designated for "whites only." They were also Jim Crowed at most restaurants. In a few places, even the pay telephone was Jim Crowed. Finding a hotel for the night was an equally grueling task.

While visiting Seattle, Washington, the Monarchs lodged at the U.S. Hotel in the local downtown section of the city. The hotel was owned by a Japanese American named Joe Genki Miyagawa. The family also owned a local produce company. Miyagawa's hotel was a familiar stopping off point for minority entertainers, athletes and railroad men in the Northwest. The team was so well attached to the Miyagawa family that their son Hiro acted in the capacity of bat boy at local games. He also traveled with the Monarchs, acting in the capacity of mascot as they toured in the region. The U.S. Hotel closed during World War II when the United States government forced Miyagawa's entire family into an internment camp and seized his property.* Some years later, the historic U.S. Hotel's 315 Maynard Street property was turned into low rent apartments.[95]

In August of 1935, the Monarchs were in the region near Missoula, Montana. That same month they won three games from the House of David in Saskatoon, Canada. And yet, before that month ended the Monarchs played their way back to Neodesha, Kansas, touring almost exclusively against the House of David. When the two teams appeared in Moberly, Missouri's Airport Park on August 23, Rogan tossed a complete game 6–2 win, a nine-hitter with four strikeouts.[96] When the Monarchs finally reached Kansas City, they were boasting a record of "101 games won out of 115" games played.[97] Another account of their record showed them as "winning 118 and losing 15."[98]

In September of 1935, the Monarchs signed Satchel Paige to their roster for the final 30 or so games of the season. By the time Paige joined the Monarchs he had already struck out more than 359 batters with Bismarck, and as a Monarch he continued to add to this total.

---

*From comments in an interview with Hiro Miyagawa in Chicago in 1996 while I was speaking at Chicago University. His father was the owner of the United States Hotel. Miyagawa had an original photograph of the 1933 Monarchs to back his claim that he had acted as a bat boy for the team during their trips to Seattle and to nearby cities in Washington state.

Paige got into many games for the Monarchs during the balance of the 1935 season. In Denver, he won, 9–0, and struck out eight.[99] Over in Omaha, the Monarchs defeated the American Giants, 6–3, in a late September game. Paige pitched the first two innings, striking out four of the six men he faced. In capturing that contest, J. L. Wilkinson's teams kept intact their record of never having lost in Omaha in more than 20 years — 15 years for the Monarchs and five for the All-Nations.[100]

In yet another game, Paige was beaten, 7–1, by the American Giants at Chicago's Comiskey Park before a crowd of 7,000. In that game Paige struck out eight.[101] When the Monarchs beat the major league All-Stars in Omaha in late October, a team that featured Charlie Gehringer, Schoolboy Rowe and Tommy Bridges, Paige struck out five batters in three innings.[102] Several days prior, on October 15, Paige's pitching whipped the Lincoln, Nebraska, All-Stars, bolstered by three members of Detroit's American League Tigers, 4–1. In that game Paige fanned Gehringer and three of his mates during his two-inning performance.[103] After that the Monarchs went south to San Antonio, Texas, where they battled La Junta at that city's Tech Field. By season's end, Paige's strikeout totals reached 500 batters — a phenomenal record in any era.

The Monarchs also got three more shots at Dizzy Dean — once in Springfield, Missouri, once in Kansas City and another in St. Joseph. When the tour's reported 20-game schedule opened, Dizzy predicted he would "make more money on this trip than in a whole season with the Cards."[104] Attendance, however, was way off compared to the previous year's barnstorming series. Cold weather helped to curtail the series as well. The fact that Dizzy and Paul weren't the national heroes they were in 1934, after leading St. Louis to a world championship, probably figured into the decrease as well.

In Kansas City, Dean's All-Stars won, 1–0, in front of a small 2,000 in paid attendance. The weather was more suited for football, and yet, "Satchel" Paige hurled the full nine innings, allowing three hits and striking out 11 batters. In the seventh, he whiffed three men in succession. Dizzy Dean hurled only one inning, the fourth. Paul Dean toiled the fifth and sixth, being relieved by Mort Cooper. Mike Ryba, another St. Louis Cardinal, pitched the first three innings. Rogan was 1-for-3 on the afternoon. His hit, coming off Dizzy, accounted for only one of the Monarchs' seven hits.[105] Henry Milton and Eddie Dwight picked up two hits each in the game. Prior to the Kansas City game, the two teams had met in Springfield, where the Monarchs downed the dynamic duo, 8–1, in front of 4,300 paid customers. The two teams battled in St. Joseph, much to the disappointment of the local fans, who wanted to see Satchel Paige more than either of the Deans.

The St. Joseph game was advertised as a Dean versus Paige classic. The pair had met only a day earlier in Kansas City, and in spite of Paige having gone the distance in that game, they assumed he would take the mound again. Equally as complex was the effect Paige was having on the rest of the Monarchs' squad. Prior to the arrival of Paige, the Monarchs were usually received as a team. With Paige grabbing all of the headlines and national press, St. Joseph fans didn't care to see any other Monarchs pitchers. When the more than 2,000 people assembled, they called for "Paige, the greatest Negro pitcher in the world."[106] When it was announced that Andy Cooper would pitch, the crowd "kept yelling for Paige." When Cooper retired after the end of the third inning, the crowd "yelled for Paige again." They got Floyd Kranson instead and the disappointment continued.

When the Deans abruptly called the game after five innings, with the Monarchs leading,

1–0, fans went away disillusioned. Explaining why Paige failed to make an appearance, one local newspaper added, "Paige's contract with the Monarchs expired a day before yesterday."[107] Confused by the demands that white fans had put on Frank Haley, owner of the local Saints team, Wilkinson admitted, "I didn't think they wanted to see Paige," he said. "I thought they came out to see the Deans."

The Monarchs finished the home portion of the summer with a big 6–0 win over the World Series All-Stars at Kansas City's Muehlebach Field. Schoolboy Rowe and Tommy Bridges pitched two innings each, and Charles Gehringer, voted the hero of the World Series, played second base.

For Rogan, the low point of the 1935 season had very little to do with baseball — it was personal. In September, his brother Willard was murdered in Kansas City, Kansas. No one was totally surprised and yet the death still came as a shock. Following Willard's pardon from Lansing, a Kansas State prison, in 1924, he returned to Kansas City and got involved with the same group that had led him into crime. This time, however, it was a fatal mistake. Willard was found shot to death — a tragic end to a life gone wrong. Having served time in both the Missouri and Kansas state penitentiaries, Willard died a broken and contrite man.[108]

Shortly after Willard's funeral, Bullet Rogan decided to restore his own faith in Jesus Christ. In late September, the entire Rogan family joined Gregg Tabernacle AME Church in Kansas City, Missouri.[109]

It was obvious that the media had calculated wrong in its appraisal of African American baseball talent. Instead of judging players based on ability, the media seemed more interested in perpetuating race superiority. Arbiters of fair play they were not. And while a few African American athletes had gotten some positive press, many, Bullet Rogan, Chet Brewer, Willard Brown and Charlie Beverly included among them, had gotten little. It would, over the course of time, prove to be an error of major league proportions. Worse yet, the end to such neglectful oversight appeared to be nowhere in sight.

11

A Hero's Farewell

Funny thing about this fellow Rogan, he never seems ready to quit. Year after year finds him in there doing his best, which is quite a bit and never once folding up under the hottest fire.— Kansas City American, *March 21, 1929*

Bullet Rogan's hitting had kept him in the Monarchs' lineup long after his arm had lost the endurance to take a regular turn in the box. By sheer ability, his transition from pitcher to position player was accomplished with relative ease. Even his career, as interesting as it had been, was nearing the seventh-inning stretch. Retirement, a logical move for most 40-year-olds, was just entering Rogan's mind. Then again, Rogan wasn't your normal 40-year-old. Even at his advanced age it would take two men to replace him—one for the hitting and another to do the pitching.

Realizing that Rogan was one of only a few active players that had started with the Negro National League in 1920 attested to his durability. League rosters had changed hundreds of times, and yet here was Rogan, a real survivor, hitting with the best of them. His eyes, the whites a little faded with time, were still eager and sharp enough for hundreds of more games. His teammate, the weary old lefty named Andy Cooper, was a survivor too.

Cooper, who had taken over as manager of the Kansas City Monarchs in 1936, was immediately consumed with rebuilding a winning team. The departure of several veterans exasperated his efforts. Chet Brewer and T. J. Young had gone to the New York Cubans, and Frank Duncan had become a member of the Pittsburgh Crawfords. The Monarchs picked up three new pitchers, two right-handers, Mike "Tudie" Berry and Willie B. Mays. They also added Woodrow Wilson, a left-hander with a submarine delivery, from Mexia, Texas. Mays, born September 16, 1916, at Prague, Oklahoma, failed to make the grade after being scouted by Frank Duncan and Eddie Dwight, who recruited him from Kansas City's Brooklyn Giants. Mays recalled, "in kangaroo court the old timers wanted part of my eating money."[1]

It was the trickery of one of his buddies, however, that put him on the outs with manager Andy Cooper. "In Springfield, I believe, a guy hit a home run off me, and another guy got a hit," recalled Mays. "Then I heard a whistle. A whistle was the signal manager Cooper gave when he wanted to change pitchers. It sounded like Cooper's whistle too." Mays whirled his head and saw "Tudie" Berry coming to the mound, and naturally he handed the ball to his relief. When he reached the dugout, Cooper, who had been preoccupied with something else, looked up and said "What are you doing little man?" Cooper took one look at the mound and responded, "That red son of a bitch!" On the very next batter, Berry gave up a home run.[2]

Wilkinson had also sought the services of Satchel Paige in 1936. "I tried to sign Paige but couldn't afford to pay him $500 a month, which is what he'll get at Bismarck, North

Kansas City Monarchs, 1936. Seated, from left: Newt Allen, Harry Else, Wilber "Bullet" Rogan, Henry Milton, Eddie Dwight. Standing, from left: Andy Cooper, Pat Patterson, Woodrow Wilson, Curtis Harris, Floyd Kranson, Bob Madison, Willard Brown, LeRoy Taylor. Taylor, in spite of a chronic knee injury, was a highly regarded outfielder. "Taylor would be chasing a fly ball or running a base when that trick knee would jump out of place," George Giles recalled. "He would have to stop and pop it back into the socket, then proceed with the play."

Dakota."[3] A catcher named Harry Else who joined from the Monroe Louisiana Monarchs and collegiate infielder Pat Patterson were recruited as well for the 1936 roster. Patterson had come from Pittsburgh's Crawfords; prior to that he'd played for Pittsburgh's Homestead Grays. As a collegian he'd been a track and baseball star at Wiley College. With Patterson, Milton and Taylor of Wiley College, Wilson and Kranson from Piney Woods College, the Monarchs were one of the most intellectual barnstorming teams on the road. Further additions to the roster were made as the season progressed.

Bob Webster, a left-hander, joined from Buffalo, New York, in late August. Hilton Smith and Barney Morris, two additional pitchers who arrived in September, came to the Monarchs from Bismarck, North Dakota, along with Quincy Trouppe. The new players made their presence known. Webster and Morris would establish a record by combining for 20 strikeouts in a game at Peoria, Illinois — Wilson getting 12 all by himself.[4]

Rogan was responsible for scouting at least two of the Monarchs' young prospects when he signed Ollie Boyd in 1933 and Mike "Tudie" Berry in 1936. Berry, a product of Kansas City's Lincoln High School, remembered how Rogan helped him to become a Monarch. "I was playing for the Boulevard Donkeys in Kansas City, Kansas," Berry recalled, "and after the game Rogan, who was there with trainer James 'Jew Baby' Floyd, asked me if I wanted to pitch for the Kansas City Monarchs." Neither Boyd nor Berry survived the rigors of Negro leagues play, though both were later stars for Harry Crump's famous Colored House of David team.

The Monarchs remained strictly a road club in 1936. Only nine games were played in Kansas City, the remainder being played on the road. In some months the team's total mileage exceeded that which many National and American League teams traveled in an entire season — spring training included. Their traveling conditions, as compared to those of the major leaguers, were clearly second-rate. "The team travels in two specially made traveling hotels," wrote the *Springfield News Leader*, "large rooms on wheels which include two lower and two upper berths, hot and cold running water, plenty of closet space for suits, shoes and hats, wash basins, and even a shower."[5]

Early April found the Monarchs in Enid, Oklahoma, where they battled Nick Urban's powerful Eason Oilers. Always troublesome, the Oilers defeated the Monarchs by a 9–6 score. In that game, Hugh Willingham, who used to patrol the infield for Chicago's White Sox and Philadelphia's Phillies, poled a home run. Milt Perry, Enid's ace pitcher, held Kansas City to seven hits. Mayweather, with two of his team's hits, also hammered a home run. The Oilers "got sweet revenge to the tune of 9-to-6 for some drubbings handed the local team in past years,"[6] wrote a local newspaper. One of the losses had occurred in the 1934 Denver Post tournament.

After four games in Springfield, Missouri, in late May, the Monarchs began June by visiting Madison, Wisconsin. From there they traveled to Peoria, Illinois, and back across to Sheboygan, Milwaukee and Green Bay in Wisconsin. In Green Bay, they defeated the Green Sox of the Northern State League by an excessive score, 12–0. That night, Kranson, who reportedly entered the game having won "10 games in 11 starts,"[7] captured the victory. While the Monarchs were spanking 19 hits, of which 11 went for extra bases, Kranson and Andy Cooper combined for a two-hitter.[8]

After that outing, the Monarchs worked their way to Spokane and over to Olympia, Washington. On June 28, they were in Casper, Wyoming, where they blanked the Casper Merchants, 9–0, behind the combined four-hit pitching of Kranson and Andy Cooper. In praising the Monarchs' pitchers, a local writer said, "Kranson, a young right hander in his second season with the Monarchs, pitched a nice game until relieved by manager Cooper himself. The youngster has a mighty fastball as well as a nice hook. He allowed only one hit, that a double by Guy Huey in the fourth."[9] Earlier, in Springfield, Missouri, Kranson had struck out 12 of that city's Western Association team.[10] He would nearly duplicate that feat with a ten strikeout performance in Vancouver, Canada, on July 8, where the Monarchs defeated the local U.D.L. team, 17–4. Their beating the locals in spectacular fashion — 15 hits, six of them for extra bases — prompted one local newspaper to note, "The colored boys played errorless ball, a smart, fast entertaining game that stamps them as probably the greatest touring team ever to perform here."[11]

As July turned into August, the Monarchs were in Regina and Swift Current, Saskatchewan, playing tournaments. The Acme Giants and Boston Giants, two rival African American teams, were simultaneously touring the same territory. When the Acme Giants failed to arrive for one of their scheduled games against the Boston Giants in Swift Current, a local white team decided to play a distasteful joke on its fans. "The local Cardinals stepped into the breach and appeared on the field all 'blackened' up,"[12] wrote one local newspaper, "and for a few minutes even fooled the home fans." The article further stated, "Galbraith, with a shock of red hair sticking out from under his cap, hardly made a hundred percent Negro, but on the whole the locals masqueraded quite well." Two days after that so-called "comedy de luxe" the Monarchs appeared at that same park and thumped the House of David. In capturing a 6–2 victory, Kranson limited the House of David crew to three hits, all of which came in the sixth inning, when the hits combined with a walk gave the House of David their two runs.[13]

A temporary stop in South Bend, Indiana, for a series against the Homestead Grays was another highlight of the season. It was the Monarchs' first meeting with the Homestead Grays in over four seasons. The series visited South Bend, Toledo, Indianapolis, Louisville and Dayton for a potpourri of night games.[14] After that series the Monarchs returned to Kansas City.

Although the travel had been extensive, player salaries suffered. Eddie Dwight's case was typical. "His salary was $125, and he earned an extra $25 a month by driving the bus. But after living on the road and sending money home, he had $45.73 coming to him at the end of the 1936 season."[15]

Oddly, 1936 was one of Rogan's best pitching campaigns in several seasons. That year, however, the arm had started to stiffen. He could still take a regular turn in the pitcher's box, it just took longer to recuperate. After games he massaged the arm with alcohol and wintergreen. The wintergreen made the alcohol hot and soothed the arm. The mixture allowed Rogan to pitch often — more than he had pitched in years. Ironically, two of his wins had come in towns known for their history of racial hatred — Monett, Missouri, and Springfield, Missouri.

In 1894, Ulysses Hayden, an African American, was taken from police custody and hanged from a telephone pole, for an alleged murder of a young white man. After the lynching, whites forced all African Americans to leave Monett, after which time they hung a sign, "Nigger, Don't let the Sun Go Down."[16] Similarly, whites in Springfield, the prime city of the Ozark Mountains, staged a triple lynching of three African Americans on Easter Sunday, 1906.[17]

In defeating Monett's Red Birds of the Arkansas–Missouri League, Rogan opened the game from the mound, pitching three innings of one-hit scoreless baseball. At-bat, his hit accounted for two of the Monarchs' seven runs.[18] Rogan returned to the mound in Springfield, Missouri, where he beat that city's Western Association League Cardinals, 8–5. In that game he allowed six hits and three runs in three innings and struck out a pair of batters.[19]

Motoring to Illinois, on May 30, Rogan pitched middle relief in the Monarchs' 7–3 loss to the Chicago Mills semiprofessional team.[20] He returned on June 29, and limited Billings, Montana, to seven hits in a well-pitched 7–0 win. Rogan also pitched successfully on July 13, when the Monarchs won, 9–4, over the House of David team in Helena, Montana. Rogan made yet another appearance on July 28, when he beat the Swift Current team in Saskatchewan, Canada. During an August 18 appearance in Charles City, Iowa, Rogan was credited with the victory as a pitcher and also hit a four-ply blast in his Monarchs' 9–3 win.[21] Rogan struck out eight members of the House of David during his outing. He returned to the mound on August 22, in the Monarchs' 7–5 loss to Madison at that city's Breese Stevens Field. Pitching in relief of Wilson, the losing pitcher, Rogan allowed four hits in two innings. Rounding out another return to star status, Rogan allowed three hits in three frames and struck out six Peoria batters in another performance.[22]

As a pitcher, Rogan reversed the clock on Chicago's American Giants twice in 1936.

The first of the two games was pitched at Muehlebach Field on August 31. In that contest Rogan pitched his last home win as a member of the Kansas City Monarchs. He allowed just three hits and no runs in six innings before giving way to a relief pitcher. The game ended in a 14–0 win for the Monarchs.[23] In a second game, an event that was played in Chicago on Labor Day, Rogan hurled nine innings of eight-hit ball. Disappointedly, only 500 people showed up for the holiday festivities, a stark contrast to the early 1920s, when the mere mention of Rogan going against Chicago's American Giants was sure to set attendance records nearly every time he pitched.

In nine games at Kansas City's Muehlebach Field, Rogan's batting average was .444. In spite of it all, the biggest news of 1936 wasn't wins, it wasn't even night baseball. It was home runs coming off the bats of Rogan's youthful teammates Pat Patterson and Willard Brown. It would have been a three-way slugging bee if Mayweather had not broken his leg in Borger, Texas, on May 12. "Mayweather pounded into home sliding feet first safely," pronounced the *Borger Daily Herald*. "As he hit the plate his right leg twisted acutely and he was carried from the field suffering from a broken bone in his ankle."[24] "The player who replaced the injured Monarch first baseman Mayweather in the fifth inning was none other than Rogan," penned the *Daily Herald*, "probably the widest known Negro baseball player in the country. He is a pitcher by trade and has aged, baseballically speaking, on the mound but still has enough activity to participate in the game with considerable ginger. In witness to his versatility he covered the first sack efficiently and slammed a single into center in the ninth."[25] Speaking of injuries, Curtis Harris, on the mend after breaking his finger two weeks earlier, replaced Mayweather at first base for the balance of the season.[26] Injuries were a common occurrence because of the African Americans' aggressive style of play.

Newt Allen recalled, "The majors wouldn't allow some of the things those players did — myself included. We didn't play by any books."[27] Allen added that he "had a habit of stepping on a baseman's foot when running the bases. Eventually, however, he seriously injured another player and it changed his playing style."[28]

Patterson and Brown pounded the ball at a lively pace throughout the entire summer, though prior to the 1936 season neither was recognized for his consistency of power. An adjustment in their stances, a change of bats and some new inspiration had changed their approach to hitting. Batting back-to-back, fourth and fifth in the lineup, Patterson and Brown started slugging in May and kept swinging right into October.

Patterson landed one of his first home runs against the Omaha Robin Hoods of the Western League in early May. He slammed another in Madison, Wisconsin's, Breese Stevens Field during a May 27 visit. In early June, Patterson blasted three home runs in a single game in Chicago.[29] The next week he hit home runs in Madison, Wisconsin, and Rock Island, Illinois.[30] He added another long ball in Green Bay on June 11, in the Monarchs' 12–0 win.

A local newspaper called that home run "one of the longest home runs ever hit at the [Joannes] Park."[31] By early July, when Patterson went 5-for-6 in Spokane, Washington, the one home run he hit was reported as his 25th of the season. The night before, in Kellogg, Montana, he had hit number 24. Patterson had also hit two home runs in a Tuesday night game at Vancouver's Athletic Park on July 8. On August 18, Patterson had slammed a pair of home runs in Charles City, Iowa, in a big 9–3 Monarchs win. Willard Brown, his slugging teammate, wasn't lagging far behind.

Brown was popping them just as frequently. In May he'd hit a home run when the Monarchs defeated the Western League's Springfield Cardinals, 5–4, at the Western League's White City Park. "Brown pounded out a homer over the right field fence with one on in the first inning to give the Monarchs a lead they never lost," penned a sports writer who had witnessed the blast.[32] In early July, Brown hit another in Billings, Montana. At East Helena's Legion Park, Brown hammered two more home runs. When the Monarchs swiped both ends of a doubleheader in Spokane, Brown ousted "the ball out of the park three times."[33]

In Vancouver, on July 9, Brown banged home run number 25. A day earlier he'd hit a pair of home runs, a double, and a triple, when the Monarchs beat yet another opponent in Vancouver.[34] On July 28, Brown's home run total reached 31. That's where the *Kansas City Call* stopped counting them, but it wasn't where Brown stopped hitting them. An August 28 edition of the *Kansas City Star* reported, "Brown, at short, has gained a world of confidence and his fielding has improved a hundred percent. He is hitting the old apple at a merry clip and is pressing Patterson closely for batting honors."

In a return trip to Madison, Wisconsin, Brown's long ball helped the Monarchs to a lopsided 13–0 win. In Peoria, Illinois, Brown homered and pushed three runs across in the Monarchs' 20–4 drubbing of that city's All-Star team.[35] One of Brown's home runs, the only one that was hit at Kansas City's Muehlebach Field, came on August 30. He hit it off Sug Cornelius in the Monarchs' 10–4 win over Chicago's American Giants.

Brown and Patterson both homered over 40 times in 1936. Their totals revealed yet another tragedy of racism in professional sports. Brown's contemporaries, Joe DiMaggio and Ted Williams, both members of baseball's Hall of Fame, combined for only 29 home runs that year. Williams and DiMaggio were dubbed rising stars, but Brown and Patterson went unnoticed. To prove his legitimacy, after major league integration, Brown hit ninety-five home runs in five years of minor league play, 1950 and 1953–1956.[36] He hit another 101 home runs in the Puerto Rican Winter League, which included a league record of 27 in a single season.[37] To top that off, Brown hit the first home run ever by an African American in the American League, on August 13, 1947, while playing for the St. Louis Browns.

No aspect of baseball was spared in this great omission of African American talent, especially pitchers. Chet Brewer, Satchel Paige, Sug Cornelius and Barney Morris were more than qualified not only to make, but to excel on any major league team. Big league managers, though, acted as if these men didn't exist and continued in their arrogance. "If [I] had another hurler that was only half as good as Dizzy [Dean]," stated Frankie Frisch, Cardinal manager, "the Cards would have the National League pennant sewed up each season by September 1."[38]

The Monarchs' new-found home run punch was manifesting itself in batting averages as well. In one important game at Wichita, numerous hits had led them to an impressive 14–4 victory over the National Negro All-Stars, winners of the Denver Post Tournament. Locking horns at Lawrence Stadium, Barney Morris' ten-hitter got the better of Bob Griffith, who allowed the Monarchs 17 hits. In that game, Brown went 3-for-5 and Patterson 4-for-5 to aid in the victory. In winning the game, the Monarchs extended their record to 39 games won in Wichita and only two losses over a 12 year span.[39]

In spite of the Monarchs' superior wealth of hitting and pitching, on several occasions they were bumped by antagonistic rivals. In an April 22 encounter in Enid, Oklahoma, they were edged, 9–6. On July 6, they were shut out, 4–0, in Yakima, Washington, by the local Indians team, a member of the Northwest League. In that game, Floyd Kranson took the loss in spite of pitching a six-hitter with 11 strikeouts.[40] Unfortunately for Yakima, the Monarchs returned a week later, and Kranson redeemed himself with a 12-strikeout, 8–6, shellacking of this same Indians opponent. A number of Monarchs starred in that encounter. Curtis Harris and Newt Allen both homered, Rogan went 2-for-4, Patterson was 3-for-5 with a pair of runs, and Brown was 3-for-5 with two runs scored.[41] The Monarchs were also defeated in Olympia, when the locals trounced the touring African Americans by a 6–5 score.

For the summer of 1936, the House of David team had changed their name to the Israelite House of David. Grover Cleveland Alexander was no longer associated with the club. Consumed with life outside baseball — and it wasn't very pleasant — Alexander was found unconscious in a gutter in the Evansville, Indiana, business district. At first it was believed he was dying, but a later diagnosis revealed a slight concussion and a big hangover. When asked about it, Alexander commented, "I was drinking beer at Lauteuschlager's Tavern and then I started downtown about 3:30 a.m., after that it's all a blank." The Davids, even without Alexander in their lineup, were still pleasing large crowds.

Fred Lawson, a member of that year's Israelite House of David team, remembered. "They [the Monarchs] were tough, and their roster boasted several players of major-league caliber. One afternoon we were scheduled to play them in the Canadian town of Hershel. When we arrived, we couldn't believe what we saw — just a crossroads on the prairie with a couple of buildings. When the Monarchs arrived, their manager and John [Tucker] took

John R. Tucker and Doc Tally (first and second, respectively, on the left) with two unidentified men. Tally was the Davids' great home run hitter. An outstanding first baseman, Tucker was capable of playing big league baseball, but his loyalty was first and foremost to the House of David.

a look at the deserted bleachers and decided to pull out and take a day of rest. Then a big redheaded Canadian walked up. 'Wait a minute!' he thundered. 'I've got a contract with you guys. You'll play or else!' He looked pretty tough, so we decided we'd better play, crowd or no crowd. But it wasn't long before people started arriving in wagons and buggies from all directions. Before the day was over, there were over 1,500 people there — and were they ever — wild fans! At the end of the nine innings, they still had not had enough and couldn't understand why we didn't just keep on playing."[42]

The Monarchs stopped momentarily for the 1936 East-West game in Chicago, something they hadn't done in the past. As expected, there was a history behind the Monarchs' boycott of the annual East-West festivities.

The East-West game was the invention of Pittsburgh Crawfords owner Gus Greenlee. On July 6, 1933, the American and National leagues had staged the first-ever All-Star game at Chicago's Comiskey Park, during the World's Fair. That same year Greenlee staged a similar event and called it the East-West game. The first East-West game was played in September of 1933 at Chicago's Comiskey Park. Supposedly, a ballot system was used to select players for the first East-West game.

Not surprisingly, the always-popular Rogan jumped into an early lead in that year's balloting. Uniquely, he was the only player selected for two positions — pitcher and outfield. On August 12, the *Chicago Defender* reported, "Old Bullet Rogan may be all washed up with some fans, but not so with those that have sent in early choices for the all-star game to be played in Comiskey Park the afternoon of September 10. So anxious are they to have the great pitcher-outfielder named, some are nominating him for an outfield berth, while others wish to see him pitch as of old. Like Babe Ruth, Rogan remains a big favorite with the fans throughout the country."[43]

In late August, Al Monroe, writing for the *Associated Negro Press*, noted that Bullet Rogan appeared certain for one of the outfield posts on the all-star team. Shortly thereafter Monroe wrote that Rogan suffered in fan appeal as "Chicago's voting ladies and gents got busy over the week-end and as a result [Steel Arm] Davis pushed him [Rogan] down to fourth place."[44]

Chicago and Kansas City had fairly well dominated the voting. Hard-hitting T. J. Young was selected over Chicago's Larry Brown at catcher. Adding in Kansas City's George Giles at first base and Newt Allen at second Kansas City had three of the top vote-getters. The *Defender* concluded, "Fans who also figured on reserve power, placed [Leroy] Morney, the Honus Wagner of the West, as first utility, and named [Mule] Suttles and Rogan, who is now in the twilight of a brilliant career as his running mate."

Negro League representatives felt that the players should have received a percentage of the gate from the East-West game. Greenlee decided against paying the players a percentage of the gate and the Monarchs boycotted the game.

On the day of the first-ever East-West game, Rogan, Brewer and Giles gave All-Star performances, but it wasn't in Chicago, it was reportedly in Wichita, Kansas.[45] That afternoon Brewer pitched an eight-hitter, and Rogan and Giles plowed home runs. Bill Gibson, writing in the *Baltimore Afro-American*, noted, "Newt Allen of Kansas City was reported to have been with the [East-West] team but didn't get in the game. Young, Brewer and Giles lived up to their word and didn't come here to play." Reports of attendance anywhere from 15,000 to 23,000 were carried in the press releases. In a statement coming directly from Harry Grabiner of the Chicago White Sox, who was in charge of the park's affairs that day, showed that only 11,380 fans entered the park for that first East-West game. Grabiner's total had included the pass gates as well as the paid admissions.

And while there were no current Monarchs in the 1935 lineup, their presence could be felt by the many former Monarchs that appeared in the lineups. For the East, George Giles, and the West's James "Cool Papa" Bell, Willie Wells and Norman "Turkey" Stearnes all made appearances.

All had changed in 1936 when Rogan, Eddie Dwight, Henry Milton, Newt Allen, Harry Else, Willard Brown, Pat Patterson, Floyd Kranson, Andy Cooper and Curtis Harris came to Chicago representing the Monarchs in that summer's East-West game.

The crowd that visited Comiskey Park realistically numbered 30,000. Rogan went 0-for-1 in his only appearance at the plate, and the West lost 10–2.[46]

Rogan and Harry Else were also participants for the South in the annual North-South classic in 1937. The North-South series, unfortunately for its originators Doctor J. B. Martin, L. S. N. Cobb, Doctor B. B. Martin, Tom Wilson and Gus Greenlee, never achieved the popularity of the East-West game. The first game was played on October 7, 1934, in Nashville, Tennessee. In 1935, the event was staged on September 29 in Memphis, Tennessee. By the time Rogan suited up for the North team in the North-South classic, it had become a series with games in Birmingham, Memphis, Atlanta and Nashville. That year the North won rather handily.

The 1937 East-West Classic, millions of dollars' worth of major league talent. Rogan appears in the front row, third from the right. This was his only appearance in the All-Star classic.

All-Star games, World Series and playoffs, Rogan had done it all, and yet, he did not possess any obvious signs of wealth. His car was not flamboyant and his home wasn't a mansion either. He drove a black, four-door Buick Master 8, trunk in the rear with spare tires mounted on both sides. Rogan lived in the heart of Kansas City at 1308 Michigan. It was a modest two-bedroom structure with a living room and a big kitchen that stretched across the whole house.

In 1937, long-time Monarchs Eddie Dwight and Newt Joseph retired. For Joseph, it was the end of a well-traveled 16 year career, most, if certainly not all, of which was spent with Kansas City's Monarchs. Who could have imagined that Joseph would attain such celebrity status in sports?

Joseph was born in Montgomery, Alabama, in 1899 into a family of seven brothers and one sister. His mother died in 1902. His father, Edward Joseph, quickly remarried and left the care of the children with Ida, their stepmother. The family eventually relocated to Muskogee, Oklahoma, where Joseph attended the segregated public schools of that city. In fact, Joseph lived right across the street from the local high school for African Americans. Nelson Dean, Henry Williams and Wilson "Frog" Redus were among the other future Monarchs attending this same school. In 1921 Joseph separated himself from the pack, and joined the Sandcrabs of Galveston, Texas. His big break came the following year when Bartolo Portuando broke his leg, leaving the Monarchs desperately in need of a third baseman. Joseph joined the Monarchs in 1922 and ultimately beat his Cuban counterpart out of the position, to become the team's regular third baseman until 1937. Willard Brown described Joseph as a "chatter box on the infield. He had one of the best arms you ever wanted to see. When I first came up, I only wanted to be like Newt Joseph and Newt Allen."[47]

In those early years, third base was considered by many to be the most difficult position on the infield. "I admit that short is a very hard position," responded Pete Hill, a former manager of the Detroit Stars, "but to my mind, third base is worse." Bill Francis, a onetime infielder from Chicago's American Giants, concurred, "The toughest position on the infield? You know what I think, third base."[48]

In leaving the Monarchs, Joseph was content to invest his time with running his prosperous Monarch Cab Company. He had started the business with two or three Fords in 1929. At one time or another, Bullet Rogan and Newt Allen drove cabs owned by Joseph during the offseason. During the winter of 1932-1933, Joseph bought 13 new cabs, FOB from Detroit. The new cabs had giant baseballs on the side. In 1934 he also opened a gas station.

Joseph was famous for having hit the first home run of the 1924 Negro World Series. He had also hit for the cycle, with a single, double, triple and home run in a single game on Christmas Eve of 1928, during a Cuban Winter League game. His younger brother, Wilson, was a ballplayer also, having played for a number of teams that included Gilkerson's Union Giants.

Wilkinson also took his team off the barnstorming circuit in 1937. He converted the Monarchs from a strictly barnstorming team and placed them into the newly formed Negro American League. This move increased Monarchs home games from ten in 1936 to 29 in 1937.

Even at an advanced age of 44, with the Monarchs back in an organized league, Rogan wasn't about to call it quits. He wasn't going to stop playing professional ball until he had added two more illustrious seasons to his already brilliant record.

The Monarchs' 1937 season was packed full of adjustments. After opening spring training in Monterrey, Mexico, where they "played 14 games, winning 12 and losing two," Kansas City returned stateside.[49] Early in the campaign, during a two-game series in Kansas, the Monarchs were defeated by the Water Works team — their first loss to a local semi-professional team in 17 years of visiting Wichita. The Watermen featured Al Nusser, who had reportedly turned back the Monarchs on three occasions in 1936, while hurling for the House of David.[50] Directly following the loss at Wichita the Monarchs manhandled Enid, Oklahoma, by the score of 9–6. In that game, Hugh Willingham hit two home runs, one off Woodrow Wilson, the other off Hilton Smith. According to one article, Kansas City's Monarchs were "seeking some revenge on the locals, for two defeats last season."[51]

The Monarchs were also bumped off in a 9–7 clash in Pampa, Texas, despite Rogan's 3-for-5 day at bat and two RBIs.[52] Before May had ended, Enid's Eason Oilers had gotten their own revenge. In a massive 14–2 blowout, Kansas City's Monarchs were held to three hits by Enid's Milt Perry. The Monarchs' only scoring had come in the fourth, on an Allen single and a Willard Brown home run.[53] Perry, a thorn for the Monarchs, had beaten Kansas City on a three-hitter in 1936. Enid's Eason Oilers took the 1937 series of three games from the Monarchs with a final victory in mid–June. In spite of Mayweather's home run and Rogan's 2-for-4 performance, that had included a double, the limitation of seven hits, three double plays and numerous batters striking out helped Enid to beat Monarchs ace Hilton Smith.[54]

The most notable of the new faces in 1937 were those of Jess Brooks of Tacoma, Washington, Byron "Mex" Johnson of Little Rock, Arkansas, Packing House Adams of St. Louis and Ted Strong, a Chicago native whom the Monarchs got from the Indianapolis ABCs. The most important change, however, was Hilton Smith, who ultimately would replace Andy Cooper as the Monarchs' pitching ace.

You couldn't help but notice the similarities between Hilton Smith and Bullet Rogan. Both were excellent right-handed pitchers. Both were equally outstanding hitters. Neither was flashy. Both were deadly in the clutch.

Hilton Smith was born on February 27, 1912, in Sour Lake, Texas, the oldest of six children born to Professor John H. and Mattie Smith.* His father had been an educator at Prairie View College. "Even as a child," according to one of Smith's sisters, "Hilton loved to take rocks and hit them with broom sticks." After graduating from Giddings Texas High, which was followed by a brief stay at Prairie View College, Smith joined the Senators, a team based in Austin, Texas.

In 1932 he reportedly won 32 consecutive games. That total included two wins over the champion Monroe Monarchs of Louisiana in the Dixie Series. The following year he joined the Monroe Monarchs of Monroe, Louisiana. In November of 1934 he married Louise Humphrey in Monroe, Louisiana. The next year the Monroe Monarchs toured the upper Midwest, all the way into parts of Canada. When the team ran into financial troubles, Smith connected with the Bismarck, North Dakota, team and ultimately a deal was struck with the Kansas City Monarchs to bring him to Kansas City in 1936.

Smith was a pitcher who was capable of having Rogan-type days in the batter's box.

---

*Hilton Smith said that he was born in Giddings, Texas. An older sister, Norva Burdine, informed me that Hilton was born in Sour Lake, Texas.

Smith offered, "I could have probably made it into the majors as an outfielder; my hitting was so good. I was one player they didn't have a pinch hitter for."[55] It seemed as though Rogan and Smith were chipped from the same flint. For instance, Smith batted 5-for-5, with two doubles and three singles, in the Monarchs' 16–1 win over the Indianapolis ABCs in 1938. He came back and struck out 12 of the ABCs in yet another game in the same series.

On August 14, 1937, Smith drove in the first two Monarchs runs when he doubled to the left-field wall and went on to win that game by striking out nine batters. In a 1938 game at Enid, Oklahoma, he and Byron Johnson plastered back-to-back home runs to beat a strong Eason Oilers team.[56]

Smith recalled, "I had a fastball estimated at 95 miles per hour and one of the best curveballs that has ever been in baseball."[57] If ever there was a man destined to fill Rogan's shoes it was Smith — a statement that was confirmed by many of his teammates.

"[Smith was an] outstanding pitcher, great, great curveball, one of the best I've ever seen," said John "Buck" O'Neil. "He was an outstanding hitter, could wear the ball out. For a span of maybe five or six years Hilton Smith may have been the best pitcher in the

Floyd Kranson (second from left) and Hilton Smith (to the right of Kranson) with two unidentified men, 1939. In 1937 Smith pitched a no-hitter in Kansas City. Georgia Dwight, who was in attendance that night, remembered, "No one paid much attention until the seventh inning. Then we realized that no one had been on base. Then it got very quiet. In the ninth when Smith got that last out, we acted like we were insane."

world." Connie Johnson agreed. "The first time I saw Smith was in Fort Wayne, Indiana. He looked funny out there with the uniform on, he just didn't look like a ballplayer. Before the night was over I found out who Hilton Smith was. Nobody ever threw me three of the fastest balls or hit me as hard as Hilton Smith hit me that night. To tell you the truth, I think Hilton Smith was the best pitcher I have ever seen."[58]

Several of that year's Monarchs also performed in the annual East-West game. Newt Allen, Willard Brown, Henry Milton, Hilton Smith and Andy Cooper were all selected to the squad.[59]

Smith went on to post a 9–1 record at Kansas City's Muehlebach Field. On May 15, he added a no-hit game when he beat Chicago's American Giants at Kansas City.

Slugger Willard Brown posted a .406 average (52–128), with six doubles, seven triples and 13 home runs at Muehlebach. Brown would also post his second consecutive 40-plus home run campaign in 1937. According to one source, Brown had cracked "42 home runs in league warfare last year."[60]

Infielder Byron "Mex" Johnson had been discovered while playing semi-pro ball with the DuBisson Tigers in his home town of Little Rock. He then moved up to the professional Little Rock Stars, in the

Byron Johnson. A great fielding shortstop, he joined the Monarchs in mid-season 1937 from Wiley College and immediately had difficulties because of his inability to hit curve balls. "Rogan and I would go to the park early when everyone else was sleeping and he would throw me hundreds of curve balls — tell me how to stand and things like that. Rogan changed my stance at the plate and that's how I learned to hit curve balls." By 1938 Johnson was the West's selection at shortstop for the annual East-West Game.

meantime earning a teaching degree from Wiley College, where he played football and baseball under the legendary Fred Long. Johnson had arrived in mid-season as a shortstop replacement for Willard Brown. Johnson recalled, "Brown couldn't make the double play well. Manager Cooper looked at Brown and said 'Sonny,' they used to call Brown Sonny, 'you better get your glove and go to centerfield, I have found a shortstop.'"[61]

Willard Brown had established himself as one of the premier home run hitters in baseball. With the possible exception of Josh Gibson, nobody was hitting the ball any further, or any harder, than Brown. His first home run of the season, a three-run shot, was hit at Shreveport, Louisiana, on April 11, against the Shreveport Tigers. On Sunday, May 2, Brown hit yet another home run in the opening game of a doubleheader in Memphis, Tennessee, against the Red Sox. He added another round-tripper on May 20, in Wichita, Kansas.[62] In a double header against the Birmingham Black Barons, on May 30, Brown homered three times — twice in the first encounter and again in the nightcap.[63] In Indianapolis, Brown homered over the scoreboard to help the Monarchs to a 10–5 victory over the ABCs on June 13.[64] Against the St. Louis Stars at Muehlebach Field, Brown homered in the Monarchs' 5–3 win on June 20. On July 25, Brown homered in the second half of a double header versus Chicago's American Giants. Brown hit his homer "immediately after the announcement that an Eighteenth Street Jeweler would present to the hitter making the first home run a diamond ring."[65]

Willard Brown and Henry Milton contributed home runs in a game in Manhattan, Kansas, against Chicago's American Giants. "Willard Brown, Kansas City clean-up batter and the league's leading home run hitter, ran his season's total to 23 when he smashed out a home in the seventh with the bases empty," wrote a local newspaper.[66] In Cincinnati, on August 15, Brown's solo shot went an estimated 402 feet.[67] In that same double bill Brown had gotten six hits out of eight times up. On August 29, against Satchel Paige's All-Stars, Brown blistered the well-known Paige for another home run.[68] Against the All-Leaguers, a team made up of Kansas City Blues and Kansas City, Kansas, semi-professionals, Brown hit two home runs on September 27, at Kansas City, Kansas', Ward Field.[69]

Brown took such a liking to Ward Field that he returned October 3 to hit four home runs and led the Monarchs to an 8–1 decision over Kansas' Semi-Professional All-Stars. In that game, Brown's four home runs were responsible for seven of the Monarchs' eight scores.[70] And this was only a sampling of his overall performance. Rogan's average would top .389 inside Kansas City's Muehlebach Field and he was still an everyday contributor.

In spite of the Monarchs' many games at home and their new berth in the Negro American League, their love affair with touring the highways never ended. Barnstorming's lucrative allure forced the Monarchs to return to areas where they once battled regional opponents. In cities where they had subdued the locals many times, promoters had begun asking for a schedule of Negro American League games. Such was the case when the Monarchs battled the Indianapolis ABCs in front of 2,000 in Marysville, Kansas, winning 8–5 as Andy Cooper pitched seven-hit ball. Although Cooper got credit for that victory, Hilton Smith did most of the hurling, tossing six innings after starting the game as the Monarchs right-fielder.[71] Ted Strong was the big noise for Indianapolis, slamming a home run. The Monarchs also battled the American Giants in Manhattan, Kansas, before another lively crowd of 2,000 at that city's Griffith Field. The two teams had also battled in Trenton, Missouri.

While much had changed, some things remained the same. The Monarchs won the first half of the split schedule and Chicago's American Giants the second half. It set the stage for yet another Monarchs-American Giants playoff series.

The playoffs opened in Dayton, Ohio, where the American Giants won, 5–4, in ten innings. Game two, an event of historic significance at Chicago, was called by darkness. The Chicago event was a pitchers' battle between Andy Cooper of the Monarchs and Sug Cornelius of the Giants that lasted 17 innings. Cooper, who hurled the entire game for the Monarchs, allowed ten hits and Cornelius nine, before he was relieved by Willie Foster, who tossed the remaining six and ⅔ innings for Chicago. Each team tallied all their runs in a single inning. Chicago scored its two runs in the first inning, and the Monarchs tied it up with two of their own runs in the seventh. At the end of 17 innings the game was stopped because of nightfall, with the score tied at 2–2.

Rogan was in left field for the Monarchs in that historic game and was completely unable to help his team, finishing 0-for-6. Among the features of the game were five lighting-fast double plays, three by the Monarchs.[72] "Many thought the two teams had played in a record game but it was not," wrote the *Kansas City Call*. "In 1920 the Bacharach of New York and the American Giants played a twenty-inning game with the Giants winning 1-to-0. In 1931 the [American] Giants and St Louis Stars played an eighteen inning game that ended in a 4–4 tie. The Homestead Grays and [American] Giants, playing in Pittsburgh in 1935, battled in another eighteen inning game."[73]

Game three, played at Milwaukee's Borchert Field, had a more bizarre ending. Down 7–5, with none out in the last half of the eighth, Kansas City rallied for three runs, but the third run was protested by manager Candy Jim Taylor of the Giants. Taylor claimed the runner was out and refused to permit his team to finish the game. The umpire forfeited the contest to the Monarchs. After some wrangling, Major R. R. Jackson, president of the Negro American League, ordered the contest be continued the next night as a preliminary to the fourth playoff game.[74]

The Monarchs returned the following night and won the disputed contest, 10–7, and they also won the scheduled encounter by a 4–1 score to take a 2–1 edge in the series. The double victory assured Kansas City fans of at least one game at home.[75] When the series moved to Indianapolis, the Monarchs won again. As the series moved to Kansas City's Muehlebach Field, only one game was needed to secure the pennant. That night, 1,600 paid their 40 cents admission as the season drew down to the last half of the ninth inning in a 1–1 tie. Frank Duncan opened that frame with a walk and advanced on an error by the Chicago second baseman. Willard Brown followed with a double to right, and Duncan scored with the winning tally and the pennant in one fell swoop. After a bit of impromptu celebrating, it was announced over the loud speakers that the pennant had been awarded to the Kansas City Monarchs. After suffering a setback in the opener, the Monarchs had won four consecutive games, with a tie sandwiched in between.[76]

An interesting sidebar was that year's barnstorming series against a team formed from members of the American Association Kansas City Blues. Representing the Kansas City Blues were Norman "Red" Branch, Al Piechota, Herman "Ham" Schulte, Bid Breese, Jim Oglesby, and Ray French. John Dellasago, Joe Egnatic, a Nashville minor leaguer, and Joe Novasel rounded out the club.

The tour traveled to parts of Kansas, visiting Junction City, Manhattan, Dodge City,

Larned, Hays, Salina and Kansas City. Piechota recalled, "Oglesby asked the fellows if they wanted to do some barnstorming and that's why I joined."[77] Schulte's memories were far more descriptive. "Only three major leaguers could be on a team after the season ended during exhibition play. Wilkinson arranged the tour with a 60–40 split for the winner. In Larned, Kansas, the Monarchs used their own lighting equipment. Willard Brown hit a ball that should have been a home run, but it hit the wire and bounced back onto the playing field and we tagged him out at second. Was he ever surprised! He complained that someone had pulled a ball out of their pocket."[78]

The game in Manhattan, Kansas, was an 11-inning affair that featured 21 strikeouts, 13 by Branch, and five home runs — the Blues All-Leaguers winning by a 6-to-4 score. It was a pitchers' battle between the Monarchs' Eugene Bremmer and Blues ace Red Branch. Five different players — Al Piechota, Branch and Oglesby of the all-Leaguers, and Mayweather and Byron Johnson of the Monarchs — hit for the circuit. Mayweather led the hitting with a double, triple and homer in five times at bat.[79]

Published results from the contest at Salina, Kansas, included no home runs. Off to a 2-to-0 lead early, the Blues looked solid, but the Monarchs took the lead in the fifth when Dwight, Rogan and Mayweather cracked doubles. The Blues proceeded to tie the score on a double by French and a single by Breese, and later took the lead when Novasel, Branch and Egnatic singled. In the seventh, it was Dwight who singled, stole second and scored on Brown's single to tie the game. Johnson scored the winning run an inning later after banging a single to start the frame. The Monarchs captured a 6–5 victory, Markham getting the win, Branch the loss.

The results of the remaining games, according one publication, were: In Junction City, Monarchs 5, Blues 4, in ten innings; in Dodge City, Monarchs 7, Blues 2; in Larned, Blues 4, Monarchs 0; in Timken, Blues 6, Monarchs 0; in Hays, Blues 5, Monarchs 0; in Kansas City, Kansas, Monarchs 8, Blues 6.[80] After the Blues series there were only a few games remaining but they were to be among the most publicized of the summer.

On October 8, 1937, Bob Feller, sensational Cleveland American League Indians pitcher, from Van Meter, Iowa, matched his All-Star team against the Monarchs in Cedar Rapids, Iowa, and gained a 6–5 win. On that night, Feller did not pitch; instead the honor went to big leaguers Lou Fette, Mace Brown and Lon Warneke.

On October 10, 1937, Feller brought his All-Star team to Kansas City. Feller stood out as the main attraction at Muehlebach Field. Lon Warneke, formerly with Chicago's Cubs, Johnny "Big Cat" Mize, of St. Louis' National League Cardinals, Mace Brown of Pittsburgh's Pirates, Fette and Vince DiMaggio of the Boston Braves, all remained with Feller's All-Stars the night they arrived in Kansas City. Rollie Hemsky, St. Louis Browns catcher, was also a member of the elite All-Star aggregation.

Like most of the players of his time, Feller respected Rogan and the entire Kansas City Monarchs team. If he had not actually seen Rogan in action, he'd certainly heard the name in many of the favorable writeups that accompanied Rogan whenever the team came to Iowa. On one such occasion, a Davenport newspaper had written. "Rogan's name, undoubtedly, is the most famous one in Negro baseball of this or any other day. He has terrific speed, a fast-breaking curve and has mastered the 'fade-away,' the delivery that made Christy Mathewson famous."[81] On yet another occasion, a Council Bluffs, Iowa, newspaper wrote, "But for his color Rogan might have been a member of one of the major league teams, and might have been rated along with Mathewson and Johnson as one of the world's great hurlers."[82]

Though the contest would result in a 1–0 victory for Bob Feller's All-Stars, this particular game provided more thrills than anyone had expected. Feller started the game, and during his stay he struck out five men and allowed one hit — a single to Rogan. Rogan didn't like to be upstaged, and Feller wouldn't upstage him that night either. Warneke followed Feller on the mound and he struck out six men, with Harry Else getting the only safe hit. In the seventh, Mace Brown took up the pitching and held the Monarchs scoreless for the rest of the game. I. V. Barnes pitched a wonderful game for the Monarchs, and he might have won if Willard Brown, Henry Milton, Frank Duncan, Hilton Smith and Newt Allen, who were in Chicago playing against the Homestead Grays, had been in the lineup.

Barnes, born December 23, 1912, in Silver Creek, Mississippi, was a recent graduate of Piney Woods College.[83] He was in his rookie year with the Monarchs in 1937 but never looked very inexperienced. Against Feller, Barnes was superb, and the rangy Kansas City pitcher finished with 11 strikeouts. "Big Cat" Johnny Mize, a first baseman who batted .364 and collected 204 hits for St. Louis in 1937, was held to a solitary hit. All totaled, the four pitchers, three for the All-Stars and one for the Monarchs, struck out 26 batters that night. For the Monarchs, Rogan's 3-for-4 day, the last hit two hits coming off Mace Brown, was the Hall of Fame performance that fans had expected from Feller. To add to the fans' disillusionment, the grand old Rogan also stole a base. From Kansas City, the series also visited Oklahoma City, where Hilton Smith rejoined the team, leading the Monarchs to a 10–0 win over Feller's All-Stars.

Years later, when Rogan's son, Wilbur, was introduced to Bob Feller, Feller said, "Your father was the best pitcher I ever saw." After a moment of pondering Feller added, "that includes the white ones too."[84]

The pennant and Bob Feller's exhibition game were high points in Rogan's 1937 season. In some ways, however, it had been a year of great humanitarian concern. All along the highways were people escaping the Dust Bowls of the Midwest. "It wasn't a pretty sight," recalled Newt Allen, "Every thing was burnt up. Hot weather in the Dakotas had people packing up and moving west. Every day you'd see people with stuff on the top of their cars, trucks. In 1937, during the drought, everything was so hot we played seven-inning ball games."[85] In Oklahoma and Texas, most night games started after 8:30 P.M.

Shortstop Bryon Johnson recalled another unforgettable event from that period. "Once, in Kansas, the team had stopped at a road house to gas up and eat. They had just started putting gas in the cars when the owner told us he wouldn't let us come in to eat," said Johnson. "The Monarchs manager insisted the owner take back his gasoline. They tried to get that gas back out of the cars. It was awful. There was gas everywhere. But the next year, we were driving through and recognized the place. When we stopped, they told us, 'Come right on in.'"[86]

By 1938 Rogan was down to his final season of professional play. That same year, the old ballpark, Kansas City's Muehlebach Field, changed its name to Ruppert Stadium to honor New York Yankees owner Jacob Ruppert, the park's new owner. Ruppert had purchased the Kansas City Blues team from Johnny Kling, owner of Kansas City's Dixon Hotel. Interestingly, Rogan had almost changed teams in early January when Detroit became a bidder for his services.

James Titus, owner of the Detroit Stars, made overtures to J. L. Wilkinson to trade Wilber "Bullet" Rogan and Frank Duncan for catcher Shirley Petway, a relative of legendary Bruce Petway and a member of Detroit's 1937 Stars. Wilkinson countered by asking for infielder/catcher Roosevelt Cox, also a member of Detroit's 1937 Stars.[87] Titus hinted that, "if Rogan comes to Detroit he will probably be given managerial reins."[88]

The deal ultimately failed when Detroit was not offered a Negro American League franchise, leaving Cox available to be picked up for the 1938 Monarchs. The Monarchs also captured Stearnes, following his release from Chicago's American Giants in early July. In Stearnes, the Monarchs had recruited a natural-born winner. Born May 8, 1901, in Nashville, Tennessee, Stearnes was already an illustrious home-run hitter and a legendary figure prior to his arrival in Kansas City. "I hit so many [home runs], I never counted them," said Stearnes. "And I'll tell you why: If they didn't win a ballgame, they didn't amount to anything. It didn't make any difference if I hit four or five over the grandstand, it didn't make any difference to me, as long as I hit them to try to win the game. That's what I wanted; to win the game."[89]

Commenting on how he got his famous nickname, he offered, "when I was a kid, I was all chest, no hips and no legs. So the boys on the team thought upon Turkey as the nickname and it has stuck with me ever since. Now I would be lost without it."[90] As one of the greats of baseball, "Stearnes was a highly-paid player. He earned $500 to $600 a month, a big salary at that time."[91] Prior to joining the Monarchs, in 1938, Stearns had clouted a homer, triple and single with four runs batted in in a game against his soon-to-be Monarchs teammates.[92]

Andy Cooper was back as Monarchs manager in 1938. Several new members were added prior to the club leaving for their annual Southern spring training tour. Among the outfielders that were featured in Kansas City's 1938 campaign were Willard Brown, Norman "Turkey" Stearnes and Henry Milton, three of the fastest outfielders in baseball and one of the Monarchs' top starting outfields ever.

The Monarchs carried a staff of seven to eight pitchers in 1938. John Marcum, Hilton Smith, I. V. Barnes, Andy Cooper, Floyd Kranson, and Dick Bradley were mainstays of the group. They also picked up a young first baseman, John "Buck" O'Neil, a native of Carrabelle, Florida and a graduate of Edward Waters College of Jacksonville, Florida, and added yet another infielder with the acquisition of Junius A. "Rainey" Bibbs, a one-time member of Cincinnati's Tigers who had formerly played fullback with Indiana State University. Bibbs began 1938 with the American Giants, but ended up in Kansas City in a deal that sent Frank Duncan to Chicago.

Bibbs' vivid memories of the Indiana State gridiron were not among his most pleasant. "Many times my own teammates would not block for me and got a kick from seeing me get hit." Bibbs continued, "Once, Evansville, the opposing team, did everything imaginable to me, and by the half I was bleeding from both ears, beaten and bruised all over. Wally Marks, our coach, asked me if I wanted to play the second half. I told him the biggest lie ever — I said, 'Yes.'"[93]

O'Neil was a college player too, having attended Edward Waters College. Reflecting on his pay for that first season, the Monarchs' new first baseman offered, "I came here making $100 a month. But wait, let me tell you, they would give me a dollar a day for meal money. That's $30 came out of that $100. So I got $70. But even at that, I was able to kick some money home."[94]

With talent like that, Rogan was lucky if he played at all. Yet, in spite of the challenge, Rogan played the last cards in his winning hand. As O'Neil put it, "Rogan could [still] throw the ball by you, and he had one of the greatest curves too."[95] He rarely pitched in 1938, but one such opportunity did present itself at Houston, Texas, when Rogan's pitching helped defeat the Philadelphia Stars by a 7–1 score.[96] It was as a pinch-hitter and outfielder, in that final season, that Rogan truly excelled.

Pinch-hitting is how Rogan most often entered the game when he wasn't in the starting lineup. In Kansas City's season-opener at Houston, Texas, Rogan pitched and slammed a single. On that night, fellow pitchers Floyd Kranson and Dick Bradley combined for 16 strikeouts in Kansas City's 7–1 win over Philadelphia's Stars.[97] In Dallas, on April 24, Rogan batted in the ninth inning for McLemore, a recruit attempting to make the team, but failed to hit safely.[98] In mid–May Rogan's three hits, stolen base and RBI defeated Monarchs nemesis Milt Perry in Enid, Oklahoma. Prior to that game Perry had defeated the Monarchs twice, leading Enid to win over the Monarchs in four of their last five games played against the Negro team.[99]

Rogan had another trio of hits and a trio of runs in Peoria, Illinois, when the Monarchs thumped a local All-Star team on May 24.[100] Elmer Ambrose, a one-time House of David hurler, was Peoria's losing pitcher. On July 3, in the first game of a doubleheader, batting for Andy Cooper in the ninth, Rogan started the rally that tied the score and eventually gave Kansas City an 11–10 win over Memphis' league-leading Red Sox. Rogan returned that afternoon and went 1-for-2.

On July 4, Rogan went 2-for-5, with a double, against the Memphis Red Sox. He followed that game with a 1-for-5 performance that included a double, at Enid, Oklahoma, on July 6.[101] In Manhattan, Kansas, Rogan collected one of the Monarchs' eight hits and collected an RBI in a big 12–3 win over the Birmingham Black Barons.[102] Only days prior, Rogan had gone 1-for-3, with a double and a stolen base, against Manhattan, Kansas', Chastains.[103] In a July 30, game against Chicago's American Giants, Rogan pinch-hit safely for Cox in a 2–1 Monarchs loss. On August 20, against the Atlanta Black Crackers, Rogan, who was stationed in left field, went 1-for-5 and scored two runs. Rogan's only hit that night, a single, had produced the first two Monarchs runs of an eventual 13–2 Kansas City win.

With a lineup of youthful stars, there would be many outstanding Monarchs games in which Rogan failed to appear. One such game was played on August 1, in Davenport, Iowa, when the Monarchs faced the Illinois–Iowa League All-Stars. That night the Monarchs defeated a team led by Johnny Valsoana, veteran Western League hurler and pilot. Milton's batting was featured in that game. He went 3-for-5 with a stolen base. When speaking of the Monarchs' big first sacker, a local newspaper offered, "John O'Neil, giant first sacker, played great ball around the initial sack, his long reach saving several errors."[104]

In that final season, Rogan visited all the cities of personal importance to his career in baseball. On June 6, he appeared with the Monarchs in Oklahoma City, Oklahoma, the place of his birth. In early August, Rogan appeared in his last game in Wichita, Kansas, a city in which he had pitched some of the most fabulous barnstorming games of his career. In mid–August, he played in Kansas City, Kansas, the city where he had grown up. When the Monarchs met the White Eagles in St. Joseph, Missouri, on August 15, Rogan made his last appearance in that familiar city.[105] He had also made a trip to Springfield, Missouri, where the Monarchs "drove out four doubles and a single" in the ninth to defeat Indianapolis's ABCs 13–12 on August 9.[106] Shortly thereafter, the Monarchs visited St. Louis after an absence of seven years. While in the city they lost a 9–5 encounter to the St. Louis Giants.[107]

On August 19, Rogan went 1-for-5, with two runs scored, in his last game in Topeka, Kansas, a town he had visited as a member of the All-Nations back in 1917. And finally, on August 21, 1938, Rogan played his last game in Kansas City's Ruppert Stadium. That afternoon Rogan, stationed in his familiar left field position, went 0-for-4 and 0-for-3 in a doubleheader against the Atlanta Black Crackers. That mediocre performance was not up to Rogan's standards. As much as Rogan hated to admit it, it was time to retire. On September 4, he made one final visit to Chicago, Illinois, the city where he had pitched his first professional game back in 1920. After 18 illustrious seasons, 45-year-old Wilber "Bullet" Rogan was finally stepping down.

When Rogan's professional baseball career came to an historic end, his lifetime offensive totals beamed with greatness. Rogan had collected more than 2,500 hits, over 400 doubles, better than 200 triples, over 350 home runs and more than 500 stolen bases. On the mound, Rogan's lifetime totals included more than 350 games won and more than 2,000 batters struck out. He left baseball with the most victories in Negro National League history. He was also one of baseball's most successful player-managers, his teams having won over 600 games and a Negro National League pennant.

There had been players who were better for a day, week or even a season, but over the course of a career, Rogan's overall totals were the most illustrious all-around set of numbers ever recorded. If for no other reason than a love for baseball, Rogan had pitched, fielded, run and slugged his way into the hearts of baseball fans everywhere.

12

The Supreme Monarch

Triple threats are not often mentioned in baseball, but there is no shorter cut to describe Rogan's ability. Bullet could pitch, Bullet could play the outfield and Bullet could hit that apple.—Baltimore Afro-American, 1932

Rogan's time as one of the world's greatest unrecognized baseball player had passed. Life outside baseball, as rewarding as it should have been, was bittersweet. Unable to separate himself from the game he loved, he eventually returned to the diamond as an umpire. When National and American League organizations started purchasing young Monarchs for their teams, Rogan sought a big league coaching job. Self-proclaimed liberals, like Branch Rickey, expressed no interest whatsoever in Rogan's knowledge. Bill Veeck shunned Rogan altogether.

Conditions of the day had left Rogan disenfranchised. The big leagues wouldn't hire him, and by the time his umpiring career ended the Negro Leagues were in decline. His legacy was also fading. Not surprisingly, journalists had started to claim that Leroy "Satchel" Paige was the superior of Rogan and other legendary Negro League greats. For Rogan, there were no endorsement deals to tide him over, and as far as collectors were concerned, his autograph wouldn't command more than 25 cents.

During Rogan's absence from the field he was able to spend more time at home with his wife Kathrine. Most weekends they would travel down to Duncan's Point in the Missouri Ozarks to fish. Rogan had purchased a summer cottage there some years earlier, in an area that was strictly segregated from affluent whites that were earning similar incomes.

After many years away from baseball, Rogan returned to umpire Monarchs home games in 1946. He took his umpiring just as he had his playing—seriously. Unlike ballplaying, umpiring was an unappreciated job. It was an occupation that was totally overlooked until there was a controversial call. The pay was decent and there was no travel, so Rogan, Frank Duncan, Hurley McNair and Robert Boone of the old Kansas City, Kansas, Giants, donned umpires' uniforms at Monarchs home games. There still remained that hazard of a player's backlash if an athlete felt cheated. Although Rogan and his crew were highly respected by the home team, it was the visiting teams that caused most problems for Kansas City's umpires. Thus a side note to McNair's long career was his being perhaps the only umpire that was ever booted from a Negro League baseball game. It happened in 1946.

In a game between Kansas City's Monarchs and Birmingham's Black Barons, a dispute between Tommy Sampson and McNair over a call at first base became legendary. Sampson started it all when he began pushing McNair. McNair responded by pulling a knife out his pocket. Sampson wheeled and made a beeline for his dugout with McNair in hot pursuit, waving his blade. Sampson snatched a bat from one of the players and regained the offensive, chasing McNair back across the diamond, whacking him once on the back of his leg. When the brawl was finally broken up, McNair was removed from the field, but Sampson remained in the game. As negative as the incident had been, it ultimately ended McNair's illustrious career in Kansas City sports. Within two years, December 2, 1948 to be exact, McNair died at his home on Brooklyn Avenue on Kansas City's east side.

Rogan was virtually anonymous throughout most of his umpiring career, which lasted

The Monarchs always got their man. In this photograph Tom Baird (at center, light-colored suit) is in Miami, Florida, looking over a list of top Cuban prospects. In 1937 Baird purchased a half interest in the Monarchs.

12. The Supreme Monarch

from 1946 to 1950. During his off time, Rogan would visit local parks and playgrounds helping youngsters who were attempting to learn baseball. Though he was mostly unknown to them, there were others much older that could attest to numerous well-worn stories of his legendary feats of the past. Occasionally, his name would reappear as a member of someone's all-time All-Star selection.

Such was the case in 1945, when Cumberland Posey, owner of Pittsburgh's Homestead Grays and Executive Secretary of the Negro National League, selected Bullet Rogan, along with Satchel Paige, Dick Redding, "Smokey" Joe Williams, Willie Foster and Dave Brown,

From left are Wilber "Bullet" Rogan, Robert Boone and Hurley McNair. Veteran players, acting as umpires, helped to draw big crowds to games. Boone had started his Negro National League umpiring career in 1923. Frank Duncan and Dink Mothell would also umpire games after they could no longer play ball.

On the bench with Monarchs greats. From left: John "Buck" O'Neil, Frank Duncan, James "Jew Baby" Floyd and Wilber "Bullet" Rogan.

as pitchers on his immortals All-Star team. In 1947, Tweed Webb writing in the *St. Louis Argus*, nominated Bullet Rogan, Andrew "Rube" Foster, Leroy "Satchel" Paige, "Smokey Joe" Williams, John Donaldson and José Méndez as pitchers on his legendary list of all-time baseball greats.[1]

In 1950 a book entitled *Your Kansas City and Mine*, with the help of J. L. Wilkinson and Tom Baird, featured an all-time Monarchs team. The team included the following players: Frank Duncan catcher, John O'Neil first base, Newt Allen second base, Walter "Doby" Moore shortstop, Newt Joseph third base, Oscar "Heavy" Johnson left field, Hurley McNair center field, Cristóbal Torriente right field. John Donaldson, Wilber Rogan and Satchel Paige were selected as the team's best pitchers and Andy Cooper its manager.[2] Rogan's recognition, though, was not limited to Kansas City.

Rogan was appearing on everybody's legendary list of pitchers and so was Leroy "Satchel" Paige.

In popularity polls, Paige beat Rogan and every other African American player hands down. As early as 1934, Paige had been the focus of feature articles in such prestigious magazines as *Look* and *Life*. Most fans, especially modern ones, were not as familiar with Rogan's talents. Paige's career was simply better documented. Paige was shocked that he was even being compared to Rogan. "He, Rogan, was the onliest pitcher I ever knew, I ever heard of in my life, was pitching and hitting in the clean-up place," was Paige's response.

Their contemporaries were highly expressive in their comparisons of Rogan and Paige, especially the catchers. Otto "Jay Bird" Ray, Rogan's catcher in 1920 and 1921, assured everyone that Rogan was better. "Paige made it into the majors, but I honestly believe that Bullet Rogan was an even better pitcher than 'Ol Satch,'" declared Ray in 1963. "It's just too bad he didn't get a crack at the big time."[3] Unlike Ray, who had caught only for Rogan, Frank Duncan had caught for both Rogan and Paige in their prime. Duncan's comments were even more interesting. "Rogan was faster than Paige and the better athlete," was Duncan's belief. "But then Satch could do a lot of things on that mound." Duncan added, "I'll tell you how fast Rogan was. I used to buy two steaks before the game when he was going to pitch. You could buy a steak in those days for ten cents. I'd start the game catching [Rogan] in the first inning with that steak next to my glove hand. After five-innings the steak would be beaten to shreds. So I'd replace it with the second steak."[4] In another interview, with author John Holway, Duncan added, "I'd say Rogan and Satchel threw the fastest balls I ever saw, but Rogan also had a great curve with a three-foot drop on it. Bullet had a little more steam on the ball than Paige, and he had a better breaking curveball. The batters thought it was a fast ball heading for them and they'd jump back from the plate, and all of a sudden, it would break sharply for a strike. I've never seen a pitcher like him and I've caught some of the best."

"[Rogan was] the best pitcher I ever saw in my life," was Chet Brewer's analysis. When Rogan was compared to Paige, Brewer's response was, "no comparison." Brewer added, "Rogan invented the palm ball. He was the master of that no-wind-up pitch. He wasn't as colorful as Satchel. Satchel was always in the media's face telling them some kind of joke or something and he sold papers. They are still quoting things that Satchel said. Satchel was a thrower — he would just throw the ball by you. But if you hit his fastball he didn't have anything else to go to. He had pin-perfect control. He could thread a needle."[5] Recalling on his many years of experience J. L. Wilkinson acknowledged, "Next to Rogan the greatest Negro pitchers were John Donaldson, who was with my club for years, and 'Satchel' Paige."[6]

James "Cool Papa" Bell, a member of Baseball's Hall of Fame at Cooperstown, New York was certain that, "He [Paige] was faster than anyone I've ever seen."[7]

Knowing that Rogan was probably a better pitcher than Paige and that Paige almost certainly won more games and struck out more batters in a season than Hall of Famers Bob Feller or Dizzy Dean speaks volumes about Rogan's prowess on the mound during the 1920s and 1930s.

As the debate over Rogan and Paige raged on, Rogan continued to work at the United States Post Office as an elevator operator. It wasn't the greatest job, but it was better than some of the jobs his former teammates were working. Wade Johnston, a man who was once considered among the greatest leadoff men in baseball, sold earthworms in Stubenville, Ohio. Sam Crawford, perhaps the greatest manager in Kansas City Monarchs history, peddled newspapers on the corner of Thirty-fifth and State Street in Chicago. After 15 years as a news vendor at 43rd and State streets, in 1955 Crawford "shot and fatally wounded Pete William DeGraw, as the latter advanced on him in a threatening manner shortly after Crawford opened his stand."[8] Crawford was living at 4311 State Street at the time of the shooting.

Sylvester Foreman, Rogan's catcher in 1921, worked as a taxi dispatcher at Newt Joseph's Monarch Cabs. George Carr, a player that had visited Japan on three different occasions to play baseball, was frying steaks and French fried potatoes as a cook for the Missouri Pacific railroad.[9] George Sweatt, one of only two players to appear in all of the first four Negro League World Series (1924–1927), was employed as a postal delivery worker in Chicago.[10] Pitcher George Mitchell was proprietor of the Main Street Restaurant in his home town of Sparta, Illinois.[11] Rogan took his elevator job as seriously as he took his baseball, and within a period of time he was promoted to night watchman.

The local sporting community wasn't always kind to Rogan either. He was always overlooked at Sammie Dubin's Nite of Sports, held annually at Kansas City, Kansas', Town House Hotel. The purpose of the dinner, according to its organizers, was to "Honor the men of the Greater Kansas City area who devoted many hours of coaching and teaching and added to young athletes' character, sportsmanship, citizenship and good Christian ideals."[12]

A joyous reunion, 1948. From left: Newt Joseph, Frank Duncan, T.B. Watkins, Newt Allen and Wilber Rogan. Sports was the theme when these men got together in the home of T. B. Watkins for shrimp and a discussion of the Monarchs (Black Archives Mid America).

12. The Supreme Monarch

In 1953, Dubin's annual dinner featured such celebrities as baseball's Ralph Houk, Walker Cooper, Glenn Wright, Dutch Zwilling and others — but not Rogan. Leroy "Satchel" Paige was always invited. It was the eighth consecutive year that the organizers had failed to invite Rogan, in spite of the fact that Tom Baird, owner of the Kansas City Monarchs, was one of its premiere sponsors. In 1958, however, 11 years after the event was originated, Dubin broke down and honored Rogan with one of his organization's sportsmen's awards.

On May 2, 1958, the Heart of America Elks Lodge #149 honored Rogan. Some 200 Elks and well wishers saluted the former great pitcher. That night he received a "bronze plaque from the M.K. Goetz Brewing Company and a trophy from the Heart of America Elks Lodge."[13] It was the second time the Elks had so honored the great pitcher. Over the years, however, people seemed to forget all about Rogan.

Rogan encountered an even greater setback on November 28, 1961, when his wife Kathrine died. It was a yet another difficult adjustment for "Bullet." Kathrine had been his life-long companion for nearly 40 years.

Rogan, though, was alive and well. That long life gave him the opportunity to witness some of the fruits of his lifelong efforts. He had witnessed a Kansas City Monarch named

Monarchs player reunion, 1954. From left: Otto "Jay Bird" Ray, Forrest Smith, Bullet Rogan, Newt Allen, unknown, Eddie Dwight, unknown. Former Monarchs pose after an evening of recognition at a local Elks Club banquet.

Jackie Robinson joining the Brooklyn Dodgers in 1947, Larry Doby's first home run title in 1952, Don Newcombe's league leading 27 wins in 1956 and John "Buck" O'Neil's selection as the National League's first African American coach in 1962. African American athletes were finally enjoying first class accommodations in hotels, restaurants and transportation. Rogan took pride in knowing that his dedicated play had yielded tangible results. In 1965 Rogan witnessed "Satchel" Paige's return to the American League. It was only fitting that Rogan would be honored with Paige on the eve of that historic event.

The last time Rogan was prominently featured in the news was during the Kansas City Monarchs–Kansas City Blues player reunion that was held to boost attendance for Satchel Paige's return to the American League. That September, Charles O. Finley, owner of the Kansas City Athletics, signed Leroy "Satchel" Paige to pitch for his struggling American League team in a game against the Boston Red Sox. To highlight Paige's return, Finley invited former members of the Monarchs and Blues to play a three-inning exhibition prior to the game.

When Bill Veeck got the news of Paige's return to American League play he responded with apprehension. "I don't think he'd [Finley] want to embarrass Leroy in that manner."[14] But most people could see right through Veeck's flimsy excuse. Satchel was no longer known by his first name, Leroy, and when Veeck used his first name he sent a powerful message of disrespect. Paige hadn't used the name Leroy since the 1930s. Most people didn't even know that Paige's first name was Leroy — all they knew was Satchel Paige. And the fact that Paige was coming off an appearance in Chicago's East-West game, where at age 58 (Paige was born July 7, 1907) he pitched three innings, struck out six, gave up two scratch hits and no runs didn't seem to matter either. Evidently, Veeck didn't think much of the East-West game either.

Paige was out to prove that Veeck and everyone else that did not support his return was wrong. And true to the "Satchel" tradition, he accomplished the feat.

That night, September 25, 1965, Paige, wearing the A's famous Kelly-green and gold uniform, made the Boston Red Sox see black and blue as he held them to three scoreless innings, allowed but one hit and struck out a batter. John "Buck" O'Neil observed to a *Kansas City Times* reporter, "He's the last one. When he goes it'll never be the same."[15] If anyone had been embarrassed it wasn't Paige — it was the Boston Red Sox. Seated in the grandstand nearby, Rogan was cheering Paige onward with glee.

The *Times* held true to their historic convictions of not putting photographs of the Negro League's top stars into its newspaper — only the Blues reunion team photograph was printed. Thus Rogan ended his career by having his photograph in the local newspapers only twice, perhaps three times, in his lifetime. The fact that Kansas City's newspapers had neglected him only added to the insult of the A's denying him free admission to American League games. Tom Baird, long-time Monarchs owner and booking agent, was having his own issues and problems with integration.

Tom Baird, J. L. Wilkinson's long-time partner and the man Wilkinson sold the Kansas City Monarchs to in 1948, was attacked by civil rights groups that protested his "for whites only" policy at a local bowling alley he owned. Baird was losing the confidence of many Monarchs ballplayers as well. In a personal letter to Lee MacPhail of the New York Yankees, dated January 10, 1949, Baird was on record as writing, "there isn't an outstanding Negro player that anybody could recommend to step into the big leagues and hold down a regular job. Several years ago I could have named several players that could more than hold their own in the big leagues. In fact, several would have been stars, but now I know of not one that would stick."[16]

Ironically, back in 1922 when then Kansas Governor Henry Allen launched an undercover investigation on Ku Klux Klan activity in the state, Baird's name appeared on the membership list of the local Kansas City, Kansas, chapter.[17]

In his final years, Rogan moved into a low-income, high-rise apartment building on Kansas City's east side. Georgia Dwight and her husband Eddie visited Rogan on many occasions during this period. "It was frustrating to visit Rogan," Mrs. Dwight recalled. "The elevators were undependable and dirty, and the complex was overrun with prostitutes and alcoholics. It wasn't the lifestyle that Rogan was accustomed to living, but he made it the best home he could until he died."

On Saturday, March 4, 1967, at age 73, Wilber "Bullet" Rogan quietly passed into the hereafter at his Kansas City apartment. The *Kansas City Call* was quick with a response. "During Rogan's tenure in the game the Kansas City Monarchs were endowed with some of the fastest and cleverest performers to ever hit the diamond in the Midwest. In this aggregation, Rogan was considered the 'King of Kings' by many of his fellow players and opponents," wrote the *Call*.[18]

Rogan's funeral, which was held at Watkins Chapel on Eighteenth and Benton in Kansas City, Missouri, was less than a mile from where Association Park once stood. In that

Wilber Rogan and grandchildren in Minneapolis, Minnesota, 1955. Standing: Karen Rogan. Seated, from left: Carl Rogan, Wilber Rogan and Casandra Rogan (Black Archives Mid America).

park Rogan had won many great victories, a fact that was attested to by the well-known faces that stood among the crowd on this eventful occasion. The services opened with a hymn, *I Need Thee Every Hour*, a prayer, and a second hymn, *Just a Closer Walk with Thee*, followed. Joe Thomas, a former member of the Jimmy Lunceford Orchestra, delivered a heartfelt solo. The organist that afternoon was Mrs. Margaret B. Sparks. The Rev. C. E. Phillips delivered the eulogy and recalled some of the great feats that Rogan had performed on the baseball diamond.

The crowd that gathered at Rogan's funeral was a virtual who's who of the greatest names in Kansas City baseball. Frank Duncan, the other half of the Monarchs' wonderful battery, was there. And so was Booker T. McDaniel, the first African American pitcher signed by the Chicago Cubs. Jesse Williams, a shortstop for the 1940s Monarchs, Percy Staples, legendary infielder of Brown's Tennessee Rats, and Connie Johnson, the first African American pitcher to hurl an opening day game for the Baltimore Orioles, were also in attendance. Newt Allen and Eddie Dwight, two of Rogan's teammates from the 1920s, were also among the many dignitaries and friends. Ruben Benton, representing the sports staff of the *Kansas City Call,* and Arthur Bryant, the man whose barbecue had made Kansas City famous for that delicacy, were just a few of the more than 500 people that crowded into Watkins' main auditorium to witness the last rites for their popular Monarchs' hero.[19]

Paul W. Fisher fairly summarized the scope of Rogan's popularity in a column written in the *Kansas City Times*: "Go a hundred or so miles in any direction from Kansas City and stop in

Wilber Rogan stands in the driveway of his home at 2516 Harrison in Kansas City (Black Archives Mid America).

any one of 200 or more towns south as far as Texas, east to the Rockies, north well into Montana, and east to the Mississippi. Ask a thousand or so men and women if they were living in that particular town in, say, 1927, or 1929, or 1933 when Bullet Joe Rogan and the Kansas City Monarchs came to play. And if they had, there will be a sudden animation and an astonishing number of them will volunteer 'I'll never forget how Bullet Joe...' or 'I can see him now...' or '...almost 40 years ago and yet every detail is so clear.'"[20] For years these small rays of hope had kept Rogan's interested in baseball, in spite of the segregation he most assuredly faced every time he took the field.

For hundreds-of-thousands, regardless of how you kept the score, Rogan was a winner. He had fought segregation and beaten the odds. He had battled isolation and become one of the best-known players of his generation. His stardom, in spite of racism, and in spite of major neglect by the American press, remained secure. Everyone knew that the sportswriters' definition of fair play hadn't included equality, but men like Bullet Rogan always found ways to persevere.

Obviously, owners of the famous National and American League teams were as blind as any sportswriter. Imagine how much revenue Rogan might have added to their major league ledgers. Ultimately, the owners' actions supported the claim that African American athletes had achieved very little in baseball and deserved no real recognition. Thus, they denied millions from intimately knowing about players like Rogan. On the field, though, Rogan's lifetime totals seemed to suffer little, and yet how long would it take for most people to accept the fact that he was one of baseball's greatest all-around players?

In retrospect, the Kansas City Monarchs provided entertainment for fans of all races in an era when most African Americans were denied the simple pleasure of seeing their photograph in a daily newspaper. For many of that period, a day at the ballpark included dress-up, a small wager on the game, a pack of 15 cent Camels or Chesterfields, a 20 cent beer and a ballplayer named Wilber "Bullet" Rogan. They grew to love baseball and they loved the man named

Wilber Rogan, with scrapbook, reflecting on his life in baseball (Black Archives Mid America).

Wilber "Bullet" Rogan Hall of Fame plaque (Baseball Hall of Fame Cooperstown, New York).

Rogan — a love that persisted even when he whipped the home team — many times a white team — into obvious submission. They realized that his was a unique talent and his ethnicity appeared to matter little. His God-given ability is what they really worshiped — a fact that was substantiated by many of baseball's most renowned personalities.

In 1971, when the Baseball Hall of Fame in Cooperstown, New York, got around to inducting players from the Negro Leagues, Satchel Paige's popularity was the only explanation for his being chosen first. Twenty-seven years later they finally got around to nominating Rogan. In 1998, after decades of oversight, a veterans committee of baseball players and sportswriters saw fit to honor Wilber "Bullet" Rogan with a long-overdue Hall of Fame induction. He was the 15th Negro Leaguer to be enshrined in Cooperstown.

In spite of the sketchy facts on his Hall of Fame plaque, Rogan's Cooperstown induction stands as one of the most monumental and well-deserving in sports history. As a consequence, Wilber "Bullet" Rogan is unrecognized no more. His status among baseball's legends is forever secured — a fact that no amount of racism, no quantity of bigotry and no great magnitude of segregation could deny.

Chapter Notes

Chapter 1

1. Comiskey, Charles A. (1910, April 17). "Ty Cobb best of diamond heroes. 'Old Roman' Comiskey picks Tiger as greatest player of All Time," *Chicago Tribune*, p. C1.
2. *Macmillan Baseball Encyclopedia*. Comparison of totals taken from this baseball publication.
3. Census records. Two versions of the census were checked. The first was the census of 1890 taken in Oklahoma City. It identified Rogan's date of birth and listed his name as Charles Wilbern Rogan. The second was the 1910 census, taken in Kansas City, Kansas, which also identified Rogan's date of birth.
4. Lillie Ann Gates Owens (personal communication, October 9, 2004). Leon Walstean, Wilber Rogan's step brother, was her grandfather. In the interview she said that Ophelia's last name was Walstean prior to her marriage to Richard Rogan. Lillie also stated that Leon, perhaps because of the long association with the Rogan family, later changed his last name from Walstean to Rogan. Leon died in California but the actual date of his death is unconfirmed.
5. Information obtained from the 1915 Kansas State Census. Volume 329, section 4, p. 11.
6. According to Thatcher's Mortuary in Kansas City, Kansas, Willard Rogan was born November 9, 1899, and died September 7, 1935, at age 36. Willard's Lancing Kansas prison record listed his age as 23 in April of 1919. That would put his year of birth at 1896 or 1897.
7. Orrin Murray (personal communications, 1986, March) Murray had grown up in the same neighborhood as Rogan's family.
8. T. Roosevelt Butler (personal communications, 1982–1985). Butler was Tobe Smith's son in law.
9. "Sam Lanford and Topeka Jack in fight to draw" (1921, August 27). *Chicago Whip*, p. 7.
10. Richard, Pullam, Jr. (personal communications, 1984–1986). Richard was the son of Monarchs catcher Chick Pullam.
11. "K.C.K. Giants to invade East. Will meet fastest Semi-pro teams in the country" (1909, July 27). *Kansas City Journal*, p. 8.
12. "Leland Giants to meet K.C. K., Giants" (1909, August 25). *Kansas City Journal*, p. 8.
13. "Leland Giants apply brush. Defeat K.C. K., Giants in fast game — score 5–0" (1909, August 26). *Kansas City Journal*, p. 8.
14. "Giants on even terms. Kansas team won second game with Lelands 3–1" (1909, August 27). *Kansas City Journal*, p. 8.
15. "Kansas Giants champions. Defeats Leland of Chicago in final game, 5 to 4" (1909, August 28). *Kansas City Journal*, p. 9.
16. Advertisement in the *Indianapolis Freeman*, Sports section, various dates in 1910.
17. Susan Greenbaum, *Afro-American Community in Kansas City, Kansas*, p. 64.
18. William Boone, A History of Black Education in Kansas City, Kansas, p. 25. Kansas Room, Kansas City, Kansas Public Library.
19. Orrin Murray (personal communications, 1982–1988).
20. Fred Langford (personal communications, 1982–1986).
21. "Amateur Baseball" (1911, April 20). *Kansas City Journal*, p. 9.
22. "Amateur Baseball" (1911, April 17). *Kansas City Journal*, p. 6.
23. "Amateur Baseball" (1911, April 24). *Kansas City Journal*, p. 6.
24. "Amateur Baseball" (1911, April 24). *Kansas City Journal*, p. 6.
25. Fred Langford (personal communications, 1983–1986). Robert Austin is buried in Kansas City, Kansas' Westlawn Cemetery, Section 17SWD, Row 25, Plot 5. His burial date was July 25, 1966. His age was listed as 73 at the time of his death.
26. Fred Langford (personal communication, December 10, 1983).
27. "Amateur Baseball" (1911, August 27). *Kansas City Journal*, p. A11.
28. "Blues beat Leavenworth, play Indian team today" (1911, October 5). *Kansas City Journal*, p. 9.
29. "Blues beat Leavenworth; play Indian Team today" (1911, October 5). *Kansas City Journal*, p. 8.
30. "Win in tenth, 3–2 and tie next 0–0" (1911, October 9). *Kansas City Journal*, p. 8.
31. Janet Bruce, *The Kansas City Monarchs, Champions of Black Baseball*, p. 9. Originally credited to a *St. Louis Post-Dispatch* clipping in the Robert Peterson File at Cooperstown, New York.

Chapter 2

1. Letter from Bertran T. Beagle at the Negro Leagues Museum, Kansas City.
2. Bert Gholston, "A leader for the Monarchs" (1926, March 19). *Kansas City Call*, p. 7.
3. Letter from Bertran T. Beagle at the Negro Leagues Museum, Kansas City.
4. John H. Nankivell, *The History of the Twenty-Fifth Regiment United States Infantry, 1869–1926*, p. 138.
5. William "Big C" Johnson (personal communication, 1984).
6. John H. Nankivell, *The History of the Twenty-Fifth Regiment United States Infantry, 1869–1926*, p. 171.
7. Letter from Bertran T. Beagle at the Negro Leagues Museum, Kansas City.

8. "All-Americans defeated" (1916, December 30). *Chicago Defender*, p. 5.
9. Letter from Bertran T. Beagle at the Negro Leagues Museum, Kansas City.
10. "Great army ball game" (1915, October 16). *Indianapolis Freeman*, p. 7.
11. "Great army ball game" (1915, October 16). *Indianapolis Freeman*, p. 7.
12. "Diamond Flashes" (1914, June 29). *Oakland Tribune*, p. 6.
13. "Big time planned for Hap Hogan in Honolulu" (1914, October 1). *Oakland Tribune*, p. 13.
14. John H. Nankivell, *The History of the twenty-fifth Regiment United States Infantry, 1869–1926*, p. 172.
15. "Great army ball game" (1915, October 16). *Indianapolis Freeman*, p. 7.
16. "Francis Barney fails to stop Wyman's crew," 1915, October 19). *Hawaiian Gazette*, p. 8.
17. "Twenty-fifth hands up mark for hitting" (1915, November 9). *Hawaiian Gazette*, p. 8.
18. "Home run beats Olympic club, 2–1" (1916, March 18). *Chicago Defender*, p. torn page, no page number listed.
19. "Rogan strikes out eighteen men and twenty-fifth wins from All-Stars" (1916, November 25). *Chicago Defender*, page torn, newspaper page number unknown.
20. "Bullet Rogan" (1922, July 1). *Chicago Whip*, p. 7.
21. "Who is greatest of ball players" (1916, March 3). *Hawaiian Gazette*, p. 8.
22. "Tin Lai to make local debut, Chink to join White Sox here" (1915, January 17). *Oakland Tribune*, p. 56.
23. "McCredie signs up Chinese tosser" (1914, November 11). *Oakland Tribune*, p. 10.
24. "Andrew has had enough baseball" (1916, March 17). *Hawaiian Gazette*, p. 8.
25. "Wasedas defeat Nipponese and twenty-fifth turn trick..." *Hawaiian Gazette*, April 25, 1916, p. 8.
26. John H. Nankivell, *The History of the twenty-fifth Regiment United States Infantry, 1869–1926*, p. 172.
27. "Mills proves to be fast runner" (1916, February 8). *Hawaiian Gazette*, p. 8.
28. "Soldier runners are stars at Alexander field athletic meet" (1916, March 14). *Hawaiian Gazette*, p. 8.
29. "Soldier runners are stars at Alexander field athletic meet" (1916, March 14). *Hawaiian Gazette*, p. 8.
30. Wilbur Rogan, Jr. (personal communication, 1990)
31. Bert Gholston, "A leader for the Monarchs" (1926, March 19). *Kansas City Call*, p. 7.
32. Fred Langford (personal Communication, December 10, 1983)
33. "All-Nations team to play Taylor's ABCs" (1917, August 30). *Indianapolis News*, p. sports.
34. "Twenty-fifth and Thirty-second tied" (1917, January 16). *Hawaiian Gazette*, p. 8.
35. "Wreckers wallop thirty-second, 14–1. (1917, January 23). *Hawaiian Gazette*, p. 8.
36. Wreckers win big post league pennant at Schofield Barracks" (1917, January 30). *Hawaiian Gazette*, p. 8.
37. "Wreckers defeat Portland again, doings are weird" (1917, March 2). *Hawaiian Gazette*, p. 8.
38. "Hawaiians coming in March" (1916, December 9). *Fort Wayne News*, p. 4.
39. "Topeka 'Jack' Johnson turns cop" (1915, April 20). *Kansas City Journal*, p. 8.
40. "The Negro Stars to pitch today" (1917, April 29). *Kansas City Star*, p. A17.
41. "A rival for Donaldson" (1917, April 27). *Kansas City Times*, p. sports.
42. "Amateur baseball" (1917, May 3). *Kansas City Journal*, p. 8.
43. Cy Sherman, Hitting the high spots on the sporting pike" (1917, May 8). *Lincoln Daily Star*, p. 9.
44. "All-Nations again put skids under Indiana" (1917, May 7). *Kansas City Post*, p. 5.
45. Ferdinand Gottlieb, "Notes of the Sport World" (1917, May 31). *Pleasanton Observer Enterprise*, sports.
46. John H. Nankivell, *The History of the Twenty-fifth Regiment United States Infantry, 1869–1926*, p. 143.
47. William "Big C" Johnson (personal communication, 1984).
48. "The History of the World's Greatest Colored pitcher" (1919, July 9). *Chicago Whip*, p. 7.

Chapter 3

1. "ABCs open with twin win over Giants" (1920, May 3). *Indianapolis Stars*, p. sports.
2. "Kansas City Defeats St. Louis Giants, 4–2" (1920, July 5) *St. Louis Globe Democrat*, p. 13.
3. Dave Wyatt, "Rogan stops the American Giants" (1920, July 10). *Chicago Defender*, p. 9.
4. Charles A. Starks, "Food for fans" (1920, July 10). *Kansas City Sun*, p. 8.
5. "Near riot as Chicago Giants beat Monarchs" (1920, August 1). *Kansas City Journal*, p. B9.
6. "Monarchs won in 12 innings" (1920, August 2). *Kansas City Times*, p. 8.
7. Charles A. Starks (1920, August 7). *Kansas City Sun*, p. 8.
8. Monarchs beat Dayton in second game, 4–1" (1920, August 9). *Kansas City Journal*, p. 7.
9. "Monarchs lose close game to Dayton Marcos, 4–3" (1920, August 10). *Kansas City Journal*, p. 7.
10. "Armors lose" (1920, September 13). *Omaha Daily News*, p. 10.
11. "Rogan holds ABCs safe; Monarchs win" (1920, September 26). *Kansas City Journal*, p. B10.
12. "Monarchs again in field" (1921, April 17). *Kansas City Times*, p. A18.
13. "Blacks play to 616,000" (1920, December 5). *San Antonio Light*, p. 9.

Chapter 4

1. "The California winter league" (1920, December 11). *Chicago Whip*, p. 7.
2. Article. (1921, April 30). *Kansas City Sun*, p. 8.
3. "Night baseball makes its debut here tonight" (1930, August 17). *St. Joseph Gazette*, p. 5.
4. "Detroit Stars may lose ball park" (1921, October 21). *Chicago Whip*, p. 2.
5. "American Giants drop two games to Kay Sees" (1921, July 9). *Chicago Defender*, p. 11.
6. "Owner Wilkinson writes" (1921, May 14). *Kansas City Sun*, p. 8.
7. *Kansas City Sun*, April 2, 1921, p. 8.
8. "A new catcher" (1921, June 11). *Kansas City Sun*, p. 8.
9. Dan Burley, "Giants take 2 from Monarchs" (1934, June 1). *Kansas City Call*, Tulsa edition, p. 6.
10. Dan Burley, "Foster tames Monarchs before 8,500 Chicago Fans" (1934, June 1) *St. Louis Argus*, p. 5.
11. Frank Duncan Jr. (personal communication, November 15, 1986).
12. Frank Duncan Jr. (personal communication, November 15, 1986).

13. "New Monarchs can't touch oldsters—Carr" (1946, August 2). *Kansas City Call*, City edition, p. 22.
14. "A slugfest to the Monarchs" (1921, June 4). *Kansas City Sun*, p. 8.
15. "Monarchs won in ten innings" (1921, June 4). *Kansas City Sun*, p. 8.
16. "Ray's Negro population" (1921, October 13). *Richmond Missourian*, p. 7.
17. "Al Munroe picks all star ball team" (1922, October 7). *Chicago Whip*, p. 7.
18. "Two Monarchs hurlers hold team hitless" (1923, August 6). *Kansas City Journal*, p. 5.
19. Rogan's shutouts for 1923: April 9 at Galveston, April 28 vs. American Giants, May 6 vs. St. Louis Stars, May 20 vs. Detroit Stars, June 9 vs. Cuban Stars, September 18 vs. Birmingham and October 7 vs. Wichita Western League.
20. "Not so bad at that" (1921, August 18). *Osawatomie Graphic*, p. sports.
21. "Rogan saved the K.C. team from defeat in a 8 to 6 win" (1921, October 6). *Osawatomie Graphic*, p. sports.
22. "Negroes easy for Tramways" (1920, October 18) *Kansas City Post*, p. 8.
23. "The sport news section" (1922, May 4). *Osawatomie Graphic*, p. sports.
24. "Monarchs 12, Maryville 2" (1922, September 21). *Advocate Democrat*, p. 1.
25. "Monarchs easy victors" (1923, August 13). *Topeka Daily Capital*, p. 7.
26. "Burlington no match for Kansas City Monarchs" (1923, August 21). *Daily Republican*, p. 1.
27. "Monarchs won game" (1923, August 20). *Junction City Daily* union, p. sports.
28. "Monarchs win from Jacksons 9 to 2 in loosely played tilt" (1922, May 18). *Jackson Citizen Patriot*, p. sports.
29. "All-Nations defeat Sioux" (1922, August 30). *Sioux Falls Press*, p. 8.
30. "Sioux lose second game" (1922, August 31). *Sioux Falls Press*, p. 8.
31. "Hall hurls Bears to win as Rogan meets waterloo" (1922, October 2). *Rocky Mountain News*, p. sports.
32. "Bears drop 4-1 contest to Kansas City Monarchs" (1922, September 28). *Rocky Mountain News*, p. sports.
33. "K.C. team plays Denver Bears in Morgan Thurs." (1922, September 23). *[Morgan] Evening Times*, p. sports.
34. "Wichita plays Monarchs here tomorrow p.m." (1923, October 1). *Parsons Daily Sun*, p. sports.
35. "Monarchs won 12 to 8" (1923, June 23). *Fort Scott Tribune*, p. sports.
36. "Negroes play Enidites today" (1927, September 22). *Enid Morning News*, p. sports.
37. "Monarchs here to play Newton" (1927, September 19). *Newton Evening News*, p. 5.
38. "Antique dealer's hobby keeps him on the road" (1936, May 3). *Springfield News Leader*, p. B4.
39. Ernest Maun (personal communication, 1984).
40. American Association 1921 Record. (1922). Reach Official American League Guide, 281–291.
41. Bruce Dudley (1922) *The "Little World Series." Spalding's Official Base Ball Guide*, 187–199.
42. Charles A. Starks, "Negro Baseball breaking down the race prejudice" (1922, November 3). *St. Louis Argus*, p. sports.
43. Rube Currie, "Rube Currie derides big leaguers' alibi" (1922, December 15) *Kansas City Call*, p. 6.
44. "Antique dealer's hobby keeps him on the road" (1936, May 3). *Springfield News Leader*, p. B4.

Chapter 5

1. Charles D. Marshall, "Will colored umpires be given a tryout?" (1920, March 27). *Indianapolis Freeman*, p. sports.
2. "Sport Hits" (1921, October 21). *California Eagle*, p. sports.
3. "Kansas City the first city to use Negro umpires in the league" (1923, April 21). *Kansas City Sun*, p. 8.
4. *Kansas City Call*, 1924, date unknown.
5. Taken from George Sweatt's un-published autobiography. A copy was provided by Dick Johnson. Sweatt died on July 19, 1983 in Los Angeles, California. The autobiography is not dated but the information shows that it was probably written in 1982.
6. Article taken from Wilber Rogan's scrapbook. Newspaper and publication date unknown.
7. William "Big C" Johnson (personal communication, 1984).
8. "Monarchs blank Detroit Stars, 6-0" (1923, May 21). *Detroit Free Press*, p. sports.
9. "All-Nations defeat Sioux" (1922 August 30). *Sioux Falls Press*, p. 8.
10. "The Monarchs won" (1923, August 16). *Marysville Advocate Democrat*, p. 1.
11. "Fredonia split with Monarchs" (1922, August 29). Fredonia paper not named, p. sports.
12. "Kansas City wins second game off Black Barons, 7-0" (1923, September 19). *Birmingham Herald*, p. sports.
13. "Monarchs won 12 to 8" (1923, June 23). *Fort Scott Daily Tribune*, p. sports.
14. John B. Holway, *Blackball Stars*, p. 193.
15. Taken from George Sweatt's un-published autobiography.
16. John B. Holway, *Blackball Stars*, p. 51.
17. Fred Langford (personal communication, December 10, 1983).
18. Eugene McFarland (personal communications, 1908–1988).
19. Article taken from Wilber Rogan's scrapbook. Newspaper and date unknown.
20. Alberta Penn Gilmore (personal communication, 1986).
21. "Brilliant play and loyal fans make Monarchs club great" (1928, July 27). *Kansas City Call*, Progress edition tenth anniversary, p. 15.
22. "Q. J. Gilmore is rated high by N.N.L" (1928, February 17). *Kansas City Call*, p. 5.
23. "Kansas City Monarchs, fielding prejudice" (1981, August 2). Vibrations, Sunday Magazine of the *Columbia Missourian*, p. 5.
24. "Stars-Monarchs open baseball championship series here Saturday" (1925, September 18). *St. Louis Argus*, p. 1.
25. "Stars win two games from the Monarchs" (1925, September 25). *St. Louis Argus*, p. 7.
26. "Monarchs nose out the St. Louis Stars" (1925, October 2). *St. Louis Argus*, p. 7.
27. "Monarchs are defeated in opening game" (1925, October 2). *Kansas City Journal*, p. 8.
28. "Hilldale club in win over Monarchs," Philadelphians take 3-1 game in ten-inning battle. (1925, October 4). *Kansas City Journal*, p. 10A.
29. "Monarchs drop another to Hilldale" (1925, October 5). *Kansas City Journal*, p. 6.
30. "Monarchs improving" (1925, October). *Kansas City Call*, Baseball extra, p. 1.
31. "Monarchs win second game of big series" (1925, October 11). *Kansas City Journal*, p. 11.

32. "Monarchs beat locals" (1923, June 29). *Wichita Eagle*, p. 14.
33. "Didn't bother the Monarchs very much" (1926, July 22). *Oberlin Herald*, p. 1.
34. Carl Beckwith, "Receipts for World Series fall way off" (1925, October 23). *Kansas City Call*, p. 6.
35. Fay Young, "Eastern Club cops two straight games to end play with Kansas City" (October 1925). *Chicago Defender*, p. Part 2, Page 6.
36. Fay Young, "Kansas City was Weaken 20 per cent. Eastern Club cops two straight games to end play with Kansas City" (October 1925). *Chicago Defender*, p. Part 2, Page 6.
37. John B. Holway, *Voices from the Great Black Baseball Leagues*, p. 23.
38. "A worlds championship goes on a visit to Philly" (1925, October 16). *Kansas City Call*, p. 6.
39. Taken from George Sweatt's un-published autobiography.
40. "Kansas City here for five game series and fight for first place in league race" (1926, May 29). *Chicago Defender*, part 2, p. 4.
41. Jinx C. Broussard, "One of baseball's great New Orleans University Grad. Date unknown," Alumni Spotlight.
42. Willie Foster taped recorded interview with Charles Whitehead, recorded late 1970s.
43. "Zinn proves nemesis of Monarchs players" (1926, October 11). *Pittsburg Daily Headlight*, p. 3.
44. "Didn't bother the Monarchs very much" (1926, July 22). *Oberlin Herald*, p. 1.
45. "Monarchs defeat Legion team in a fast game" (1926, July 23). *Wymore Arbor State*, p. unknown.
46. "Bert Gholston's All-Star team" (1926, August 27) *Kansas City Call*, p. 7.
47. Taken from George Sweatt's un-published autobiography.

Chapter 6

1. "Bullet Rogan to manage Monarchs" (1926, March 12). *Kansas City Call*, p. 6.
2. "Triden-Monarch game a thriller" (1923, August 19). *Morning Chronicle*, p. 1.
3. Holly Hiller, "A baseball memoir George Giles" (1984, May 27). *Manhattan Mercury*, D1.
4. "Kansas City Monarchs, fielding prejudice" (1981, August 2). Vibrations, Sunday Magazine of the *Columbia Missourian*, p. 5.
5. Doolittle Young (personal communication 1984).
6. "Large crowd attends last rites for Geo. Mitchell, professional ball player" (1953, November, 17). Sparta, Illinois, news paper unknown.
7. Newt Allen. (personal communications, 1982–1987).
8. A. D. Williams, "Claims Crawford one of the best baseball trainers" (1931, January 9). *Kansas City Call*, p. Sports 2B.
9. Walter Judge, "Defeat Denver A.C., 4 to 3" (1934, August 6). *Denver Post*, p. sports.
10. Local Sporting News. (1923, June 15). *Chanute Daily Tribune*, p. 8.
11. Bert Gholston, "Rogan, Duncan and picked on Bert Gholston's 1927 All-Star team" (1927, September 23). *Kansas City Call*, p. 6.
12. Bert Gholston, "Diamond Dust" (1928, February 24). *Kansas City Call*, p. 4.
13. George Giles (personal communication, October 12, 1985).

14. "Dizzy's dope on baseball" (1932, March 19). *Pittsburgh Courier*, p. 4, second section.
15. James McCary, "Article in Call gets response" (1931, October 30). *Kansas City Call*, p. Sports 2B.
16. "Local boy to start contest here Saturday" (1928, June 14). *Wichita Beacon*, p. 11.
17. Frank Duncan Jr. (personal communication, March 26, 1983).
18. Stella M. Cooper, "Army" Cooper's wife (personal communication, December 15, 1984).
19. "Hallie "Art Shires" Harding is back in the States unsigned; and here, folks, is story" (1932, April 1). *Chicago Defender*, p. sport.
20. Doolittle Young (personal communication 1984).
21. John "Buck" O'Neil (personal communications, 1982–2003)
22. Jesse Williams (personal communication 1984).
23. "Antique dealer's hobby keeps him on the road" (1936, May 3). *Springfield News Leader*, p. B4.
24. Newt Allen. (personal communications, 1982–1987).
25. "Stars new 2nd baseman" (1931, April 17). *St. Louis Argus*, p. 7.
26. Frank Duncan Jr. (personal communication, November 15, 1986).
27. "Kansas City Monarchs, fielding prejudice" (1981, August 2). Vibrations, Sunday Magazine of the *Columbia Missourian*, p. 4
28. George Giles (personal communications, 1982–1990).
29. "Kansas City Nears League Title..." *Chicago Defender*, 7-9-1927, p. 9.
30. Ted "Double Duty" Radcliffe (personal communications, 1982–1999).
31. "Kansas City, American, Chicago Team Wins Pennant" 9/13/1982, p. 5.
32. "Locals lose both games" (1928, August 27). *Russell Record*, p. 1.
33. "Boosters hold Monarchs to 4 hits; lose 2 to 0" (1928, September 14). *Atchison Daily Globe*, p. 6.
34. "Monarchs win two when misplays by locals are costly" (1928, June 18). *Wichita Eagle*, p. 2.
35. "Monarchs easily win from Comar" (1928, June 21). *Tonkawa News*, p. sports.
36. "Fast nine to play Monarchs" (1928, September 21). *Arkansas City Daily Traveler*, p. 7.
37. Dizzy Dismukes, "Olde Stove League" (1928) George Giles' scrap book, newspaper unknown.
38. Dizzy Dismukes, "Judge Hueston re–Elected President" (1929, January 10). *Kansas City American*, p. 5.
39. George Giles (personal communications, 1982–1993).
40. George Giles (personal communications, 1982–1993).
41. "First homer is worth $35 to Bullet Rogan" (1929, May 31). *Kansas City Call*, p. 12.
42. Jack Etkin, *Innings Ago*, p. 102.
43. "Livingston jailed in Texas; Forced to pay fine for (?)" (1929, December 27). *Kansas City Call*, Sports p. 10.
44. "Livingston jailed in Texas; Forced to pay fine for (?)" (1929, December 27). *Kansas City Call*, Sports p. 10.
45. "Professional Stars face Monarchs today" (1929, June 9) *Muskogee Daily Phoenix*, p. 13.
46. Richard Bak, *Turkey Stearnes and the Detroit Stars*, p. 184.
47. Richard Bak, *Turkey Stearnes and the Detroit Stars*, p. 184.
48. "Mac Park Ruins are scoured for Possible Fire and Panic Victims" *Kansas City Call*, 7/12/1929, p. Sports.

Chapter 7

1. The Rube Foster Ledger (author's collection), p. 130.
2. "Blues vs. Monarchs" (1921, October 8). *Kansas City Sun*, p. 8.
3. The Rube Foster Ledger, p. 130.
4. Ibid.
5. Ibid., p. 123.
6. Ibid., p. 124.
7. Ibid., p. 125.
8. From George Sweatt's "My Life," an unpublished autobiography.
9. Paul W. Fisher, "Talk of the Times" (1967, March 10). *Kansas City Times*, p. 21.
10. "Locals lost but gave Monarchs good game" (1927, July 29). *Great Bend Tribune*, p. 7.
11. Holly Hiller, "A baseball memoir George Giles" (1984, May 27). *Manhattan Mercury*, D1 & D6.
12. Bob Finnigan, "Baseball runs in their bloodline" (1990, June 28). *Manhattan Mercury*, D1 & D6.
13. "Antique Dealer's hobby keeps him on the road" (1936, May 3). *Springfield News Leader*, p. B4.
14. Donn Rogosin, *Invisible Men*, p. 18.
15. "Monarchs won. Clinton team worried colored champions" (1926, August 12). *Henry County Democrat*, p. 7.
16. "3,500 saw Larned Monarch Game" (1926, August 26). *Larned Tiller and Toiler*, p. 1 section 2.
17. "Monarchs lift eight balls from park" (1927, July 28). *Salina Journal*, p. 12.
18. "Negroes blank local players" (1927, September 23). *Enid Morning News*, p. 10.
19. "Give Monarchs a real Battle" (1928, September 21). *Arkansas City Daily Traveler*, p. 8.
20. "Chick pitches winning game but mates lose" (1927, September 12). *Trenton Republican Times*, p. 1.
21. "Merchants beaten 13 to 1 by Monarchs" (1928, August 11). *Trenton Republican Times*, p. 1.
22. "Monarchs easily defeat Advertisers" (1926, August 13). *Wichita Beacon*, p. 14
23. "Monarchs take three from Wichita pros" (1927, September 23). *Kansas City Call*, p. 5.
24. "Monarchs win from All-Pros in night game" (1930, June 3). *Wichita Beacon*, p. 21 and "Monarchs win over all-pros for second time" (1930, June 4). *Wichita Beacon*, p. 3.
25. "National League Stars seeking to stop Monarchs" (1936, September, 22). *Wichita Beacon*, p. 16
26. Article. (1926, April 19). *Salina Journal*, p. sports.
27. "Kansas City Monarchs trounce Miners by 19-12 score" (1927, September 12). *Joplin News Herald*, p. 8.
28. James W. Loewen, *Sundown Towns*, p. 93.
29. "Late rally fails to upset K.C. Players" (1928, April 22). *Springfield Daily News*, p. 11.
30. "Midgets down Monarchs in opening game, 8-7" (1927, September 8). *Springfield Leader*, p. 9.
31. "Monarchs trim Midgets in second, 9-1" (1927, September 9). *Springfield Daily News*, p. 6.
32. "Midgets easy for Monarchs" (1927, September 9). *Springfield Leader*, p. 14.
33. "Monarchs trim Midgets in second, 9-1" (1927, September 9). *Springfield Daily News*, p. 6.
34. "Monarch club in an easy victory" (1928, October 1). *Monitor-Index and Democrat*, p. 2.
35. "Monarchs vs. Morland" (1928, August 30). *Morland Monitor*, p. 1.
36. "Monarchs win in 12th inning" (1928, September 17). *Concordia Blade Empire*, p. 3.
37. "Monarchs so fast they are bothered by weak imitators" (1928, June 9). *Wichita Eagle*, p. 5.
38. "Big League Base Ball at Great Bend" (1928, June 14). *Great Bend Tribune*, p. Sports.
39. *Missouri's Black Heritage*, p. 148.
40. *Missouri's Black Heritage*, p. 149.
41. *Missouri's Black Heritage*, p. 149.
42. "Girl's lie caused Coffeyville riot" (1927, June 10). *Seattle Enterprise*, p. 1 and 4.
43. "Crowd sees champs" (1922, August 24). *Iola Daily Register*, p. 8.
44. Ernest Maun (personal communication, 1984).
45. "The Monarchs won" (1922, October 12). *Iola Daily Register*, p. 8.
46. "A victory in Meusel's homer" (1920, October 10). *Kansas City Times*, p. 10.
47. "Food for fans" (1920, October 16). *Kansas City Sun*, p. 8.
48. "Monarchs easy winners" (1928, October 8). *Atchison Daily Globe*, p. 2.
49. "Colored team wins by a score of 11 to 0" (1926, August 26). *Dodge City Journal*, p. 2.

Chapter 8

1. "Hansox will play K.C. Monarchs" *Hannibal Daily Courier Post*, 8-15-1930, p. Sports.
2. "Baseball talk" (1914, August 24). *Austin Daily Herald*, p. sports.
3. "Cubans beat Kansas City" (1930, April 19). *San Antonio Light*, p. 9. "K.C. Defeats Cubans, 9-2" (1930, April 20). *San Antonio Light*, Sports p. 1 and "K.C. to Meet Black Indians" (1930, April 21). *San Antonio Light*, p. 11A.
4. Roy Waller (personal communication, 1985).
5. "Kansas City Monarchs cop 3 more games" *Chicago Defender*, 5/30/1930, p. A15.
6. "And so, there'll be no game tonight" *The Arkansas City Daily Traveler*, June 10, 1930, p. Sports.
7. "Enid gets first glimpse of night baseball when Kansas City Monarchs drub Phillips" (1930, April 29). *Enid Morning News*, p. 6.
8. Donn Rogosin, *Invisible Men*, p. 128
9. "Thousands turn out to see baseball at night" (1930, May 7). *Waco News Tribune*, p. 6.
10. John B. Holway, *Blackball Stars*, p. 336-337.
11. Richard Bak, *Turkey Stearnes and the Detroit Stars*, p. 191.
12. "Our First Nite Game" *Cleveland Gazette*, 7/19/1930, p. Sports.
13. "12,000 See Night Game" *Kansas City Times*, 7/19/1930, p. Sports.
14. "Night baseball makes hit with local fans" (1930, August 8). *St. Joseph Gazette*, p. 5.
15. "Like night baseball" (1930, August 8). *St. Joseph News Press*, p. 16.
16. "Monarchs stage field day smothering Hansox by 16-1" (1930, August 16). *Hannibal Courier Post*, p. 8.
17. "Night baseball great game especially for lost balls" (1930, September 16). *Manhattan Morning Chronicle*, p. 1.
18. "Lose to Monarchs" (1930, September 18). *Manhattan Republic*, p. 5.
19. "Night baseball great game especially for lost balls" (1930, September 16). *Manhattan Morning Chronicle*, p. 1.
20. "Champions beat local Negro nine" (1930, April, 11). *Galveston Daily News*, p. 13.
21. John Coates, "Hancock looks back some 50 years at Negro baseball," Sioux City, Iowa, newspaper unknown.

22. "Kansas City Monarchs defeated Mohawks here" (1922, June 7). *Jefferson City Daily Capital News*, p. 1.
23. "Monarchs headed by great hurler" (1931, September 24). *Council Bluffs Nonpareil*, p. 1.
24. "Colored team's hurler baffles local batsmen" (1931, July 11). *Wisconsin Rapids Daily Tribune*, p. 7.
25. "Red Sox drop ragged tilt to Monarchs" (1931, July 20). *Crookston Daily Times*, p. 5.
26. "Negro team wins" (1931, July 17). *Burlington Standard Democrat*, p. sports.
27. "K.C. Monarchs trim locals" (1931, July 31). *Wymore Arbor State*, p. sports.
28. "Colored team's hurler baffles local batsmen" (1931, July 11). *Wisconsin Rapids Daily Tribune*, p. 7.
29. "Monarchs win 9–0; play again today" (1931, October 4). *Kansas City Kansan*, p. 11A.
30. "Monarchs top Grays." (1931, August 29). *Akron Beacon Journal*, p. 11.
31. "Grays split double bill with Kansas" (1931, August 31). *Cleveland Press*, p. 24.
32. "Monarchs defeat Cubans in contest" (1931, September 28). *Council Bluffs Nonpareil*, p. 6.
33. "Trent is "dub" then hero in hurling 6–5 win over Monarchs in 12 innings" (1931, September 11). *St. Louis Argus*, p. 14.
34. "Canaries suffer first home loss since June 7; Monarchs winners 12–5" (1931, July 23). *Daily Argus-Leader*, sports.
35. "Brandon hits homer, triple as mates win" (1931, July 24). *Sioux City Journal*, p. 13.
36. "Strikes out 27 batters" (1930, August 3). *Kansas City Star*, p. 3B.
37. Cum Posey, "Posey's All-America ball club!" (1931, October 10). *Pittsburgh Courier*, p. 5, second 2.
38. Cum Posey, "Posey's All-America ball club!" (1931, October 10). *Pittsburgh Courier*, p. 5 section 2.
39. "Fast Negro team drops first game in Topeka" (1931, September 10). *Topeka Daily Capital*, p. 9.
40. "Monarchs are easy victims of locals" (1931, July 30). *Advocate-Democrat*, p. 12.
41. Jerry E. Clark, *Nebraska Diamonds*, Making History press, Omaha. (1991) p. 13.
42. "Jamestown baseball club will open season May 8" (1932, April 21). *Jamestown Sun*, p. 6.
43. "First season game won on windy Sunday" (1932, May 16). *Jamestown Sun*, p. 6.
44. "Jamestown to play New Rockford here on Tuesday night" (1932, May 23). *Jamestown Sun*, p. 6.
45. "Cassell allows only two hits in entire game" (1932, May 25). *Jamestown Sun*, p. 6.
46. "Jamestown club plays good ball to beat visitors" (1932, May 31). *Jamestown Sun*, p. 6.
47. (1932, July 5). *Jamestown Sun*, p. 6.
48. Al Monroe, "Panic is seen within the ranks of organized baseball" (1932, August). *Abbott's Monthly*, 16–17, 48.
49. Quincy Trouppe, *20 Years Too Soon*, p. 66.
50. "Stars new moundsman" (1931, April 10). *St. Louis Argus*, p. 7.
51. Phil Dixon, and Cool Papa Bell, "A legend in his own time" (1991, March 21–27). *St. Louis American*, p. 1B & 3B.
52. J. Bell is fastest man he's ever seen in baseball, says Paul Waner. (1933, January 13). *Kansas City Call*, Southwest edition, p. 1B.
53. "Negroes exhibit speed and hitting strength in win" (1932, August 5). *Daily Argus-Leader*, p. sports.
54. "Monarchs' great team beat Red Sox 7 to 0 before huge crowd Thursday" (1932, July 22). *Crookston Daily Times*, p. 5.
55. "Colored artist impress in win" (1932, July 23). *Winnipeg Free Press*, p. 7.
56. "Brewer pitches Monarchs to 8–0 win over Red Sox" (1932, August 8). *Grand Forks Herald*, p. 2.
57. "2,000 Milwaukee fans see Monarchs trip Davids, 11–4." (1932, September 23). *Kansas City Call*, Southwest edition, p. 2B.
58. "Monarchs set for battle" (1932, September 28). *Wichita Beacon*, p. 11.
59. "Monarchs put up very fine ball exhibition" (1932, August 2). *Jamestown Sun*, p. 6.
60. "Team defeated only 7 times in 1932 season" (1932, August 15). *Jamestown Sun*, p. 6.
61. "Jamestown baseball season one of greatest in history; Hancock leads bat average" (1932, August 23). *Jamestown Sun*, p. 6.
62. John Coates, "Hancock looks back some 50 years at Negro baseball" Sioux City, Iowa, newspaper unknown.
63. "Lefty Holmes due to handle mound duties" (1932, September 28). *Wichita Evening Eagle*, p. 6 and "Monarchs win over S.K.S.L. in Fast game, 11–0" (1932, September 29). *Wichita Beacon*, p. 13.
64. "The Skelly loses to colored nine" (1932, October 1). *El Dorado Times*, p. 4.
65. "Monarchs win over All-Stars, 17 to 7" (1932, October 9). *Joplin Globe*, p. 8.
66. "Giants and K.C. split in even split in four" (1932, September 3). *Chicago Defender*, p. sports.
67. "Monarchs make it 73" (1932, October 3). *Kansas City Times*, p. 10.
68. "Senator first baseman picks All-Stars to win tilt" (1932, October 10). *Wichita Beacon*, p. 10.
69. "Monarchs win over Major Stars" (1932, October 11). *Wichita Beacon*, p. 12.
70. "Monarchs take five out of six from the Aztecas, leading Mexico City club" (1932, November 11). *Kansas City Call*, p. 1B.
71. Quincy Trouppe, *20 Years Too Soon*, p. 69.
72. Johnnie Porter, "Porter Grams" (1933, May 26). *Southwest American*, p. unknown.
73. "Indians win from Monarchs, 9 to 3" (1933, May 28). *Joplin Globe*, p. 10.
74. "Monarchs add to string" (1933, July 5). *Kansas City, Times*, p. sports.
75. "Record crowd sees Monarchs defeat Duluth" (1933, July 10). *Duluth Herald*, p. 10.
76. "Colored boys get 21 hits to local's 8" (1933, July 13). *Wisconsin Rapids Daily Tribune*, p. 5.
77. "Monarchs take second series game, 8–0" (1933, September 14). *Wisconsin Rapids Daily Tribune*, p. 5.
78. "Kansas City Monarchs here" (1933, July 28). *Jewell County Monitor*, p. 1.
79. "Large crowd see Monarchs" (1933, August 4). *Linn-Palmer Record*, p. 1.
80. "Kansas City ball club faces Imps here tonight" (1933, August 7). *Des Moines Register*, p. 5.
81. "Brewer hurls stellar game" (1933, August 8). *Des Moines Register*, p. 7–8.
82. "Monarchs bump All-Stars in wild tilt" (1933, September 11). *Wichita Beacon*, p. 9.
83. Janet Bruce, *The Kansas City Monarchs*, p. 83.
84. "Monarchs in 14–3 victory over Demons" (1933, August 11). *Kansas City Call*, Southwest edition, p. 2B.
85. "Monarchs's fire-ball star tames Senators" (1933, August 24). *Topeka Daily Capital*, p. 8.

86. "Monarchs slip Grover Alexander 1–0 lacing" (1933, August 18). *Kansas City Call*, p. unknown.
87. "House of David and K.C. Monarchs play great ball" (1933, August 11). *Winnipeg Evening Tribune*, p. unknown.
88. "Monarchs win again" (1933, August 25). *Topeka Daily Capital*, p. 10.
89. Monarchs win over Davids, 6 to 2" (1933, August 21). *Wichita Beacon*, p. 9.
90. "Monarchs meet well known House of David club here tonight" (1933, September 19). *Kansas City Kansan*, p. 6.
91. "Monarchs out to battle majors" (1933, September 25). *Wichita Beacon*, p. 9.
92. "Beat the bearded boys" (1933, October 2). *Carthage Evening Press*, p. 6.
93. "Dizzy ready for work" (1933, October 2). *Kansas City Times*, p. sports.
94. "Dizzy ready for work" (1933, October 2). *Kansas City Times*, p. sports.
95. Western Historical Manuscript collection, University of Missouri–St. Louis, April 6, 1970, Oral History T-015. Interview with James "Cool Papa" Bell, Interviewed by Dr. Arthur Shaffer and Dr. Charles Korr, Black community Leaders project.
96. "Sitting in on the sports game" (1932, September, 29). *Wichita Evening Eagle*, p. 8.
97. Article from the Wilber Rogan scrapbook. Black Archives Mid-America, newspaper unknown.
98. "Fans want Negroes in big leagues, report suggest" (1933, February 17). *Kansas City Call*, Southwest edition, p. 1B.
99. "Rogan's hit to right breaks up a ball game that almost gives the fans heart disease" (1933, October 6). *Kansas City Call*, Southwest edition, p. 1B.
100. Pete Lightner, "Just in sport" (1934, October 11). *Wichita Eagle*, p. 8.
101. See the Kansas City All-Star game of October 8, 1933 for this quote. Check *Journal, Times, Star* and *Post*.
102. "Famous outfielder believes team fastest barnstorming club on tour" (1933, October 12). *Wichita Beacon*, p. 10.
103. "Negro hurler fans 14 men, blanks stars" (1933, October 12). *The Oklahoman*, p. 12.
104. "Major leaguers beat Monarchs" (1933, October 13). *Wichita Evening Eagle*, p. 20.
105. Frank Duncan Jr. (personal communication, November 15, 1986).
106. "Coming Sunday, July 18, one of baseball's greatest attractions" (1926, July 15). *Oberlin Herald*, p. 1.
107. "Semi-pros hope to stop Monarchs club" (1933, October 22). *Kansas City Kansan*, p. 9A.
108. "Win 134 games, lose 14" (1933, October 18). *Kansas City Times*, p. 10.

Chapter 9

1. Charles Whitehead's interview with Dave Malarcher, interview date unknown. Malarcher died May 11, 1982.
2. "Donaldson in 1917 debut" (1917, April 26). *Kansas City Times*, p. 11.
3. "The White Base Ball and Amusement Association, new name; Goodwin field manager" (1921, October 15). *California Eagle*, p. sports.
4. Ed O'Malley, "Walter Mails gets jarring" (1920, November 22). *Los Angeles Times*, p. Section 2, p. 9.
5. Chet Brewer (personal communication, 1987).
6. "Cops prevent battle at Los Angeles park" (1929, February 22). *Kansas City Call*, p. 8.
7. "Bobby Meusel to be with All-Stars" (1920, November 5). *Los Angeles Times*, Section 3, p. 3.
8. "All Stars cop ball game" (1920, October 25). *Los Angeles Times*, Section 1, p. 6.
9. "All Stars are slapped" (1920, November 11). *Los Angeles Times*, Section 1, p. 8.
10. "All-Stars are bumped" (1920, November 15). *Los Angeles Times*, section 2, p. 8.
11. "Mails is after sweet revenge" (1920, December 9). *Los Angeles Times*, section 3, p. 2.
12. "Mails is to pitch this afternoon" (1920, November 21). *Los Angeles Times*, section 1, p. 8.
13. "White Sox thump Mails" (1920, December 13). *Los Angeles Times*, Section 1, p. 8.
14. "Walter Mails gets jarring" (1920, November 22). *Los Angeles Times*, Section 2, p. 9.
15. "White Sox skunk Ralls's All-Stars" (1921, January 24). *Los Angeles Times*, section 2, p. 8.
16. Rogan's 1920 California Winter League home runs. #1 vs. Major League All-Stars (1), #2 11/20/1920 vs. Major League All-Stars (1), #3 1/1/1921 vs. Fisher's All-Stars, #4 2/19/1921 vs. Rall's All-Stars (1).
17. Article from the Wilber Rogan's scrapbook. Black Archives Mid-America, newspaper unknown.
18. "Baseball" (1921, February 5). *Kansas City Sun*, p. 8.
19. "Baseball" (1921, February 5). *Kansas City Sun*, p. 8.
20. "Hard luck for Rogan" (1921, April 2). *Chicago Whip*, p. 7.
21. "White Sox grab game from Giants" (1921, March 27). *Los Angeles Times*, p. 18.
22. Clint Thomas (personal communication, 1983, August).
23. Chet Brewer (personal communication, 1985, September).
24. *Smoke*, p. 247.
25. *Smoke*, p. 251.
26. "Giants take it" (1926, January 18). *Los Angeles Times*, p. A8.
27. "Kings 9: Giants 0" (1926, February 8). *Los Angeles Times*, p. A8.
28. See Kansas City Call for Winter League of 1926–27 for this quote.
29. "Cleveland Gts. Champions of Coast League" (1929, March 8). *Kansas City Call*, p. 13.
30. James Newton, "Chet Brewer is leading coast pitcher" (1929, February 22). *Kansas City Call*, p. 7.
31. "Giants win as Joseph hits out home run" (1929, October 25). *Kansas City Call* City Edition, Second section sports, p. 11.
32. "Bullet Rogan halts attack of big league heavy hitters" (1929, November 8) *Kansas City Call*, Main edition, p. Second section sports, p. 12.
33. "Rogan shines as club loses two games in California Winter League — other Monarchs going great in coast League" (1929, November 29). *Kansas City Call*, Main edition, p. 7B.
34. "Monarchs head for home with 14 victories in bag" (1932, November 18). *Kansas City Call*, Southwest edition, p. 1B.
35. Taken from John Holways' interview of "Dink" Mothell.
36. Taken from John Holways' interview of "Dink" Mothell.
37. R.H. Barber writes in the Philadelphia Tribune. (1929, February 21). *Kansas City American*, p. sports.

38. Taken from John Holway's interview of Dink Mothell.
39. "Monarchs lift eight balls from park" (1927, July 28). *Salina Journal*, p. 12.
40. "Monarchs are held to 16–0" (1927, September 22). *Arkansas City Daily Traveler*, p. 10.
41. Email with author William McNeil. (2002, August 3). He has credited Rogan with a 42–14 pitching record for his winter years in California.

Chapter 10

1. Bob Boyd, "Foster makes majors eat from hand" (1931, October 9). *Kansas City Call*, p. unknown.
2. "Troubadours lose to Kansas City Monarchs by 8–1 score" (1934, June 5). *La Crosse Tribune* and *Leader-Press*, p. 12.
3. "Steve shows promise as relief hurler" (1934, June 2). *Wisconsin State Journal*, p. 11.
4. "Revamped Blues lose 8–4 decision to Monarchs" (1934, June 1). *Wisconsin State Journal*, p. 17.
5. "Troubadours lose to Kansas City Monarchs by 8–1 score" (1934, June 5). *La Crosse Tribune* and *Leader-Press*, p. 12.
6. "Monarchs win 2 from Mills, 3–1 and 5–3" (1934, September 17). *Chicago Tribune*, p. 23.
7. "Morris tames Kansas City Monarchs" (1934, June 16). *Bismarck Tribune*, p. 10.
8. "Jamestown defeated Kansas City Monarchs Thursday, 5 to 1" (1934, June 15). *Jamestown Sun*, p. 6.
9. "Monarchs halt hot try by Davids in ninth for triumph" (1934, July 15). *Daily Missoulian*, p. 5.
10. "Monarchs in 4–0 victory over H. of D.'s" (1934, July 20). *Kansas City Call*, Southwest edition, p. 6.
11. "Monarchs whip House of David nine in close game; Beverly, Brewer, Rogan star" (1934, August 3). *Kansas City Call*, Tulsa edition, p. 7.
12. "House of Davids batter colored Monarchs into subjection by score of 15–1 at Henderson park Monday" (1934, July 17). *Lethbridge Herald*, p. 10.
13. "Kansas City Monarchs in double win" (1934, June 8). *Kansas City Call*, p. 12.
14. "Morris tames Kansas City Monarchs" (1934, June 16). *Bismarck Tribune*, p. 10.
15. "Monarchs whip House of David nine in close games; Beverly, Brewer, Rogan star" (1934, August 3). *Kansas City Call*, p. 7.
16. "Colts, Davids are whipped by Monarchs" (1934, October 5). *Kansas City Call*, p. 6.
17. "Stearnes is added to K.C. team lineup" (1934, August 3). *Kansas City Call*, Tulsa edition, p. 6.
18. "Greeley Advertisers downed by colored club; score 12 to 1" (1934, August 2). *Denver Post*, p. sports.
19. "Defeat Denver A.C., 4 to 3" (1934, August 5). *Denver Post*, p. sports.
20. "Defeat Denver A.C., 4 to 3" (1934, August 5). *Denver Post*, p. sports.
21. Walter Judge, "Humble Oilers are defeated by bearded beauties, 8 to 2" (1934, August 13). *Denver Post*, p. sports.
22. (1934, August 11). *Denver Post*, p. sports.
23. Leonard Cahn, "Too much Satchel Paige; K.C. Monarchs drop 2 to 1 game to House of Davids" (1934, August 17). *Kansas City Call*, City edition, p. 12.
24. Robert Gamzey, "Monarchs extended to beat fighting Eason Oilers, 5 to 4" (1934, August 13). *Denver Post*, p. sports.
25. Walter Judge, "Kansas City Monarchs lose championship game" (1934, August 14). *Denver Post*, p. sports.
26. Walter Judge, "Kansas City Monarchs lose championship game" (1934, August 14). *Denver Post*, p. sports.
27. Walter Judge, "Kansas City Monarchs lose championship game" (1934, August 14). *Denver Post*, p. sports.
28. George Giles (personal communication, 1984).
29. "House of David team wins Denver baseball tourney" (1934, August 14). *Benton Harbor News Palladium*, p. 8.
30. "House of David team wins Denver baseball tourney" (1934, August 14). *Benton Harbor News Palladium*, p. 8.
31. "Monarchs again unable to beat bearded men in 10" (1934, August 24). *Kansas City Call*, City edition, p. 11.
32. "House of David nine wins contest from Negro stars" (1934, August 21). Colorado Springs daily newspaper, sports.
33. "Monarchs see win over Davids" (1934, August 25). *Wichita Beacon*, p. 5.
34. "House of David certain of win over Monarchs" (1934, August 26). *Wichita Beacon*, p. 8B.
35. "House of David certain of win over Monarchs" (1934, August 26). *Wichita Beacon*, p. 8B.
36. "Monarchs win before huge crowd" (1934, August 27) *Wichita Beacon*, p. 9.
37. "Monarchs, Davids play ten frames to 8–8 deadlock" (1934, September 21). *La Crosse Tribune*, p. 10.
38. "Bewhiskered club defeats Monarchs" (1934, September 30). *Tulsa Daily World*, p. sports.
39. "15,000 storm park to see Dizzy and Daffy" (1934, October 11). *Daily Oklahoman*, p. 17.
40. "11 to 0 count on famous men from big teams" (1934, October 8). *Jamestown Sun*, p. 6.
41. "Lyons touched for 11 hits for winning runs" (1934, October 6). *Valley City Times-Record*, p. 6.
42. "Dean boys entertain vast crowd by baseball feats" (1934, October 12). *Wichita Eagle*, p. 8.
43. "Monarchs beat Deans" (1934, October 13). *Kansas City Times*, p. 14.
44. "Dean obliges Kansas City nut vendor" (1934, October 13). *Des Moines Register*, p. 6.
45. "Dean all-Stars beaten 9–0 by Monarch team" (1934, October 14). *Des Moines Register*, section 7, p. 1.
46. "Dean all-Stars beaten 9–0 by Monarch team" (1934, October 14). *Des Moines Register*, section 7, p. 1.
47. "Deans capture semipro game" (1934, October 15). *Chicago Tribune*, p. unknown.
48. "Dean & Dean get $5,000 pitching for Mills team" (1934, October 15). *Chicago Tribune*, p. 19.
49. "Deans in city post series take 14,000" (1934, October 15). *Milwaukee Leader*, p. sports.
50. "Dizzy Dean heads All-Stars Monday" (1936, September 27). *Wichita Beacon*, p. 12B.
51. "Deans may take plane to Wichita" (1934, October 8). *Wichita Eagle*, p. 8.
52. "Elden Auker is no admirer of the boasting Dean brothers" (1934, October 21). *Kansas City Times*, p. 4B.
53. "Dead bandit identified as Lem Hawkins" (1934, September 7). *Kansas City Call*, City edition, p. 1.
54. "Lem Hawkins goes to Chicago" (1928, June 21). *Kansas City American*, p. unknown.
55. Lemuel Hawkins File; Inmate Case Files; United States Penitentiary-Leavenworth; Records of the Federal Bureau of Prisons, Record Group 129; National Archives and Records Administration-Central Plains Region (Kansas City).
56. Quincy Trouppe (personal communications, 1982–1996).

57. "Charleston puts his okay on Henry Milton" (1932, April 8). *Kansas City Call*, p. (need)
58. "All-Star club out to snatch second of set" (1936, June 9). *Peoria Star*, p. 12.
59. Taken from article in George Giles scrapbook. Year of publication unknown.
60. "Locals lose both games" (1928, August 27). *Russell Record*, p. 1.
61. Georgia Dwight (personal communications, 1982–2003).
62. Fred McDaniel (personal communication, November 4, 1987).
63. Jack Etkin, *Innings Ago*, p. 103.
64. The Major League guides give Brown's date of birth as 6/26/1915. According to Brown, this was not his correct date of birth. The new date was presented in order to make him appear younger.
65. Willard Brown (personal communication, May, 1987).
66. Willard Brown (personal communication, May, 1987).
67. Jack Etkin, *Innings Ago* p. 103.
68. "Great hurler will arrive with players" (1936, May 11). *Pampa News*, p. unknown.
69. "Crack colored team battles All-Stars" (1936, June 7). *Peoria Star*, section 3, p. 1.
70. The Monarchs had the following home attendance totals in 1935: 5/5 (1,200), 5/19 (2,500), 8/25 (3,000), 9/2 unverified, 9/4 (3,000), 10/11 (2,000), 10/13 (2,200) and 9/29 (3,000) a total of 16,900 the 18,000 total is an estimate based on the missing game.
71. "Great hurler will arrive with players" (1936, May 11). *Pampa News*, p. unknown.
72. "Leading Negro players clash in season's first big game" (1935, April 25). *Wichita Beacon*, p. 14.
73. "Monarchs down Giants in second" (1935, April 27). *Wichita Beacon*, p. 5.
74. "Monarchs in 5 wins and one defeat" (1935, May 3). *Kansas City Call*, p. 7.
75. "Monarchs win 4 to 3" (1935, May 22). *Emporia Daily Gazette*, p. 10.
76. "Dusky Missourians in Merchants double win" (1935, May 27). *Denver Post*, p. 10.
77. "With the Monarchs" (1935, June 7). *Devil Lake Journal*, p. unknown.
78. "Kardow loses third of season on eleven hits; Silvey gets home run" (1935, June 10). *Devil Lake Journal*, p. unknown.
79. "Colored team here tomorrow" (1935, June 11). *Valley City Times Record*, p. unknown.
80. "Monarchs win game Friday by score of 16-6" (1935, June 15). *Jamestown Sun*, p. 2.
81. "Deans vs. Paige will draw crowd" (1935, October 6). *Kansas City Journal-Post*, p. 13A.
82. Donn Rogosin, *Invisible Men*, p. 100.
83. "Trouppe leaves Monarchs" (1935, June 7). *Kansas City Call*, p. 7.
84. "Kansas City Monarchs in scoreless tie; Joseph hits for 3 sacks then dies there" (1935, June 21). *Kansas City Call*, p. 6.
85. "Paige, Brewer, hurl double shutout" (1935, June 7). *Winnipeg Evening Tribune*, p. 15.
86. "Kansas City Monarchs nose out Bismarck" (1935, June 8). *Winnipeg Evening Times*, p. 25.
87. "Bismarck nine divides doubleheader with Monarchs" (1935, June 17). *Bismarck Tribune*, p. 6.
88. "Kansas City Monarchs play here this evening" (1935, July 8). *Tacoma News Tribune*, p. 7.
89. "Kansas City Monarchs play here this evening" (1935, July 8). *Tacoma News Tribune*, p. 7.
90. "Monarchs defeat Tigers" (1935, July 9). *Tacoma News Tribune*, p. 14.
91. "Monarchs trim tribe" (1935, July 17). *Yakima Morning Herald*, p. 5.
92. "Fast Negro nine crushes Indians" (1934, July 11). *Yakima Morning Herald*, p. 5.
93. "Running catches and long drives entertain crowd" (1935, July 21). *Daily Missoulian*, p. 6.
94. "Monarchs in west winning ball games" (1935, July 19). *Kansas City Call*, p. 6.
95. "New homes in old setting for downtown old-timers" (1970, December 13). *Seattle Times*, p. G2.
96. "Monarchs win double victory" (1935, August 24). *Moberly Monitor-Index*, p. 5.
97. "Monarchs to return home Sunday to meet House of David club" (1935, August 24). *Kansas City, Kansan*, p. 6.
98. "Monarchs play four with Chicago Giants" (1935, August 31). *Kansas City Journal-Post*, p. 6.
99. "Beards take first contest by 4–3 score" (1935, September 16). *Denver Post*, p. 20.
100. "Monarchs win from Chicago at Omaha, 6–3" (1935, October 4). *Kansas City Call*, p. 6.
101. "Chicago beats Monarchs in rally, 7 to 1" (1935, September 27). *Kansas City Call*, p. 6.
102. R. S. Simmons, "Monarchs in 8–2 win over Omaha Stars" (1935, October 25). *Kansas City Call*, p. 6.
103. "Rowe, mates lose to K. C. Monarchs" (1935, October 17). *Albert Lea Evening Tribune*, p. 12.
104. "Dean barnstorming junket flops" (1935, October 9). *Springfield Daily News*, p. 7.
105. "Paige loses hurling duel to Dean boy" (1935, October 11). *Kansas City Call*, p. 6.
106. "Monarchs win over Deans, 1–0" (1935, October 8). *St. Joseph Gazette*, p. 6.
107. "Monarchs win over Deans, 1–0" (1935, October 8). *St. Joseph Gazette*, p. 6.
108. Interview with Bill McCallop of Thatchers' Mortuary, in Kansas City, Kansas. Willard's date of birth was November 9, 1899. His date of death was September 7, 1935, at age 36. Willard was living at 428 Minnesota Avenue, in Kansas City, Kansas, at the time of his death.
109. Wilbur Rogan, Jr. (personal communication, 1985–2003).

Chapter 11

1. Willie B. Mays (personal communication, December 7, 1985).
2. Willie B. Mays (personal communication, June, 7, 1987).
3. "Antique Dealer's hobby keeps him on the road" (1936, May 3). *Springfield News Leader*, p. B4.
4. "Monarchs pop all-Star club in 6–5 battle" (1936, September 4). *Peoria Star*, p. 10.
5. "Antique dealer's hobby keeps him on the road" (1936, May 3). *Springfield News Leader*, p. B4.
6. "Oilers defeat Monarchs 9–6" (1936, April 23). *Enid Morning News*, p. 8.
7. "Ace colored team faces Green Sox Thursday evening" (1936, June 10). *Green Bay Press-Gazette*, p. 15.
8. "Kansas City Monarchs in easy victory over Bays" (1936, June 12). *Green Bay Press-Gazette*, p. 15–16.

9. "Monarchs bunch runs to blank Merchants by 9-to-0 score in Sunday battle here" (1936, June 29). *Casper Tribune Herald*, p. unknown.
10. "Monarchs wallop Cardinals in second game, 11 to 1" (1936, May 3). *Springfield News* and *Leader*, p. B4.
11. "Kansas City crew clouts four homers" (1936, July 9). *Vancouver Province*, p. unknown.
12. "Locals pull a fast one" (1936, August 4). *The Swift Current Sun*, p. 1.
13. "Monarchs beat bearded team" (1936, August 4). *The Swift Current Sun*, p. 1.
14. "Grays, Kaysee series set" (1936, August 8). *Pittsburgh Courier*, p. 5, section 2.
15. Janet Bruce, *The Kansas City Monarchs*, p. 86.
16. James W. Loewen, *Sundown Towns*, p. 95.
17. James W. Loewen, *Sundown Towns* p. 344.
18. "Kansas City Monarchs play thrilling game" (1936, May 1). *Monett Times*, p. 1.
19. "Monarchs take three from Springfield club" (1936, May 8). *Kansas City Call*, Southwest Edition, p. 6.
20. "Monarchs whip Mills, 12–1, then lose second, 9–7" (1936, May 31). *Chicago Tribune*, p. B5.
21. "Negro Sluggers beat David club" (1936, August 19). *Mason City Globe Gazette*, p. 19.
22. "Monarchs maul Peoria outfit for 20–4 duke" (1936, September 5). *Peoria Star*, p. 6.
23. "A sweep for Monarchs" (1936, September 1). *Kansas City Times*, p. 12.
24. "Local drop 5–1 decision to Kansas City Monarchs team" (1936, May 13). *Borger Daily Herald*, p. unknown.
25. "Local drop 5–1 decision to Kansas City Monarchs team" (1936, May 13). *Borger Daily Herald*, p. unknown.
26. "Monarchs win twice; Mayweather breaks his leg in a slide" (1936, May 15). *Kansas City Call*, City Edition, p. 15.
27. "Kansas City Monarchs, fielding prejudice" (1981, August 2). Vibrations, Sunday Magazine of the *Columbia Missourian*, p. 4.
28. "Kansas City Monarchs, fielding prejudice" (1981, August 2). Vibrations, Sunday Magazine of the *Columbia Missourian*, p. 4.
29. "Monarchs win two" (1936, June 1). *Chicago Tribune*, p. 25.
30. Eddie Dwight's scrap book, publication and publication date unknown. K.C. Monarchs beat Madison club, 6 to 5 (1936).
31. "Kansas City Monarchs in easy victory over Bays" (1936, June 12). *Green Bay Press Gazette*, sports p. 15–16.
32. "Monarchs team [in] second battle" (1936, May 2). *Springfield Leader* and *Press*, p. 4.
33. "Monarchs play tonight" (1936, July 6). *Yakima Daily Republic*, p. 11.
34. "Kansas City crew clouts four homers" (1936, July 9). *Vancouver Province*, p. unknown.
35. "Monarchs maul Peoria outfit for 20–4 duke" (1936, September 5). *Peoria Star*, p. 6.
36. C. C. Johnson (1974, June 7). Sporting News Publishing Company.
37. Caguas Criolls year book. 1985.
38. "Diz Dean heads Stars in Exhibition" (1936, September 24). *Wichita Beacon*, p. 19.
39. "Dizzy Dean heads national stars in Game Monday" (1936, September 23). *Wichita Beacon*, p. 17.
40. "Monarchs upset in pitching duel" (1936, July 7). *Yakima Morning Herald*, p. 5.
41. "Strikeouts stops rally by Yakima" (1936, July 15). *Yakima Morning Herald*, p. 9.
42. *Old Time Magazine*, publication date unknown.
43. "Slugger-pitcher gets two places" (1933, August 12). *Chicago Defender*, p. unknown.
44. Al Monroe, "Davis moves up to replace vet Rogan" (1933, August 26). *Chicago Defender*, p. unknown.
45. "The East vs. West game is no All-Star game" (1934, July 13). *Kansas City Call*, p. 6.
46. Fay Young, "East defeats West, 10–2, in annual All-Star game in Chicago before 26,000" (1936, August 28). *Kansas City Call*, City edition, p. 1.
47. Willard Brown (personal communications, 1983–1990).
48. Dave Wyatt, "The most difficult fielding position on the diamond" (1920, March 13). *Indianapolis Freeman*, p. unknown.
49. "Famed black hurler will take mound" (1937, May 25). *Pampa News*, p. unknown.
50. "Nusser slated to face Monarchs" (1937, May 17). *Wichita Beacon*, p. 14.
51. "Monarchs play Oilers tonight" (1937, May 18). *Enid Morning News*, p. 10.
52. "Sammy Baugh to join team in weekend" (1937, May 27). *Pampa News*, p. unknown.
53. "Oilers Defeat Monarchs" (1937, May 29). *Enid Morning News*, p. 10.
54. "Clowers beats K.C. Monarchs" (1937, June 24). *Enid Morning News*, p. 10.
55. "Kansas City Monarchs, fielding prejudice" (1981, August 2). Vibrations, Sunday Magazine of the *Columbia Missourian*, p. 3.
56. "Monarchs trim Oilers 13 to 5" (1938, July 7). *Enid Morning News*, p. 6.
57. "Kansas City Monarchs, fielding prejudice" (1981, August 2). Vibrations, Sunday Magazine of the *Columbia Missourian*, p. 3.
58. Connie Johnson (personal communications, 1983–1990).
59. "East-West game Sunday in Chicago" (1937, August 6). *Kansas City Call*, City edition, p. 13.
60. "Monarchs bring fast ball team" (June 5, 1938). *Wichita Eagle*, p. 5A.
61. Bryon Johnson (personal communication, November 12, 1987).
62. "Al Nusser scheduled to hurl for Wichita at stadium" (May 20, 1937). *Wichita Beacon*, p. 18.
63. "Two for the Monarchs" (1937, May 31). *Kansas City Times*, p. 8.
64. "Monarchs in 10–5 victory over Indianapolis A.B.Cs" (1937, June 18). *Kansas City Call*, National Edition, p. 6.
65. "The Monarchs win two" (1937, July 26). *Kansas City Times*, p. 10.
66. "2,000 see the Monarchs win" (1938, July 28). *Manhattan Morning Chronicle*, p. 5.
67. "Monarchs fail in bid" (1937, August 16). *Kansas City Times*, p. 10.
68. "The Monarchs beaten" (1937, August 30). *Kansas City Times*, p. 10.
69. "Monarchs win 8–6 game in ninth inning" (1937, September 28). *Kansas City Kansan*, p. 9.
70. "Brown hits 4 home runs as Monarchs win" (1937, October 8). *Kansas City Call*, City Edition, p. 14.
71. "2,000 see Monarchs beat Indianapolis" (1937, September 2). *Marysville Advocate-Democrat*, p. 3.
72. "Monarchs in a long tie" (1937, September 13). *Kansas City Times*, p. 13.

73. "Thriller stopped by darkness" (1937, September 17). *Kansas City Call*, National edition, p. 7.
74. "Monarchs' game protested" (1937, September 14). *Kansas City Times*, p. 14.
75. "Series lead to Monarchs (1937, September 15). *Kansas City Times*, p. 13.
76. "Pennant to Monarchs" (1937, September 18). *Kansas City Times*, p. 20.
77. Al Piechota (personal communication, September 1985).
78. Herman "Ham" Schulte (personal communication, October 5, 1985).
79. "All-Leaguers beat Monarchs" (1937, September 22). *Manhattan Morning Chronicle*, p. 2.
80. "Liell to face Monarchs on mound for Blues here tonight" (1937, September 27). *Kansas City Kansan*, p. 5.
81. "Kansas City Monarchs to meet All-Star semi-pro team at stadium tonight" (1939, August 1). *Davenport Democrat*, p. 8.
82. "Monarchs headed by great hurler" (1931, September 24). *Council Bluffs Nonpareil*, p. 1.
83. Sarah Barnes (personal communication, January 19, 1985).
84. Wilbur Rogan, Jr. (personal communication, 1998).
85. Donn Rogosin, *Invisible Men*, p. 131.
86. "Talkin' baseball" (1994, April 5). *Rocky Mountain News*, p. D3.
87. "Detroit, Monarchs dicker for a trade" (1938, January 15). *Chicago Defender*, p. 9.
88. "Detroit stars seek player deal with Monarchs" (1938, January 22). *Chicago Defender*, p. 9.
89. John B. Holway, *Blackball Stars*, p. 248.
90. Bill Bagby, "Bill-O'-Fare" (1940, July 5). *Kansas City Call*, Texas Edition, p. 6.
91. "Turkey Stearns" (1979, September 15). *Michigan Chronicle*, p. unknown.
92. "Chicago Giants beat Monarchs in Negro clash" (1938, April 25). *Dallas Times Herald*, section 2, p. 2.
93. Phil Dixon, *Negro Baseball Leagues a Photographic History*, p. 184.
94. Jack Etkin, *Innings Ago*, p. 11.
95. Donn Rogosin, *Invisible Men*, p. 13.
96. "Kansas City wins 7–1 tilt from Phillips" (1938, April 16). *Chicago Defender*, p. 8.
97. "Kansas City wins 7–1 tilt from Phillies" (1938, April 16). *Chicago Defender*, p. 8.
98. "Giants drub Monarchs in clash here" (1938, April 25). *Dallas Morning News*, section 2, p. 3.
99. "Monarchs edge Oilers 3 to 1" (1938, May 18). *Enid Morning News*, p. 7.
100. "All-Stars conclude set with Monarchs" (1938, May 25). *Peoria Star*, p. 14.
101. "Monarchs trim Oilers 13 to 5" (1938, July 7). *Enid Morning News*, p. 6.
102. "K.C. Lads in 12 to 3 victory (1938, July 9). *Manhattan Morning Chronicle*, p. 3.
103. "Monarchs take exhibition game" (1938, July 6). *Manhattan Morning Chronicle*, p. 6.
104. "Monarchs win 6 to 1 battle from All-Stars" (1938, August 2). *Davenport Democrat*, p. 11.
105. "Monarchs here" (1938, August 15). *St. Joseph Gazette*, p. sports.
106. "Monarchs in rally to beat ABC club by 13 to 12 score" (1938, August 10). *Springfield Leader and Press*, p. 10.
107. "Giants beat KC Monarchs" (1938, August 26). *St. Louis Argus*, p. 10.

Chapter 12

1. The All-Star information came from the Annual book that I have from 1945.
2. *Your Kansas City and Mine*, p. 127.
3. "Ex-baseball star now in second retirement," from the Jay Bird Ray's scrapbook, newspaper unknown.
4. Article. (1965, September 26). *Kansas City Star*, p. sports.
5. Chet Brewer (Personal Communication 1983).
6. "Antique dealer's hobby keeps him on the road" (1936, May 3). *Springfield News and Leader*, p. B4.
7. Western Historical Manuscript collection, University of Missouri-St. Louis, April 6, 1970, Oral History T-015. Interview with James "Cool Papa" Bell, Interviewed by Dr. Arthur Shaffer and Dr. Charles Korr, Black community Leaders project.
8. "Sam Crawford, ex-ballplayer, held in fatal Chicago shooting" (1955, March 26). *Chicago Defender*, p. 11.
9. "New Monarchs can't touch oldsters — Carr." (1946, August 8) *Kansas City Call*, City edition, p. 22.
10. Taken from George Sweatt's non-published autobiography.
11. "Large crowd attends last rites for Geo. Mitchell, professional ball player" (1953, November 17). Sparta, Illinois newspaper unknown.
12. The motto of the organization appeared on the rear of their printed program.
13. "Wilber "Bullet" Rogan to be honored next Saturday by Heart of America Elks" (1958, April 25). *Kansas City Call*, National edition, p. 10.
14. "Veeck still worries over LeRoy" (1965, September 12). *Kansas City Star*, p. 2B.
15. "Satchel's old eyes look ahead" (1965, September 25). *Kansas City Times*, sports.
16. Letter from the files of Kansas University, Tom Baird Monarchs collection.
17. Tim Rives, "Jackie Robinson's Klansman." Paper presented at the 7th annual meeting of the Jerry Malloy Negro League Research Conference. Cleveland, Ohio (2004, July 24).
18. "Last rites held for one-time Monarchs ace, Wilber (Bullet) Rogan" (1967, March 17–22). *Kansas City Call*, p. 12.
19. Names of people attending the funeral were taken from the signed roster in Rogan's in memoriam book.
20. Paul W. Fisher, "Talk of the Times" (1967, March 10). *Kansas City Times*, p. 21.

Bibliography

Books and Manuscripts

Bak, Richard. *Turkey Stearnes and the Detroit Stars.* Detroit: Wayne State University Press, 1994.

Bruce, Janet. *The Kansas City Monarchs, Champions of Black Baseball.* Lawrence, Kansas: University Press of Kansas, 1985.

Dixon, Phil, and Pat Hannigan. *The Negro Baseball Leagues: A Photographic History.* Mattituck, New York: Amereon House, 1992.

Etkin, Jack. *Innings Ago: Recollections by Kansas City Ballplayers of Their Days in the Game.* Marceline, Missouri: Walsworth, 1987.

Figueredo, Jorge S., Mario Figueredo, and Augusto Jose Tuva. "Year by Year Performances of Negro Players in Cuban Baseball from 1903 to 1960." Report Prepared for the Negro Baseball Hall of History, 1980.

Greenbaum, Susan D. *The Afro-American Community in Kansas City, Kansas.* Kansas City, Kansas: City of Kansas City, 1982.

Greene, Lorenzo J., Gary R. Kremer, and Antonio F. Holland. *Missouri's Black Heritage.* Revised edition. Columbia, Missouri: University of Missouri Press, 1993.

Holway, John. *Blackball Stars.* Westport, Connecticut: Meckler, 1988.

_____. *Voices from the Great Black Baseball Leagues.* New York: Dodd, Mead, 1975.

Johnson, Lloyd. *The Minor League Register.* Durham, North Carolina: Baseball America, 1997.

_____, and Miles Wolff. *The Encyclopedia of Minor League Baseball.* Durham, North Carolina: Baseball America, 1994.

Loewen, James W. *Sundown Towns.* New York: New Press, 2005.

McNeil, William. *The California Winter League: America's First Integrated Professional Baseball League.* Jefferson, North Carolina: McFarland, 2002.

Nankivell, John H. *The History of the Twenty-Fifth Regiment, United States Infantry, 1869–1926.* Fort Collins, Colorado: Old Army Press, 1972.

Nemec, David. *The Great Encyclopedia of Nineteenth Century Major League Baseball.* 2d Edition. Tuscaloosa, Alabama: University Alabama Press, 2006.

O'Neil, Buck, with Steve Wulf and Dave Conrads. *I Was Right on Time.* New York: Simon & Schuster, 1996.

Ribowsky, Mark. *A Complete History of the Negro Leagues, 1884 to 1955.* New York: Carol, 1995.

Robinson, Ray. *Ted Williams.* New York: Putnam's, 1962.

Rogosin, Donn. *Invisible Men: Life in Baseball's Negro Leagues.* New York: Atheneum, 1983.

Rucker, Mark, and Peter C. Bjarkman. *Smoke: The Romance and Lore of Cuban Baseball.* New York: Total/Sports Illustrated, 1999.

Spink, C.C., and Paul Macfarlane. *Daguerreotypes.* St. Louis: The Sporting News, 1981

Sweatt, George. "My Life." Unpublished manuscript, 1982.

Trouppe, Quincy. *Twenty Years Too Soon: The Autobiography of Quincy Trouppe.* Los Angeles: S and S Enterprises, 1977.

Whitehead, Charles. *A Man and His Diamonds: A Story of the Great Andrew (Rube) Foster, the Outstanding Team He Owned and Managed, and the Superb League He Founded and Commissioned.* New York: Vantage Press, 1980.

Newspapers

Akron Beacon Journal, Albert Lea Evening Tribune, Arkansas City Daily Traveler, Atchison Daily Globe, Austin Daily Herald, Benton Harbor News Palladium, Birmingham Herald, Bismarck Tribune, Burlington Standard Democrat, Carthage Evening Press, Casper Tribune Herald, Chanute Daily Tribune, Chicago Defender, Chicago Tribune, Chicago Whip, Cleveland Press, Columbia Missourian, Concordia Blade Empire, Council Bluffs Nonpareil, Crookston Daily Times, Daily Missoulian, Dallas Morning News, Davenport Democrat, Denver Post, Des Moines Reg-

ister, Devil Lake Journal, Dodge City Journal, Duluth Herald, Emporia Daily Gazette, Enid Morning News, El Dorado Times, Fort Scott Tribune, Galveston Daily News, Grand Forks Herald, Great Bend Tribune, Green Bay Press-Gazette, Hannibal Courier, Hawaiian Gazette, Indianapolis Freeman, Iola Daily Register, Jamestown Sun, Jefferson City Daily Capital News, Jewel County Monitor, Joplin Globe, Joplin News Herald, Kansas City American, Kansas City Call, Kansas City Journal, Kansas City Kansan, Kansas City Post, Kansas City Sun, Kansas City Times, La Crosse Tribune, Lethbridge Herald, Linn-Palmer Record, Los Angeles Times, Manhattan Mercury, Manhattan Morning Chronicle, Marysville Advocate-Democrat, Mason City Globe Gazette, Michigan Chronicle, Milwaukee Leader, Moberly Monitor-Index, Monett Times, Morgan Evening Times, Morland Monitor, Newton Evening News, Oakland Tribune, Oberlin Herald, The Oklahoman, Pampa News, Parsons Daily Sun, Peoria Star, Pittsburg Daily Headlight, Pittsburgh Courier, Rocky Mountain News, Russell Record, St. Joseph Gazette, St. Louis American, St. Louis Argus, Salina Journal, San Antonio Light, Seattle Enterprise, Seattle Times, Sioux City Journal, Southwest American, Springfield Daily News, Springfield Leader, Swift Current Sun, Tacoma News Tribune, Topeka Daily Capital, Trenton Republican Times, Tulsa Daily World, Valley City Times Record, Vancouver Province, Wichita Beacon, Wichita Eagle, Winnipeg Free Press, Wisconsin Rapids Daily Tribune, Wymore Arbor State, Yakima Morning Herald

Interviews and Personal Communications

Newt Allen, Sarah Barnes, Chet Brewer, Willard Brown, T. Roosevelt Butler, Stella M. Cooper, Frank Duncan, Jr., Georgia Dwight, George Giles, Alberta Penn Gilmore, Byron Johnson, Connie Johnson, William "Big C" Johnson, Fred Langford, Ernest Maun, Willie B. Mays, Bill McCallop, Fred McDaniel, Orrin Murray, Richard Pullam, Jr., Lillie Ann Gates Owens, William F. McNeil, Al Piechota, Wilbur Rogan, Jr., Herman "Ham" Schulte, Clint Thomas, Quincy Trouppe, Roy Waller, Jesse Williams, Doolittle Young

Index

A. A. Productions xi
Acme Giants 163
Adams, Babe 91
Adams, Packinghouse 73, 171
Afro-American (Baltimore, Maryland) 107
Airport Park (Moberly, Missouri) 158
Akana, Lang 23
Akron, Ohio 102
Alexander, Grover Cleveland 5, 96, 105–106, 115, 144, 147, 167
Alexander's Giants (California Winter League) 125
Alexandria, Louisiana 72, 154
All-Chinese 17, 20, 23,
Allen, Henry (Kansas Governor) 189
Allen, Newt, Jr. x
Allen, Newton Henry "Newt" x, 2, 4, 50, 56, 60, 67, 69, 74–75, 79, 81, 98, 108, 113, 144, 162, 186–187; All-Nations 86; All-Star team: (1928) 80, (1931) 103, (1950) 184; California Winter League 129–130, 132, 134; Denver Post Tournament award 145; East-West game 168, 169, 173; home runs 101–102, 167; on league play 165; Rogan's funeral 190; on Satchel Paige 156
Alliance, Ohio 102
All-Nations x, 26–29, 31, 61, 75, 86, 97, 180
All-Star team selection: (1920) 34, (1926) 64, (1927) 70, (1928) 80, (1931) 103, (1945) 183, (1947) 184, (1950) 184
Almendares (Cuban Winter League) 125, 128
Altrock, Nick 123
Ambrose, Elmer 179
American Association 14, 45–47, 49, 111, 118
American Giants (Chicago) 34, 36, 43, 49, 52, 54, 57, 60–61, 63–64, 69–70, 76, 78–79, 85, 112, 133, 136, 151, 152, 155, 159, 165–166, 170, 173; fight with Monarchs 50; first game against Rogan 32–33; Negro National League (West) 31; play-offs (1937) 175; twenty-inning game 175
American League x, 19, 31, 44, 92, 131, 138–139, 163, 168, 176, 188, 191
Ames, Leon 46
Amos 'n' Andy 143
Anderson, Aaronetta xi
Anderson, Louis xi
Anderson, Theodore "Bubbles" 50, 86
Anson, Adrian "Cap" 5
Anthony, Kansas 64
Arkansas Baptist College 64, 78
Arkansas City, Kansas 90, 98, 137
Arkansas City Daily Traveler 80, 98
Arkansas-Missouri League 164
Arlett, Buzz 120
Arlington, Nebraska 103
Artillery Brigade 27
Ashwill, Gary 41
Asian (The Mauis) 17
Asman, Herb 111
Associated Negro Press 47, 168
Association Park 8, 28, 34, 36, 41, 51–52, 86, 93, 189
Atchison, Kansas 51, 80, 91, 93, 100
Athletic Park: Burlington, Wisconsin 101, Hawaiian Islands 17, Vancouver, Canada 165
Atlanta, Georgia 169
Atlanta Black Crackers 179–180
Attucks Elementary School 37
Augustine, Leon 49
Auker, Eldon 104
Austin, Minnesota 97
Austin, Rob 13–14
Austin, Texas 171
Austin Senators 171

Babe Ruth All-Stars 105
Bacharach Giants 63, 101, 175
Baird, Floyd x,
Baird, Frances (56)
Baird, Thomas Younger "T. Y." x, 29–30, 56, 116, 182, 184, 187–188
Baker, Nonnie 64
Ball, Walter 9–10
Baltimore, Maryland 54, 60
Baltimore Afro-American 168
Baltimore Black Sox 55, 101
Baltimore Orioles 190
Bancroft, Frank 20
Bankhead, Sam 142
Barber, Ralph H. 136
Barfoot, Clyde 129

Barnes, I. V. x, 178
Barnes, Jess 52
Barnes, Sarah x
barnstorming 85–86, 95, 101
Bartlesville, Oklahoma 40
Bartley, James Homer 52
Beagle, Sgt. Bertram T. ix, 16–17, 19
Beaver Athletics 11
Beckwith, John 34, 132
Bell, Clifford x, 63, 70
Bell, Dorothy x
Bell, James "Cool Papa" ix, 3, 64, 71, 108–110, 112–113, 117, 152, 169, 185
Bell, William 54, 58, 64, 67, 70, 80, 91, 97, 101
Beloit, Kansas 33
Benedict, Kansas 52
Benton, Ruben 190
Benton Harbor, Michigan 142, 146
Berry, Mike "Tudie" ix, 161–162
Bertha, Minnesota 107
Beverly, Charlie 4, 83, 101–104, 108–109, 111–114, 116, 118, 120, 141, 147, 149, 152, 155, 160
Bibbs, Junius A. 178
Billiken Cigars 125
Billings, Montana 164, 166
Birmingham, Alabama 169
Birmingham Black Barons 53, 57, 67, 69, 76, 174, 179, 181
Birmingham Herald 52
Bismarck, North Dakota 141, 156, 171
Black Archives of Mid-America xi,
Black Buffalos (Houston, Texas) 82, 97, 102, 155
Black Giants (Dallas, Texas) 98, 155
Black Sox scandal 47, 103
Blackburn, Hugh 29, 42
Blackwell, Joe 111
Blade Empire (Concordia, Kansas) 91
Blount, Tenny 31
Blue, Lu 123
Bobo, Willie 58, 108
Boldridge, E. C. ix
Boldridge, Manville ix
Bono, Gus 46, 51
Booker T's Baseball Team xi,
Boone, Robert 10, 181, 183
Borchert Field (Milwaukee, Wisconsin) 109, 149, 175

209

Borger, Texas 165
Borger Daily Herald 165
Borrow, Ed 123
Boston Braves 52, 176
Boston Giants 163
Boston Red Sox 2, 188
Boulevard Donkeys 162
Bowman, Joe x, 120
Boyd, Donald x,
Boyd, Ollie x, 113, 116, 162
Bradley, Dick 178–179
Branch, Norman "Red" 175–176
Branch, Rickey 181
Brandford, Claude 103
Breese, Bid 175–176
Breese Stevens Field (Madison, Wisconsin) 164–165
Brewer, Chester Arthur "Chet" 4, 37, 92–94, 97, 109, 113, 118, 123, 134, 144, 148, 152, 154, 160, 166; Crookston, Minnesota 101, 107; home runs 117; on Jose Mendez 69; on Nelson Dean 60; New York Cubans 161; play-offs (1926) 63; on Rogan and Satchel Paige 185; shutouts 111–112, 117, 141, 148; strikeouts 103, 105, 115, 119, 135, 141, 147, 151; on Walter "Doby" Moore 52; Washington Pilots 108; wins 116; Winter League record 133
Bridges, Tommy 159–160
Brief, Anthony "Bunny" 45–46
Broadnax, Maceo x
Brooklyn Dodgers 3, 119, 123, 129, 134, 188
Brooklyn Giants (Kansas City, Missouri) 161
Brooklyn Royal Giants 151
Brooks, Jess 171
Brown, Dave 41, 183
Brown, Jim 64, 136
Brown, Larry 168
Brown, Mace 176
Brown, "Three Finger" 9
Brown, Willard "Home Run" ix, 4, 82, 152, 154–155, 157, 160, 162, 165, 169, 170–171, 173–174
Brown's Tennessee Rats 190
Bruce, Janet 1, 3
Bruce Elementary School 75
Bryan Park (Richmond, Missouri) 40
Bryant, Arthur 190
Buffalo, New York 162
Burlington, Kansas 44, 155
Burlington, Wisconsin 101
Burlington Daily Republican 44
Bush, Joe "Bullet" 35
Butler, T. Roosevelt ix
Buxton Wonders 100

Caldwell, Ray 51
Caldwell, Roy 120
California Eagle 49, 124
California Winter League x, 59
Camp Steven D. Little 28
Campbell, Lon 151

Capitol Records 37
Cardenas, Matanzas 55
Carey, Max 123–124
Carey Lake Field 89
Carr, George 29, 31, 37, 39, 51, 53, 60, 122–123, 125, 129, 132, 186
Carr, Wayne 41
Carrabelle, Florida 178
Carrolton, Missouri 52
Carter, Nick 46
Carthage, Missouri 117
Casey Stengel's All-Stars 93, 124
Casper, Wyoming 163
Casper Merchants 163
Cawker City, Kansas 42
Cedar Rapids, Iowa 176
Centennial Methodist Church 42
Centralia, Missouri 52
Chanute, Kansas 151
Charles City, Iowa 164–165
Charleston, Oscar 35, 51, 136, 152, 154
Charleston, Porter 130
Chattanooga, Tennessee 69
Chelsea Athletic Club 28
Chicago Cubs 9, 66, 68, 120, 124, 176
Chicago Defender 18, 20, 26, 36, 60–61, 74, 78, 85, 98, 115, 168
Chicago Giants 18, 31, 34, 36–37, 43
Chicago Mills 102, 104, 114, 164
Chicago Union Giants 6; W.S. Peters 26–27
Chicago Whip 23, 26, 30–31, 35, 41
Chicago White Sox 19, 26, 83, 148, 163, 169
Childress Field League Park (Joplin, Missouri) 111
Chocolate Whizbang 144
Cincinnati, Ohio 101, 174
Cincinnati Reds 43, 55, 70, 97, 125
Cincinnati Tigers 178
City League 17
Cleveland, Ohio 102
Cleveland Giants (Winter League) 132, 134
Cleveland Indians 112, 120, 156, 176
Cleveland Tate Stars 36, 39, 72
Clinton, Missouri 64, 76, 89
Cobb, L. S. N. 169
Cobb, Ty 5–6, 28, 35
Cockrell, Pete 54
Coffeyville, Kansas 9, 92
Cold Springs, Minnesota 107
Colorado Springs, Colorado 146
Colored Championship of the United States 9
Colored House of David 101, 162
Columbia, Missouri 92
Columbus, Ohio 72, 99
Columbus Buckeyes 36
Comiskey, Charles 26
Comiskey Park 159, 168, 169

Compton Cubs 108
Concordia, Kansas 91, 100, 115
Concordia Travelers 137
Cooper, Alfred "Army" 73, 76, 103
Cooper, Andrew "Andy" 4, 33, 73, 79–80, 97, 113–114, 117, 119, 130, 132–134, 143–144, 152, 159, 161–163, 169, 171, 173–175, 178–179, 184
Cooper, Mort 159
Cooper, Walker 187
Cooperstown, New York 4, 8, 193
Cornelius, Sug 166, 175
Cot Tierney's All-Stars 106
Cotter, Lefty 119
Cotton States League 83
Council Bluffs, Iowa 101, 103, 176
Courier Post (Hannibal, Missouri) 96
Cox, Dick 129
Cox, Roosevelt 178
Cramer, Roger 148
Crawford, Sam 29, 31, 34, 69, 78, 93, 139, 143, 152, 155, 186
Creacy, Dewey 71
Crescent, Oklahoma 97
Crookston, Minnesota 101, 109, 112
Crookston Daily Times 109
Crookston Red Sox 101, 107, 109
Crump, Harry 162
Crutchfield, Jimmy x
Cuban Giants 85
Cuban House of David 101, 103
Cuban Stars 31, 36, 100, 112, 114
Cuban Winter League 125, 128, 170
Cudahy's 73
Currie, Ruben "Rube" 29, 31, 37, 44, 47–48, 64, 74, 123, 125, 129

Daily Oklahoman (Oklahoma City, Oklahoma) 148
Daily Register (Iola, Kansas) 93
Dakota League 44, 52
Dallas, Texas 29, 69, 83, 98, 179
Dallas Giants 14
Dalton, Georgia 152,
Darby, Pennsylvania 60, 103
Davis, Carl 91
Davis, Dick xi
Davis, Oscar 13
Davis, Roosevelt 141
Davis, Walter "Steel Arm" 64
Day, Clyde "Pea Ridge" 90
Day, Connie 132
Dayton, Ohio 164, 175
Dayton Marcos 32, 34, 36, 39
Dean, Jay "Dizzy" 117, 120, 147–148, 159, 185
Dean, Nelson x, 59–60, 70, 170
Dean, Paul "Daffy" 148
Deason, Eva 146
death 189
DeGraw, Pete William 186
Dell, Wheezer 124
Dellasago, John 175
DeMoss, Elwood "Bingo" 33–34, 73, 75, 78, 136

Index

Dempsey, Jack 6, 123
Denver, Colorado x, 44
Denver Athletic Club 143, 155
Denver Bears 44
Denver Post 142–143, 145
Denver Post Tournament x, 69, 141–142, 146–147, 150, 156, 166
Des Moines, Iowa 28, 115, 149
Des Moines Register 149
Detroit News 84
Detroit Stars 29, 31, 34, 36, 41, 49–50, 52, 54, 57, 67, 73, 76, 82, 101, 145, 170, 178
Detroit Tigers 44, 70, 147–148
Devils Lake Journal 155–156
Dials, Lou x
Dihigo, Martin 128
Dillard (New Orleans University) 62
DiMaggio, Joe 166
DiMaggio, Vince 176
Dismukes, William 80, 152
Dixie Series 171
Dixon, Arthur xi
Dixon, George "Tubby" 34, 136
Dixon, Herbert "Rap" 129, 132
Dixon, Dr. Kerry xi
Dixon, Wendolyn xi
Doan, Ray L. 142, 146
Doby, Larry 188
Dodge City, Kansas 117, 175–176
Dodge City Journal (Dodge City, Kansas) 95
Donaldson, Billy 49, 51
Donaldson, John, W. xi, 26, 28–29, 31, 33, 44, 52, 69, 86, 101, 103, 107, 122, 139, 141, 147, 151, 184–185
Donaldson All-Stars 112
Doswell, Raymond xi
Douglas, Eddie 10
Drake, William P. "Plunk" 32, 34, 41, 60, 66, 86
DuBisson Tigers 173
Duffy Florals 101, 104
Duncan, Bernice x
Duncan, Frank x, 2, 37, 50, 67, 74, 76, 81, 87–88, 95, 97, 99, 101–102, 108, 113, 125, 130, 132–133, 175, 178, 181, 183–184, 186; All-Star team: (1926) 64, (1927) 70, (1928) 80, (1950) 184; Pittsburgh Crawfords 151, 161; on Rogan and Satchel Paige 185; Rogan's funeral 190; traded to Kansas City 37
Duncan Point 181
Dutch Ralls' All-Stars 124
Dwight, Georgia x, 172, 189
Dwight, Edward "Eddie" "Pee Wee" x, 2, 37, 72, 76, 80, 147, 149, 152–153, 155, 159, 161–162, 164, 169–170, 176, 187, 190
Dyer Act 151

Eagle Pass, Texas 33
Eason Oilers 144, 163, 171–172
East Grand Forks, Minnesota 157
East St. Louis Cubs 108
East-West Game 168–169, 173, 188
East-West League 107
Eastern Colored League 18, 54–55, 63, 82, 132
Eckley, Elizabeth 72
Edward Waters College 178
Egnatic, Joe 175
El Dorado, Arkansas 152
El Dorado, Kansas 111
Elba, Nebraska 105
Elmwood Park (Sioux Falls, South Dakota) 103
Else, Harry 162, 169
Embry, William 49
Emporia, Kansas 155
Enid, Oklahoma 90, 98, 144, 163, 165, 171–172, 179
Enid Morning News 98
European War 28
Evans, Frank 9
Evers, Johnny 66

Fabrica de Cigarros 125
Fagan, Robert, T. 17, 23, 29
Fargo, North Dakota 114
Fargo Moorhead Twins 107, 114
Farrell, Fran 14
Federals (Omaha, Nebraska) 75
Feller, Bob 176, 185
Fette, Lou 176
Fields, Margaret xi
Finley, Charles, O. 188
Finner, John 32
First Field Artillery 17
Fisher, Paul, W. 190
Fitzpatrick, Jack 119
Floyd, James "Jew Baby" 29, 162, 184
Flynn, Jim 10
Forbes Field 99, 102
Force, William 41
Ford, Henry 73
Foreman, Hazel x
Foreman, Sylvester 37, 107, 186
Foreman, Zack x, 40
Fort Huachuca Museum 21, 22, 24–25
Fort Leavenworth 16
Fort Morgan, Colorado 45
Fort Morgan Evening Times 45
Fort Sam Houston 16
Fort Scott, Kansas 28, 45, 52, 54, 112
Fort Scott Daily Tribune Monitor 52
Fort Smith, Arkansas 113
Fort Wayne, Indiana 171
Fort Worth, Texas 10, 83
Forth Worth, Black Wonders 12
Foster, Andrew "Rube" 9, 31–32, 36, 40, 49–50, 54–55, 61, 69, 85–86, 108, 136, 184
Foster, William Hendrick "Willie" "Bill" x, 37, 62–64, 67, 78–79, 101–103, 130, 141–142, 155, 175, 183
4th Cavalry 17
Francis, Bill 170

Frank Lowe's Pool Hall 11
Franklin, C. A. 116
Fred Long's All-Southwestern Football Eleven 74
Fredonia, Kansas 52
Freeman, Bill 107
French, Larry 119–120
French, Ray 175–176
Frisch, Frank 149, 166
Funk, Liza 119

Galveston, Texas 97, 170
Galveston Sand Crabs 51, 97, 170
Garden City, Kansas 100
Gardner, Floyd "Jelly" 63, 78
Garland, Lou 118
Garner, Beatrice Joseph x
Geer, Cliff 119
Gehrig, Lou 6
Gehringer, Charlie 159–160
General Hospital #2 58
George E. Lee Jazz Orchestra 37
Gholston, Bert 16, 26, 49, 57, 64, 66, 70, 82–83
Gibson, Josh 174
Gibson, Bill 168
Giddings, Texas 171
Giddings Texas High School 171
Gilbert, Clyde 23, 26
Giles, George ix, 66–67, 70, 76, 80, 87–89, 92, 108, 113, 118, 120, 141, 144–145, 151, 162, 168–169
Gilkerson's Union Giants 29, 57, 80–81, 107, 152, 170
Gilmore, Quincy x, 56–57, 113, 135, 150
Glasgow, Missouri 26
Glass, Carl "Lefty" 66, 132
Gleason, James "Jimmy" x, 120
Go Devils (Iola, Kansas) 11, 40
Goliah, Fred 17–19, 22
Goliah County, Texas 10
Good, Wilbur 46
Good Year Park (Los Angeles, California) 110
Goodell, Willie 83
Goodwin, Alonza Alfred "Lonnie" 123, 130
Grabiner, Harry 169
Graham, Art x
Graham, J. H. 122
Graham, Lefty 111
Grand Forks, North Dakota 109
grand slam home run 111
Grange, Red 6
Grant, Leroy 33
Gray, Roosevelt "Chappy" 37, 39
Great Bend, Kansas 64, 87, 92
Great Bend Tribune 87
Greeley Advertisers 142
Green, Dalbert, P. 23
Green, Guy 28
Green, Joe 31, 36
Green Bay, Wisconsin 163, 165
Green Sox (Green Bay, Wisconsin) 163
Greenlee, Gus 168–169
Green's Nebraska Indians 28

Index

Gregg Tabernacle AME Church 160
Gregory, Louis 11
Griffith Field (Manhattan, Kansas) 174
Grigsby, J. B. 82
Groomer, Evelyn 86
Grove, Lefty 102, 150, 157
Gunn, Raymond 92
Gutierrez, Tomas 125
Gutteridge, Don 111–112, 119

Haley, "Gyp" 83
Haley, Red 107, 141
Hall, Sterling 42
Hall of Fame 192–193
Hall of Fame Veterans Committee 2
Hampton, Eppie 82
Hancock, Charley W. 100, 107, 109, 111
Haney, Fred 126, 129, 134
Hannibal, Missouri 96, 99
Hannibal Courier Post 99
Harbold, Lt. 17
Harding, Hallie 73–74, 76, 81–82, 91, 99, 101
Hardy, Arthur W. 55
Harney, George 64, 130–131
Harris, Curtis "Popcycle" 101, 108, 111–113, 162, 165
Harris, John, N. 11, 14
Hartford, Kansas 44
Havana (Cuban Winter League) 125
Hawaiian All-Stars 155
Hawaiian Gazette 23, 27
Hawaiian Island Championship 17
Hawaiian Islands 15, 20, 23
Hawkins, Lemuel xi, 17, 19, 22–23, 37–38, 50, 55, 70, 123, 150–151
Hayden, Ulysses 164
Haynes, Sammie x
Hays, Kansas 176
Heart of America Elks Lodge #149 187
Heath, Mike 135
Helena, Montana 164, 166
Hemsky, Rollie 176
Henry Clothiers 90,
Hensley, Eggie 78
Herman, Babe 126, 129
Hershel, Canada 167
Hewitt, "Buck" 50
Hiawatha, Kansas 87
Higgins, Pinky 148
Highland Park (Crookston, Minnesota) 108
Hill, Dewey 116
Hill, John Preston "Pete" 9, 170
Hilldale 54–55, 58–60, 103
Hines, John 64
Hogan, Happy 19
Holdrege, Nebraska 109
Holland, William "Bill" 41
Holling, Carl 124
Holloway, Crush 129–130, 134

Holmes, Lefty 111
Holway, John B. x, 185
home runs 27–28, 81–83, 90, 100, 107, 111, 115, 119, 124, 128, 164
Homestead Grays 99, 101–103, 105, 107–108, 162, 164, 175, 183
Honolulu, Territorial Hawaii 16–17, 137
Honolulu Advertiser 19
Honolulu Brewing and Malting Company 20
Honolulu Star-Bulletin 27
Hooper Field (Cleveland, Ohio) 99
Hopkins, Marty 148
Hopwood, Reginald 72
Horn, Jimmy 119
Horton, Tank 120
Hotel Cosmos (Mexico, City) 112
Houk, Ralph 187
House of David x, 105, 109, 111, 115–117, 141, 144–145, 147, 158, 164, 167, 179
Houston, Texas 16, 82, 97, 102, 179
Houston, William 9
Hovlik, Ed 45
Howard, Frank 122
Howard, J. C. 32
Hubbard, Jess 129
Hubbell, Carl 119
Hudspeth, High Pockets 129
Hueston, William Clarence 65
Huey, Guy 163
Huggins, Miller 123
Hugo, Colorado 42
Humble Oilers 143–144
Humboldt, Kansas xi, 40
Hunter, Bertum 108, 111, 113
Hunter, Frank "Spike" 116–117, 144, 146
Hynes, Johnnie 72

Illinois-Iowa League All-Stars 179
Indiana State University 178
Indianapolis, Indiana 164
Indianapolis ABCs 29, 34, 39, 47, 49, 52, 59, 85, 152, 171–172, 174–175, 180
Indianapolis Freeman 9, 20, 32, 49
Indianapolis Ledger 32, 136
Indianapolis News 26
Ingram, Mel 141
injuries 59
International League 120
Iola, Kansas 11, 40, 92
Isbell, Frank 104
Island Park (Wichita, Kansas) 60, 90, 111, 115, 120
Israelite House of David 167

Jack Griffin's Oilers (Iola, Kansas) 92
The Jackie Robinson Story 2
Jackson, Edgar 107
Jackson, Michigan 44
Jackson, Maj. R. R. 175

Jackson, Sanford 63–64
Jackson, Tut 8
Jackson, Wilbur "Ashes" 10
Jackson Citizen Patriot 44
Jacksonville, Florida 178
Jamestown, North Dakota 107, 109, 111, 114, 141, 148
Jamestown Sun 111
Jamison, Caesar 49
Jasper, Sgt. 17, 19, 22, 24
Jeanette, Joe 8
Jefferson City, Missouri 27
Jeffries, Jim 41
Jenkins, Fats 143
Jensen, Forest 119
Jewell County Monitor (Mankato, Kansas) 114
Jim Crowed 158
Jimmy Lunceford Orchestra 190
Joannes Park (Spokane, Washington) 165
Johnson, Byron "Mex" ix, 73, 171, 173–174
Johnson, Clifford "Connie" ix, 173, 190
Johnson, Jack (boxer) 8
Johnson, Jack "Topeka" 6, 9–10, 27, 61, 136
Johnson, James 61, 65
Johnson, Opal (Lemuel Hawkins' wife) 151
Johnson, Oscar "Heavy" 17, 20–21, 23, 29, 51–52, 57, 125, 184
Johnson, Tom 49
Johnson, Walter 96, 111, 150
Johnson, William "Big C" ix, 17–18, 22, 28 51
Johnson, William "Judy" x, 54, 134
Johnston, William Wade x, 55–57, 70, 72, 78, 90, 185
Jones, Ducky 123
Jones, Sherman "Road Block" 2
Joplin, Missouri 80, 90, 91, 119
Joplin Globe 5
Joplin Tournament All-Stars 111
Joseph, Walter Lee "Newt" 50, 56, 64, 73, 78–79, 97, 103, 111, 117, 130, 134–135, 147, 157–158, 170, 184, 186
Joseph, Wilson 170
Junction City, Kansas 44, 175–176

Kansas City, Kansas ix, 6, 10, 12, 14, 27, 30, 72–74, 84, 102, 113, 147, 162, 174, 176, 179, 186
Kansas City Allies 29
Kansas City American 66, 79, 96, 136
Kansas City Athletics 2, 188
Kansas City Baseball Trivia Quiz 1
Kansas City Blues x, 14, 33, 39, 45–47, 54, 118, 175, 188
Kansas City Board of Trade 152
Kansas City Call xi, 20, 47, 50, 59–61, 66, 70, 77, 84, 86, 89, 111–112, 115–116, 118, 123, 127, 135, 139, 151, 158, 166, 175, 190

Index

Kansas City Chiefs 2
Kansas City Globe 14
Kansas City Journal 6, 11, 13–14, 35, 59, 156
Kansas City Kansan 6, 14
Kansas City, Kansas, Giants 8–12, 14, 27–28, 55, 100, 181
The Kansas City Monarchs, Champions of Black Baseball 1
Kansas City Post 6
Kansas City Public Service 77
Kansas City Star xi, 6, 26
Kansas City Sun 16, 30, 33–35, 37, 41, 49, 86, 93, 125, 150
Kansas City Tigers 37
Kansas City Times 6, 28, 33–35, 82, 115, 117, 119–120, 122, 149–150
Kansas Daily Globe (Atchison, Kansas) 91
Kansas Daily Headlight (Pittsburg, Kansas) 49
Kansas Legislature 11
Kansas Stage Lines Team 111
Kansas state law 10
Kansas State Normal College 40
Kansas State Prison (Lansing, Kansas) 160
Kansas Supreme Court 11
Kansas University 65
Kardow, Paul 156
Katy Park (Waco, Texas) 98
Keating, Ray 124
Kellogg, Montana 165
Kellogg Miners 141
Kemp, Dave xi
Kendrick, Bob xi
Kenyon, Harry 64
Kerr, Johnny 120
Kildare, Texas 63
King, Martin Luther 2
King Fish (Amos 'n' Andy) 143
Knobnoster, Missouri 29
Knox, Elwood 32
Kranson, Floyd x, 152, 157, 159, 162–163, 167, 169, 172, 178–179
Kress, Ralph 148
Ku Klux Klan 189
Kuhel, Joe 112, 120

La Crosse, Wisconsin 141, 147
La Junta, Colorado 159
La Lucha 128
Ladies Day 85
Lai, William Tin 23
Land, Beryl 115
Landis, Kenesaw Mountain 47
Lane, Bill 101–103
Langford, Fred ix, 12, 14, 55
Langford, Sam 8
Langston University 40
Larned, Kansas 90, 176
Lawrence Stadium (Wichita, Kansas) 155
Lawson, Fred 167
Lazzeri, Tony 106, 134
League 3 & 2 2

Leavenworth, Kansas xi, 9, 16, 100, 151
Lee, Fred 9
Lee, Julia, M. 37
Lee, Julie x
Legion Park, (Helena, Montana) 166
Leland Giants (Chicago) 9–10, 14, 17–18, 85, 100
Lenora, Kansas 60
Lethbridge, Alberta, Canada 141
Levis, Oscar 128
Lexington, Missouri ix, 10, 28–29, 32, 107
Lexington Athletics 40
Lexington Tigers ix, 100
Liberal, Kansas 100
Liberty, Missouri, Tigers 11
Lieb, Fred 2–3
Life magazine 185
Lightner, ___ 29
Lincoln, Nebraska 28
Lincoln High School 37, 75
Linder, ___ 17
Lindimore, Howard 111
Lindsay, Robert "Frog" 9
Lindsay, William "Bill" ix, 8–10, 26
Linn, Kansas 115
Little Falls, Minnesota 107
Little Rock, Arkansas 171, 173
Little Rock Stars 173
Livingston, Bill xi
Livingston, Larry "Goo Goo" 72–73, 79–81, 83, 99–100, 130, 134
Lloyd, Curtis "Bingo" ix, 104
Lloyd, John Henry "Pop" 35
Lone Rock, Iowa 107
Lone Star League 83
Long, Fred 174
Long Beach, California 132, 135
Look Magazine 185
Los Angeles, California 122
Los Angeles Daily Times 131
Los Angeles Times 91, 123–124
Los Angeles White Sox 122–124, 129
Lou Koupal's Major League All-Stars 130
Louisville, Kentucky 164
Lowe, William x, 25
Lowry, Herbert G. 19
Lucas, Charles xi
Ludolph, Willie 44
Luque, Adolfo 125
Luther, Oklahoma 64
lynching 11, 92, 164
Lyons, Jimmy 34
Lyons, Ted 148

M. K. Goetz Brewing Company 187
Mack, Connie 20
Mack Park (Detroit) 33, 36, 40, 52, 83
Mackey, Raleigh "Bizz" 33, 59–60, 128–130, 132, 134, 136
Macon, Georgia 38

MacPhail, Lee 188
Madison, Bob 152, 162
Madison, Wisconsin 141, 163–166
Mails, Walter "The Great" 124
Major League All-Stars 103, 119, 129
Malarcher, Dave "Gentleman" x, 50, 63, 78–79, 122, 136
Manhattan, Kansas 66, 99, 104, 108–109, 114, 174–176, 179
Manhattan All-Stars 99
Manila, Philippines 16
Mankato, Kansas 114
Mansfield, Noah 14
Manush, Heinie 148
Marianio (Cuban Winter League) 125
Markham, Johnny 96, 98–99, 176, 178
Marks, Wally 178
marriage 42
Marshall, Charles D. 49
Marshall, Jack (Chicago, Illinois) ix–x, 104, 155
Marshall, Jack (Kansas City, Missouri) 41, 52, 74
Marshall, Missouri xi
Marshall, Texas 14, 72
Martin, B. B. 169
Martin, Millie Johnston x
Martin, Pepper 98, 117–118
Martin, Speed 93, 123–124
Marysville, Kansas 44, 52, 102, 104, 174
Marysville Advocate Democrat 44
Maryville, Missouri 92
Mason City, Iowa 114
Mathewson, Christy 176
Maun, Ernest x, 45, 92–93
Mays, Carl 51
Mays, Willie B. 161
Mayweather, Eldridge E. "Chili" 56, 152, 154–155, 158, 163, 165, 171, 176
McAdoo, Tully 9–10
McCampbell, Ernest, J. 9
McCampbell, Thomas 9
McCary, James 72–73
McClure, Robert 33
McCredie, W. W. 125
McDaniel, Booker 190
McDaniel, Fred x
McDonald, Webster 64, 107
McFarland, Eugene x
McGee, Lorraine x
McGraw, John 26, 45, 101
McHenry, Henry 83, 96, 101–103
McLemore, ___ 179
McMullen, Hughie 129
McNair, Emma 68
McNair, Hurley Allen ix, 4, 14, 29, 31, 34, 51–52, 67–68, 70, 73, 90, 123, 124–125, 139, 151, 153, 181–184
McNeil, William, F. x, 129, 132, 135, 138
Meadows, Lee 93
Meeker, Roy 106

Index

Meharry Medical College 100
Memphis, Tennessee 63, 98, 169, 174
Memphis Red Sox 25, 63, 67, 179
Mendez, Jose 4, 28–29, 31, 35, 43, 55, 58, 65–66, 69–70, 78, 80, 86, 93, 122, 125, 184
Mercy Hospital 54
Merrick, Owen 27
Meusel, Bob 54, 93, 123–124, 126, 129–131, 134
Meusel, Irish 93, 123–124, 134
Mexia, Texas 161
Mexico City 112–113, 136
Meyers, George 41
Mickey Mantle League 3
Midland Life Club (Oswego, Kansas) 111
Mid-Pacific Carnival 23
military enlistment 16
Miller, Bobo 72
Miller, Buck 64
Miller, Henry "Dimp" 37, 74
Mills, Benjamin, H. 23, 26
Mills, Charlie 31
Mills Stadium (Chicago, Illinois) 149
Milton, Henry 4, 73, 152, 159, 162, 169, 174–175
Milwaukee, Wisconsin xi, 72, 109, 163, 175
Milwaukee Bears 36, 43, 49–50, 52
Milwaukee Giants 108
Miners Park (Joplin, Missouri) 114
Minneapolis, Minnesota 189
Missoula, Montana xi, 141, 158
Missouri Pacific Railroad 186
Missouri River 8
Missouri State Penitentiary 100
Mitchell, Clarence 114
Mitchell, George 66–67, 70, 73, 87, 186
Mitchell, Robert 67
Miyagawa, Genki 158
Mize, Johnny "Big Cat" 176
Moberly, Missouri 91, 158
Molina, Augustin 128
Monarch Cab Company 56, 186
Monarchs Billiard and Recreations Parlor 56
Monarchs Cab Company 170
Monett, Missouri 164
Monett Red Birds 164
Monroe, Al 168
Monroe, William "Bill" 85
Monroe Monarchs 171
Monrovians (Wichita, Kansas) 60, 73
Montgomery Wards Monitors 42
Moore, Walter "Doby" 17, 22–23, 29, 31, 34, 44, 46, 51–53, 60, 62, 76, 123, 125, 184
Moose Jaw, Saskatchewan, Canada 141
Morland, Kansas 91

Morland Monitor (Morland, Kansas) 91
Morris, Barney 141, 156, 162, 166
Morris, Milton x
Mosolf, Jim 120
Mothell, Carroll Ray "Dink" ix–x, 3, 28–29, 31, 59–61, 64, 69, 70–71, 81–82, 86, 99–100, 102–103, 108, 111, 113, 115, 130, 132, 134, 136–137, 147, 151, 183
Mothell, Scottie 81
Motley, Don xi
Moulder, Dorsey x, 147
Muehlebach, George 47
Muehlebach Field 43, 49, 52, 54, 64, 81, 86, 98, 112, 117, 155, 160, 165–166, 173–174
Muller, Ray 117
Municipal Stadium (Cleveland, Ohio) 102
Murphy, Art 141
Murray, Orrin ix, 11
Murray County Herald 26–27
Muscatine, Iowa 142
Muskogee, Oklahoma 83, 113, 170
Muskogee Chiefs 83

Nashville, Tennessee 169, 178
Nashville Elite Giants 98
National Archives and Records Administration-Central Plains Region xi
National Association 14
National Baseball Hall of Fame 4, 9, 193
National League x, 5, 12, 19, 31, 43, 92, 119, 138–139, 147, 163, 168, 191
Nebraska State League 114, 117
Ned Ideas Team 14
Negro American League 175, 178
The Negro Baseball Leagues: A Photographic History, 1867–1955 1, 3
Negro Leagues Baseball Museum xi
Negro National League (East), 183
Negro National League (West) 5, 16, 18, 24, 30–31, 33–34, 37, 43, 66, 70, 79, 98
Negro National League attendance totals 31–33, 36, 51, 82, 85
Negro Southern League 107
New Orleans, Louisiana 49, 62
New Orleans Eagles 12, 100
New Orleans University *see* Dillard
New Rockford, North Dakota 107
New Tribune (Tacoma, Washington) 158
New Ulm, Minnesota 96
New York, New York 49
New York Black Yankees 74, 123, 150
New York Cubans 161
New York Daily News 118
New York Giants 45, 92, 114, 119
New York Harlem Stars 101
New York–Penn League 119

New York Yankees 35, 54, 105, 130, 188
Newcombe, Don 188
News Herald (Joplin, Missouri) 91
News Palladium (Benton Harbor, Michigan) 145
Newton, Kansas 91
Newton Evening Republican 91
Nicolai, Fritz 119
night baseball 96
9th Cavalry 16–17
Nogales, Arizona 28
no-hitter 42–43, 51, 98, 102
North-South Game 169
Northern League 115
Northern Pacifics 114
Northern State League 163
Northwestern League 158, 167
Novasel, Joe 175–176
Nusser, Al 171

Oahu League 23
Oakland, California 49, 124
Oakland Tribune (California) 19
Oberlin, Kansas 64
Oberlin College 56
Oglesby, Jim 175–176
Oklahoma City, Oklahoma 6, 119, 179
Oklahoma Indians 113
Oklahoma Monarchs 100
Oklahoma Normal School of Agriculture 40
Oldham, Red 123–124, 130
Olms, Alejandro 128
Olympia, Washington 163, 167
Olympic Club 20
Omaha, Nebraska 102, 114, 159
Omaha Armours 34
Omaha Packers 115
Omaha Robin Hoods 165
O'Neil, John "Buck" ix–x, 2, 37, 76, 92, 172, 178–179, 184, 188
O'Neil, Ora x
Orange, Grady 73, 100
Osawatomie, Kansas 43–44
Osawatomie Graphic 43
Osborn Stadium (Winnipeg, Canada) 157
Oswego, Kansas 111
Overton, Texas 143
Owantonna, Minnesota 96
Oxford, Nebraska 95, 109, 114, 118

P.A.C.s 20
Pacific Coast League 27, 119, 124, 129, 132
Pacific Coast News Bureau 131
Padron, Juan 41
Paige, Leroy "Satchel" 69, 76, 142, 144, 156, 158–159, 161, 166, 181, 183–185, 187–188
Palace, Fred ix, 12–13
Palace Colts ix, 11–12, 15, 26–27, 41
Palmer House Hotel 104
Pampa, Texas 171

Index

Park Owners Association (Chicago) 31
Parnell, Roy "Red" 82
Paseo Rats 75
The Pastimes 11
Patterson, "Pat" x, 73, 162, 165, 169
Paul Quinn College 52
Paulette, Gene 93
Payne, Felix 8
Payne, Milton x
Pekin Tigers (Cleveland, Ohio) 12
Penn, Alberta Gilmore x, 56
Penn, Steve xi
Peoria, Illinois 162, 164, 166, 179
Perkins, William "Bill" 141–142
Perry, Milt 163, 171, 179
Perticia, Bill 124
Pettus, William 10
Petway, Bruce 37
Petway, Shirley 178
Philadelphia Athletics 70, 106, 148
Philadelphia Giants 85
Philadelphia Giants (Los Angeles, California) 129
Philadelphia Phillies 93, 163
Philadelphia Royal Giants 108, 134–135
Philadelphia Stars 150, 179
Philadelphia Tribune 136
Philippine Islands 16, 45, 137
Phillips, The Rev. C. E. 190
Phillips University (Enid, Oklahoma) 98
Phillis Wheatly Elementary 2
Phoenix, Arizona 108
Phoenix Giants 108
Pick, Eddie 123
Piechota, Al x, 175–176
Piney Woods College 162
Pirrone, Joe 123–124, 129
Pitcher, Oklahoma 87
Pittsburg, Kansas x, 61, 89, 111
Pittsburg Normal College (Kansas) 40
Pittsburg Pirates (Pittsburg, Kansas) 64
Pittsburg State University (Kansas) x, 40
Pittsburgh, Pennsylvania 103
Pittsburgh Courier 143
Pittsburgh Crawfords 139, 150, 157, 162, 168
Pittsburgh Keystones 36
Pittsburgh Pirates 93, 108, 119, 130, 147, 176
Plank, Eddie 5
play-off attendance (1925) 58
play-offs: (1925) 58, (1926) 67–68
Pleasanton, Kansas 28
Poles, Spotwoods "Spot" 35
Pollock, Syd 114
Port Arthur, Texas 101
Portage la Prairie, Manitoba, Canada 144
Porter, Dick 148
Portland Beavers 23, 125

Portuando, Bartolo 31, 34, 46, 55, 170
Portuguese Athletic Club 17
Posey, Cumberland "Cum" 99, 103, 107, 183
Post League 17, 20, 27
Powell, Willie x, 79
Prairie View College 171
Prescott, Arkansas 62
Prim, Randolph 62
prize fighters 8
Pueblo, Colorado 10
Puerto Rican Winter League 166
Pullam, Arthur "Chick" 8–9
Pullen, Neal 129–130, 132

Quindaro Athletic Club 113

Radcliffe, Alex 155
Radcliffe, Theodore "Ted" "Double Duty" x, 78, 141, 156
Ragland, Herlen 32, 37, 55
Rand, Charlie 39
Raper, Jack 83
Rawlings, Johnny 126, 129
Ray, Otto "Jay Bird" 29, 31–32, 36–37, 42, 123, 185, 187
Ray County (Missouri) 40
Reardon, Beans 123
Red Lake Falls 114
Redding, Dick 183
Redus, Wilson "Frog" 170
Regina, Saskatchewan, Canada 141, 163
Renfroe, Othello x
Reno, Kansas 11
Republic (Manhattan, Kansas) 99
Richmond, Missouri 40
Richmond Giants 40
Rickey, Branch 123
Rickwood Field 52
Riley, Jim x
Riseberg, Swede 103
Riverside Park 8–10, 13, 16, 27
Rives, Timothy xi
Robinson, Bobby x, 36, 84, 98
Robinson, Jackie 3, 5, 188
Rock Island, Illinois 165
Rocky Mountain News (Denver) 44
Rodriquez, Jose 31
Rogan, Anna 6
Rogan, Beatrice Walstean 6
Rogan, Carl ix, 189
Rogan, Casandra 189
Rogan, Johnson 6
Rogan, Karen 189
Rogan, Kathrine McWilliams 43, 187
Rogan, Leon Walstean 6
Rogan, Ophelia Walstean Clark 6–7, 10, 27, 84
Rogan, Richard 6–7, 27
Rogan, Wilbur "Little Bullet" ix, 58
Rogan, Willard 6, 27, 160
Rogers, William "Nat" 63, 101, 103–104
Root, Charley 135

Ross, Pam xi
Rowdy Ann 4
Rowe, Schoolboy 159–160
Royal Americans (Kansas City) 52
Royal Giants (Los Angeles, California) 126, 131–132, 137
Rue, Joe 29
Ruppert Stadium 180
Russ, Pythias 61, 64
Russell, Kansas 80
Ruth, Babe 5–6, 46, 51, 54, 61, 105, 125, 150, 168
Ryba, Mike 159

Salina, Kansas 62, 137, 176
Salina Millers 90
Salmon, Harry 69
Salt Lake City, Utah 124
Sam Houston College 61
Sammie Dubin's Nite of Sports 186–187
Sampson, Tommy 181–182
San Antonio, Texas 33, 97
San Antonio Black Broncos 100
San Clara Sun 125
San Francisco, California 20
San Luis Cuban All-Stars 97
Sanders, Roy 43–44, 54
Sanford, Jay x
Santa Clara, California 27
Santa Clara (Cuban Winter League) 125, 127–128
Santa Fe, New Mexico 10
Santa Fe Railroad 136
Santa Maria, California 125
Saskatoon, Canada 158
Satchel Paige All-Stars 174
Saunders, Effie 55
Sawyer, Tom 99
Schmelzer Sporting Goods 11
Schmidt, Walter 93
Schofield Barracks 16–17, 23
Schorling Park (Chicago) 36, 54, 63, 67, 78, 82, 85–86
Schulte, Herman "Ham" x, 175–176
Scott, James T. 92
Scott, Jim "Death Valley" 19
Scott, Walter 85
Seattle, Washington 157
Sedalia, Missouri 41
Sedbrook, Leonard 119–120
Seibert, Harry 14
Seibold, Dutch 120
Sewell, Luke 148
Shackleford, John 72
Shannon, "Spike" 14
Sheboygan, Wisconsin 163
Shell Oilers 129, 131, 135
Shellenback, Frank 123
Shibe Park (Philadelphia, Pennsylvania) 54
Shreveport, Louisiana 82, 154, 174
Shreveport Tigers 174
Shur, Gus 134
shutouts 28, 33–34, 54, 57, 90, 127, 164, 165
Silva, Pedro 41

Index

Simms, Willa x
Sioux City, Iowa 103
Sioux Falls, South Dakota xi, 44, 52, 101–102, 109
Sioux Falls Canaries 102–103, 114
Skinner, Andrew 10, 100
slavery 6
Slayton, Minnesota 26
Sloan, Bruce 119–120
Smaulding, Bazz Owen 66–67, 70
Smith, Earl "Oil" 147
Smith, Forrest 187
Smith, Hilton ix–x, 156, 162, 171, 173–174, 178
Smith, Kevin x
Smith, Louise x
Smith, Mattie 171
Smith, Reggie 2
Smith, Tobe ix, 6, 8
Snaer, Lucian 49
Society of American Baseball Researchers (SABR) xi
Songer, Chub 89
Songer, Don 89
Sour Lake, Texas 171
South Bend, Indiana 164
Southwestern League 90
Spanish-American War 11
Sparks, Margaret, B. 190
Sparta, Illinois 67, 186
Sparta, Wisconsin 114
Sparta High School 67
Sparta Stars 67
Speaker, Tris 28
Spokane, Washington 141, 163, 165–166
Springfield, Missouri 74, 80, 90–91, 159, 161, 163–164, 166, 179
Springfield Cardinals 166
Springfield Midgets 90
Springfield News Leader 163
St. Cloud, Minnesota 101
St. Joseph, Missouri 28, 35, 99, 113, 171, 179
St. Joseph Gazette 35, 99
St. Joseph Saints 115
St. Louis, Missouri xi, 3, 12, 31
St. Louis Argus 47, 80, 184
St. Louis Browns 166, 176
St. Louis Cardinals 90, 111, 144, 147–148, 159, 176
St. Louis Giants 11, 28, 31, 36, 107, 180
St. Louis Stars 50, 57, 67, 69, 71, 78, 98, 174–175
St. Louis University Saints 20
St. Paul Gophers 12
St. Petersburg, Florida 2
Stack, Eddie 68
Staples, Percy 190
Starks, Charles 33, 47
Starks, James 74
Stark's Shoeshine Parlor 55
Starkville, Mississippi 108
Stars of Cuba 100
Stars Park (St. Louis) 52, 58
Stearman, Tom 9
Stearnes, Norman "Turkey" 64, 101, 113, 130, 132, 142, 145, 155, 169, 178
Stengel, Casey 93, 129
Sterling, Colorado 44
Steubenville, Ohio 72, 186
Stevens, Paul "Jake" 54
Street, CeLois x
Street, Felix x
Street, Roma 102
Streeter, Sam 69
Street's Hotel 51
strikeouts 20, 33–34, 36, 90, 128, 164, 165
Strong, Ted 171, 174
Sumner High School 11
Suttles, George "Mule" 64, 76, 155, 168
Sweatt, George ix–xi, 11, 40, 51, 55, 60, 63, 86, 186
Swift Current, Saskatchewan 163–164

Tacoma, Washington 157–158, 171
Tally, Doc 167
Taylor, C. I. 29, 32–33, 36, 69
Taylor, James "Candy Jim" 78, 154, 175
Taylor, John 34
Taylor, Leroy Ben 71–72, 81, 91, 99, 134, 157, 162
team bus 140
Tech Field (La Junta, Colorado) 159
Tennessee Day 85
Tennessee Rats 153; *see also* Brown's Tennessee Rats
Tenth Cavalry 16
Texan Day 85
Texas Colored League 100
Texas League 105
Texas-Oklahoma-Louisiana League 57, 82–83
32nd Infantry 27
Thomas, Alfonse 148
Thomas, Chet 123
Thomas, Clint x, 125
Thomas, Joe 190
Thomas, Max 156
Thompson, Samuel "Sam" 101, 119
Thompson, Sandy 104
Thorpe, Jim 113
three-home-run games 20, 76, 158
365th Infantry 49
Three-I League 83
Thurston, Hollis 119, 134
Thurston, John "Sloppy" 124
Tierney, James "Cot" 11, 93, 106
Timken, Kansas 176
Titus, James 178
Tobe Smith's Transfer Company 8
Toledo, Ohio 164
Toledo Tigers 36, 39
Tonkawa, Oklahoma 80
Topeka, Kansas 3, 9, 27–28, 44, 62, 81, 89, 104, 117
Topeka Capital Journal 28
Topeka Giants 28–29, 136
Topeka Senators 53
Torriente, Cristobal 28, 34, 60–61, 64, 70, 184
Town House Hotel 186
Traynor, Pie 147
Traynor, Poncho 147
Treadwell, Harold 41
Trent, Theodore "Ted" 78, 103
Trenton, Missouri 90, 105, 174
Tronick Park (La Crosse, Wisconsin) 147
Trouppe, Quincy ix, 108, 112–113, 151, 155–156, 162
Tucker, John, R. 167
Tulsa Oilers 147
Tunney, Gene 6
Tuskegee Relays 152
25th Infantry "Wreckers" ix, 15–17, 20–22, 27–29, 31, 38, 73
24th Infantry 16
two-home-run games 23, 51, 82, 90, 107, 144
Tyler, William "Steel Arm" 66
Tyler College 74
Tyree, Rube 11, 29

Union Giants 102
Union Pacific Park (Kansas City, Kansas) 113
United States Army 15–16
United States Army Series 20
U.S. Hotel 158
University of Missouri-Kansas City 3
University of Nebraska 115
Urban, Nick 163

Valley City, North Dakota 148, 156
Valley City Times-Recorder 156
Valsoana, Johnny 179
Van Meter, Iowa 176
Vancouver, Canada 165–166
Vann, Johnny 107
Vanoy, Myrtle x
Vassar Roofing Company 11
Vaughn, Harold 74
Veeck, Bill 181, 188
Venice Tigers 19
Vincennes, Indiana 49
Vine Street x
Virden, Manitoba, Canada 141
Virginia League 83

Waco, Texas 52, 98
Waco Cardinals 98, 155
Waco Times-Herald 98
Waddell, Rube 5
Wagner, Honus 168
Wakefield, Bert 9
Walker, Admiral "Deacon" 66
Walker, Hoss 133
Waller, Roy 97
Waner, Lloyd 112
Waner, Paul 108–109, 119
Ward, Ann x
Ward, John W. xi
Ward Field (Kansas City, Kansas) 174

Ware, Willie 72
Wareham Ice Team (Manhattan, Kansas) 114
Warfield, Frank 136
Warneke, Lon 176
Washington, Edgar "Blue" 4, 29, 31
Washington High School (Luther, Oklahoma) 64
Washington Park (Indianapolis, Indiana) 31
Washington Pilots 108
Washington Senators 45, 112, 120, 148
Watkins, T. B. 186
Watkins Brothers Funeral Parlors 56–57
Watkins Chapel 189
Waxahachie, Texas 40
Webb, Normal "Tweed" xi, 184
Webster, Bob 162
Weingarner, Ralph 112
Welch, Jesse 119–120
Wells, Willie 108–109, 112–113, 130, 169
Wesley Park (Winnipeg, Canada) 115–116
West End Hotel 58
Western Association 80, 83, 90, 163
Western League 44–45, 51, 53, 102, 111, 114–115, 118–119, 165–166, 179
Westlawn Cemetery 13, 84, 100
Wheat, Zack 106
White, James, P. 122
The White Base Ball and Amusement Association 122
White City Park (Springfield, Missouri) 166
White Eagles 179
White Kings 129, 131
White Sox Park (Los Angeles, California) 125–126, 130, 132
Whitworth, Richard Henderson "Dick" ix–x, 12–14, 26, 30, 41–42, 74, 108
Whitworth, Roger x
Wichita, Kansas 45, 60, 64, 73, 80, 98, 112, 117, 120, 146–147, 155, 168, 171
Wichita Eagle 80, 91, 111, 118, 148
Wichita Evening Eagle 117
Wickstrom, Harriet x
Wilberforce College 57, 74
Wiley College 73–74, 101, 152, 162, 173–174
Wilkins, West 9
Wilkinson, J. L. 4–5, 28–29, 31, 37, 43, 45, 48, 54, 56, 75–76, 79, 89, 108, 113, 116, 136, 139, 146, 154, 161, 184–185
Williams, A. D. 69
Williams, Charlie 64
Williams, Henry 170
Williams, Jesse x, 76, 190
Williams, Joe "Smokey Joe" 103, 105, 151, 183–184
Williams, Ted 166
Williams, Tom 33, 107
Willimgham, Hugh 163, 171
Willis, Corporal 19
Wilson, Bill 109, 112
Wilson, Herbert, "Tack" 73
Wilson, Tom 98, 169
Wilson, Woodrow 161–162, 171
Winnipeg, Alberta, Canada 109, 114–115, 139
Winnipeg Evening Tribune 116, 157
Winona, Minnesota 114
Winter League (Los Angeles, California) 124
Winters, Jesse, "Nip" 54
Wisconsin Rapids 101–102, 114
Wishkeno, Willie 83
Wood, Charley 111
World Series: (1924) 54–55, 170, (1925) 58–60, (1934) 147
World War I 16, 29, 40
World's Fair 168
Worten, Leroy 151
Wright, Bearcat 8
Wright, Glenn 46, 119–120, 187
Wrigley Field 126
Wyandotte County 10
Wyandotte Weekly Herald 14
Wyatt, Dave 136
Wymore, Nebraska 64, 102

Yakima, Washington 157–158, 167
Young, Fay 60, 73, 85
Young, Maurice "Doolittle" ix–x, 66–67, 70, 76, 94
Young, Thomas Jefferson "T. J." x, 4, 57, 73, 80–82, 95, 99, 101–102, 108, 113, 117–118, 130, 134, 155, 157–158, 161, 168
Your Kansas City and Mine 184

Zinn, Jimmy x, 46, 64, 156
Zwilling, Edward "Dutch" 46, 115, 187